THE NAKED SAILOR

THE NAKED SAILOR

NORMAN COUTTS

atmosphere press

© 2024 Norman Coutts

Published by Atmosphere Press

Cover design by Felipe Betim

No part of this book may be reproduced without permission from the author except in brief quotations and in reviews. Some names and incidents may have been altered to protect the innocent.

Atmospherepress.com

To my friends and fellow travellers: Captain Rob who invited me on this adventure and John who made it possible. There would have been no story without you both.

FORE

A)   **Naked** (neikid): adj. *1) having the body unclothed; undressed, 2) having no covering, exposed, 3) with no qualification or concealment: the naked facts, 7b) lacking some essential condition to render valid; incomplete.* (Collins Canadian Dictionary, 2004.)

[Noteworthy: To Canadians, anything minus a fleece parka might be considered naked.]

B)   **Sailor**: n. *1) any member of a ship's crew, esp. one below the rank of officer, 2) a person who sails, esp. with reference to the likelihood of his becoming seasick: a good sailor.* (Collins Canadian Dictionary, 2004.)

C)   **Naked Sailor**: [Google] Ah, yes...whoa, what the...that's more pop-up than anyone needs to see. H-m-m-m-m, that must be Photoshop.

Add: Define **'Naked Sailor'**: Okay, let's see... **Urban Dictionary**: **Naked Sailor**: adv. *The act of having sexual intercourse without a* *condom; as in, "He forgot to bring the protection, so they had sex naked sailor."*

That was a turn I wasn't expecting, but truthfully, no metaphor could better define the act of going off to sea. You know you shouldn't, but you can't help yourself; unprotected skin assaulted by the mixed ambrosia of salted wind, the charge of dry heat, and the ecstasy of a cool, wet spray; they penetrate the pores, tempt the soul, and the mind dims the perils with every wave you part. In the exhaustion of the conquest, the worries begin. How many times lucky in and out of port? When will Sea Transmitted Disasters strike? Will my rudder fail? Can I get the anchor up? Will there be an unexpected swell? You know you shouldn't, but when opportunity knocks, off you go again.

Unprotected sailing? Here's another truth: there is no protection for anyone who goes off to sea. Have you seen it out there? Typhoon seas, tsunamis from hell, and Alaskan king crabbing; on any given day, sailing is jumping in and hoping for the best. In the end, perhaps it's a statement on life itself.

For me, the physical part of naked was pretty simple; unbuckle, unzip, drop, step out, and watch the disappearing act. But it was the "Exposed and vulnerable, without qualification...lacking some essential conditions..." naked definitions gleaned from the world of jurisprudence that, metaphorically for me, alarmingly fit. When it came to experience in motoring and sailing, I was naked as that proverbial jaybird of dubious nesting grounds. Until this journey, I had never been to sea. I had not grown up by the sea nor had a lifelong yearning to go. Somehow, I had a firmly entrenched fear of the sea altogether. It was culled, perhaps, from some Dewey website anchored in my brain; sails, sailboats, and sailors, a sad disgruntled sailor, "...for a man who would go to sea for pleasure would go to hell for a pastime."

Even if you are not familiar with the geography, the naked factor should help you conclude that I was not watching penguins marching or ice calving from an Alaskan glacier. But, for those like me who might be location-challenged, grab a globe (that pre-Google round sphere covered in dust with a map of the world on it), spin it with your finger on the equator (the widest girth of the ball), and let it sail through Ecuador, the mouth of the Amazon in Brazil, across the Atlantic, through the narrowing midriff of Africa from Equatorial Guinea and Gabon to Somalia, over the Indian Ocean (watch out for sharks), and bring it to a stop in the cluster of islands starting with Indonesia. If you are in New Guinea, back up a sea short of Borneo. Somewhere in there, you will see Singapore on the tip of a feeble peninsula occupied by Thailand and Malaysia. There is a narrow thread of water here called the Straits of Malacca that leads to the South China Sea. Head north to the Philippines, northwest to Hong Kong and northerly still to Beijing in China, and you have pretty much traced the route.

I was hoping the title would put you in the right frame of mind. For me, getting naked mid-South China Sea meant not having to unzip a snowsuit, unwind a scarf, or pull aside a sweater or two to simply find it...skin that is...worthy of a "pinch me, am I really here?" But that aside, it was the glorious sunshine and unrelenting heat that made me realize tropical viewing was best done near-au naturel.

There is nothing like a recipe of tropical seas, coconut palms, and all the colours sunsets and dawns can muster to jump-start the libido. Add the elixir of the East Indies islands, one exotic yacht, and three good friends. Throw in some sneaker waves, Willy Willie winds, big fish stories, monkeys in heaven, and hot Indonesian sauces to crank up the heat. Stir in mythical ports, Singapore slings, and the Wild Man of Borneo. To enhance, try a few naked gods, your choice of exotic fruits, and a dose of gym socks. Let swing free and easy. Serve steamy hot, with a few shooters of apprehension and, for me, a stiff mug of fear.

To this end, there were moments in the three months of travel that threatened a *Heart of Darkness* journey. Four typhoons raged to the north, and an earthquake sent a tsunami from the south. Sea junk came close to sinking the boat, and although they never materialized, pirates were always a threat. If this voyage was my river, my soul of complacent ignorance had been my Kurtz, exposed in the end and transformed in a thousand paper cuts of renewal. The sea had called and invited me in. Little did I realize to accept was to be reborn from the birthing seas of our planet. In the end, concerning the sea, I was hooked. More importantly, the voyage was a wake-up call in its reflection of life...my life for sure. Too soon we are old and resting in port!

There comes a time in a man's life when he hears the call of the sea.

"Hey, YOU!" are the sea's exact words.

If the man has a brain in his head, he will hang up the phone immediately.

– Dave Barry, Captains Uncourageous
(*Miami Herald*, 1992)

1

THE SEND-OFF
SPOTLIGHTS AND PIRATES
THE END IS NEAR

...LABOUR DAY WEEKEND, SEPT. 2009

Like all great adventures, there was a send-off. It did not have the splash of a great ship being christened off to sea, but alcohol was spilled, glasses clinked, and some sort of speech was proffered towards my Bon Voyage and safe journey. It was the kind of farewell party where the celebrated guest is met with a boisterous cry of "Sur-r-p-r-i-i-i-se" from a host of boisterous surprisers. In this case, the surprisers were mostly my relatives with partners and offspring all dressed like pirates. They were not the pinstripes of Wall Street, but the kind made famous by Johnny Depp. I was soon decked out in a skull-and-crossbones scarf, eye patch, and a stuffed felt parrot pinned to my shoulder. It is the custom of Canadian surprisers to humiliate their celebrated guests, especially if the guest has announced he is leaving for a three-month cruise to the Far East and none of them have been invited.

For the rest of the afternoon, most conversations started with an "A-a-r-r-g-g-h, matey" or a gargled caw followed by

"Polly want a cracker." Within an hour or so and after several private toasts to "You lucky bastard," the parrot hung forward from my shoulder in a drunken stupor, charged to an erect position occasionally by tucking my T-shirt into my shorts and tightening the belt. The eye patch without glasses disoriented me toward an inebriated walk and I was forced to tilt my head back to peek out at those who were speaking. Nose in the air and staggering with a drunken parrot prompted, it seemed, some truly heartfelt "good lucks" and two-handed goodbyes...shakes held longer than usual with thoughts that suggested this was the end.

There was a cake as well, lovingly prepared by my niece, decorated with a man walking a plank or being eaten by a shark. I can't quite remember. I was surprised all right. The party fed upon my discomfort of pointed attention and, worse, a newfound phobia of pirates.

I loathe being the center of attention. Close friends find this surprising, considering my school days of speeches or my choice for a television career, which required me to call for quiet on the set. I am not inclined toward the adoration of centre stage. It's the eyes, I think. Eyes fixed on your every move, sparkling with anticipation, eventually dulled by reality. I am not a wallflower; I simply don't seek the limelight. Writing in a darkened room with a dog and cat at my feet suits me fine.

You see, along with my introverted tendencies, I have a speech impediment, actually, a brain malfunction that moves words and letters around in my head without my consent and Jabberwocky spoonerisms leave my lips. A toast to the bride and groom at my niece's wedding came out as a "Toast to sex," not "success" as was intended, sending the guests into layers of guffaws and laughter as it was explained and repeated into the distant corners of the room. Some conversation about a new Korean *truck factory* came out as a *fuck tractory* and a sale at Miracle Food Mart escaped as Miracle Mood Fart. Barely a day passes without some distortion of words bypassing my brain's editor. It is better, my wife has reminded me, to fut the shuck up.

Secondly, no one knew at this bon voyage party to what extent I had worked myself into a lather over the issue of pirates. Pirates had never been one of my lifelong fears. I had never met any outside the beer and hot dog vendors at the baseball games, but due to my sailing announcement, pirates had been elevated to fill some unknown fear I had of death by walking the plank, shark bites, and the inability to breathe due to drowning. Damn the internet. It's not like I went looking for pirate possibilities. They simply popped up with every conversation.

"I am leaving for Thailand to help a good friend move his yacht to the Philippines," was my answer to questions of what the hell I was doing. Hell, it seemed, was tossed into the conversation to set the tone. Everyone assumed, smugly, that I wasn't doing anything useful. I was writing. With the sailing announcement, eyebrows lifted, eyeballs shifted, and sallow cheeks inflated like a blowfish. Inevitably, the word "pirates" came out with a prolonged whistle and a lemon pucker.

"Whoa, what about the pirates?" That might be quickly followed by "I hear there are a lot of pirates in that part of the world," in case the nail had not been driven deep enough with the first blow. The questions and queries were delivered with the same serious demeanour as those who launch into horror stories about ten days in labour for a fifteen-pound baby when a young mother pie-eyed with fear announces her first pregnancy. These pirate stories, lifted from some dark chamber in the user's warehouse of the brain, were about crews left for dead, wives sold into slavery, or men buggered for days before being fed to the sharks. Maybe if I had puked fear on their sandals, they might have got the point; that pirates, unlike sharks, poisonous jellyfish, and all the forms of natural sea disasters they could muster into one conversation, were my greatest concern.

It didn't help that while waiting at the immunization office for special shots (every disease east of India), I happened onto a *National Geographic* magazine featuring modern-day pirates in full colour. These were the real-life thieving and murdering scum in the seas of New Guinea, Borneo, and Indonesia and... oh...wait a minute, wasn't this close to where we were going? "Oh crap, while you are at it, give me a shot for lead poisoning and sword lacerations!" And then, curiosity killed the cat, and I had to open the door to the internet. Shiver me timbers, I didn't need to know that. Close the laptop and Google me gone.

To lighten the mood, mine especially, I tried to laugh off talk about pirates with an "A-a-r-r-g-g-h, Billy b'Jesus, theys be messin' with fire if theys be messin' with me," knowing damn well that I had no idea how to stave off an attack of "after me booty" buccaneers. It was the amazing regularity at which the subject of pirates came up that astonished me. It was as if the whole world had no opinion on global warming but knew something or someone who knew about bloodthirsty pirates. It wasn't merely this party, but nearly every person I had met since announcing my travel plans who seemed to raise the issue. Even my doctor couldn't help strafing my fears with cheerful words of encouragement.

"Three months on a yacht? In the Far East? I hope you get buggered by pirates!" It was finished with a laugh, a tetanus shot, and a handshake wishing me well.

What is it about our need to rain negatively on the plans of others? For some, it seems, the announcing of a new vocation, a wedding, or even a walk in the park is justification to open the septic sluice for discussions on disaster. Getting accepted to dental school can be fair game for a conversation on professional suicides. Don't mention the police academy or army cadets unless you know much about body bags, and wannabe pilots and bankers need not open their mouths. Most people, I suppose, think it is their civic duty to give fair warning, even if they have never gone into deep space, dove fathoms into the sea, or hunted grizzly bears with a bow and arrow. You are going to get an earful just the same about death from bends in a space suit while being chased by a bear with an arrow in its ass. Perhaps their concern stems from plain old jealousy: if we see a crab pulling itself out of the communal clam bake pail that is life, let's make sure we pull the pretentious dreamer down so we can all bake together.

I don't believe, however, that there was anything beyond fun intentions from the family party. After all, I had never shared my fears with anyone, not even my wife. I was afraid she might have laughed herself silly then rescinded her blessings for the trip, handing me back that frilly French maid's outfit that she loves me to wear when she comes home from work. The party had ended in hugs and goodbyes tightly squeezed with, "Be careful. Take care," and of course an obligatory "A-a-r-r-g-g-h, bye" and "Billy b'Jesus" for a laugh. I survived the pirate party, but the damage of doubt had come and stayed.

I might be classed as a nervous traveler to start with, especially at departures. If it says be there three hours before takeoff, well, by God, three and a half it is, but I had avoided acquainting myself with the headline terrors that could face travellers beforehand—"Murdered in Mexico," "Robbed in Romania," "Gassed and stripped naked in your own RV"—because it took the fun out of travel, though I might give RVing a second look. For all the nervous tension in preparation, the special visa for China, medical shots, packing for a three-month trip for extreme hot and cold weather (I would be heading for northern China in November to see my nephew), insurance, travel papers, a last-minute will, fond farewells, and party gatherings, I was rather calm when my wife dropped me off at the airport two hours early for a domestic flight to Edmonton. She gave me a hug and a kiss, softly cooing, "I'll see you in three months, love you, take care and...watch out for the pirates." Hey, was she laughing and letting her hair down when she laid rubber on departure?

I entered the parting doors of the airport, wondering if I had made the right decision, doubting my abilities to survive on the high seas.

2

GATHERING THE CREW
28 HOURS IN...
JUMP OFF THE BRIDGE OR PUSH

SEPT. 7ᵀᴴ DEPARTURE

Rob and I had been friends since the first day of grade three. It was a new school for us both, my third in three years, and recess found us shuffling and kicking stones by the playground, watching as other kids—kids with friends—tried to bump each other off the teeter-totter. There was a lone wolf on the high end with four of his buddies sitting on the other, crashing wood into the ground so that the lone individual was bucked and eventually dislodged from his seat and flew like a human cannonball, pie-eyed with fear and adrenalin, toward the four boys bellowing with delight. It was called the royal bumps. I was horrified. Rob screamed with laughter, hoping at some point to become the "one." The problem was he didn't have four good friends with the kindness of trying to break his neck. While we watched, I offered him a chocolate marshmallow cookie. That was an act akin to the rituals of blood brotherhood. We had been two lost souls on the playground, but the snake-eyes tumble of friendship has lasted over sixty years.

Our true bond went back to grade four when I became his school-to-home buddy in case of nuclear war. There was, apparently, a crisis with Cuban missiles causing Russian threats with shoe banging at the UN. It was complicated. Amidst the rehearsals of hiding under our desk, where archeologists would have extracted rows of teeth from huddled piles of glowing ashes, Rob and I were assigned to walk to his place together (if annihilation was not immediate), since I was a bus person and all buses would be charred embers, unable to ferry us home. Without understanding, we both hoped for the sirens and explosions after which I could follow him home, he could show me his dog, and then we would deliver his wagonload of *Toronto Star* newspapers proclaiming the end of the world. Thankfully we never had to make that walk home, but we remained friends all the same.

Rob liked the idea that I lived on a farm, where he understood that kids chased chickens and jumped in piles of hay. Dick and Jane had done that in our grade one reader. I liked the idea that the only chore he had was to deliver a bunch of papers. Beaver did it on TV. Buoyed by the greener fields in each other's yards, we visited. I was dazzled by his running water and flush toilets, heating from things hanging on the walls and not having to carry wood to make it happen. There wasn't anything he didn't like at the farm, "like camping, but better," since there actually were chickens (which he chased) and hay bales that made forts, ropes to swing on and a river to be damned with a raft to be built, sheep to be sheared, horses for riding, and…well, I won the battle of interesting. We became inseparable, and, for a while, he was a constant addition to my family of two brothers, two sisters, a half-brother with two other full siblings to the half, which I guess made them quarters to me. That too was complicated.

Rob was now an accomplished veteran of the cruising

ports of Southeast Asia and co-owner (with his estranged wife) of the *Sea Horse* trawler yacht. When his family was quite young, he had moved them west to Vancouver Island, where he bought a trailer park and some building land, which he subdivided and sold, leaving him pleasantly well-off. I had spent years in television production, then moved on to design-build renovations and carpentry. Our paths had yielded different dividends, but we both were a long way from our working-class childhoods. Neither of us had gone through life with nostalgic glimpses to childhood, though with the advantage of hindsight, I realize mine wasn't as dark as it seemed. Most kids, I was told, were beaten within an inch of their miserable lives. It was the law of the straight and narrow.

I had best-manned his wedding to Catherine and stayed tight by their side a few years later, while their son's life hung by a thread. Some while later, after his miracle survival, I helped pack their U-Haul for Vancouver Island, where they started a whole new life. Thirty-five years later, we got excited together about their plans to buy the boat. In all those years, we had seen each other less than a dozen times, but each time it was as if we had met the day before. We had never measured our friendship with time or distance.

Rob and his wife Cathy's relationship had always seemed solid—the "You're in good hands, Gibraltar" solid—but in one short visit, I had seen the train wreck coming. It was in Cathy's eyes; the paralyzing fear of the unknowns when plans were being made for buying the boat. Exciting as that was, it meant leaving the family home, their grown-up kids, and all the tried and proven benefits of earned retirement for the unknown adventures in travel far from home. This had been Rob's idea right from the get-go, and Cathy could never find the brakes, thinking perhaps it was a toked dream from the homegrown. She didn't stop the train's momentum because she didn't want to be that stick-in-the-mud, stuck in time and pulled out for the show-and-tell of "If" and "Only."

The idea had started as a boat for travelling along the

British Columbia coast, maybe as far north as Alaska or daringly down south to Panama and out to the Atlantic for cruising the Caribbean. It grew to buy a boat built in mainland China at half the North American cost. That changed everything. Boating would now occur in the South China Sea. Whisperings from friends, blogs on pirates, and rhymes of experienced mariners filtered in. But only Cathy was listening.

Expectations have a way of dictating truth. I had read their travel blog and felt the tone melting month by month.

Rob showed up one day in June while the spring flowers were giving their last hurrah before the heat of summer arrived in Toronto. I thought he and Cathy were still cruising somewhere off the shores of someplace in an area of the world I was somewhat unfamiliar with (okay, I had no idea, in fact). I was happy to see him and immediately jealous of his wiry tanned physique, Willy Nelson beard, and bleached blond hair tied back in a ponytail. There was a large black guitar case slung over his shoulder. I didn't even know he played.

"Yeah, I taught myself," he confessed to my surprised reaction at being handed the instrument. "There's a lot of nothin' to do on the boat sometimes." There had to be a country and western song in there somewhere, I remember thinking, pulling a welcome beer from the fridge.

He was on a trip home to Canada to see Catherine, he explained, whom I thought was still somewhere "over there" as well. Via e-mails, Catherine had made me aware of Rob's midlife crisis with arguments for and against leaving him. It was the fear of being alone. They had spent a lifetime together. When I pressed Rob on plans of divorce or reconciliation, he would only say, "She still loves me to pieces you know... she's just so dependent. I have to make all the decisions about everything. I was so tired of looking out for the two of us." I saw it from both sides and so I had to bite my tongue.

We spent some time talking about the trip and especially the boat. I already knew a fair amount about it, or at least the species he had bought, since on my last trip to their home in Qualicum Beach on Vancouver Island, we had spent several days shopping around for used trawler boats, both online and in-the-water offerings at the various marinas on the island. Those may have been pinch-me moments for us both; boarding yachts with the possible intent to buy.

And then, out of the blue, he dropped the question.

"How would you like to crew my boat, first mate, Thailand back to the Philippines?" he said. "I need a crew to help me cross the South China Sea," he added with ease as if talking about moving apartments across town. He briefly explained the need to have someone at the helm at all times, especially during the four-day, no-anchored journey across the South China Sea that required a crew by maritime law. I made a mental note to check the atlas and see where exactly this was. Somewhere in a sea, south of China, I presumed. His tone was slightly sarcastic.

"Hell, there are young kids that sail solo around the world all the time," he blurted out, but left it at that. The kids were added, I think, to humble the request to child's play.

He had had me at Thailand, or maybe "How would you like to," my body reacting in usual form. My heart skipped a beat with anticipation; my brain warned the sphincter to be prepared. I managed a holy-shit reply.

"The Filipino first mate I used the last time got his green card for the U.S., and he is no longer available," he continued, and, before I could raise the obvious question of what the hell do I know from a hole in the ground on first-mating a boat, he added, "I can teach you what you need to know. It's simple...automatic pilot...easy as falling off a bike." I wasn't sure I cared for the analogy.

"I think it's 'riding' a bike."

"Whatever," he said, ignoring my correction, as he had done all of my life. He had appreciated that I studied arts and science in high school, calling me a brainer, referring to himself as "just a techie." "Yeah, not bad for just a techie," he had said when he told me he was buying a yacht. It was cupped in pride, of course, with a healthy dose of pointed sarcasm. He was retired, a millionaire, and I was neither.

"You don't need to worry nothin' about cost, except getting to Thailand and sharing food." That had the same playful enthusiasm as a friend who had constantly invited us to his cottage in the process of being built, "bring your tools" inferred in the innocence of "We'll swim, drink, water ski… and maybe do a little work." It always fell in the reverse.

"I don't need to know today," Rob said, "but let me know as soon as you can. Me and you can talk later."

It all sounded so simple, like a nonstop, share-the-wheel drive to Florida during March break. I had never made that trip with Rob. In fact, I realized we had barely travelled anywhere together beyond a horse-to-stable lead-footed rocket ride from Toronto to Vancouver Island by car; Cathy, his pail of oats, promising to make up for the lost month he had spent back in Ontario.

Kim was the replacement, a Filipina.

"A real sweet girl," Rob had said. "You'll meet her when we get to Subic. I left her money to pay the rent. By the sounds of it, there are already a dozen people living there." He had laughed in a way that I knew he was smitten. "It's a whole different world over there, Norm."

He had neglected to reveal her age, and I hadn't pressed. It wasn't any of my business until he decided to share, and even then, he never shared wanting opinions or advice. Kim was a bar find from Barretto, the wedge that drove Cathy back to their home on Vancouver Island. The boat at the time of his visit was dry-docked in Phuket, Thailand.

I drove him to the airport, where he would hopscotch from Toronto to Vancouver to Seoul, Korea, and finally to Manila. He would wait for my answer, all communications to go by e-mail. If my answer was yes, we would meet in Phuket sometime in September.

Meanwhile, I stewed.

My answer, which should have been instant, took a few weeks for me to digest.

Southeast Asia...so remote to my travel knowledge that I had to thumb through an atlas. Borneo, Indonesia, Thailand, Singapore, Philippines; these were countries of my collective schooling memories...Dutch East Indies, buccaneers, hot spices, and media exposures of earthquakes, war zones, Imelda Marcos and her two thousand pairs of shoes...without much heed to their location.

And then, of course, there were the questions. What about pirates, sharks, tropical diseases, typhoons and tsunamis? Isn't it unbearably hot? And what did I know about motoring yachts? I had never been to sea. I was not working at the moment, which was opportune for travelling, but hence, no pool of money, which wasn't. Doubt, to self-doubt, to excuses, and I nearly missed the boat...no proverbial downwind tack intended. The eventual "yes" caused sweat and sleepless nights, with the yin-yang duo doing battles in my head.

"Go, it's the chance of a lifetime."

"Pirates, typhoons...lost at sea."

"Don't listen to him. He's your idiot side of the brain. Life is too short. *Carpe diem!*"

"Shark'd eat 'em!"

"You're such an idiot!"

"Bite me!"

My departure meant teaming up with another friend, John from Edmonton. We had all been primary school chums in Toronto, but now lived on that thin line of populated existence from Toronto to Vancouver Island. It had been John who made it all possible. Rob had called him, trolling for a second mate, and John had accepted immediately. He called me in mid-July to say he had bought me a ticket for departure in September, an internet sell-off. It was off-season for travel. "Monsoon or typhoon season or something," he said.

"We can't afford to stay home."

John had been retired for years on wise investments. He could have signed on without me, but I was the best friend and comfort link to them both. Of course, I couldn't say no, but it added to the sweat and insomnia of doubt.

Both John and I had been cast into the same rooms through elementary and high school, eventually bonding as lifelong friends. Our high school girlfriends were best friends; had been for years, spilling beans between them and comparing notes, whispered into our ears in back seats, which left us comfortably aware of each other's intimate shortcomings, without ever talking between us. We played euchre in his parents' basement and drank pink lemonade and gin, which I puked up and was reminded of by his mother for years to come. Thankfully I am missing the gene that would allow me to be an alcoholic, but also the brain cells of memory that would remind me not to drink.

Our paths widened and crossed occasionally after high school until I invited him to join me for a backpacking tour in Europe when I finished university. True to form (I think my body was telling me something), John watched as I hurled sangria and paella in Barcelona, perhaps regretting his decision to accept my invitation to travel. Thankfully, that was not the European highlight, as we took our rail passes to all the treasured corners of the continent. However, three months together, twenty-four hours a day, scavenging for cheap food and shelter, shared sleeping bags, a claustrophobic pup tent, noisy hostels, and daily cultural overload caused rifts that had scabbed but never seemed to heal.

In later years, John had become a seasoned traveller of sorts. After hearing his stories, I have come to suspect that he has ADHD or other issues defying labels. He travels like a ball through a pinball machine. On separate travels, he has spent weekends in Buenos Aires and Berlin, three nights in Shanghai, and a day in Bangkok. He has stopped for afternoon tea in London and breakfast in Sydney with acquaintances and then moved on with another pin flag for the world map. Adventure to him, it seemed, was like dragging a drumstick through hot water and calling it chicken soup. The boat, I hoped, would slow him down. You can't just up and leave, or so I thought.

This had been part of the rift of the three months in Europe. He never seemed to grasp carpe diem; that *saisir l'instant croissant en Paris* fresh from the oven, *den augenblick nutzen kaffee* in Vienna, or standing in the shadow of Michelangelo's *David* or nose to nose with *Mona Lisa* and *The Kiss of Rodin*. Of course, these were my dreams come true that I hoped he might enjoy, but he never did. We ended up quarrelling a lot and it took months after returning before we spoke to each other... but then again, we were backpacking kids out of school, lacking the art of compromise that marriage instills. A few years later, with our significant others, we met up in Greece, where I swore, never again.

But here we were thirty years later, now aged vintages with nosings of eccentric and stubborn, meeting in Edmonton, midlifers helping a friend through a crisis, with connecting flights for Vancouver, Tokyo, Bangkok, and Phuket. My wife had assured me, catching me gritting my teeth and rubbing my forehead as if I had a bad headache, that I was ruminating on ancient history and that we were "mature adults, for Christ's sake." I believed her assessment. It was made while barely looking up from her computer, perusing the stack of bills with the same eagle eye of vice principal she had used for the eight hundred report cards back in June. I knew her assessment had all the I's dotted and T's crossed in weighing the "could we afford it" against "I don't want to be accused of standing in the way of your once-in-a-lifetime." There may have been a healthy dose of a double-arm pump—Yes—...three months of quiet and solitude on her part; nearly forty years of marriage can prompt such a response.

John greeted me at the stopover gate in Edmonton, head shaved to disguise the balding that gave him that joyful twinkle of the Dalai Lama, countered by a shirt and tie that belied said first impressions. He eyeballed my comfy clothes for travel. Nothing was said. Everything was understood. I was a slob. He was pompously overdressed. Our complex vintages, I guess, had cured in a batch of oak with hints of smoke and fire.

"Three bags...good God...this is all I ever travel with," he said, hoisting his single gym bag as we headed through Vancouver Gate C 51 for AC003 to Tokyo. I explained that one bag was for the electronics—laptop, cell phone and camera, with all the charging and user paraphernalia that goes with them—and books for reading: five, with a portfolio of relevant documentation and a file with my writing papers for my book-in-progress. There was another small carry-on with a change of clothes and toiletries...just in case. And, well, since I was staying for nearly three months, venturing to China to visit my nephew in the cold of November, I defended a backpack full of clothes that reflected my winter needs. He clucked, shrugged, and pointed to his nylon bag dangling weightlessly from one hand. "It's all Tilley clothes, light, wash in the hotel sink and wear again the next day." I had no desire to wash clothes every day for three months, but said nothing.

"I don't think that lounge card of yours will work over here," he said. "I paid a thousand bucks for mine," producing a card that got us into showers and a private sushi-sake bar at Japan's Narita airport. I refused to pull mine out in case he was right. Mine was a gift for paying an outrageous user fee for my credit card. It had worked perfectly well in Paris, London, and Stockholm for beer, dried nuts, and a quiet place to wait. I bit my tongue, mindful of my status as "mature adult."

"Yellow shorts? In the lounge? This is Japan," he scoffed.

"But we are going to Bangkok," I said, slightly bewildered. "It's going to be bloody hot and humid."

He dismissively shrugged and rolled his eyes.

"Online hotels are never what you think they will be," John chastised as we stepped from the taxi into the bustle of our adopted neighbourhood in Bangkok. "Not the area I would have booked."

"What did I tell you?" he said when we pulled back the curtains in the hotel room and found it didn't look out on the pool. A window on a brick wall two feet away allowed the filtered light of a ten-storey building next door.

Twenty-eight hours into a three-month trip and I was looking for a bridge...jump or push? *Keep my mouth shut and things will settle*, I told myself. I chalked it up to jet lag, but I should not have been surprised, having travelled in Europe with him twice before, once with our future spouses. His need for control was given by his wife as a reason why they rarely travelled together, while his take was that she could never be relied upon to be organized for the daily tours...amounting to the same thing, I suppose. It had crossed my mind that, since he had bought both of our tickets from a hundred thousand travel miles, "he who pays the piper gets to call the tune," but only for a short senior moment before I gave it a reality check. My soul wasn't for sale. I intended to pay him back eventually.

"This place is fabulous," I said, defending my choice of novelty hotel that came with statues of happy Buddhas by the pool, smiling pigs, and a whole open-air temple of ceramic monks at prayer. I had asked for a room with a window (which technically we had) that looked out over the pool. Perhaps it had once, I thought. The online pictures showed such rooms with happy patrons enjoying the view.

"Oh well, it's a place to sleep," I said, pulling on a multicoloured shirt to go with the banana-yellow shorts. "At least the air-con works. Bangkok here we come."

John wore safari beige, Tilley.

Had I probed the anxiety a little further, I may have admitted to being uneasy about the voyage to come. The issue of pirates still weighed heavily even though I had half-heartedly convinced myself it was no big deal. In my hollow blustering to the concerned well-wishers back home, I had pointed to commercial ships with big payloads, noting that we didn't qualify for pirate attention. I showed them patches for sea sickness and described medical certificates for malaria, yellow fever, and bat-induced rabies for their cheerful assault on death by rare diseases, but I could only stare dumbly without answers for shark bites and poisonous jellyfish. I endured the good-natured ribbing about wearing a body suit in the bars. "I am too old for that shit" was my usual reply...knowing curiosity kills the cat; knowing I was curious. And now here we were, about to take our first steps into Bangkok, a city known to swallow its victims whole.

3

BANGKOK...THE CITY OF SIN?

SEPT. 8-12, 2009

Bangkok, the city of sin... Many cities qualify for this title, including the seemingly conservative and chic sophisticated London and Paris. Rio has Mardi Gras, Vegas has gambling, and Amsterdam has red-light canals, but ask someone what Bangkok has and the answer will be some variation on perversion, pornography, and dirty old men. Bangkok has plenty to offer, and it was a sad title, I first thought, for a city of twelve million, adorned with the structures of a rich and colourful history. This was evident in the magnificent royal palace, sumptuous parks, grand plazas, and gold-clad Buddha temples on every bend in the river Chao Phraya that snakes with massive force through the city. But maybe the river was the key. If rivers wash away the sins of man, then Bangkok, being at the river's end, is the catch basin of all sins flushed from the north. Based on what I saw, there must be a dark world upriver in the heart of Thailand.

John and I passed the gauntlet of human sale in Bangkok, for the most part unscathed. It was offered up like fast food... plastic menus of sex specials—one-on-one, two for one, one of each, quality quickies, priced to stay or go—barked from street corners, pulled from purses, dealt from cab drivers and owners of three-wheeled tuk-tuks (pronounced *took-took*), which is Thai talk, so named, possibly, for the sound of the two-stroke engine. It's a motorcycle with a covered seating area on the back that carries four tourists or twelve locals. It was easy to dismiss these third-party offers. There were no soft brown eyes trolling for weaknesses, caressing hands, or *Parfum D'homme Savage* strategically daubed to melt girds of steel. The tone in their voices and the furrowed brows when we declined their offers suggested we must be a pair of space aliens who had landed in Bangkok by mistake. Of course, it was thought that if no sex was required, we must need a suit. Why else would two grown men wander the streets? Temples and ruins? Ha, likely story!

"The finest suits for you, sir, I get you best deal." The menus of sex, some with photo illustrations, were quietly folded away. Embossed cards of gentlemen tailors magically appeared. Offers of massages with happy endings and floor shows with ping-pong girls rolled with elegant tones toward the finest Italian wool, Thai silk, Egyptian cotton, and crisp linens, craftsmanship by family tailors with histories predating the invention of the loom. You could feel the silk blend weave against your skin and the sculpted suit lifting you from polyester tourist to haute-couture celebrity. Women, fast cars, fame and fortune...a man of multiple suits...the addiction of fine tailoring like heroin in your veins.

"No suits, thank you," a Canadian brush-off. Others, Aussies and Kiwis, boldly told them to "fuck off, mate."

"You want taxi...tuk-tuk? Good deal." Cards, of course, followed.

The air-con on our first outing and return to our room had failed—or, rather, we had failed to understand the connection between taking the room key card out of the slot, which gave us light and, as we found out, sweet, cooled air. They were linked. This was easily manipulated with some cardboard to leave the air conditioning running after we turned out the lights, undone by room service, who had experienced this bit of brilliance before. Cool the room, go for a walk, and come back to an oven.

On our last evening in Bangkok, John and I decided to venture out for a night of look-see in Patpong, one of the world's most infamous red-light districts and a driving force to Bangkok's nearly twenty million tourists each year.

There was no question of whether we had arrived. No directions were required. The air hummed with the buzz of neon and cranked music from nightclub doorways and the megaphone calls of showgirl hawkers wanting to pull tourists exactly like us into their showrooms. It wasn't a stroll past a bar or two; there were hundreds of bars, possibly thousands, on large avenues, lesser streets, and cul-de-sacs, each claiming the most beautiful bodies, male or female, combined groupings, or variations thereof. There was a movement of erotic anticipation. The hypnotic beats of electronic music worked its magic…exciting heartbeats of rising desire, blood pulsing engorged veins…a rhythmic throbbing chosen carefully to vibrate the tequila-juiced libidos pressed into the silk camisoles, laced thongs, or the sensual nakedness of nothing under at all. The light cottons revealed hardened desires in both genders alike.

We were immediately pulled into a tidal flow of humanity as we stepped out of the tuk-tuk, pushing aside outstretched arms and unhooking hands that were determined to drag us in. We moved quickly, hoping we could find a bar and nurse drinks while watching the nightlife go by. This was not that kind of neighbourhood. There was no room for passive coffee shop voyeurs.

Hoping to avoid the mob, we scrambled into a side street. It was, as it turned out, a trap. The road was dead ended. We were immediately stopped dead in our tracks, surrounded by a web of street hawkers selling the show inside. Their voices were oddly husky.

"What you 'fraid of…big, handsome man? We no hurt you. You no think we pretty?" It wasn't that they weren't, but there was something different for sure. I could see makeup had been applied with a shovel; their skin had the waxen hue of mannequins.

"Come in and see. You know you want to."

It wasn't the words but the flesh pressed in well past the space of comfort that caught us by surprise. There were multiple faces and hands clad in baubles and rings. Fingers massaged the neck. Fingers raked the scalp. Fingers twisted the hairs into curls and tugged gently as one might in foreplay, wanting to send signals to move the head down…down, please…way down. Hands caressed and patted our faces and when the resistance became minimal, as we hoped to show no fear (we were mature adults after all); hands moved to caress earlobes, pinching nipples, then moved downward toward vulnerable thighs. Lips moved close to my ears and whispered something teasing. A wet tongue rimmed my ear. Less than fifteen seconds had passed, but blood was flowing. There was the sensation of melting flesh. I think it was mine.

"You like? You want more?" I stopped a hand before it could stroke my groin, but another one slid up my shorts and grabbed a cheek.

We relented, knowing that if we didn't, we might be ravaged on the street or, worse, exposed as excited in our light cotton shorts. In truth, we had no excuse, nor could we protest our innocence. We were in Patpong, after all, knowingly, but we were caught off guard by the shameless, forward speed of lightning foreplay and our even faster capitulation. We had been two lambs too easy to the sacrifice.

As we headed through the gauntlet of groping flesh toward the nightclub entrance, I saw the street gang high-fiving and throwing their heads back in gales of laughter. One removed half a padded bra to wipe away the tears. Of all the streets and nightclubs to wander into, we had found the one that catered to the cross-gender crowd. Maybe they all did—who knows? I could feel sweat beading and starting to roll. I was far beyond my zone of comfort, though curiosity chased the cat.

Inside, a tall, lean man dressed in black silk welcomed us in. His shirt was opened, and several gold chains sparkled under a strobe of blue light from above. His large Adam's apple moved like a piston with every word he spoke.

"Good evening, gentlemen. Welcome to our club." The words were delivered slowly, with a haunting of late-night Vincent Price. He sported a black goatee that hung from a chiseled face, hatchet-thin veins and their tributaries disappearing into the hollows of two bony sockets and inkwell eyes. A thinning tuft of black hair ringed a scalp so tight it seemed transparent. The skeletal frame suggested a cross of the grim reaper caught without his cloak and scythe with a vulture waiting to dive into a feast of fresh roadkill.

Maybe we should have begged out, claiming wives were waiting or the tuk-tuk taxi was expecting us back, but our ruse of brave maturity prevented a hasty retreat. We had been corralled by the street hounds like two village idiots, and now it seemed that maître death was pushing us further into this iniquitous den of forbidden fruit. As if reading my mind of cut and run, our host caught our shoulders with bony fingers covered in large, gaudy rings and asked if we would like to be seated by the stage. "For a closer look?" We declined in hasty unison. We intended to be personas non-conspicuous, grata or not.

Our attention was quickly diverted to a stage. In the tradition of hammering large brass gongs, a sculpted man of oriental extraction let loose one stroke that hung in the room like Big Ben in a thick London fog. At center stage was a line of men, teak-brown, oiled and muscled, some naked, others with thongs or strips of loincloth, who raised number cards to the audience. There was polite applause from the audience and a wolf whistle that set some men posturing in a Mr. Atlas pose. A second gong prompted them to turn like chickens on a rotisserie and flash their cards and personal amenities in the opposite direction. The well-endowed used extra hip swagger to accentuate the obvious while the "have-nots," which were few, tried not-so-subtle primping. On the stroke of three, the men filed off-stage...meat market gladiators back to their cells. A few were intercepted before leaving the room and escorted to waiting tables.

My brain battled with the ethics of being entertained in a place like this. Back home, I had resisted most offers in my life to go see peelers and pole dancers, terms of labelling that ignored that they were women first. Patrons that I had known of such establishments had no desire to be lectured.

"Fuck off! What are you, fucking gay?" That logic defied further argument. If you liked women, you were gay. If you didn't like women, you were gay. Relenting was a lesson in the anthropological study of men, post-Darwin chimp, pre-homo-erectus, sometimes called the high school gym class that lasts about forty years.

We men don't want to be seen as getting excited in a strip club. "What, not getting any at home?" It's a rhetorical question since best buddies would have spilled the beans more than once over a salvo of beers...hence the reason you are at the strip club in the first place. Besides, they are probably married and have kids as well.

We like to drink beer loudly...talk sports over a round of pool, acknowledging occasionally an overly large set of jugs, a tight bod, or a nice piece of ass, and only after the opening rack of splitting balls might we point to a great rack before lling a red ball to the side pocket. We go to such places use this is where men supposedly bond with testosterone, gain, don't get a chub on because that might make you We get to tell stories about what happened in Vegas or

Vegas-like scenarios, which should have stayed in Vegas but came back in embellished tales of longer and larger for occasions such as these.

"Next thing I know, I am getting down and dirty in a threesome with my best buddy and his girlfriend, who took us both at once. A real skank!" Men are horny. Women are whores.

Calling strippers anything but women enables us to employ demeaning locker-room expletives to distinguish between naked "hoes" and our sacred mothers...a miserable, dumb motherfucker being the lowest form of man in our eyes, next to a cock-sucker, though this rule apparently does not apply in prison.

If we have any line of defense on ignoring strippers glued to a pole, it is showmanship. There is none. Long gone, of course, are the days of exotic burlesque when there was the seductive show of skin from a glitz of disappearing feathers. Strippers, not burlesque artists, arrive in heels and not much else, strutting like hot cats on a din of music and 80 Proof, grinding on a pole as if they had a bad itch. They bump, grind, and gyrate to titillate our fantasies, stir the blood to the nether regions, get a rise, and then send us packing. Touching is a Class-A offence and will get you dragged to the street protesting your innocence. What you are left with are the haunting memories of your favourite love songs, debased to butt-flossing with leopard-print thongs by a girl named Candy, Tasha, or Angel, while holding your cue, chalking your tip, and missing pink with a hard shot, leaving two balls floating.

Here, however, in the battle of conscience, the side of looking outside the straight box of the staid and responsible won out. The half-brain of Puritan rebuke told me to leave, but we were already being ushered to seats by a waiter, summoned by the snap of the buzzard's beak.

My eyes began to adjust to the dim light as we climbed upward, past the settings of tables and chairs. The room was not what I expected. The stage was surrounded by seating pushed to the ceiling, like an arena. Looking across the tiers of darkness, the room appeared to be full, and beyond the front tables of gawking men, evenly cast with both men and women; couples sharing tables, drinks in hand, casual as piano bar patrons in a five-star lounge. The theatre had the air of a Toulouse Lautrec painting where top hats and gowns had lent an appearance of civility to a grotesque circus of tawdry cabaret. We were seated at a table that was as high and far back as the building would allow, in the shadows, out from the view of judgment, I hoped, and when I checked, I found all eyes thankfully trained on the stage, which was now being lit with torches, carried by a fresh cast of nubile bodies moving in a rhythmic dance to African drums. On the final beat, all feet snapped to attention, waiting. From the darkness deep beneath the arena, a Sudan chair borne by four strong men bearing a sequined Cleopatra emerged. Two slaves followed, carrying large palm leaf fans, and they in turn were followed by a man who looked to be wearing a sword. I was wrong. It was not a sword.

There were only so many positions, I had thought, that could be performed in the act of sex. These players were out to prove me wrong. Had they been street buskers, they may have billed themselves as Ivan the Impaler and Cleo the sword-swallower, though this act had no place on the sidewalks of the world. This was a live sex show, after all, and the performers wasted no time in conjugating the act.

The house for the most part remained unmoved—until, that is, Cleo, the impaled, wrapped his legs around Ivan the Impaler's waist (having absorbed the entirety of what had appeared to be a lengthy rapier), facing hands-down, and was forced in the style of a wheelbarrow race to crab-walk around the stage and then out into the audience. There was a gasp, and not one I think of empathy or disbelief at how much had been sheathed in the human scabbard. Up to this point, it had been a viewing, like watching XXX video, without the close-ups. The action was conveniently far away. Brought into the audience, it became a 3D flick asking for the audience to reach out and touch. There was noticeable squirming at many of the tables visited, not the least being ours.

The gladiators had come looking for a thumbs-up approval in the form of Thai baht currency tucked into their...well, that was the problem—there was no place to tuck a baht. Strippers, at least, wore G-strings. I tried staring anywhere else but at the acrobatic contortion that confronted us, but it was impossible to ignore what might have once been a dark circus sideshow attraction: it was that mythical Cuban pinga hung on a slim, muscled Asian and, judging from my view of what had unfolded on stage, he was the smallest of the pair. The eyes of the house were on us, watching, waiting possibly for some move that none of the other tables had been willing to provide. John quickly passed me a 100-baht denomination to hand over, hoping, I think, that this contortion would leave faster than they had come. As I reached out, the crab's hand shot forward like a lizard's tongue, drew my hand to his engorged member, and forced me to squeeze, holding it in place for all to see. He could feel my resistance, sense my judgement in the quick struggle that ensued to pull my arm back, as if I had been forced to grope a leper. His was the gaze of a snake, eyes trained on a cornered rat. *Dare you judge me*, they said, *you Peeping Tom of misery. If only you knew...if only you knew.*

Indeed, if only. Was this the child—now a young man as the stories ran—sold by desperate parents into the slavery of the sex trade? Had they known his fate? Had they even cared? Which monster was greatest; the ones who paid the silver or the ones who took it? And was this to be his entire life, a human reduced to a wheelbarrow crab-walk, conjoined in sodomy, forced to perform to crowds of casually interested, mildly amused voyeurs, multiple times a day? How long before youth and beauty faded and disease ravaged the body?

How many thousands were there, where do they come from, and where do they go? My head swarmed with questions.

I looked for answers in his face, a face polished like a cold marble bust of a Greek warrior, chiselled beauty, with dark, hollow eyes absent of the individual. As if reading my thoughts, in a final gesture of resistance or contempt, he rose off his arms and, held by his partner, stretched his long, sinewy body toward our table. His head twitched side to side, and he flicked his tongue with lascivious curls like a two-headed multi-limbed sea serpent of Hollywood design (though Hollywood's version could never come with the hard prop this one offered), luring Jason and his sailors into the clutches of doom. The body glistened with sweat, still hard, still menacing, still tempting, challenging all those who would look down in condemnation from their good fortune, with his athletic prowess and muscular virility. As he was lowered back to the floor, he broke into a thin smile and spun, giving a guttural laugh, and, with his partner still providing legs, crabbed down the stairs into the theatre of darkness. He had managed to skim the money from my hand, but I never saw where it went. I couldn't wait to return to the street.

The tuk-tuk ride back was quiet, as quiet, I guess, as a stressed 2-cycle Kawasaki leaving a trail of blue smoke could be. John and I sat in silence, watching the city around us. There were thousands of other tuk-tuks and taxis moving humanity to dark destinations all over the city. The travel brochures said that Bangkok never sleeps. I began to see why. Patpong had still been going strong when we left somewhere in the wee hours of the morning.

A tuk-tuk driver had informed us that we were lucky—"or maybe no's, dependings on youse ideas for funs time"—that we had missed the mid-April celebrations of Songkan. This is when all of Thailand celebrates their astrological New Year; a three-day festival and celebration of water play. "No's safe while on the streets," we were told. Tourists and locals alike are hosed from pickups or mopeds with mammoth water guns or dumped on with pails of water. It is a continuous pool party with thousands of tourists attending. The light white cottons reveal all, see-through advertisements of what's beneath. Street clothes are stripped to bathing suits, and in some corners of play, eventually, nothing at all. If good-natured was not your chosen stance, staying home was the sage advice.

Mother Nature offered up this festival daily. The day's humidity turned into a warm night rain. Unlike the summer rains in Toronto, which usually brought a cooling freshness, the Bangkok air became heavy and thick, with the sun-baked asphalt, still warm, turning the splashes of moisture into a steam bath. My clothes of light cotton clung to the beading perspiration. John's safari browns melted into stripes of sweat, though in truth, some was spray from the road. Arriving fresh in this city had to be an art form.

I tried not to let my mind wander too far into the perceived bleakness of our night's entertainment because, truthfully, I didn't know what to think. My mind was a battleground of contradictions. I tried convincing myself on the long ride across the city that, like hunger or any of the dozens of afflictions that curse mankind, I had not created the carnie of lust; that it had been around since that snake and apple routine and would be there long after I was gone. Deviant behaviour was labelled as such, according to whose rules of human engagement? My struggle to retrieve my arm was based on a lifetime of social behaviour; sexual desires were private, undercover retrievals from the brain's library of mostly un-vetted dreams.

In Toronto the Good, a billboard ad for risqué lingerie was cause for scandal, TV stations warned viewers of possible sexual content (knowing a suggestive warning kept the viewers glued), and a continent was drawn into debates about a Janet Jackson wardrobe malfunction that showed the square root of sexual nothing. If this sexual mass frenzy of a jungle was so wrong, as my social conscience suggested it was, not only the symbiotic need of circus act and viewer, but the entire concept of such complete sexual freedom, why, then, did Bangkok, a city of millions in a nation of many more, condone it, proudly wear the badge, wrap it around them like the flags of freedom carried by battle-scarred rebel victors over sexual tyranny? And what was the suggestion of multiple millions visiting Bangkok each year? In lands of fanatic theocracies or states where theologies were the basis of law, this behaviour was driven underground, punishable by imprisonment and even death. But those needs, those dark desires, did not go away. This may have accounted for the strong presence of Middle Eastern tourists who brushed shoulders as we wandered through Patpong. The audience, I noticed, had been a Babel of cultures. What did it say, however, about the large numbers of Western tourists, blessed with "liberal democracies," lined several deep in anticipation of the raw, dark, and salacious? They were, perhaps, countries and places that did the talk while Bangkok's exotic distance provided the walk of the dark-room glory holes for anonymous sex.

There were no answers, I told myself, when it came to quenching the thirsts of our deepest desires of animality. We pursued them and filled them in the end, like a pride of hungry lions devouring the young calf; temporary gratification, but never enough to satisfy the hunger, left prowling, always with a gnawing ache for more.

Neither John nor I wanted to sleep. We wandered the streets of our neighbourhood, Khaosan Road, famous to Westerners because it was Westerners who hung out there, preferring to hang out with Westerners over the locals. The small cache of locals kept it exotic among the offerings of Aussie and American breakfasts for reluctant tourists. As we walked, revellers staggered from bars, girls teased half-hearted invitations (wanting to sleep but hoping to get paid to do it) from strobe-lit doorways, and we watched money pass hands for unknown transactions while shop owners swept sidewalks in anticipation of the better day ahead. We found a thatch-covered sidewalk café, dimly lit with colored lights, still serving. The beer was cold and welcomed. John diverted my attention to a rat climbing stairs down the road, while he kicked away a very large one by my feet. He knew, had I known, there would have been a scene.

After nearly a week in Bangkok, we were off to exotic Phuket, billed as Bangkok with beaches. We surrendered our souls to Captain Rob, tired, frayed slightly at the elbows, mind and soul craving a jolt of familiarity.

4

PHUKET
FEAR OF MOTORBIKES
TSUNAMI REVISITED
THE MUPPET SEND-OFF

MID-MONSOON SEASON, A DRY EVENING, SEPT. 17

Captain Rob was found at the Royal Phuket Marina, a thirty minute taxi ride from the airport. He was wandering along a floating concrete pier, one of many that ran perpendicular to a sprawling rise of modern condos, on the backs of exclusive shops. We had been greeted by crisp salutes from the men at the roadside guardhouse and welcoming salutations as uniformed doormen reached for our luggage under a canopy of teak and bright lights at the clubhouse doors. There were smiles of welcome from security, all of which shouted excess and exclusivity long before we breached the gates to the harbour.

If fine cars are showcased baubles to mansions they inhabit, it was the opposite here for the luxury condos and shops. First glance revealed sailboats and launches that proclaimed status by the foot, from nations that created wealth by the barrel; Singapore, Hong Kong, Malaysia, the who's who of Far East power, now Near East, since I was here.

It was here in the wash of gleaming yachts, fluttering halyards, and tailored help in pressed whites that the sight of Rob refreshed the spirit in the same way, perhaps, a bag lady found peering through the glass of a Fifth Avenue icon humanized the road of greed and pretension. Our fearless leader, captain-to-be of the high seas and lord of all that was moored in berth C10, blond hair cascading toward the small of his back, with rugged good looks in chiselled, tanned flesh, was shirtless and without pants, clad only in flip-flops and bright orange SpongeBob boxers. He was moving a bag of semi-crushed beer cans to a teak and plexiglass trash bin designed to go unnoticed.

He acknowledged our approach with a wave, suggesting we join him where he stood.

We moved down teak walkways until we arrived mid-harbour, where there were welcomes all around. Through the chit-chat, I stopped to breathe it all in.

It was like standing, I presumed, in center field at Ascot, where the highborn of royalty, the power brokers of wealth, and the daily flavours of fame were displayed in their polished vestments of class. Again here, the notables of attention were yachts, not people. Little notice might be given to three artful dodgers wandering in their midst.

And, among the yachts of fantasy, named in progressive enormity, *Ladies* and *Princesses* to *Queens* and *Empresses*, rays of sunshine to fiery constellations, kingdoms on earth to points in the universe, gods of the deep, rulers of the heavens, expressions of want, desires of need—the name *Bob-the-Boat*, our chariot and home for the next couple of months, stood out—plain, yet not unobtrusive. Moored among the gleaming whites and dark navy blues, smoke-tinted windows, elaborate portals, and sleek designs of longer and larger, the squared lines of *Bob-the-Boat*, bathed in lime yellow and white, trimmed in chrome, suggested attention and reserve, like a sequined suit at a black-tie gala.

I dragged luggage aboard (John marched smartly with his ten pounds of gym bag) and we accepted our first beer with a heartfelt thanks. It was hot. It was impossible, as we swigged down the beer, not to be overwhelmed by the luxury of the surroundings, though perhaps that was only me. We had entered from the outside through a set of double doors from the stern. They were closed quickly behind us.

"Gotta keep these doors shut tight. I've got the air-con going at full tilt," Rob had said as we entered. John and I dropped sighs of relief.

It was the wood—inlaid teak on the floor, panels on the wall, solid cabinet doors, and a beamed ceiling—that caught my attention. John fawned over the galley with blue pearl granite countertops, the four-burner gas-top stove, stainless steel hood, microwave, and fridge. Doors popped open to reveal a washing machine, an ice maker, and a flat-screen TV with a DVD player. Two padded chairs faced a teak coffee table that lifted to dining height in front of the wraparound sofa. Natural light filled the entire space. The large windows were trimmed in lined draperies. The rest of the boat's interior followed suit, with a teak spiral staircase leading down to staterooms with queen beds and two fully equipped heads with showers. Golden teak reigned supreme.

The helm was centred with a large six-spoke captain's wheel and a dozen gauges and switches below a gray panel the size of a laptop that read *Ray Marine*. It, we were told, was the key, the lifeblood and brain of all navigation on the boat.

"Electronic map, sonar and radar. Lay in the waypoints of where you are heading, tweak for visible land masses, shoals, coral reefs, submerged rocks, buoys, lights, lighthouses, shipwrecks, oil wells, drilling platforms...yeah, that's about it... then hit this button and *voila*...automatic pilot. I will teach you how it works in good time...you will need to know, but first," he said, "let's drink. Tomorrow we will rent some motorbikes for you guys, and I'll show you a little bit of Thailand."

Right up there with sharks, on par with pirates, a notch lower than appendage-shrivelling STDs...out of left field came motorbikes. Didn't people—tourists, for example—die horrible deaths on those things? Crushed cadavers with pavement burns...heads found up the ass of a roadside water buffalo? The fact that I had never ridden a motorbike created a temporary knot in my sphincter. I had never driven in England or Japan because it meant stepping out of comfort into a zone short of terror, all to learn how to drive on the opposite side of the road. Besides, that's what taxis were for. Yet there it was, two challenges thrown to the wind to separate chaff from the men. It was not a gauntlet thrown deliberately, but it rose as such. To that was added the nightmare of having to learn in a circus of traffic at high noon, since that was when we were scheduled to sign waivers for death, dismemberment, and full replacement destruction, before taking possession of the bikes.

A day later, with the driving force of fear and paranoia, I slipped into the lava flow of buses, dump trucks, and ten thousand motorbikes; all pressing for precious road space, all unwilling to share, all vying, it seemed, for "kill the tourist of the month" award. As the fear beaded, it rolled from the crown of my head and wet my shorts.

Rob had a motorcycle licence. Well, of course he did! He had ridden for years. Here, he already knew the terrain, having spent time touring about with Cathy, and he never listened to his inner "what if" self-preservation mechanism that kept grown men from philandering or licking frost-covered pipes in the dead of winter (an act I had witnessed during recess in grade four). His departure was fearlessly executed, like a diving instructor demonstrating a backflip jackknife double twist two and a half rotations no-splash pool entry...never looking back. If you drive, they will follow. Simply learn by doing. His final instructions had been "Gas right, signals left, brake with both. Got it? Good. Follow me!" Gone!

After several days, I was praising myself for this life achievement. I had cheated death twice and became fairly proficient at moving around town. At the first traffic circle from the rental shop, I hit a bus. At the second it was a van. At ten and a half miles per hour, the crashes were non-life-threatening. Falling to the pavement and being run over was more likely. The bus never knew I hit it. The van driver gave me the up-yours and never stopped. It was later agreed that a) I had to let go of the gas when I hit the brake, and b) whoever had the most lug nuts got the right of way.

From the bike shop, we rode up a mountain and visited a very large Buddha that stared with peaceful calm over Chalong Bay. We stopped and paid for the privilege of feeding an elephant that covered us in mashed banana and massaged my head with its trunk. We went to a beach and watched tourists parasail, then played in the surf of the white-foam waves. I stripped to my underwear and then changed back to my dry shorts to prevent chafing where one should never be chafed. We ate coconut soup and climbed serpentine roadways over small mountains and hills in pursuit of the next ocean-view vista. They were breathtaking. And we shopped.

"We need supplies for the boat," it was explained matter-of-factly, so we detoured to a food outlet where the locals shopped. Parking lots are a disaster at the best of times, but a bargain basement food depot lot is a shark frenzy, especially with the horse-to-the-stable-death-to-those-who-get-in-my-way home-bound patrons of Phuket...even without a hint of blood in the water.

We exited "The Big Cheap" (I can't remember the real name, but it's not on tourist maps of places to see for good reason) with a cart full of supplies, cases of water, cases of beer, and nonessential foodstuff. Of course, I had wondered where it would go on the scooters but had not asked.

"Stack the cases between your legs. The other stuff can go under the flip-up seat and into the two backpacks." If Rob had been able to put it where I suggested, he would not have been able to sit. I refused, citing fear, citing self-preservation, citing the fifth, pleading the fourth, not to put cases of whatever between my legs. I agreed to wear the largest backpack, stuffed with ten pounds of deboned chicken, a bag of unshelled shrimp, six oblong yams, a dozen dwarf bananas, green oranges, yellow cucumbers, boxed milk, bagged cereal, canned tomatoes, jars of jam and peanut butter, twenty pounds of rice, whole almonds, crushed cashews, hot Thai sauce, and frozen fish. If I had leaned backwards, gravity would have taken me off the back of the bike. The other two were thus loaded to death-defying limits (as if mine wasn't).

On the expressway, we rode shoulder to hubcap with 18-wheelers, cement trucks, missile Mercedes and the occasional three-wheel tuk-tuks adapted with platforms for carrying bags of rice, mounds of palm leaves, and possibly a pig or two and/or seven passengers where three should fit...sometimes driving towards us—against traffic. It was not unusual to round a corner and find a dog had wandered onto the road, sitting, defiant, unfazed by traffic, licking its balls. (And let's face it, in a showdown, I knew the dog would be fine and I would be dead or dying or found twisted in a dog-mimicking curl as if licking my own!)

Supplies were stuffed in crannies and recesses, cleverly disguised as hatches and holds in the boat. Beer—the better part of a case—was consumed, and the minor gambits of the day became Herculean triumphs spun into cocktail nuggets of future happy hour glee. Introspection deepened with each can crushed...*pfsst...slurp*...until I sat face to face with the naked truth—*swig, gulp*. The shame of showing terror of the unknown, plunging thought and heart into darkness...*pfsst, gulp, slurp*. The soul, my soul, had rubbed shoulders with the bleakness of self-doubt...*slurp*...despair...*gulp*, and then in Robert Duvall's *Apocalypse Now* bravado...*pfsst, slurp*...I had snatched conquest from defeat...*slurp*...won the battle of the rising bile...*b-u-r-r-p*, and finally, like napalm on the morning battlefield...*swig, gulp, b-u-r-r-r-r-p*, claimed the smell of victory over fear.

"Another beer, Norm? Christ, you're full of shit! It's just a bloody moped," Rob said with a hint of derision. He may have wondered what kind of pecker-less first mate he had hired on.

Over the next few days, we explored the entire island of Phuket. We rode two hours into the interior of Thailand to a mountain waterfall where we swam in the cool waters of descending pools. We visited several beaches, swimming in one and heeding the red-flag warnings of dangerous undertow at the others. We watched planes take off, a pastime we all had as kids, growing up in the shadows of Toronto's Pearson Airport. John had lived under the flight path and had never lost his fascination for planes. He could tell the kind of airplane by the airstreams at thirty thousand feet. "That's a 747," (four streams), "most likely Thai Air or Cathay Pacific...most airlines have stopped flying them in favour of the Boeing triple seven with two engines" (two streams). A single plume from the tail was likely a Lockheed something or other, "and that there is the French Fokker...complete rip-off of the..." and so it went. I never questioned because I knew he knew. We ate the street meat of numerous vendors and never asked what. Got lost and never cared where. Found places and never knew how. But one place begged the question... Why?

It was to be our treat, Rob had said; a place he had saved until last, like a fine bottle of wine to say farewell to Phuket and toast our venture to sea. It was rather poetic, especially for Rob. It was Patong, the jewel of Phuket beaches, a beach with great swimming, lively bars, massage parlours, pleasures for whatever your preference and shopping for whatever your needs. We arrived midday, having taken the bikes through a hill and dale of twists and turns, past villas and hotels tucked away in clusters of bougainvillea and lush palms, cultured and wild. Had I been looking, there were signs. Whole beach fronts were empty, and fields had cement block pilings that had once housed buildings. We rode past a sign that read *Welcome to Patong Beach* with Thai script below.

It never registered completely...it took parking the bikes on the busy street facing the surf and walking the miles of beaten track filled with tourists. I had never been here before, but there was a recognition that nagged. The other beaches had been quiet retreats of surf and sand, but Patong was a malthusian venture in bars and shops offering expensive replicas of things that were half-price up the street. It morphed into back alleys and duplicate main drags with signs for hotels, pizza, massage, Thai cuisine, Chinese food, Asian noodles, Aussie steaks, American breakfast, handcrafts, authentic souvenirs, T-shirts, fine tailors, bike rentals, car rentals, scuba lessons, travel agencies, coffee bars, coffee houses, Starbucks, KFC, Burger King, Danish, Swiss, Swedish, Norwegian...and then it hit me. It may have been the open courtyard of pillars and arches or one particular street running perpendicular to our path, but something tweaked a synapse of recognition that rolled video in my brain. It had been on this very beach, shot high from a hotel balcony, December 26, 2004, that the killer tsunami had rolled over the sand, over the tops of palm trees, over cars parked in orderly rows, through shop windows, through courtyards of tourists, up streets of hawkers, into bars of dancers, over stools of drinkers, chairs of gawkers, pushing with tidal force; children, parents, lovers, old, young, towards some destination inland and then, with awesome draw, sucked the lifeless bodies of the thousands who had never seen it coming back out to sea. The lucky dead were buried by loved ones. Others, never found, were lost to the tides of the Indian Ocean.

Standing in the sunshine, five years later, listening to the patter of commerce, watching the waves crash on shore and roll without menace back down the sandy beach, to hear the children's laughter and to know that if that same wave happened today...if it was my family...my children making sandcastles...I would be as helpless as they all had been. For a moment, I sensed the pang and wretched suffering of parents who had tried to gather doomed children into their arms or those who had pushed loved ones to a higher perch only to be swept away themselves. Families ripped apart forever. Generations were lost; from India to Indonesia, more than 230,000 dead. The sheer terror of such thoughts made me feel the insignificance of my power, the smallness of my being, the hugeness of nature...and then I moved on, refusing to relinquish my senses to "what if" But of God, if one believed in such omnipotent power, one could surely ask... Why?

And maybe it was here that started me thinking of why I was about to go off to sea in the first place...why, if things happened for good reason, this "chance of a lifetime," as my wife had explained it, had landed in my lap. Pondering this tragedy of monstrous proportions was asking me to challenge my views of the world, of others, especially of myself, through what I came to realize was a very narrow scope of vision, evident possibly in my reaction at the Bangkok nightclub or my resistance to riding a motorbike. I caught myself viewing, assessing, and pronouncing judgements as if I was still in my easy chair at home, living life vicariously through the lens of others. Looking for the familiar, the safe, the well-trodden path, was like seeking out a McBurger in the hills of Tuscany or Rome. What I wanted to find, I wasn't sure, but I knew I wasn't seeking the comfort of beige, the known of familiar, the safe of well-trodden. This beach that I stood upon that had seen it coming and watched it go reminded me that life was too precious to watch it from afar, too huge to leave it to all the others, too terrifying to take it for granted, too fragile not to care, and too infinite and finite in the same breath not to make of it what I could; a case for carpe diem. But that said, it would be a work in progress, like diverting the Thames around London or getting a Republican to give a damn about the plight of the poor.

⚓ ⚓ ⚓

Subic Bay in the Philippines was two and a half thousand miles of wake from Thailand. The pull was minimal as the push began. Captain Rob announced our departure date from Phuket, like a travel host giving the next port of call on his last cruise.

"We need to leave by noon tomorrow. High tide...and there will barely be ten feet of water in the bay, even at that. I've given notice at the front office...so expect to get up extra early. We'll need to prep." At some point, he mentioned that Langkawi in Malaysia would be our first stop, with Singapore our goal in a week. There were a couple of other stops in between that I missed.

The previous day had been dedicated to tying up loose ends. We made a second run for water and beer, and without fear, I had accepted my share of the cases, propped between my legs. We then returned the scooters to the shop, leaving ourselves at the mercy of buses and schedules they never posted or kept in an effort to return to the yacht club. It rained on us—not for the first time on this trip, but now we stood with the locals, waiting for tarp-draped trucks offered as buses. We packed in between veiled women with bags of groceries and crates of wet chickens, school kids in uniforms of blue and white, some in excited chatter, others dozing, heads bobbing, while others were busy picking two-thumbed texts on cell phones to unseen friends. A phone rang and the leathery hand of a Buddhist monk pulled a phone from a satchel, but not in time for the call. A text message was forwarded. It was a simple act of quiet communication I had never done.

Our final approach to the five-star yacht club of Phuket was a long, increasingly wet walk from the main highway. With scooters, it had taken only a minute or two. Our arrival in the state of wet dogs may have gladdened the hearts of those who ran the front office, I think, informed of our imminent departure.

There is nothing like departure, it seems, for bringing out new sea lore from the yachtsmen who are staying tethered; stories of disaster and near-misses, ships sunk, men lost, eight-meter waves or no wind for a week. And so it was on the night before our departure, announced in "potluck bring booze make merry fashion," to be one evening hence, which was now upon us.

The event started with a gathering around a guitar, and then two, as Captain Rob brought out his, then, gradually spread from off the back of the large catamaran called *Oshili Nawa*, toward boats in either direction. "*Oshili Nawa*" is a Namibian greeting like "G'day mate" from Australia or "Howzit" in South Africa. The boat and crew, it turns out, were South African. The gathering became a pier party as it flowed towards the floating gangplank for the wharf, with more owners turning on their lights and hanging off sofa-lined decks and teak swim platforms. It didn't hurt, of course, that beer was being offered up, a joint passed around or the possibility of a night in the sack with Liz, the bikini-clad woman, was dangling like a participle...*bouncing seductively through the crowd, the sailors eyed the prize*, and, perchance the dangle should fall, there was the waiting crew of the catamaran, all young, "at sea" single and silver-tongued, capable of making the catch. The captain was odds on to succeed, with Greek God features—corkscrew blond hair dipping to his shoulders, Paul Newman eyes, tanned to the nether regions, white cotton shorts strategically balanced to drop at the slightest hint of yes. He played guitar in practiced jest, at times arm swinging like an Elvis windmill for single chord repeats, shaking the box to give a shiver to the sound, and when he pulled his face into a hurtin' grimace, his perfect teeth shone perfect white. My body, in a state of Buddha advancement, easily took me out of the running, so I concentrated on the cruiser load of Swedes that had docked earlier. My wife is Swedish (another good reason for pursuit retreat, though not the Swedish part). Their English bad, my Swedish worse, we picked through conversations that became bolder as the beer flowed between shots of Swedish paint stripper called schnapps. To an outsider listening to the conversation, they may have thought they had fallen into a Muppet movie with the Swedish cook.

"Yah yah, urn dee burn dee urnin burnin, eller hur?" (*Yes, those are a nice set of pontoons, don't you think?*), nodding toward the party catamaran, as ample D-cup Liz, the party girl, breezed by in a bikini that had become smaller as it dried.

"Yahveest yah, inky burnin, finky holy doodee!" (*Yes, they are, fine indeed!*)

"Hahaha." (*Hahaha.*)

"Ewl?" (*Beer?*)

"Yahveest yah, inky meenden om yawg yurden." (*Absolutely, don't mind if I do.*)

We were last heard in slurred exchanges of "Eye loves youse man," washed down with the quick shot skål of Akvavit dedicated to Hell and Gore.

And so, the conversation digressed, until I quietly slipped back to the boat in anticipation of the following day. It promised the beginning of an adventure like no other. And it was.

5

FINALLY, TO SEA
THE DUEL OF CAPTAIN AND CONDUCTOR
MUSIC IN THE WIND

QUICK FIRST IMPRESSIONS

This was the first time that John and I were out to sea. There had been ferry rides over harbours and inlets in various parts of our travel worlds, but they didn't seem to count, since, on those rides, we were passengers in large hulks of steel that barely caused a ripple in our gut, and we had no input to our own well-being. This was a fibreglass hulled trawler yacht, fifty-three feet of intimate space that rolled with every wave it entered. We got to untie, unhook, and remove the polyform fenders, spin the wheel, slow the engine, turn right and left...sorry, move to starboard and port, read buoys and distant lights, hoist binoculars to consider oncoming or crossing traffic, watch sonar for depth and radar and the electronic displays for boat traffic that moved all around us. We got to do all that for about half an hour out of the harbour and then automatic pilot kicked in and we watched as Bob motored himself. He still needed us, however, to tweak his movements around other boats and to park—no...sorry again...moor and tether him at the end of the trip.

We weren't long out of the gate, it seemed, before I began to feel something deep inside of me, some primordial stirring, like the first land fish with lungs rediscovering its gills, though probably it was closer to a young male hound sniffing the air, getting a boner, and never knowing why. There must be a good reason we crave salt or our fluids ooze salty flavour. I had no immediate words or understanding for what some sailors mournfully miss, sitting on park benches, waiting for those unsuspecting wedding guests to hear their stories and share an albatross of guilt and shame. Maybe it was that endless dive and swish of parting waters, that pushing thrust of the boat as the waves were intersected, that short glide before the next wave parried with resistance, the thrust again and again, a seductive rock and roll of conquests that never seemed to end. In relatively short order I began to develop an appetite for the thrust and parry of boat and sea.

Reliable sources might ignore thoughts of magic in the clouds and the winds that carried them. Rational minds would disregard suggestions of poetry in the pulse and rhythms of the waves, reaching for the practical of science and mechanics to explain. In the beginning, that was me. But the seduction of the heart and mind by the sea is mostly unexplainable, like chords of music that make you cry, or a scent that pulses desire into action. Long before we sighted the first exotic port and its people, my mind began to gather notes, first impressions, large observations and emotions. I like to think of myself as a two-feet-solid-to-the-ground kind of person with a mind that strives towards dependable narration, but somehow, the sensations of the sea…sights, sounds, and smells, even tastings of salty air…bypassed the logical mind with vibrations measured only by the heart and soul. It was tapped possibly by stirrings from long ago when all the world was a stage of lovers and innocent possibilities.

If music could be the measure and best describe this journey, it would be classical. Country hurtin', rock slammin', head bangin' doesn't cut it as a new moon is rising over the swell of the sea. Rob had downloaded nearly sixteen hundred songs before the journey began, from Abba to ZZ Top. Admittedly, they kept us in the familiar, kept us awake through the dark vigils of night, but they failed somehow to complement this grand stage into which we motored, sets changing, moods swinging on the fly.

In Hollywood, it took a full symphony of brass—trumpets heralding the coming winds and French horns billowing sails—to push a fleet of windjammers out to sea. Strings worked wonders for a three-mast schooner or a Chinese junk slipping into a setting sun, although the junk required a hint of strangled cat to denote the Orient. Wagner worked well with warships and airships and Tchaikovsky covered the exchange of cannonballs. Mozart could tickle a rowboat with petticoats undone, but not at sea and not the seas of the Far East especially. This, after all, was serious pirate country; no harps or pastoral flutes allowed. And maybe, had there been a magical surround of music for our trawler yacht, a duelling solo of farting tubas or a ripple of burbling bassoons might have done the trick. Not quite the poetic send-off one might desire, but in the end, it wasn't the ships that called the tunes, or the instruments, but the vast world of sea around them. Thunder, rain, a folding wave, and a dolphin's splash while playing tag diminished even the largest vessels to single notes of play. And, often, outside the burble of our boat, it was the hushed quiet that left that magic ringing in my ears.

Once out of the harbour, past last goodbyes, waves, and wanton wishes (Double-D Liz emerged from the catamaran as we were leaving), past the miles of markers and buoys, we could say we were officially at sea. Forward, south by southeast, it was glorious sunshine; behind, wind, rain, and black clouds settled over Phuket. I was surprised at how warm it was—actually, very bloody hot—but the wind from the movement kept us from melting. Waves parted, danced off the bow and reunited in the wake, churned white initially, then fell off to the azures and grays or greens and navy blues…depending. Sometimes, it seemed the wake lasted forever until the currents brushed it aside like empty lines of music; a staff waiting to be inscribed.

A flotilla of islands, tall, gangly, volcanic creations, carved by millenniums of relentless seas, were anchored portside, a playground to tourist boats promising Asian memories. Hidden galleons flying British, Dutch, and Spanish flags had chased pirates here, had chased each other, fleets of clippers wrapping tendrils of ownership around routes of trade for tea and spices. I stared the islands down until they were distant markers of our beginning. Like the icebergs in Newfoundland, these islands are the signature of the natural wonders for exotic travel in Southeast Asia.

At one point, a school of flying fish came and went. They broke the water's surface like rounds of bullets, wings keeping them temporarily aloft for a few wavelengths, unable to change direction in the air. One had the bad luck to rise and fly as our boat crossed its path. I found it on deck, flat-nosed, with a look of "What the hell was that?" Occasionally, dolphins played in the wake and disappeared. At one point, we witnessed hundreds of dolphins chasing a school of fish, a collective white-water frenzy I've been told is rare to be seen. And once only, a solitary whale stitched a long thread past our bow.

Fishing boats entered our radar and passed. Two in tandem meant there was a net in between, which meant caution was required. Tugs appeared towing barges. Barges are dangerous because they don't have lights, just the tug. Freighters came. Freighters went. Oil freighters, supertankers, cargo frigates, container ships, compressed gas.

Nightfall was a Rhapsody in Fire. Clouds at times hid the final exit of the sun. Night, then, was immediate with no romantic dusk.

Nocturne, moving to the same tympanic beat of the day.

Not as black as I thought it would be, lights on boats, lights on shore, and lights on buoys...one blink, two blink, three blinks, four. There was the soft light of our guiding light—Sonar Radar Electronic Map. Starlight, moonlight, the light of our running lights—red light, port (PORT wine should be LEFT alone when it is RED), green light, starboard. I needed these rhymes to remember what was what and justify my position as first mate. City lights are a warm glow in the distance. Fluorescent lights of a hundred squid boats, like fire screened through the smoke of burning trees, or streetlights in a fog. A dredge boat of work lights, a cruise boat of twinkling lights. Oil platforms of seething gas light, the dull pulse of light on abandoned wells, and phosphorescent light from particles in the sea.

Usually, there was no second melody outside the drumroll of the diesel motor, the swish of waves parting on the bow, and the burble of exhaust in the wake. When I closed my eyes, I was alone in the concert hall that rose to infinity. It was music in the key of freedom.

The sea, when we stopped to swim, was eerily quiet. The waves rolled and seldom broke. The wind catchers of pastoral symphonies—winds in willows and whispers in pine trees—don't exist out here. I wondered...when waves break in the ocean and there is no one to hear them, do they make a sound? There were no seagulls to announce arrivals, no barking seals to say goodbye. No whale music. Rainfall made a sound. Patter, patter on the boat, crinkling plastic wrap on the water. Even the sheet lightning was silent. Ships piled twenty stories high, islands of moving merchandise, passed on the horizon. They too were silent.

The magnificent sea, as I came to understand it (and does anyone truly grasp its meaning?), is magical and mysterious, and, of course, massive beyond telling. It sighed, it heaved, it seethed, it sucked...all in perfect harmony. If Darwin is to be believed, it is the first symphony of life. Bigger than all music ever written, it's a lullaby in the calm. In its fury as seen in storms and seas by the poles...ten thousand kettle drums could not recreate. It gives—witness the fishing fleets we passed all day and through the night. It takes at will. The maps were marred with wrecks. It is so complex it is beyond our greatest abilities to know it entirely. The moon has got its number. It calls the tune. It is simple. It travels in circles. It goes up and down, in and out. It is strong...cities of steel float on it. Sharp... continents have been carved by it. Weak...man is killing it. The waves carry refuse; trails of oil and debris, plastic bottles and plastic bags. Every shoreline on our journey is a testimony to man's wanton disregard for nature.

Coconuts...lots, floating on the currents, and palm trees rose from every shoal.

And then there was that special relationship the sun has with the sea. On shore, it appears the earth is in constant rebuke; chastised for things beyond its control by a sun that sits at the heart of the trouble; that, and man of course. It is not so evident in these tropics where there is abundant growth, but look around. Cracked sections of dried-up riverbeds, shifting sands of encroaching deserts, baked fields, receding ice... cooked, dried, diminished, then overcompensated with flooding rains; erosion and changing landscapes. But the sea... the sea basks. Rays filter. Life spawns. You could feel it, like growth on the first hot days of spring. The ocean gives up its vapours willingly to a sun begging forgiveness for its arrows of overpowering heat and sends torrents crashing back in a daily show of mutual respect. Hence, perhaps, the rainstorms we encountered daily. If the sun smiles, the waters sparkle. If it hides behind the clouds, the sea has tantrums. There are magnificent cloud formations and thunderheads that climb thousands of feet. Some islands are surrounded by circles of puffy white clouds like carefully blown rings of smoke. Storms bring closed blinds of gray and blue, laced with rain. The sun and the sea, Apollo and Poseidon, Icarus misread them both. The big picture, viewed from our boat, was extraordinarily beautiful. And on that, my observations narrowed.

Lamenting the absence of classical inspiration in our taped collection of music, it occurred to me, over the long nights and days of the voyage, that our captain, and perhaps any captain, had much in common with the grand master of the symphony, the conductor, and the only name that appears on the music cover, though a thousand musicians and voices are involved. So, in keeping with my thoughts of poetry, my mind wandered.

Concerts may take an hour or two. A voyage will take what it takes. The success of the journey is in the hands of the captain and conductor. Failure is, as well. And possibly I was high-handed duelling the pair, but there is a rhythm to a boat in a voyage to the sea that requires a conductor's ear, as navigating through a symphony needs a captain's resolve. There is a pulse to a propeller turning, a tempo in an engine spinning, and a tone to liquids cooling. It's a sound, a harmonic language, and every boat has one. A captain knows that sound and can hear the dropped note in a single instrument; a change in oil pressure, the rise in temperature, and even the resonance of dishes clinking in a cabinet.

I imagined a symphony conductor stepping up on the podium, exquisitely honed voices and instruments to the front and an auditorium of discerning patrons to the back. With a nod to the first violin, the conductor lifts the baton, the instruments rise, and the lungs fill. Ahead are thousands of notes, stanzas, and phrases to be played; behind them, the multiple hours of training, practice, and rehearsal. Once the baton drops, the fusion begins. While the directors conduct the score, the drama unfolds on the screen filled with the adventures of a captain called Rob, his yacht, the South China Sea, and two first mates who have never trawled an inch in their lives.

Our trip in reality was a series of several movements. Like

a symphony, they were woven by the ships we passed, the people we met, and the constant change in weather patterns. They didn't necessarily match in pace or performance, and we meandered through the musical glossary daily. Given that we were only a few degrees off the equator, they usually settled on hot like a Spanish rhapsody and quiet plodding, like the first ten minutes…well, actually, the whole of Ravel's *Boléro*.

But there is a rhythm caught in my mind. It is the long rise of the cresting bow, followed by the dip and melodic swish of the dividing wave in the hollow, like a crash of cymbals on the relentless drumroll that is the engine, always churning, never wavering from the 1,400 rpm, always there from day to night to day again, until the ensemble finds an end in port. The sounds are forever, like dawn is to light, etched into my mind with symbiotic reverence, in much the way the soothing cry of a seagull is followed by the sound of a slow-breaking wave on shore, or what the sight of a large frigate pushing through pea soup fog, followed by the two-toned sigh of a foghorn, is for others, like comfort food.

6

MARCO POLO
LANGKAWI EID
SMUGGLING AND DEATH
TIME OF INNOCENCE

SEPT. 21-22...? ALREADY LOSING TRACK

The Straits of Malacca, squeezed like toothpaste between the mainland peninsula of Thailand, Malaya and Singapore, and the long Indonesian island of Sumatra, is the busiest strait in the world, with over eighty thousand boats a year. We were glued to the helm. All that ocean and we still had close calls. Half a mile is close, especially at night. If you can see the crews waving frantically for you to go around their nets, you know you've breached some law of space.

The Malaccan Strait has possibly hosted every circumnavigating ship and explorer in history, negating, of course, the few like Captains Henry Hudson and Jacques Cartier who were duped into the frigid waters of the Arctic, thinking there was gold, spices, and alohas with hula leis waiting beyond. Marco Polo made this trip, in reverse to our travels, over seven hundred years ago, sailing from Shanghai for the sunshine of the Persian Middle East. This had been his ride home to Venice, a voyage that took him two and a half years. Later, he made references to the bounty of fish and the problem with cannibals, and though we had not tested the waters thoroughly, fish seemed to have been removed from the equation over the centuries. I was hoping the fate of the former held for the latter. Marco Polo had started with fifteen ships in China and ended with only two when he arrived in what is now Iran.

It might be worth noting that Marco Polo took around twenty-five years to finish his tour, from Venice to China and back. Most friends, family, and neighbours could be forgiven for thinking he had perished, but Marco knew he had not been forgotten when he heard kids in the pool next door, shouting his name. That may have been the reason why he left Venice once again to battle Genoa, where he was imprisoned and told his story to a scribe. That, and the fact there was a pile of waiting mail (mostly bills; the gas company had cut him off and his international camel licence had long since expired).

On our first night out, the tide sucked, and the wind pushed. We hit eight knots and rolled into Langkawi, our first port of call, two hours early. It was the first stop of four before we ventured into the South China Sea. It had been our first night at sea, our first night of shared navigation in three-hour watches, our first night...where no one slept.

Langkawi was the first real chance for John and me to hang the fenders, cast ropes, and second-guess the captain's docking skills...our first chance to perform as sailors. Up until now, we had been guests admiring the view. The sun was barely awake and reluctantly cast light on our presence. The docking failed because the bow thrusters malfunctioned. Bow thrusters are built-in propellers that can push the bow left or right as needed. The tide was pushing us towards disaster. Rob gunned the engine and tried again but failed. He moved us to a safer spot on the outer edge of the pier built for yachts that exceed a hundred feet. We comfortably filled half the space.

Within two hours the thrusters were repaired. With the

help of diving gear and three minds churning, the small props were removed, redesigned, and reinstalled. It meant working in the harbour water, with currents pushing and pulling, and being swamped by the wakes of several large boats. It is here I believe a bacterial infection started on my skin. I smelled like a dead fish, and the boys were not amused.

Langkawi is a duty-free port, one of the first islands located inside the Malay Peninsula, southeast of Thailand. This long, thin leg of land is shared by Myanmar, Thailand, Malaysia, and Singapore and would fit into Southern Ontario but supports a population nearly double that of Canada, which has the second largest land mass in the world, and this tidbit has been included in case it took you three hours to get to work in your city and you think things are getting crowded. Langkawi is also an immigration port, so we chopped into Malaysia. "Chopping" is the term for going through customs, immigration, and the port authority. It is the modern version of the ancient form of Chinese signature blocks; fingerprints and clay pestles in ink or wax for identification. I think "chop" refers to the sound of the big ink stamps used to mark the passports. There were dutiful uniforms in Customs…*Chop! Chop! Chop!* Serious uniforms in Immigration…*Chop! Chop! Chop!* Happy ladies covered in colourful scarves at Port Authority for boat clearance…*Chop! Chop! Chop!* Chopping leaves large ink squares, which are to be dated and initialled with "Bob the Boat" written in pen below.

Malay paperwork included this dire warning: **The Penalty for Smuggling Drugs is DEATH.** There was no attempt to obfuscate the message. I could not imagine Canada having such a warning. It would be an apologetic *Sorry for the inconvenience, Excuse this reminder, but Please don't smuggle drugs,* with a number for a tax-paid lawyer, just in case.

John wondered again if he should declare his pills for high blood pressure. I say again because he nearly answered yes to the question on the Japanese immigration form before landing in Tokyo. It asked *Are you carrying any weapons or drugs on your person?* It was so unlike John's methodical mind, but occasionally I felt that his eccentric one was pushing to make decisions, making sure that the execution of exemplary fiduciary duty would be dutifully executed. I just didn't want my neck on that execution block. He was determined to answer the question on drugs to the letter of truth, a truth determined by the English ambiguities of the word drugs covering medicine. And oh, I could only imagine.

"Well, you see Mr. Customs' officer," looking for a glint of understanding, "back home we buy our medicine in a drugstore, but we store drugs in a medicine chest and, when needed, we then medicate our chests with the same stored drugs. We are allowed to drive medicated though one's drive is suspect if they are suspected of taking drugs. *Those* drugs (pretending to shoot heroin into his veins) come from holding company with drug cartels as opposed to *these* drugs (showing pills) which are the domain of a cartel of drug holding companies. Oh, and does this faux samurai sword box cutter (still dripping with self-inflicted blood) qualify as a weapon?"

I protested, refusing to sit in Japanese detention while he explained the not-so-subtle difference to a sumo inspector. He gingerly marked an "X" for NO.

It is a requirement to chop in and out of every port, even though they are all in Malaysia. You would think all the ports would be linked, wired to track whatever they are tracking, but they're not; too many jobs at stake, perhaps. As we travelled, we found these authorities in strange out-of-way places, thirty miles inland, second-floor, over a dry goods store, located in the back corner of town. It took time, something we had an abundance of, and they were not a problem to find, since Rob had been through them all before, motoring in the opposite direction.

We happened into Langkawi at the end of Ramadan, a

month of Muslim fasting followed by weeks of Muslim feasting. It was a long weekend, and, like everywhere else in the world, it was filled with holiday travelers. From our mooring at the marina, we could see that the port was busy with ferries of visitors and workers on their way home for the holidays or on tours with their family. We decided to go to town and see the sights.

The harbour was plain but tidy with a modern structure of rolling rounded roofs set behind a giant sculpted eagle in the form of the "World's Largest" that kept an eye over everything. It required a visit and photos in the same way as the Wawa Goose, the Sudbury Nickel, the Giant Ukrainian Egg, or any one of the world's largest sculptures like the Kubasa, Hairball, Pineapple, Farm Hog, Golf Putter, Potato, Pistachio Nut, Sandfly, Loaf of Bread, or the World's Largest Beaver deserved five minutes of a person's time. They're big. Small attractions are about as popular as cocktail wieners in a house of ill repute.

One road skirted the town, so we followed it for a long walk to the farmer's market. Rob had been there before on his last visit and craved some hot sauce or sauce on something hot that had him walking double time. We headed out at noon and melted!

"Exercise," Rob explained. "You gotta get it when you can, since you don't get it on the boat." The "you" seemed rather pointed, and the royal "We" was not included in the conversation.

The colourful market meandered along a small road and dried-up riverbed, finding an end of busy activity in a crowded parking lot. It hosted several food stalls beyond the normal merchants of local produce with colourful booths of cheap clothing, shoes, plastic doodads, and colourful thingamabobs, not unlike farmer's markets the world round. The food was tasty but not for the faint of heart. Flattened chicken and other meat-kebabs were prepared on smoky barbecues that would give a health inspector a heart attack. Back home in Canada, all eyes were on a scandal of listeriosis, a lethal food poisoning caused by dirty preparation facilities. The locals here must have guts of iron since mine caved a day later, saved only by a stash of Pepto Bismol.

On our return to the boat, we decided to hire a taxi for the following morning, taking us into the countryside for a gondola ride and a special mountain waterfall. I was excited about heading inland, not knowing what to expect. This was Malaysia, after all, another place I knew nothing about other than it had passed through Portuguese, Dutch, British, Dutch, British, and Japanese hands over the last few centuries, like many of the island state countries in the area. The word "Malaysia" once represented the entire region now referred to as Southeast Asia, but that feasibly is only in Western history books. The region of several proud states, collectivized under European rule, only gained freedom after WWII with the breakdown of colonial rule.

As we drove, I was fascinated to see a huge plantation of rubber trees pushing to the horizon. Every tree was a mass of lesions, exfoliating empires of car tires and condoms into small containers. I wondered if there were various species, ribbed rubber trees, or Ramses super trees for large exports to the fabled Caribbean. Of course, little did I know that rubbers are made of latex or some other poly-petroleum mixture and have no rubber in them. Most men had complained that the steel-belted radials destroyed the feel.

Although there had once been a strong Christian influence, Malaysia, we were told, was mostly Islamic. On our early-morning tour, we passed several villages where the mosques were the sole center of attention.

Ramadan requires prayer, which the locals seemed only too happy to offer up, several times a day. Our taxi passed motorcades; cars, vans, and motorcycles loaded with entire families, even a donkey cart or two and a few Mercedes, windows up,

AC cooling the back seat of elegant age, holding armloads of fawned-over young, all dressed in festive clothing. The towns were like Easter morning in Christian Middle America, or imaginably as they once were. Cars parked on roadsides with people streaming in cheerful attire towards worship…and I thought to myself that this was the picture of Islam the world needed to see.

Passing through these villages, a witness to the simple devotion, I felt slightly envious of the sense of community, the belonging, the connection of the mullah's calls and the people's happy response. It was the peace of the community, not the religion, that interested me. John pointed out the four large speakers pointing to compass extremes. These are the church bells of mullah prayers with the demand of duty trumping simple devotion. I conceded the point. He expounded on the power of mullahs and Islam in an Islamic state. I conceded again as our windows rattled from the second call to worship. Though religious, this colourful stream of humanity seemed more joyous than a dutiful act for mullah and state. Was it not simply people caught in the social grace of giving thanks for life?

"It's the end of Ramadan," John said. "They have fasted for a month. Thanks, yes, but now they get to eat!"

It seemed to me, I remarked, that some have wealth, while others are peasants. In their draw to the mosque, sceptre and crown rubbed shoulders with scythe and spade; in all colours of the silk rainbow, there was no distinction. He pointed to a chauffeur waiting in the shade of a palm tree while his employer prayed. I conceded on the lack of will to continue.

We decided to forgo the gondola. This would have taken us up Gunung Mat Chinchang, the highest mountain on the island with an above-the-rainforest canopy walk, called the Langkawi Sky Bridge. It was a holiday and every child on the island, it appeared, had been promised a ride to the top. There was better luck, however, with crowds at the Telaga Tujuh

Waterfalls, also known as the Seven Wells. The name refers to the seven natural pools, where legend has it fairies once came to bathe and frolic. Catching frolicking fairies would be great, I thought. Naked is even better.

It felt like there were five thousand and eighty-three steps up the mountainside, though I've been assured there were only three hundred—I was too busy suffering to count. Only the fittest need have tried. By five thousand and twenty, we appeared to be melting, crème brûlée under the waiter's torch. With sixty to go, I wondered what sins we had committed... penance extracted with every step.

I had a memory flash from childhood of watching Mexican pilgrims in a movie called *Mondo Cane—A Dog's World*. It might have been *Mondo Cane the sequels 1 through 36*, but never mind. The pilgrims were ascending stone steps on their knees in the reenactment of Scala Sancta, I think, the steps of Christ on his way for trial before Pontius Pilate. The reward was a plenary indulgence, which was forgiveness after confession and granted absolution. It was occasionally sold (who said you can't buy your way into heaven?) but usually granted by the Catholic Church if you did dumb things like commit murder and maintain mistresses but begged forgiveness while ascending a thousand stone steps on your knees. I think my father took us five children to see *Mondo Cane* so that we would stop wanking about the lack of running water, flush toilets, electricity for cooking, or central heating for warmth in our farmhouse. All that was despite the fact that we lived near a big cosmopolitan city in Canada where it sometimes hit -40° in the winter, two miles from where the most sophisticated fighter jet in the world was being built, called the Avro Aero. I don't think the Avro engineers shat in unheated backhouses, but who knows.

"Look how others suffer...now shut the hell up." And we did!

Conceivably, this was my yin-yang urging me forward,

crying weakly, "*If Mama Rosita who was ninety-eight and lived on a donkey could make the climb, what's the matter with you?*"

The top rise was met with relief and despair when a sign that showed a trail to a picture of a waterfall read, *1.8 km ahead*. Now I understood the taxi driver's smirk when he said, "Have fun. I go for sleep."

The water was heaven, but unfortunately not to Rob's fond remembrance. The last time he was here it had been the rainy season, but now there was barely enough water for sluicing pool to pool. It was a series of seven rocky pools connected by small waterfalls. With lots of water, it allows one to slide between pools. The water was still flowing, but great care had to be taken not to leave your behind on protruding rocks. The final waterfall fell fifty feet or more, with a warning sign and a single cable preventing swimmers from being dragged over the edge.

"The other place will be better," Rob offered.

"Other place?" I asked, thinking of another stairway halfway to hell.

"It's just a hop along the road from here, after the skip down the stairs."

At the next stop, the driver curled up for his second nap on the hood, but first blessed us on our journey. This place was home to the Durian Perangin Waterfall.

There was a small hike involved, longer than Rob's mind served him. John still declined to swim but would hold the cameras and record the moments.

Our approach wound through a series of shaded groves; vestries robed in lush growth. They were linked by a path of ascending rocks and manmade steps, hemmed by a rail of wood, the path twisting and turning beneath columns of mountain pines and trees with thick, waxy leaves. The trees rose and formed cathedral arches of intersecting vaults; a clerestory through which the sun filtered in white streams of illumination on quiet pools and eddies flowing with meditative calm to the valley below. We walked quietly and spoke in hushed tones as if intruding on sacred ground.

The canyon walls converged and revealed a vision of nature with velvet thighs, caught in the act of giving birth. A wet crevice framed in lush foliage opened high above the canopy. A narrow rush of water fell, then opened wide. The inner cascade hugged the layered rocks of the wall, while the outer veil plunged and divided into separate streams, some misting in the drop to the rocky chalice below. The sounds of motherhood were barely audible until we were standing in the baptismal mist of her breaking waters.

Once in, we were boys again, reborn in childish acts of splashing taunts. We climbed the slippery rocks, dove deep to swim against the currents, pushing with futile effort into the white foam and finally relenting, floating freely downstream. In this sanctuary, beneath a sky of solid blue, it seemed as if, like monks, we were divested with each stroke, beyond dust and sweat, the trappings of midlife constraint. Maybe it was the guilt for parents tucked away in strangers' care, the demands of homes and receding retirement funds, the microscope of parenthood and failed marriage; responsibilities of age that wedge us further from our childhood. Whatever, for a short while, we were reminded of our days as kids, building a dam across the river, flagging a flimsy raft in pirate bones, splashing the day away until we were called to supper, and lamented the passing. "It was," as the telling verse from Simon and Garfunkel's "Bookends" suggests, "a time! Time it was, it was a time...of IN...no...cence."

The return trip was subdued. We were tired from play. Our window into the world revealed new treats. A water buffalo wallowed in mud and water, lost except for its mammoth head, at the edge of a rice paddy. Small white egrets stood poised like statues in riverbeds and tidal flats, waiting for telltale signs of life in the marsh. An alligator farm trolled for tourist attention, with a large sign in Malay and English. Mosques that had been magnets of activity on our drive in stood empty, though at one, an elderly man, perhaps the imam, was spotted quietly locking the doors. Families could be seen, still in bright colours of celebration, enjoying the cool of covered porches or palms in the yard. Our taxi driver crossed the double lines on hills and curves to hurry home. His wife and two daughters were waiting. We had taken him away on this holy day; the lure of tourist dollars was too great to pass up. We tipped him handsomely to compensate. He would make the evening prayer.

7

GEORGETOWN PENANG
HOT SAUCES
MONKEYS IN HEAVEN
YIN-YANG WEALTH

THE 3ᴿᴰ WEEK OF SEPT.

We were back to sea the following day, lifting with the rising tide, slightly ahead of the rising sun. Pulau Penang, the smallest state in Malaysia, and the city of Georgetown were in our sights. Rob had told port authorities that the more distant town of Port Dixon was our destination.

"We'll be in and out of Penang before they know we came," Rob explained. "If my memory serves me, this place took us an entire day to chop in and out last time. Like I got nothing better to do! Screw 'em!"

The names Port Dixon and Georgetown, British of course, seemed gentle to the tongue, out of place with the exotic flow of Malay and Thai names we had left behind. The town of Butterworth was across the strait from Georgetown, making me want to suck on something sweet. Tanjung is the Malay name meaning "the cape," but it's called Georgetown in honour of King George the Third of England. He's the king of the Napoleonic wars, sometimes of madness, and was at the helm when Britain lost the American colonies. The yachtsmen seemed content to stick with the familiar of the English title. My father, back home, languished in elder care in a town of the same name. The mention of Georgetown pushed forward a vision of his face, smiling without understanding, when I told him I would see him in three months. He had blown a kiss and clasped his hands above his head in a bond of safe-journey-farewell-God-be-with-you-see-you-soon-I hope as I left. His fragile state had caused me to worry when I left, thinking I may never see him again. He was well, I knew—as well as ninety-three can be—otherwise I would have heard. There were cell phone towers on nearly every island peak.

The movement towards Penang was set to the metronome of time constraints. Rob had called ahead to reserve a berth. He gave the approximate time of arrival, calculated on rpms and knots per hour, with variance for tidal swells to move us forward, minus the possibility of wind holding us back. We arrived early.

This was a short, whirlwind tour of two nights and possibly two days, arriving midafternoon and leaving sometime early in the morning. The feeling of confusion here reflects the lack of sleep.

The yacht harbour resided next to a busy ferry terminal. Boats ferried around the clock in a tit-for-tat clearing of mainland tourists off the island, for returning Ramadan revellers to the island, thus avoiding the ease and expense of the Penang toll bridge, ironically designed and installed to make ferries obsolete. Our boat, like the few boats that were moored at Penang Yacht Club, rocked like a bassinet in the hands of a Hallelujah choir. Ferries crossed the harbour north-south, sending wake east-west, while stadium-sized freighters motored in perpendicular reflections, creating a whole physics class in wake modulation and amplification study with grating matter diffraction, especially in the galley of *Bob-the-Boat*.

A trip to the head was a lesson in multiple-scattering interaction. We ate out, in town.

⚓ ⚓ ⚓

This was my first introduction to Southeast Asian culture in a restaurant setting. Rob found a place he had visited before, though several others had recommended a small hole-in-the-wall with the best seafood around. We looked at its street menu and concluded that it was overpriced. It was full...a good measure the food was great. We moved on, crisscrossing several blocks of partially familiar; "I think it's down this street... wait, I remember, no, that's wrong, it's on a main street...off a back alley, I think...I don't remember the name...so I can't ask for directions, I'll know it when I see it...yes, here it is, smaller than I remember...fuck off, it's been six months since I was here; food is great and best of all it's cheap" before we settled at a cafeteria-style amidst a busy hive of locals. They were all men, and based on their dress—casual white or brown cotton pants, mid-thigh loosely fitted white kurta tops, and trim kufi caps—I guessed they were Muslim, post-prayer and definitely over Ramadan since large helpings were set in front of them. There had been a momentary hush when we entered. Rob's blond ponytail seemed to attract that kind of attention. Two Buddha-like followers with black aviator glasses may have helped.

We quickly trolled the food bar. There was chicken cooked with various sauces, steamed rice, and variations on varieties of local foods for which I had no previous misconceptions. Rob suggested and John and I took notes.

"Avoid the red and green sauces, unless of course you like it really hot and don't mind a burning asshole for days." We moved past the red and green chicken. "The satays are usually good," pointing to several trays of skewered meats. "They could be chicken, goat, mutton, beef, pork, or fish." In this room, I knew we could rule out pork. "This could be beef rendang," Rob said, pointing to a dark stew-like dish. "It's kinda like a caramelized beef curry. It's really good, especially over a bed of rice, though that seems to be how everything gets served." I noted this one might be my choice. "And this here is sambal," Rob noted with a somewhat sombre tone, as if stopping to remember a death in the family. "If you have the hankering to shoot flames, give it a try. It's hot chilli peppers mixed with other hot chilli peppers and left to marinate in a stew of hot chilli peppers. They use it as a marinade."

We sat at our table and waited. The place was busy, and it took a while to get served. I took the time to survey the surroundings.

It was a large, open space with a view of the kitchen along the back wall. Several cooks prepared food, while three male waiters took orders, cleaned, and hurried food to the tables. Other than the lack of women, the most obvious difference to restaurants back home was that there were no plates, forks, knives, or spoons. The food was served on banana leaves, and everyone ate with their fingers. A naan flatbread was used to push the food into small piles, where it was squeezed between the thumb and first two fingers and brought to the mouth, lowered halfway to the table. When they ran out of bread, they continued to scoop with their fingers. Most diners used their left hand to eat, while the right was waved and pinched in forceful animations to emphasize their points of speech. All the tables were in lively discussions, except ours. John and I were in shock. Finger-lickin' chicken was about as far as my North American cuisine digressed to finger food…well, okay, fast foods like burgers and fries, nachos covered in jalapenos and gooey cheeses aside, but nothing with thick gravy or hot sauces unless, of course, it was poutine-covered fries and you were minus a fork…well, whatever, but I did notice constant herding of gravy and rice to stop it from flowing onto the table. There was a lot of finger-sucking and lip-smacking.

Each table was outfitted with a roll of toilet tissue. This substituted for serviettes. If ever there was an example of "green" dining, this was it.

When our food order was taken, we asked for cutlery. It was possibly needed to cut the air, since our request was not taken lightly. We caught the cooks checking us out as if the infidels (one even in banana-yellow shorts) had ordered a side of bacon. I wanted a beer, but of course there was no alcohol offered. The palm leaf wraps fell on our table without much ceremony. Bottles of water followed in like fashion. We ate slowly, quietly tasting, no conversations. It may have been an insult, I am not sure, but the restaurant cleared before we were finished. Did they leave because of us? Or had there been a call back to prayer? In the end, Rob seemed to smooth things over by telling them it was the best chicken he had had anywhere in Southeast Asia and that he would recommend the place to all his boating friends, sailing along the route. It wasn't a lie; he would. It was inexpensive and sailors love a deal. They smiled with humble acceptance as we walked out the door.

Content, we marched off to the open-air market and shopped for food. If one buys too much food while food-shopping hungry, the opposite seems to be true while shopping full. I always felt we bought too little when we were in the marketplace—a few onions, a half dozen bananas, a cucumber—when it would have made sense to rent a pack mule and fill up the boat. Good thing I wasn't in charge. Even with air-con, things went bad quickly, especially at sea when the air conditioning was off. It is probably why rice is a main staple. If cured properly, it doesn't go bad. With the backpack filled with goods, we hurried to the boat as escaped sambal peppers mixed in our lunch burned holes towards the exit.

The following day, we boarded the bus, intending to take a mountain tram up Flagstaff Hill, one of the highest peaks on the island. It was the bus for locals, so we got the residential tour. There was a lot to see.

Georgetown has a clock tower by the harbour, stuck at ten past seven. I think it probably still is. I wondered if it marked when the Japanese invaded or the English left. There were other reminders besides the sculpted stone of this proud building, of the footprints of Britain's colonial power. Our bus passed orderly neighbourhoods, London clones by British builders, sent to stamp the empire's claim to rule. Buildings for magistrates and government business, squared into monoliths of orderly rows, were fenced in wrought iron and pillars of stone. The remnants of a cathedral, laid to waste by time or possibly Japanese bombers during the Second World War, had been left to the wilds of jungle growth, but the cemetery had signs of nurtured life. Flowers circled a stone saint, perhaps James or John, standing with arms uplifted in praise to God or in defiance to the bombs from above. There were orderly green paddocks for polo ponies, nurtured lawns for bowling, stadiums that announced cricket matches and carpet-like pitches for soccer. All that was missing were the orderly pre-WWII crowds of Englishmen, buttoned tightly against tanning rays that might suggest belonging to that despised working class of "wogs," "boys" and "coolies" they deemed their right to rule. Thankfully, the arrogance of empire had been scoured from the scene by the outbreak of war.

The order of buildings, like the order of the empire, was brief. We soon rolled into neighbourhoods of small stucco and concrete dwellings mired in frantic activity. Hindu markets replaced Chinese markets and morphed into Buddhist temples or the telling arches of Muslim mosques. Turbans and saris mingled with T-shirts and blue jeans and the whites of mullahs with long, flowing beards. Again, I thought, this is what the world needs to see; the happy comingling of faiths and peoples, washed in shades of white and brown. But John noted wisely that tourists see what they want to see, and our short stay does not make us privy to the struggles of power that are sure to exist.

Our destination was the Penang tram, a train car drawn by a subterranean cable, the same mechanics that move the trolleys of San Francisco. It is pulled straight up the mountainside and splits only momentarily off the single track to allow the second car on the way down to pass. It was painted in white and the Britannia red of post boxes, telephone booths, and London double-deckers. We glided into a gray cloud like an ascent into heaven (one can only presume) where we were delivered into hawkers' hands of hot roasted nuts, which we could not refuse. If this was the gathering before heaven's gate...a note: the nuts are stale and monkeys roam freely, so if you are waiting for entry, bring food.

As we left the cloud of arrival at the tram exit, a Hindu temple came into view. It was like a multi-layered cake, frosted with pastel licks, green lion pillars and pillars of twisted cinnamon sticks, carved elephant decals, cherry and lemon flowers, lotus leaves of multiple colours, topped with deities and gods with heads of various animals and bearded cherubs come out to play. There were no warning dragons, or demonic gargoyles, or statues of men demanding penance before entry. There was almost the expectation of organ music and a carousel within, but it was largely empty, graced only with low tables of candles and incense. Uncluttered heaven, as heaven should be.

The disappointment of an intermittent view was offset by large mugs of frosted beer in a tea house, perched so that on better days, much of the city and the western approach of the island were within one bird's-eye glance. We sat on an open veranda, shaded with vines that twisted and wound over an iron arbour. Heineken was the offered choice of the heavenly host that served our table.

Our patience for being wrapped in a fog of the multi-faith Heaven-Paradise-Swarga-Cosmos (though the Buddhists have thirty-seven levels...I wasn't sure where we were) was rewarded with a glimpse through a brief opening of cloud; tall condos on white beaches, oil freighters in final approach to the refinery on the mainland, an eagle gliding in an uplifting wind and, before the mist closed, a gleaning ray of sun sweeping the gentle swells of waters below, perhaps looking for our boat. It was not our time; "Heaven can wait," it suggested. Back to earth...it was time to go.

A few miles out of the harbour, John calculated the untold millions from the first oil drilling platform we encountered—the first of many to come—and elaborated on the good fortunes of the Malaysians, Indonesians and the rogue nations that are Singapore and Brunei. "Money coming out of their yin-yang," he said. We were heading to Port Dixon with a side venture to Kuala Lumpur, a couple of hours inland by train. It would seem Kuala Lumpur is the capital of all things yin and yang.

8

PORT DIXON
KUALA LUMPUR – THE HEART OF MALAYSIA
LUXURY AND THE DARK SIDE OF PARADISE

THE LAST WEEK OF SEPT., 2009

We cruised into the yacht club harbour of Port Dixon, greeted by luxury. We were tired from thirty hours of motoring, but the view raised our spirits. It was clear that we had been slumming it at our last ports of call.

Beyond the boats moored along hundred-foot piers rose a clubhouse looking like a southern belle racetrack from the Carolinas, with Ascot aspirations. It was crisp Georgian architecture dressed in white, topped with green and softened with pillared balconies and protruding square turrets of windowed skylights. The Admiral Marina and Leisure Club looked every inch the luxury advertised in the Yacht Club directory. It warranted a "pinch me," used daily since the beginning of this journey.

The club interior had a high-sheen polish of mahogany and granite and was fawned over by a starched uniformed staff. The pool was the crème de la crème of infinity architecture, where vaulted bridges connected islands of palm trees giving shade. No wandering in SpongeBob boxers and flip-flops might as well have been listed on the long list of do's and don'ts posted by the pool.

Day two was chop in and out. This set a timetable; four days from entry to exit. Chops were delivered in town, a short taxi ride from the club. We shopped for fresh produce, and John found a post office where he sent home envelopes of receipts. These were to be used as business expenses and proof of travel files so that portions of the trip could be claimed, in part or in whole, as a business affair. He worked occasionally as a retail business consultant.

An afternoon swim was followed by relocating *Bob-the-Boat* to a pier for refueling. This was notable for a couple of reasons.

First, I had never witnessed pumping three thousand litres of diesel fuel into a vehicle, although I understand it's a daily event for some American SUVs. Boat fuel is pumped left and right sides simultaneously, for balance. During motoring, the fuel is cleaned by fuel scrubbers and streamed center, as needed.

Bob-the-Boat had a fuel capacity of 1,040 American gallons. That's 3,936 litres and, if you are reading this in imperial gallons, do the conversion math. The tanks were not empty, but the bill was a few thousand dollars. A minor bit of research reveals that some large cruise ships have a four-million-gallon capacity. That's over fifteen million litres. It can cost $200,000 a day for fuel on a seven-day cruise, and apparently, their fuel prices rise and fall as fast as a toilet seat from a gastric attack on a bad island tour. This might tempt you to sympathize with owners of those amassed fleets of yachts on the south coast of France. No? I didn't think so. Many ships are now changing over to LNG (Liquid Natural Gas). It's cheaper, cleaner and has a lower fuel density than diesel, thus less weight to carry.

Just as memorable were the moments of panic when Captain Rob's credit card was refused. Luckily, John stepped up and gave his card a "whirl," saving face. Mine would have landed us all in jail. An hour was spent on the phone with the card company where Rob managed to extract an apology from their excuses only after he threatened to cut up their card.

There had been no offer to wash the windshield or check the oil.

⚓ ⚓ ⚓

Day one set the agenda for day two as we reserved a taxi for early-morning pickup. We were heading to Kuala Lumpur.

The taxi ride followed a clean, modern highway, sans the potholes and pavement cracks that plague the roads in Canada due to hundred-plus-degree temperature changes, winter to midsummer. Roadsides here came with nurtured greenery, many of which I recognized as indoor plants I had cultivated and killed in my kitchen. Some bushes came with magnificent splays of colourful flowers, found in the city greenhouses or solariums of the wealthy back home, lending an air of the exotic to the drive.

We passed suburban villages with new suburban homes in tidy suburban rows. Some even had swimming pools. Whatever happened, I thought, to rambling villages with twisting roadways and bicycle paths, bamboo huts and thatched roofs? These were images embedded in my mind from movies and newsreels of war and mayhem or typhoons turning villages inside out like discarded lingerie on the way to the bedroom. The problem was, these camera flickers could have been anywhere from Southeast Asia—Vietnam, Cambodia, Myanmar, Thailand, the Philippines; they all fell into my same shameful lump of Far East ignorance—"over there," "somewhere in the Far East," places not on a need-to-know basis for daily living in Toronto. In my world, everyone not Caucasian or African was lumped as Asian, probably meaning China but could include Indochina, both Koreas, and, well, whatever else my ignorance wished to include—all still wrapped in palm huts and rickshaws. Most of these places, I think, had fought battles of independence while Moses had wandered about in the desert. How was it that I knew zilch about them...and when did they start building swimming pools in their backyards? I didn't even have a rubber kiddie pool in mine.

We also passed miles of palm trees, cultivated in corduroy precision on both sides of the road; plantations as far as the eye could see, our driver explained, for palm oil. There were large road signs along the way with the name *Sime Darby Berhad*—owners, the driver informed us, of nearly everything in sight, including the neat villages we passed and the wages to a workforce of over one hundred thousand employees. Palm oil had fallen into disfavour as of late, he continued, due to the high content of bad fats getting a negative ride with junk food. Our driver went on to explain the benefits of good fats and salads. He practiced what he preached, it appeared, since he was slim and fit.

The thirty kilometres ended in front of the train station of Seremban, a neat, organized building in a town that followed suit. Arrangements were made to have the taxi pick us up on return. We were his new best friends.

Despite the promise of searing heat, John dressed in long gray pants, a dark blue shirt, socks and leather shoes. "We are going into banks and towers of powerful corporations," he said. "I don't think it would be respectful to wear shorts." It was the eccentric John I knew, but the comment pricked some acorn-sized gland of mine, usually reserved for fight or flight. It made me want to go naked in defiance of stupidity.

"You guys wear what you like," he said. We did.

I wondered at my sensitivity to his remarks that had usually passed me by in my "John being John" file that my brain deemed as nonsense.

It must be the lack of sleep, I thought...nothing longer than a couple of hours of deep sleep since we left Phuket, with no chance of REM. Every watch at the helm in the middle of the night demanded full attention, each blip on the radar a potential collision. Some were closer than anyone wanted to see, especially a rookie like me. Relief, when it came at four a.m., left me in the darkness of my room, winding down in a big bed, alone. The motor hummed, the boat rocked, the corrections of left and right for the automatic pilot were piercing beeps in the dark, all night long. Turn the automatic pilot off by mistake (a short thumbprint from the other unlit buttons) and the system had a piercing fire alarm screech that raised hairs that weren't even grown. Everyone came running.

Ports should have been an oasis of calm, but there were lapping waves and the sound of a thousand fish nibbling at the bottom of the boat, slick with plankton-like hangers-on. Rob rose with the sun, at six a.m., even though his room was dark. I heard the flush, the shower on and off, footsteps on the deck above. Sunshine broke through the slits of curtains covering my two portal windows. Boats motored in and out of the harbours, and then there were the incessant ringtones of the captain's cell phones and the computer processing digital bits into notes of comprehension. These were messages from night-owl friends who lived in the Philippines or his wife, Cathy, back in Canada. When it rained, there was the patter on the fibreglass like a storm on a tent. When I turned off the air-con in the middle of the night, I was sweating two hours later. How do you turn off the brain already in super sensory overload? *Think about your feet*, I thought, *the two small toes, and wiggle them*. That was good for five minutes. The mind was slowly going mad from the lack of rejuvenating sleep. It was venturing into corners of darkness, sweeping for webs of discontent, touching buttons that the "mind shit-filters" usually let pass.

"Three trips to the toilet? I only have one a day. Toilet paper costs over a penny a sheet, you know," John said over his *Malaysia News* that he had already been out to pick up in the club reading room and was halfway through.

"You gotta go when you gotta go." I was slightly perturbed to think anyone was counting my movements.

"Oh no, you have to train your body. Give it a routine."

"Fuuuck off!" rolled out with playful contempt. *Good God*, I thought, *I am pushing sixty and I don't need a potty train*. It hung on the end of my tongue but never made it out.

"It's true. I have my coffee, read the paper, second cup, and off I go. Once a day, like clockwork."

"Okay, just plain fuck off."

"Suit yourself. Testy!"

Rob came up from down below. "Rat crawl up your ass and die? I opened the portal window in your washroom. And, oh, you left your bedroom light on again. Don't like to harp, but the light bulbs are expensive."

"In that case, I think I'll use club facilities," John piped in. "We're paying for the facilities…may as well use free toilet paper in the…fresh air while I can."

Filters were clogging, but I let it pass.

The Saturday train to Kuala Lumpur was filled to standing room only by the third or fourth stop. It was an hour's ride. The countryside was more of the same that we viewed from the taxi, fading in and out at a faster pace. Though not express, the train was very fast. It was a cross-section of all the ethnic mixes that make up Malaysia. There was an animated conversation in English between a girl who may have been Chinese and a boy who looked East African, both students, it appeared, from the satchels of books hanging from their arms. It was good-hearted banter of close friends. A Muslim family moved to vacated seats, and a boy and girl, both in their teens, laughed at things out loud. If they were siblings, I was jealous of their closeness. My two at home had always kept their distance from each other. The mom tugged periodically at her daughter's scarf. It appeared like any Saturday outing into the city by commuter train in Toronto. The exceptions here were the signs warning of fines for EATING, DRINKING, LITTERING and KISSING. The ban on kissing caught my attention, but never registered beyond an irritation. There were also good-natured signs encouraging people to give up seats to the ELDERLY, CRIPPLED and PREGNANT WOMEN. Everything was in English, Malay, Cantonese, or Mandarin. We remarked how hard it was to find a French sign outside of a bistro in Toronto or, for that matter, "Bilingual Canada," outside of Quebec.

Kuala Lumpur snuck up station by station, with buildings growing taller the closer we got. John pointed out the Petronas Twin Towers that hovered over and dwarfed all the rest. This pair was made famous (in the West) by the movie *Entrapment*, I noted, with Sean Connery and Catherine Zeta-Jones, who were two towers in their own right. Petronas, John informed us, was the state-owned oil company, the eightieth largest company in the Fortune 500 world companies, the eighth most profitable company in the world and most profitable in all of Southeast Asia. Who the hell needed Google?

We transferred from the rural train to a connection of high-speed subways, futuristic realities that would shame any competition in North America. Our brains were in correctional defragging, with the download of technological bytes of this superior ultra-modern city. There is a chance we missed it, or it wasn't ground-breaking news, but this part of Malaysia had done a technological flypast of the Western world.

The trains stopped in a precision of computerized stops, and doors opened in a precision of computerized openings. They hissed in and out of stations precisely on time.

Our escalator rose to the surface and deposited us into the sun and heat at the base of the polished nickel towers marked *1 Satu Warisan, Satu Matlamat, 1 Malaysia*. The heartbeat of Kuala Lumpur and, I guess, Malaysia started here!

It was impossible to snap a photo of the towers that included anything of identifying merit from the street. I didn't have a wide-angle lens. We headed in and explored the centre, hoping to visit the upper decks for a look-see from the top. "Sorry," we were told, "the sightseeing is all booked until Monday." We perused the shops from the seventh-floor balcony, looking down into a polished granite pit of wealth. Every big name in design was there.

The shopping concourse emptied out to a terrace that cascaded towards a reflecting pool and disappeared behind islands of lush, manicured growth. Paths led past enormous mangrove trees to connecting bridges where visitors like ourselves were trying to fit buildings into their camera view. The walk took us to a beautiful playground and water park, a long walk from the buildings but still in their shadow. I finally got the shots I wanted.

The buildings are truly magnificent pieces of architecture, sun bouncing from the high-sheen polish of nickel and stainless steel that divides each floor like cream puff filling in a waffle stack, soaring one thousand, four hundred, and eighty-two feet skyward. There were info boards in the park. It was the highest free-standing building until they built something over twenty-seven hundred feet in the Middle East. John knew that something was called Burl Khalifa in Dubai.

All this downtown property, devoted to a park, surrounded by corporate buildings...a children's playground even...millions spurned in capital building opportunities that would never be considered in most city cores of North America. The cleanliness and the feel of wealth on every corner made for lively topics of discussion over very cold pitchers of beer and something we had not had since we left home: real hamburgers with fries and ketchup at a bar called the Rum Jungle. It is a fancy business crowd-type bar, with open terraces under palms, jungle decor with large aquariums, a dance floor for evening crowds and, not for the faint of heart, cockroaches the size of my eyes of disgust, since large rats wandered without fear under the empty tables

"One of my favourite bars in Barretto has the exact same

name," Rob offered up. "A good friend of mine manages the bar...actually, he manages four of them altogether." Rob had not said much about what happened between him and his wife, Cathy, nor ventured into stories about Kim, perhaps because of guilt. I hadn't asked, figuring it was none of my business and that when he was ready, and if he wanted to, he would talk.

The conversation veered towards Barretto, a suburb of Subic and Olongapo in the Philippines, and the bar girls. Our waitress reminded Rob of one of the Mama-sans that took care of the girls at the other Rum Jungle in Barretto, "friendly enough, but tough as nails, always with an agenda to sell more beer, more ladies' drinks, more nights with the patrons...more kickbacks for her." The conversation was peddled faster than my mind of moral comprehension could adjust to.

"Whoa, back up! You mean to tell me the bars own the girls?" I asked, not quite believing my ears.

"It seems that way, but they can leave if they want. They end up on the street with nothing, however. You know, Kim was sold once for twenty-five thousand pesos. That's about..."

"Seven hundred bucks at today's rates," John threw in without stopping to calculate on fingers or toes.

"...of which she got to keep half. She had barely arrived for her shift when the Mama-san took her aside with a big hug and congratulations. She had no idea what was happening to her. It's called a steady bar fine: it takes the girl out of the bar, and she is then supported by the guy, who gives her an allowance. At his discretion of course. She was scared shitless. She was only eighteen."

"Eighteen? Good lord," John said, eyebrows raised in shock.

"The guy who bought her was seventy-two, for Christ's sake," Rob continued with a little extra steam.

"SEVENTY-TWO? You're kidding me, right?"

"I've met him! He's still around, fat and balding." There was a fire burning deep inside of Rob, beyond what was being said.

"So how long was the contract for?" I asked, thinking perhaps a subtle shift in thought might lighten the tone.

"Contract?"

"Yeah, the bar sold her. How long?"

"Life, as far I know, but I am not sure how long a steady bar fine lasts."

"LIFE? For seven...fucking...hundred dollars?" John shushed me. My voice had broken the acceptable level of bar chatter. I was beginning to see red...the indignity of it. "What the hell is this, ancient Egypt?"

"If it makes any difference, I think most guys get tired of having only one girl and end up cutting them loose." The word "life" had been delivered with complete contempt. The shift had made him angrier, but he added with a hint of calming sarcasm, "The other option, I guess, would be that they marry the girl and everyone lives happily ever after. But I think that's what most guys are running from." There was no attempt to connect himself to the revelation.

He stopped to drink some beer and there was a moment of silence. Rob looked like he might continue on his former tack, but he started in with an explanation of some of the more pertinent details of the bar life. My mind was still stewing, starting to boil in fact, but I listened as he explained the "bar scene" as he knew it.

The girls had to be eighteen to be in the bar. Bars could lose their licences if caught with girls underage. The girls had to go for check-ups every week for STDs and every six months for HIV. They didn't get paid unless they showed the signed forms, and the cost of examinations was at the girls' expense. They also got fired if they were positive. Those were government regulations—whether local or higher, he wasn't sure. This ensured that somehow the government got money. The clinics were government-run in a country where, technically, prostitution was illegal. The girls paid, giving the bars arm's-length involvement. Legalized. Sanctioned. Monitored. It was, at least, a huge step ahead of how things went down in the West, I thought. Or was it? I truly was not versed in this area of behaviour or the laws back home, but I assumed that there were no government regulations on the health of prostitutes, since governments back home did not seem to recognize the institutions of paid sex. It was guesswork on my part. Girls still hung out on corners downtown. They were cash jobs, I presumed, with no account records for government scribes. It was like that around the world, except maybe in the Netherlands, a country so progressive that drive-through quickies had been built, including one on the way to the airport. It brings new meaning to "doing things on the fly." When it came to discussions on sex, the Dutch had the long and short answers.

Rob explained that there were maybe a dozen bars with about twenty or thirty girls each in Barretto. In Angeles, close to Manila, there were probably a thousand bars. "You do the math," Rob teased, knowing that John probably would.

Next to his friend and three other assistant managers he knew, the Mama-sans wielded all the power. They recruited the girls and took care of them, supposedly protecting them from the violent patrons, but the arm didn't reach beyond the front door of the bar. And, of course, the more girls that got bar fined, the more Mama-Ssan made.

"The girls don't have to bar fine if they don't want to," Rob said, "but what choice do they have? For some, it's the difference between life and death."

"Bar fined? Explain," I said. It was self-explanatory once he explained it.

"The girls make a hundred and fifty pesos a day," Rob explained.

"Three bucks," John added.

"If you buy the girls a ladies' drink, it is double what you would pay if you had ordered it for yourself, but the girls get half. So, you have already increased their pay by a third for the day. Three drinks and they have doubled their wage."

"Six bucks," John counted.

"Now if you want to help the girls, you can give them extra money by throwing the bucket of ping-pong balls that sits on every table. For three hundred pesos, you can throw the balls and watch the girls scramble to retrieve them. Each ball is worth a few pesos each."

"Why would you do this?" I asked, knowing of course the answer was money. But it sounded demeaning as hell.

"It's a hoot to watch thirty girls scramble for balls."

"Bloody humiliating if you ask me," John added.

"Yeah, that's why I have never done it," Rob laughed, knowing that he shouldn't, and, like an off-coloured joke that catches your funny bone, he winced slightly as if to say "*It is kind of funny...sorry.*"

"These balls, they turn them into the Mama-san, who keeps records. That is what Kim does at the bar in Barretto. She is a checker...checks to see who got what. If you are feeling quite heavy in the pockets, they have large buckets that have ropes in the middle of the room. Pull the rope and you drop maybe a hundred bouncing balls into the crowd. That can cost you fifteen hundred to three thousand pesos. If you are rich, you can ring the bell and all the girls get free drinks that you pay handsomely for. You do this hoping the girls will come to you, knowing, of course, you have money. The Mama-san gets a take on everything. The big bucks come if the girls get bar fined. If you want to take a girl home, you have to pay the bar a fine, since you are taking them away from their place of work. For fifteen hundred pesos, you get to take them home. They are yours until they start work the next day."

"Thirty bucks," John said.

"The girls get half," Rob continued.

"Fifteen...not even a buck an hour, if she stays with you 'til work the next day," John chipped in.

"If you take them to a hotel, the hotel makes them pay a fine—a user fee, if you will," Rob said. "No reason given, other than they can."

"Christ, everybody makes money off the girls except the girls," John added, shaking his head in disgust.

"Gotta ask," I interjected, "if Kim was sold for life, ah... how did you two hook up?"

"The guy told her to get lost. She wouldn't go along with his kinky shit so he told her to get out. She ended up back at the bar for three bucks a day."

"This is too depressing. We should think about getting back to Port Dixon," John said, looking to attract the waiter's attention.

"Seventy-two years old," I thought out loud. "Christ, that's like putting a marshmallow in a piggy bank."

It may have been the heat or the accumulation of the day's conversations, but the ride back turned quiet. My thoughts were consumed by our discussion and the peek through the dark keyhole of the Philippines. It had been government-sanctioned, quasi-legalized prostitution of young girls and slavery we had been discussing, after all, and it stunk. The poster of the couple kissing on the train, circled with red and crossed through, seemed almost justifiable; who knew where a public kiss could lead? Perhaps the Philippines could use some state-enforced morality.

Before I allowed my mind to careen off on the road of high and mighty in favour of state-imposed laws over the freedom of the individual, I roped it in. It had always bothered me when I saw women in Toronto wearing the hijab or, God forbid, the head-to-toe burqa not because it represented any threat to me or my space, but because, I felt, it was cruel and symbolized the institutionalized hatred of women. I had once groaned in disgust, then on second thought openly cheered to see a woman in a burqa motoring down the highway in Toronto. She was driving, an activity once banned for women in Saudia Arabia. And Afghanistan...well, that's a women's prison of a darker colour still.

That government ban of a kiss, led with due process of

contemplation to the horror of the fascist, whether German Nazis, Iranian autocracy, or the Afghani Taliban. That ban on a kiss innocently circled and innocuously hung beside littering and eating food, quietly disguised the shameful practice of Sharia law a law with wide girths of interpretation that may or may not give men the moral and religious right to beat their wives for deemed improprieties...improprieties that never had to be explained. If violent acts of admonition are not forbidden in writing, are they assumed to be allowed? I was told by my Muslim friend that Western assumptions on the evils of Sharia law are unfounded. I hope he is right, but I have my doubts.

Across the Malaccan Strait in Indonesia, truckloads of police patrolled cities, looking to impart justice to unmarried couples sitting too close on park benches or women not wearing head scarves. Some infractions came with public floggings, but stoning seemed to be reserved for the females—though, in the enlightened year of 2009, in the very September of our voyage, that same Indonesia approved a law for stoning both adulterers to death.

What we had seen in Bangkok and the description of the Philippines versus Indonesia were opposing scales of morality. There was no doubt in my mind as to the wrong of sexual exploitation, but weighing that against Sharia law, it was hard to find a comfortable shade of gray. The Filipino girls were acknowledged as existing; there were rules in place to take precautions, and the Mama-sans, for bad or worse, were available to protect their interests. Women of Sharia law had protectors as well, albeit men again—but with the mandate to keep their women safe, to keep them out of the hands of predators that would sell or push them into the trade of sex. One could only hope that the men who lived by the pillars of Islamic faith were not abusive. The problem is that Sharia law grants state-sanctioned violence to those who are. These weighted thoughts were a conundrum for sure and drove my mind to consider things back closer to home.

For all our horn-blowing around democracy, liberty and the rights of the individual, were things any better in the Western world? When girls disappeared like the four dozen murdered in British Columbia or those lost daily, north and south, did anyone care? Did anyone actually give a damn? Police? Courts? Communities? Our cultured Western world had a long way to go in how they acknowledged the culture of street girls, starting with the admission that the culture actually exists and probably always will. The hatred of women, especially of those in the oldest profession, has solid roots in theologies. That's a fact, but why have those attitudes crossed all the boundaries of Eastern and Western thought? Or has the West infested it all? I was sure there were libraries filled with all the answers, but my mind was on a roll of questions. This went beyond the trade of sex, where neither East nor West had a monopoly on violence towards women.

How could men hate so violently as to rape with iron rods? Rape, kill and feed them to pigs? Use rape as bullets of war? Rape them in front of their children, their husbands, terrorize whole villages, where villages turned against them because they had been raped? How could we push victims to survive in the darkness of blame and guilt? Force them into prostitution? Write laws against them? Imprison them? Call them whores, hookers and hoes? Write it into verse? Rap it into song? Blame them for great men's defeat? Trash them in biblical verse? Bury them in earth? Stone them to death? Pin titles on the innocent young? Bully them to death? What the hell is wrong with the psyche of men? I am a man. I like women. I like sex...love sex in all its splendid variations, but sometimes I am ashamed to call myself a man!

Is it the duty of men to protect women? Of course! Men have power. That power should protect everyone, but when I hear women calling other women *whores* and *hoes*, helping men turn them out and shun them on the streets, I know this is not just a problem of men. The sisterhood, it seems, stops short with help and understanding for those of the world's oldest profession.

All this from a no-kissing poster. It all bordered on a world too dark to dwell on, but it carried my thoughts until our train delivered us to our waiting taxi.

9

THE ROAD LESS TRAVELLED
NEAR-ABDUCTIONS IN GREECE
THE REAL GLOBAL VILLAGE

A MEMORABLE FLASHBACK, ONE DAY LATER

When my wife and I travelled for a year through Europe in 1980, we did so by van—a Volkswagen van that was retrofitted with all the amenities of a home, minus a shower, toilet, central heating, and a two-car garage. The Dutchman from Utrecht, when he handed over the keys, gave us a word or two of advice, which we heeded and has stayed with us to this day.

"A good time you make yourself," he had said and then continued selling the advantage of taking the road least travelled when caught at the cross-sections of life. "Sometimes, great things happen when you least expect it, without any planning at all." Ironically, the van he sold us sent a piston through the block, and the two weeks we waited for its repair in Greece left us memories for a lifetime.

This memory surfaced when we were met by a woman at the doors of the marina on our return from Kuala Lumpur. She was the yacht club version of the cruise boat variety that organized fun.

"Tomorrow night," she explained, "we are organizing a special tour in association with all of the local hotels. There will be free food and drink, and if you are interested, drop by and sign up." It was a long, cool swim, beer and sleep that preoccupied our minds. Sleep was key or perhaps the happy hour beer, or gin and tonic, but the thought of another tour fell flat.

"Besides," said Rob, "we will be long gone. Our departure is already set."

The sobering effect of the swim followed by libations and naps brought us to the realization that indeed we would be at the marina, Rob having miscalculated by a day. We could take it or leave it, we all agreed, and gave it little more thought. Rob pulled out his guitar and sang, I harmonized, and John left for the quiet sanctuary of the deck by the pool.

By six the following evening, we were huddled with a dozen other guests in the club foyer, waiting for the bus. We had tossed the coin of why not against the cynical thought it may be a sales job to sell condos and fell soundly on the side of free food. We three cut a ragged swatch against the group dressed to the nines. There was a couple that we knew already since we had traded beers off the back of their boat flying the flag of New Zealand. They had known Rob and Cathy as a couple from some other port on the ride in the opposite direction. They had liked Cathy, and were curious where she was, but didn't push. They accepted she was visiting family back in Vancouver, nodding with understanding, all else suggesting they knew otherwise. It wasn't the first time egos and dreams had driven couples apart. It took a special person to drift the seas without terra firma to call home.

I traded quips with a man cut out of the conversation between wives over the need for a real hair salon and the awkward feel of semi-heels over the comfort of deck shoes. I pontificated, once again, over the possibility of being sold one of the twenty-seven spots left unfilled as visualized by the large model of the condominium project under glass in the foyer.

He agreed with a shrug, but parenthesized the comment with "But it's free and let the evening go where it will." The underlying meaning was *shut up, this is not the big city hustle, stop spoiling the fun, you paranoid geek!*

We were counted into the bus and roll-called down a list by the hotel organizer of fun. The swish of the closing doors got us on our way. The bus was not full, but we were stopping, we were told, to pick up more guests from another hotel.

"Thank you for coming, ladies and gentlemen," she said through a crackling microphone. The bus driver plowed through the gears. "Tonight is a very special celebration. We are the guests of the local hotel association, who have put on this evening's event to, yes, promote tourism in this area, but more genuinely, to celebrate with you, our guest, the end of Ramadan." Since we were white and European-looking, English was spoken as it was assumed all Europeans spoke English, in the same way that we Westerners assume English is spoken by everyone. Her assumption was correct. She read from a prepared script.

"The end of Ramadan, a month of fasting, is celebrated by two very special and holy days as proclaimed by Muhammad, called Eid al-Fitr—the celebration or festival of breaking the fast. You may hear Muslims proclaim '*Eid Mubarak*,' meaning Blessed Eid, much in the way much of the world might say '*Happy New Year*,' though this is not to be confused with our own New Year, Hijra. This all means, for simplification, it is the end of fasting and now we feast for the new beginning. Tonight, you will feast on the best of the best from each of the hotels, as they compete for awards for best food overall, best dishes, and best presentation. This tradition is called Buka Puasa, literally meaning 'breaking fast,' and it is a tradition for hotels to create the finest buffets." Drinks, it was explained, would be non-alcoholic, as this was a Muslim celebration. She also explained there was another celebration called Eid al-Adha, the Festival of Sacrifice, which would happen in two months.

It remembered Abraham's willingness to sacrifice his son upon God's command. This was pointed out to help non-Muslims like us understand the connections between Islam, Judaism, and Christianity. They were all born on the same rock.

"Malaysia is very proud of its four founding religions, Hindu, Buddhism, Muslim, and Christian, and we celebrate in harmony, all four new years with equal fervor." The spiel went on and then was repeated for the second group from the next hotel.

It was an hour as we drove back in the direction of Kuala Lumpur on a highway that turned into ever smaller roads, where there were no signs of towns or backcountry life. Outside the bus, minus the pollution of light from highway lighting and village windows, it was black velour darkness. My mind wandered again.

What if this was not a free evening of food at all? What if we had walked onto a bus at the promise of free food; lambs to the slaughter, wealthy yachters, into the hands of terrorists, an Al-Qaeda pocket for Malaysia? Who inquired as to where we were "really" going? We were deep in the country, going deeper. Had anyone bothered to leave a breadcrumb trail of notices as to our whereabouts? Why so far to nowhere, with the promise of something known by no one? My paranoia deepened with the darkness, imagining some cave in the black hills; being ransomed, fingers and toes offered as proof of capture. I had no money. There would be no ransom paid, and my probable fate was to be sold or traded into slavery with pirates, cabin boy to Jabba the Hutt. My mind had been hijacked by the lack of sleep and the prejudice scoured from the TV depths of fiction hell and the endless loops of bad news from somewhere in the Middle to Far East.

As addled as this mindset may seem, there was precedent for such thoughts. On that same trip to Greece thirty years ago, my wife and I, travelling with John and his future wife, Ann, had all nearly fallen into such a trap. We had wandered into the harbour square of Heraklion on the isle of Crete, walking off the effects of a late-night meal…too much sticky baklava, moussaka and tzatziki, each course cleansed with a little ouzo or pine-tainted retsina wine. Our wandering had taken us down cobbled streets where we moved in and out of numerous pottery shops; traps of China-made, Greek design, Minoan treasures. They were painted with naked archers and wrestlers and men leaping bulls, satyrs in compromising positions and gods, naked or not, offered on plates and Grecian urns alongside masks of Etruscan warriors, statues of happy centaurs, bare-breasted snake goddesses and the Minotaur being tamed by Theseus, unabashedly naked, of course. Such things can soften one's brain toward danger and intrigue. We had also spent time swapping stories with vendors, one of whom sold wool flokati rugs and had lived in Toronto.

"Fuckings cold, fuckings me," he said, lamenting his decision to return to Greece, where he worked from "fuckings sunrise to fuckings midnight, seven fuckings days a week," making less than the little he had made in his shop at Yonge and Bloor. "At least it is fuckings warm back here in Greece!" We thought ourselves privileged that a vendor could feel so comfortable with us to unleash his deepest inner thoughts, thinking we had crossed from fuckings tourists to family. We were feeling ouzo-relaxed and warmed by the locals' charms, with one invitation to dance and smash dishes until dawn with Zorba abandon. So, when hailed by a pair of sailors hanging off the gangplank of a large merchant ship, naturally we drifted in their direction.

They had tipped their bottle of whiskey towards us, downed their drinks in a single swig to an "Opa," and reached out with arms in a clawed curl as if they were scooping air into their lungs, shouting "Ella! Ella!"—an indication that we should join them. After the small talk of names and places, one sailor shouted up with the result of a third sailor coming down, four glasses in hand so we could all "Opa" together and smoke their cigarettes, all of which left the limbs to moulder towards a Jell-O-like composite. The brain too!

"Come," they had said. "We go on board. Drink 'til bottle is empty. We talk, we laugh, we play cards and wait for sun to come up," reincarnating the raspy Anthony Quinn with two arms raised, waiting for the off-screen bouzouki to strike up a dance chord. It was one of those invitations that had the promise of "the real experience," the one that did not come poetically waxed in tourist brochures to view more shards of antiquity, a "path less travelled," like the time John and I had agreed to take a ride with a Spaniard in Madrid and found ourselves surrounded by Franco's secret police, complete with an agent wearing a fedora pulled low over a trench coat, collar turned up, steel-rimmed glasses and a slow-burning cigarette gradually revealed from a darkened doorway. It was a drug bust, and we happened to pull into the wrong parking space. The best was a pair of Swedish girls in Austria who invited us back to see their beautiful country, if we were so inclined, one of whom became my wife of forty years and counting. In the spirit, four brains melded as one and we headed up the gangplank.

We were stopped mid-ascent by the sound of sirens, honking horns, and loud bombast from megaphone-sized voices hiding in a gauntlet of car lights that had appeared, it seemed, from nowhere.

"STOP, POLIS! COME DOWN FROM BOAT," shouted in capital urgency. Police came running from cars, doors thrown wide, like a scene from a surreal thriller with the Gestapo moving in on the Von Trapp family, holding edelweiss and guitars over their head. We handed our glasses to the sailors, who continued to move up the walkway, reluctant hyenas backing off the kill as the lions appeared. I flicked my cigarette into the water in case it was contraband, then followed the others in single-file procession down to the harbour wharf. A small group of tourists had gathered, thinking possibly they were witnessing a drug bust where there might be a public cavity search.

Our passports were already collected and stacked in the hands of an officer by the time a large, uniformed man appeared in a Red-Sea parting through underlings. He was shaking his head side to side, clucking his tongue as if he was the vice principal who had finally caught Ferris Bueller smoking on school property. He held each passport up to compare mug shots, then handed them back, one at a time, lips pursed, but still no introduction.

"D'you know why we stops you?" he finally asked, with the hint of a smile under furrowed brows, suggesting good-cop concern. We didn't.

"I can't say for sure this be their intentions or no, but there has been in past, bad things happen." Our blank faces must have betrayed the stupefied surprise we were feeling, since he continued, tone softening even more. "Perhaps they want to have drinks as they says...but let me tell you what could have be. You could go on boat and have drinks... Yes? These drinks, unbeknownst to you, have drugs. Before sun rise tomorrow, boat leaves harbour and somewhere out in sea you men are dumped overboard to drown. You ladies they keep, to be sold into slavery somewhere in Middle East." He paused to let this sink in.

Our reaction was a unanimous lip-paralyzing pin-dropping silence, the immensity of the "if," the unfathomable ring of "drown" and "sold into slavery" catching us cold. Slavery? Sold? Murdered? Surely, we had been unwittingly drawn into some forum theatre production by a local drama troupe, a Greek tragedy, cleverly using the largeness of the harbour setting, pulling unsuspecting persons like ourselves into their theatrical fold. The tourist chorus would break in at any moment with a singing chant of...

"Too cheap to take the Knossos tour,
Bated by the seamen's lure,

> These mortal tourists' hubris spurned,
> Nemesis exacts her vengeful fate!"

A dance would follow. There would be a battle and a God-appeasing sacrifice, and this man would drop his mask at any moment, smile large, and beg our forgiveness.

He did not.

Instead, he shook his head, sucking air through his teeth, fingertips pressed together in prayer formation below his nostrils. He made no explanations as to why they had been lying in wait, or why no arrests were made, or, pointedly, how they knew any of this for fact. We didn't ask...too stunned to move. Had I been as old as I am now, I may have filled my shorts.

"Again, I can't say if this be their intention, but you very lucky, my friends," the police inspector had said, leaving us to ponder this luck as we wandered home in the pitch of darkness that is a normal Greek summer night. It had been slightly intimidating on other evenings, trying to negotiate the unlit back streets to the campground, but it became terrifying with the possibilities of murdering slave traders at every twist and turn in the road. Each strafe of foliage, from hanging vines or grasses protruding from the roadside ditch, raised hackles of hair and goosebumps the size of pregnant nipples. But maybe that was only me. I had never gotten over my childhood anxieties of the dark. I still tend to avoid Greek restaurants in the harbour, moored bistros, or romantic night cruises with musicians playing bouzoukis.

And then, as if someone had pulled a switch, there was light. Colourful lights. Lights in trees and lights on poles and a canopy of light that created a causeway of colour, shining down on a street filled with people, so deep and crowded that our bus came to an immediate stop. It was as if the night had spawned humanity from darkness and we had been witness to the big bang of creation. We were disgorged from our bus into the welcoming hands of heads with officious hats and colourful scarves that belonged to the mayor and the governor, their wives, hangers-on of each, hotel owners, the managers and their prized possessions, the Cordon chefs. It seemed we were the guests for which the festivities could begin.

I must sheepishly confess that my imagination can sometimes get the best of me. This welcome was living proof that, of course, take the road less travelled, but that would still have left John and I floating somewhere in the Mediterranean and the wives complaining that the men, as usual, got off easy.

There were a dozen tents, strung together with lights and banners, one proclaiming *Selamat Hari Raya*, meaning Happy Eid, or Happy Breaking Fast or…I am so hungry I could eat the back end of a goat all by myself…after all, it had been a full month of fasting between dawn and dusk. Muslims loved Ramadan in Sweden when daylight lasted about three hours in December. Hunger riots were a real possibility in June and July when the sun barely set.

The tents were filled with entire families dressed in the finest silks and wool combinations, coloured not in the drab browns of the Afghani burqa or the full white of Saudi princes or piercing black of Bedouin herders, but in the best tradition of Malayan costume, a full spectrum of the rainbow. This was no ordinary potluck.

Plates and cutlery (fork and spoon) in hand, we manoeuvred toward the food. There was no use in asking what, so I stood in the middle, outside the perimeter of activity. I watched as some of the guests indulged. The last thing I wanted was waves of heat going down in a ring of fire. Bottled water was being handed out at every turn.

Guests were being summoned by chefs pushing the entree specials of their house. There was chicken, dressed in red and green, sauces of varying degrees. Rice…everyone had rice and noodles…oodles. Dishes of stewed meats steamed everywhere. My hunch was beef, lamb, or goat. There were also frittered shrimps and prawns, steamed squid and wafer slices from fish with heads, and tiny whole fish with tails. One table offered variations on pancakes and waffles filled with hot peanut sauce. I followed Rob, whose daring was legend (if only to John and me) and who basically would eat anything that didn't eat him first. We ate and returned for more, each plate a little more adventurous than the last. If we returned for seconds from the same chef, heads were nodded in thanks and smiles exchanged between servers, thanks enough for a full day of work.

Layered cakes, fruits and candied sweets were offered as dessert, along with chai and vanilla-flavoured tea to fill the holes that entrees never could.

At some point, we were summoned by electronic feedback and a hush descended, except for under the tents, where chefs still nurtured their food. A man called for our attention in English and Malay. He looked like a middle-aged Charles Bronson, rugged, face pulled to the edge of a pensive smile, dark-haired with a hint of gray. He was to be our MC for the night and began with welcomes all around. Special thanks were offered to the mayor and the governor. They spoke and were applauded. There were thanks to the hotels and their chefs and all the supporting staff. They were applauded, and they applauded themselves with whoops from the staff working in the tents. Finally, thanks were turned to their special guests, us, for blessing their gathering with our presence and with hopes that we would go back home and spread the word. We acknowledged their kind applause with nods and timid waves.

For the next two hours we were entertained by our MC-turned-singer-and-comedian. He brought on laughter with tasteless non-politically correct ethnic parodies, something that would have had him blackballed in the West and, if done in reverse from some Western stage, burned in effigy in the East. He did Elvis and Michael Jackson (no crotch-holding), and the women who lined the back rows of chairs, mostly kitchen help, cooed satisfaction with laughter and applause. It seemed he was well-known, possibly on TV. He pulled up people from the audience, mostly Westerners who were tortured with the embarrassment of singing or wearing silly hats. He caught me enjoying the music, head bobbing and legs in the motion of a jig, so he called for me to come up to the stage. Not a bloody chance in centre-of-attention hell, I thought, no matter how golden the experience of the divergent fork in the road. I averted my eyes. He struck gold with a man from our bus who loved to sing, could hold a note, and had no trouble being made the fool for entertainment's sake. It takes all kinds.

Halftime was turned over to six women with tambourine-sized drums, minus the tambourines, and a singer, all dressed in traditional Malayan folk costumes. It seemed amateurish compared to the host and his band, but I soon realized it was folk—traditional, real, and true. These were the songs of Ramadan, songs of Eid performed and passed down in festivals such as this for centuries. This was the village, not McLuhan's Global Village, but the real village, the village in which it took the whole village to raise a child, and these were the songs of thanks. Thanks for the food and thanks for the drink. Thanks for the rain. Thanks for the sun. Thanks for the leftovers the hotels were giving away. And with arms raised, thanks be to Allah, who is loving and great.

As we were ushered back to our bus, connected forever in our own village experience, we were thankful, having come to that fork in the road, we had all said yes.

10

THE ART OF THE SKINNY DIP
MIDNIGHT EID
LILLIPUTIANS IN SINGAPORE

A DAY LATER IN THE LAST WEEK OF SEPT.

Each shore leave became gradually more difficult. Our legs began to crave the roll and heave of the sea over the solid structures of roadways that had no give. Our bodies were becoming seaworthy. I looked forward to the preparation to leave Dixon. There was a system.

All loose items were secured. Toothbrushes and shampoos went into lockdown in the heads, flashlights tucked under pillows and loose change, combs, wallets and papers put into drawers. Drawers were tested with a click, and doors with a clack to make sure they were locked into place. In the galley, all breakables—plates, glasses, cups, bottles—were wrapped in towels and wedged into the appropriate cupboards and cubbyholes. Utensils that hung or stood in tall jars and appliances like the toaster, rice cooker and kettle were wrapped and wedged into plastic containers, covered with tops, and piled on the floor, fitted, wrapped or wedged between the sofa and the table. All pictures, playthings and loose what-its were placed in another container, wedged with wedges or became wedges themselves. The guitar was retired to the master en-suite and cuddled in pillows. The gas stove was covered and locked. Curtains were opened and pinned back. Porthole windows were closed and dog-eared shut, with several cranks of the ears to make sure the dogs were tight. We wouldn't want that dog taking a leak. Carpets were rolled or folded and stuffed under chairs or, occasionally, used as wedges if required. Nonslip doilies were put on the counter to hold plates, bowls, and glasses for food preparation later. Eggs and rice that had been prepared in advance and cold meats bought for fast non-stove prep meals were stuffed in the fridge. The fridge was closed, and a pin clasp secured to make sure the door could not swing open.

Canvas covers were removed from the pilot house windows. The world shone in.

One hundred feet of hose was disconnected from the marina tap, and the appropriate switch was flipped to shift the water to onboard tanks. Hydro was switched off at the pier, pins removed or loosened with screwdrivers and the fittings disengaged. Switches again were flipped to convert to ship power. All lines were coiled and put into their appropriate holds. Lights were flicked on and off to make sure they worked. The bilge pumps were tested, and the head storage tanks were flipped to at-sea disposal.

The electronics were turned on, and Rob tweaked the route in the automatic pilot. Routes were already laid in from the trip in the opposite direction, so the tweaking was short, assuming no islands had shifted or coral reefs had formed within the last six to eight months. Radar and sonar were turned on, and depth immediately was shown with harbour bottom formations digitalized in colored display. The radio crackled to life at the flick of a switch, set to channel 16, the channel for hailing and calling for help. Maydays were for dire straits. Calls were posted to the marina office, and help was signalled to send us underway. Finally, the key was inserted and the engine started. It was the purr of a tom cat, with three prospects in sight. With the motor running, the engine room was opened, and Rob hopped down to inspect meters and gauges, hoses and clamps, and felt for leaks, listened for ticks, sniffed for smoke, and proclaimed it fit for travel.

Cast-off crews arrived, un-looped the figure eights from the cleats and gave gentle pushes out from the wharf, casting ropes to us, first the bowline as the nose edged beyond the pillars of the pier, then the stern line, as the full length of the boat burbled forward into the wider waterways between piers of tethered yachts and sailboats. Assistance was required from the bow thrusters to get us perpendicular to the mooring, negating the need for a three-point turn. Once the bow hit the first wave beyond the exit channel, the soothing swish announced our entrance back to the sea. Ropes were formed into measured loops, tied and stored, and the fenders, heavy pears of rubber hanging three aside, were pulled up, untied, and crammed into the hold. Departure was textbook.

Within minutes, we were like that bead of sweat on the long neck of an ice-cold beer gathering speed towards the southernmost tip of the Malaccan Strait. Our next port of call was Singapore.

The bead paused momentarily midafternoon, and we divested ourselves of shorts and T-shirts and jumped naked into the refreshment of an afternoon swim. John insisted it was a bad idea for all three to be swimming. The boat, he said, could drift out of reach or jump into gear or who knows, as it was never explained beyond a bad idea. He watched with the eagle intensity of a mother duck introducing her brood to water. This attention to due diligence of motherhood may have come to John honestly, as I could see his mother, the mother I had known as a teen, in every action he took. Suggestions and ideas were cupped in sarcastic humour, with idiot implied, perhaps, in every "of course."

"Of course I am not swimming. Someone has to watch the boat."

Of course, he was probably right. I had grown up without a mother, and my father had been too preoccupied with survival, maintaining a family of five kids, a farm, and a job in the city, that nurturing with an ounce of prevention natter was often left to the pound cure kick in the ass. Spirited adventures as children that should have been nipped in the bud, like playing a game of tag high on the beams in the barn, sometimes in complete darkness, had played through luckily, without consequences. Little thought had been given to "what if."

John's wife, Ann, had survived a terrible accident in the North Sea, off the coast of England, which undoubtedly tempered John's approach. This may have also been on Ann's mind during our experience in Greece.

Her uncle's yacht, on which she had been a passenger, had been cut in half by a Polish trawler in the middle of the night. Her boat sank in minutes and the trawler kept on motoring. After an assumed bout of conscience, it returned and rescued them all. One can't be too vigilant, and "of course" it was this reason that we were never allowed to crack a beer while under power. However, my experiences have taught me that you must let loose sometimes.

There is something freeing about a high-in-the-sky baptism of a full sun skinny dip, although I was still languishing in the realm of ready-for-market pork that the term "skinny" pushed the envelope. This is not to say I was obese, mind you, like one of my son's clients for personal training, who lamented the fact that "He looked like shit, couldn't get his breath on the stairs, and had a pecker down there somewhere that he hadn't seen for five years." Mine came into view, now and again. That aside, the daylight skinny dip has the spiritual cleansing of finally coming out of whatever closet darkness that envelops you, to a joyous reception of a full sun disclosure of the real you. Sometimes pie-eyed witnesses to the act may be prone to suck in air and cry "Mother of God" or "Oh... sweet Jesus," though I have never been party to such a religious movement.

In my younger days, dipping off a dock in Muskoka under the cover of night had always felt daring and risqué, the body not knowing when the water would touch, and, when it did, naked with all that dangles and jiggles freely, it was surrounded by black liquid that hours before had been sunlit water but at midnight had the delicious possibility of being a vat of mulled wine, melted chocolate, or a giant vagina. Okay, maybe not chocolate or wine, but something equally naughty. Well, why else do we taunt with whispered temptations to skinny dip in the dark? It's the kind of daring first offered in the darkness of adolescent rooms to "show me yours and I'll show you mine," with the hope that showing is the all-encompassing noun of demonstration and performance where lips and tongues unleash something of the "not sex" Clinton proclamation. The problem is that the cold of midnight waters shrivels all the opportunities, a clinical cleansing scrub with all parts wet at once before the hoped-for conjugation. Cold fingertips need to be sucked to warmth before coaxing frosted parts to reappear. Here, in the waters of Southeast Asia, it felt completely natural, like the comfort of a warm bath, where a suit of any sort was as out of place as clothes on your wedding night. Besides, I had yet to see a dolphin in a Speedo. It also came minus the E-E-E-k-s and W-e-e-e-h-a-a-a-s when the water finally hit the W-o-o-h-o-o-s that had been part of the slow submersion of lake penetration preferred by my sister during daytime walk-ins from the shallow beach. The water here was deliciously warm, wrapping the body in a silk brine of comfort.

There was nothing to prove by going native; our need for a swaggering show of testosterone had long since been handed over to the generation of our sons. The sagging apparatus of middle age is not valid for the pissing contests of size. There was no excitement in the thought of being caught; there wasn't a boat in sight and land was a distant dot. It was simply the freedom of knowing that we could and being as nature intended.

I was lying on my back enjoying magnified beams of heat, so my mind wandered. Wouldn't this be the ideal place for the next G-20 summit, arms talks, peace negotiations—in fact, the whole UN charade of pretending to solve world problems?

"Strip down and jump in! Panties too!" I wasn't sure who these authorities of such demands would be; possibly smart, alert, wonderfully balanced, can do no wrong, walk on water G20 protesters who set cities ablaze and barring them...well, me. But once corralled and made to swim, minus the gray twills of business, the white cottons of fiefdoms, the embroidered silks of royalty, the crosses, the Yarmulkes, the Kufis, and minus the flags of power, the coats of arms with historical claims, pins of appointment, medals of merit, the gavels of justice, the podiums for shoe-banging, the prompters with hollow speeches from entourages of informed sources, they would all be caught naked like the five-star general chased from the house of ill repute in *Catch-22*, minus his shoulder badges of distinction and made equal with shepherds and the flotsam of life.

"Okay, you bastards, we want world peace, so get along, or this shark bait pail of fish guts goes in!" And of course, as history has been witness for an eternity, they would not, which would leave some poor press secretary to proclaim that the next G-2 1/2 conference would be held somewhere wheelchair-accessible.

But I digress.

Rob took advantage of the swim to snorkel under the boat and check the prop and rudder, then moved to the bow and hand-tested the refurbished thrusters for wobble and shake. They were still solid as stone. A captain never rests—not even for a naked moment.

⚓ ⚓ ⚓

Our one task in Singapore, other than seeing the city, was to buy new bow thruster propellers. Rob had called ahead, having made a deal with the Phuket marina for partial payment, to a marine supplier that stocked the merchandise in Singapore. When the boat had been out of water in Phuket, Rob had had the hull scraped and repainted. The painters had not reinstalled parts properly, mismatching cotter pins and grooves, causing our prop to spin uncontrolled in the Langkawi harbour.

Yachtsmen tend to love their boats to extreme distraction. Tempt their wife off to sea (please), abscond with their firstborn, but God forbid your bow should glance off the portside hull of a tethered sloop. That would be a walk the plank for the depths of hell, plunge through a platoon of ravenous sharks, stirred to a frenzy with a vat of hot blood if you were lucky. Luck and the borrowed patron saints, St. Vigilance and St. Sobriety, followed us to Subic Bay.

Or perhaps it was the spell of Eid. The last hurrah followed us until the small hours of the morning. On the final night of celebration, every small town along the coast vied for Who-Ville recognition, shooting cannons of fireworks to light up the sky. Parasols of colour momentarily split the night, imaginably blessed by the village drums, but for sure were followed by the O-O-h-s and A-A-h-s that accompanied fireworks the world over. From our distance out to sea, they were silent exclamations of hope; hope that countered the black caves and bleak minds of retribution in far-off places, colours to remind the world we were all connected regardless of faith, race, or gender of those we love. Hundreds of villages and towns were instantly bound together from our distance out to sea in a connect-the-dots of peaceful reverie, a connection only visible from our quiet point of vantage. Again, it was a moment the Western world needed to see.

Although we were thankful for this show of celebration, it reminded me of the movie *Apocalypse Now*; Captain Willard and his stoned childlike surfer dude Lance Johnson, puppy in arms, arriving at a bombed-out bridge, flares lighting a midnight sky. We could not hear music from the village bands or the whoops of joy from delighted kids, so my mind filled in the blanks with the cries and screams from the movie soundtrack. It might have been Zepplin or Sabbath on the boat stereo, I don't remember. It wasn't the Stones, that much I know.

What river were we travelling down? What Kurtz, what heart of darkness did we seek? Would the natives get restless and turn ugly? Rob's story of Kim being sold to a man named Kurt had dislodged a bleak string of thoughts, egged on again by insomnia and the strangeness of piloting between midnight and four a.m. It's amazing what can run through your mind in the small hours of the morning. Our radio, set on an open channel, sometimes emitted the sound of fishermen or other boaters chatting back and forth, laughing at jokes I didn't understand in languages quite foreign to my ears. A small girl called for her papa and then sang a lullaby while she waited for his reply. The radar was a constant wash of blips; ships in the night, some anchored, some moving, that kept the mind active enough to not fall asleep—if a momentary nod with the head crashing down on the spokes of the helm wheel could be called sleep. If that happened, it was like hitting the grooved markings on the pavement edge while driving a car. It woke you with a start, sweat beading, senses hyped, wondering for how long you had drifted off, checking clocks and speed and pressure gauges, radar and sonar, blips that hadn't moved or had moved, or were facing the boat dead-on six nautical miles ahead, vowing to stay awake, stretching, purging all thoughts of sleep...beds, soft pillows, counting sheep... until it happened again. There were no embankments to drive off, but a collision meant a date with Davy Jones somewhere at the bottom of the sea and John's ghost with an admonishing finger, mouthing "Of course" to haunt me.

The radar was blank when John showed up to take over the helm at four a.m., refreshed and blessed with a clean slate on the radar, although, having something to watch—and aim towards missing—helps to pass the quadrants of deadly plodding time. I don't remember falling into bed or my head hitting the pillow. The body crashed, then dove towards REM. It never made it, or if it did, it was pulled back as quick as a bungee jumper at the end of the taut stretch, sucked to the surface of full consciousness by discussions at the helm and a reduction in the constant that was the rhythm of the boat. We had slowed down to a crawl.

I pulled myself to the top of the spiral stairs, up from the darkness of the staterooms below into a brightness that jolted my senses and blinded my eyes. Was I dreaming? The question "What are you doing up already?" suggested I wasn't.

"What time is it?" was all I could muster in response.

"Five-thirty." So, it wasn't sunlight after all.

"What the hell is this?"

"We are approaching Singapore. We are early, probably an hour and a half out. This? This is a parking lot for ships, and I think there is a refinery here somewhere too," John had said, matter of fact, too early for "of course," though "idiot" may still have been implied. Maybe not, but my tired mind could not discern the nuances at that hour. Rob was busy plotting on the electronic chart, letting John speak.

"About half an hour after I took over from you," John said, still matter of fact, "I flipped the radar ahead to twelve nautical miles. I nearly filled my shorts. The screen filled up with a thousand blips. I thought there was something wrong with the radar, but they didn't go away. They kept growing in numbers. We've been motoring through this for a while now, but we have just now reduced the speed. It's a little hairy with all these ships."

I walked out on the deck, still trying to comprehend the view. The night sky was illuminated by floodlights, casting a hue of honey-yellow across our path, and our path was a series of crossing shadows, as if we had been caught in a thousand suns. One hundred feet off the port side of the bow, what

I had first mistaken to be an apartment building was a container ship. It was too early to count the tiers of containers high and wide. Another ship sat anchored off to our right. It was a supertanker for oil. As far as the eye could see, from the direction we had come to the direction we were heading, ships illuminated far brighter than the small cities we had passed in the night sat anchored. We were tiny in their presence, Lilliputians adrift in the land of giants. In all directions, our quiet ocean of solitude was filled with ships, and we were motoring between massive bows of cranes, anchor chains and sterns of steel rudders, tops of rusted propellers, the monstrous hulls painted with names and flags from around the world.

It was surreal, as if we had been sucked into *The Matrix*; a grid of steel island portals connected via a saline solution of conductivity, busy in the production of sinister what's-its that are the realm of science fiction. In reality, it was the most awesome display of wealth and the power of capitalist industry I had ever seen.

A city of skyscrapers, like New York, screams largeness and wealth, huge in magnitude and greatness, but the windows, eyes to the soul of the humanity within, soften the effect of the cold, hard printing presses of cash. A thousand ships, however, launched by the face of churning yen, dollars, or pounds sterling, waiting in silence to move cargoes of hundreds of millions each, no human presence to be felt, was a true unadulterated brush with the world economies generating unfathomable wealth from hulks of steel. It was humbling and awesome and beyond words for such an early hour, so I returned to bed and counted waves on the bow until I fell asleep. I may have got to three.

11

THE SINGAPORE SLING
HISTORY
HISSING OFF THE NEIGHBOUR
BIRDS OF PARADISE

ONE LONG NIGHT LATER, SEPT. 27 OR 28...NO WATCH...
NO TIME...NO CALENDAR

Singapore (*Singa Pura* meaning "Lion City" in Malay), is possibly best known to some in the world for its Sling, created at the Raffles Hotel in 1915. A true Sling is comprised of gin, cherry liqueur, Cointreau, Benedictine, grenadine, Angostura bitters, pineapple and lime juice, shaken with ice, sipped through a straw and cursed soundly for its smooth sneak-up-and-whack-your-brain after being consumed like candy. That could just be me, however, since it remains one of the most popular old-fashioned mixed drinks in the world today.

Its namesake city, unlike the drink, is a sober testament to modern architecture. It is a bustling mass of activity. The building crane should be declared the national bird. We were bordered by a nest of such birds at our new three-day perch, called One Degree 15 Marina Club. It was an exquisitely modern, exclusively appointed, recently opened yacht club. Some yachts shone oil wells, and others small fiefdoms. Ultra-fashionable condos were in states of recently moved-in to walls rising from newly poured footings. Floodlights carried construction well past the darkness that enveloped the world at six. Twelve hours of light, twelve hours of dark, twelve months of the year. This was the benefit, or not, of no earth wobble at the equator.

I had thought Singapore was a city and was surprised to learn that it's a country, in the ancient manner of city-states, like Athens and Sparta, to mildly ancient like Florence and Venice and in the same modern way as Hong Kong was and Monaco is. John explained.

"Originally it was established by the British East India Company and then became a British colony, if I am not mistaken, in the same year as Canada became a nation in 1867. The Japanese occupied it during the Second World War, and it gained independence from the British as part of Malaysia in the early 1960s. They had so many riots and troubles that Singapore was expelled from the Malaysian Federation and became their own country. Big mistake for the rest of Malaysia! Singapore struck oil and now they have money coming out of the whazoo." Apparently, money out of the whazoo was bigger than the Ying Yang of Kuala Lumpur.

This information floated freely, as we did, in the One Degree 15 Yacht Club pool. The club's name was derived from a state of fact. Singapore sits at one degree and fifteen minutes off the equator. In miles, it represented seventy-five, as each degree was sixty miles, like an hour, and the minutes—well, they spoke for themselves—one minute...one mile. Every minute was a scorching sunburn as one degree in the oven of the afternoon heat said we were baked. Beer and an umbrella were required issue if we were to survive.

While we made faces for my underwater camera, spat water fountains in the air, and explored the four-inch glass wall that gave illusions of headless bodies when viewed from outside the pool, two women sipped on martinis. Their table was in the shade of the four-storey glass and steel structure of the yacht club building. They moved with the practiced air and nonchalant coolness that comes with the self-appointed class found in wealth. Waiters dressed for royalty kept their glasses fresh. The light olive skin suggested Middle East, the tone natural rather than collected from time in the sun. The hair was dark, long, and shone like pampered silk. One had a scarf that fell with measured effect halfway down to the shoulders, suggesting the decorum of Muslim modesty, but not the complete obedience required on the street. It wasn't necessary to read labels to know the clothing was designer. The jewellery was not ostentatious—this was poolside, after all—but one ring sported a stone large enough to send out a sparkle of numerous carats now and then. Their conversations were spoken into the thin air, over each others' shoulders. Acknowledgments were given in short nods and smiles as eyes met, then crossed to focus on exclusive shop windows or pan across the vulgar antics of three sailors in the pool. Glances were brief in our direction. I guessed from the coolness that they were wives from rival yachts, finally caught in the invitations of "must do lunch" that each had hoped the other had forgotten. It all smacked of Whazoo Ying Yang, where the boredom of advantage was a burden on the mind. This was a surmising observation on my part since I had neither, and, I suppose, one should not judge a book by its cover, for, as strangers, the covers are all you see.

Chopping into Singapore had been a notable event, in that it happened at sea. We had been tailed by harbour police as we slid into the magnet of the Singapore pull. Helicopters swept overhead, between tankers and shoreline, presumably dealing with the businesses of security and commerce. It was not a long stretch to understand the jobs of the shadowing police. We said quietly between ourselves (in case Big Brother was listening) that someone or some organization intent on creating havoc could. We had motored for miles between tankers of oil and freight. We had not been bothered by a soul until we came close to the Singapore harbour.

From miles out we could see the towers of the city proper, though Rob waited until we were close to hail immigration. The yacht club knew to expect us. From his notes, he found the specific radio channel and began his call.

"Hello, Immigration, this is *Bob-the-Boat*...Charlie...Foxtrot...November...4-7-3-4... Over?"

There was silence. Radio static and crackling were followed by a voice asking for the name once again.

"This is *Bob-the-Boat*... Over?"

Was that a muffled snicker in the background? "Hello, BOB, the boat...this is Immigration. What's your destination please?"

"Hello, Immigration, this is *Bob-the-Boat*. We are heading for the One Degree 15 Yacht Club when this is over... Over?"

Between hail and counter-hail, Rob was instructed to wait. We were two in line, we determined, following requests from other captains on the radio. Two more lined up after us.

We were soon met by a boat, a PT cruiser in size, hung with tires like a tug. Before arriving, it had been communicated as to what was to be expected; passports in a plastic bag along with three copies of handwritten paperwork pertaining to the boat and its crew. John and I were passengers at this port, not crew, as crew denoted commercial, implying business, pushing up the paperwork to triplicates of everything, including fees. The boat bore down on us in the mutually agreed location, "...twin islands to starboard," where we had waited. Rob had taken the time to crawl into the engine room, pop the hood, and check the oil. We hadn't used a stitch, which was good.

The immigration boat motored perpendicular to our hull, then backed off with precision skill before touching, hanging within a foot of *Bob-the-Boat*, rolling in the wake of its approach. A young fellow dressed in shorts and a T-shirt rode the bow, holding the railing with one hand, a long fishnet pole in the other. He was in sharp contrast to the immigration crew. The driver and the officer in charge wore the dark navy-blue vestments of official issue—wool, it appeared—long pants, long-sleeved shirts over heavy, blue undershirts, single buttons loosed at the neck, heavy leather shoes not made for the teaks and rosewood decks of yachts. It was a uniform out of coordination with the equatorial sun. I was sweltering in my cotton T-shirt and shorts.

Rob appeared, dressed for the occasion. The sun was already high by nine a.m. and hot, like a wet steam sauna. The captain wore only his best SpongeBob boxers, red hearts on black and the words *The Love Angel* front and center. It wasn't any wonder the first words spoken by Immigration were addressed to John, outfitted in safari-brown shirt and shorts, sporting dark aviator glasses of authority. Busy taking photos of the event, I wasn't considered a second glance.

The papers were dropped into the outstretched net and then hauled in for observation. The boat backed off our hull by twenty feet. We waited.

The captain returned to the engine room looking for the exit of the single drip he had found beneath a cooling hose. It was condensation. We waited.

A container ship motored into the commercial lanes of shipping traffic like a car speeding onto a freeway. It was heading northwest toward India, up the strait we had just come down. Although the boat was several miles away from us, when the ship cranked the throttle to full speed, our harbour fluttered with the massive rush of air from the engines. It made windows rattle on the boat. Within a minute it was gone.

"He is probably doing twenty knots by now," John piped in.

So, to give perspective, we used the on-board Google of John's mind to do some very quick math. The large container ship was carrying three or four thousand eighteen-wheeler-sized containers (research later told me that was short by about ten thousand, so quadruple all these numbers).

"That's a forty-mile convoy, bumper to bumper, adding the tractor!"

A train puts two per car.

"Twenty miles of prairie train."

"So how does a ship that size go zero to twenty knots in a few short minutes?"

"The new ships have the largest diesel engines in the world. A train locomotive packs around six thousand horsepower. These engines in the supertankers are nearly a hundred and ten thousand horsepower. That's eighteen locomotives all accelerating at once!"

"Must be some torque," I added.

"About five and a half million pounds per foot!" he said. God, how does his mind do that? All I thought was…

"Big feet!"

"And it's all happening at over one hundred rpm." We watched the ship disappear, the air still pounding with the acceleration. "And now that the ship is up to speed, it can take ten miles to stop in an emergency." He was the whole Wikipedia of Britannica.

"How do you know all this shit?"

"Reading of course!" Perhaps "idiot," was implied with the added shrug. "This stuff interests me. Don't forget my dad used to build engines for the Avro Arrow. I find it fascinating."

"It all kind of makes *Bob-the-Boat* seem like a dinky toy."

"It is!"

"If you would both like to swim, it's fine by me," Rob chimed in. Testy captains love their boats.

Before a walk the plank could be invoked, the papers were returned with a two-thumbs-up from the sergeant, who posed for a final picture. We were in.

⚓ ⚓ ⚓

Hooking up power at our various stops had become an

Olympic event. Each slim wharf dividing berths for two boats contained a hook-up for both power and water. There were meters to measure the use of both. Each outlet had a switch, which was turned on once connected and off to remove. The electrical line for the boat was about a hundred feet long. One end was pushed into the side of the boat, twisted into place, and locked. The other end was complicated.

Some marinas required three pins, some five, and this one was a configuration of eight or something in that range that rendered our line useless. This had been the situation at each of the previous stops, but Rob had come prepared with various combinations of multi-pinned ends that only required the patience of an hour or so to disassemble one connector and add another. This connector, however, was not to be found in the boat's stash of ready supplies. The marina offered a new one for fourteen thousand Singapore dollars, equaling about four hundred Canadian dollars, which was soundly rejected and left us no further ahead. Some modification was suggested, alternatives accepted, and before long John had assembled a new configuration and was ready to plug us in. He did, with a hitch.

The power must be off when the cord is inserted and twisted into place. If it's not, things get fried. To prevent frying, John flipped off both switches at the pier, unable to discern which meter belonged to us and which belonged to the boat next door. It was only for a couple of seconds before he flicked one back on.

Our boat had been given berth between two unflagged vessels: a sailboat and a three-storey condo disguised as a yacht. The condo erupted. Smoked glass doors hissed open and a royally pissed owner hissed out. John, sitting cross-legged, electrical tools scattered around him at arms' length, was in no position to deny involvement when asked if he had turned off the power. It had only been momentary, but long enough to have created havoc.

"I have a dozen screens displaying the markets from around the world. Let me rephrase that. I *had* a dozen screens. What in God's fucking name are you doing?" It was a tirade of a blue streak, followed by descending colours in a rainbow of apologies by John. The condo hissed open. The condo hissed shut. At some point we had power.

Had this been a brain surgeon in mid-operation or a novelist who had lost an entire book, John may have laughed and shrugged it off with a *"C'est la vie."* But this was a money man in the serious indulgence of finessing numbers and rounding up bank accounts. John was mortified, driven to fall on the sword of remorse and heartfelt apologies that can only be rectified with a bottle of vintage expense, delivered with the humility of hat in hand, hissed in and out with the assurance of no harm done. The bottle of Trojan Horse would later bring him to the inner sanctum of an investor's lair, conceivably the reigning highlight of his trip to date.

My encounter with the neighbor on the opposite side was less dramatic. I asked him what he did for a living. "International finances," not expounded upon, was delivered in such tone that suggested I was an idiot for asking. He disappeared into his boat and was visited by a swarthy man of short blond hair and dark glasses who left expensive shoes on the deck. They left together, a single gym bag in hand, two hours later. My mind wandered to dark affairs, international hitmen, arms dealers, CIA. Yachts made for the perfect cover, nestled in harbours of dubious finances that brought them all together. John had cast the first doubt.

"You can't seize assets if you can't find them." Runaway investment dealers, clandestine hedge funds, derivatives gone south...who knew what lurked beyond the snake hiss of a smoked glass door? Were we hobnobbing with a pack of thieves? What devious thoughts had our neighbours about us? Village idiots made good? Three cast-offs? Rub-a-dub-dub, three men in a tub? The truth I believe...what happens behind closed hatches, nobody cares. Don't ask, don't disconnect power, and don't hiss them off.

⚓ ⚓ ⚓

Lee Kuan Yew, the first Prime Minister of Singapore, has been quoted as saying, "To understand Singapore, you've got to start off with an impossible story. It should not exist." Singapore is modern; not a show of tall buildings hiding another city behind, but nearly the whole city is twenty-first century, with barely a trace of old and used. It led me to wonder as to what had happened. Did all the shacks blow away in a storm? Had there been an earthquake or a minor Krakatoa? A fire, perhaps? Okay, the Japanese bombed it before taking control in 1942, but as far as I was able to find out, there had been no great Singapore disaster, like a quake or monstrous tsunami or volcanic eruption. Not since 1855 had there been a fire of city-wide destruction. There had been riots back in the early sixties, but there was no historical record of complete destruction.

What happened was a national vision; large investments in public education and huge manufacturing growth all backed by an aggressive oil industry. They don't have huge reserves, but Singapore refines crude imports from the Middle East and their geographical location is perfect for trading oil all over the world. They are the undisputed oil hub of Southeast Asia, with about ninety-five oil companies doing trade here, and thus that massive flotilla of oil tankers we had encountered on our way in. This has created vats of money, sheikdom-type wealth that most cities and nations can only dream about, the whazoo yin-yang money that can buy an entire country makeover, out with the old and in with the new; futuristic high-speed transit on elevated causeways and under-city subways, new highways and roadways for electric cars and buses, and state-of-the-art port facilities away from the view of glass towers that rise like crystal monoliths to a *Star Wars* world.

We saw the country/city, a journey of thirty-two high-speed train stops inland. We left the security of our gated island on the private-members-only air-conditioned bus that is the luxury of the One Degree 15 Yacht Club. We were on a mission to chop in for the port authority and find the marina office that supplied the new bow thruster propellers. Marina suppliers, one might suppose, should be near a marina, on the water, with easy access by boat or a short sailor's walk with petulant sea legs from the docks. Our supplier was found between a clover leaf and a subway stop, miles from the smell of salt and seaweed, six stories up, down a long, dark, industrial hallway, through a door with a number that had no name. A few nautical parts hung on the wall. There were displays of rope and cleats, an expensive new captain's chair, posters of yachts, and a single desk occupied by a woman who may have looked more comfortable in a wedding gown shop. But she had what we needed, so we made the purchase and left. It was high noon, lung-searing hot, so we hailed a cab.

Too early to return to the marina, we decided to play tourist and spent the afternoon admiring colourful birds at one of the world's largest aviaries, the Jurong Bird Park. It was notable for the massive collection of rare tropical birds, five thousand from three hundred and eighty species including the Froot Loops toucan, a rockhopper penguin, and a shoebill stork, most birds in colours beyond the imagination and now stuck forever in my memory, for John's total lack of interest. How could you not get excited about a lesser bird-of-paradise or a greater flamingo, macaws and cockatoos or the yellow-naped Amazon parrot? A macaroni penguin? How about a white-faced tree duck? Having dragged the drumstick (no birds from the aviary) through the broth of Singapore, he was ready to call it soup, wanting to move on toward our goal of Subic in the Philippines. Birds, I guess, were foul-feathered friends as far as he was concerned. It was interesting how, as friends, our tastes could be so different. A fairy penguin? This tour, I guess, is not for everyone.

The afternoon heat drove us back to the sanctuary of our air-conditioned boat, but first we stopped at an air-cooled mall and bought food (real French bread with butter), a bottle of penance wine (oaked in humble pie) for Chateau Hiss, and industrial strength deodorant for me. It was either that or be ditched at sea. The private air-con bus with tinted windows delivered us into the heat of the late afternoon sun at the club, where we again found refuge in their pool and gins with tonic on the boat. In a city that shouldn't exist, life was good!

12

KILLER TYPHOONS
EARTHQUAKE 7.9
TSUNAMI WARNINGS
MERRILY BACK TO SEA

SEPT. 30, 2009

It was simply another day in most parts of the world. John had picked up his usual two newspapers. The world was still unfolding as it had the day before, with war in Afghanistan raging and markets careening on roller-coaster rides in the West. President Obama was getting ready to visit this part of the immediate world in a month or so. Singapore was no different, it seemed, weathering the storms of faltering economies in far-off lands by pumping more oil, shoring up banks, and staying the course of solid financial prudence. The rest of the world could fall, but Singapore was as solid as the Rock of Gibraltar could be, sitting on the Pacific Rim of Fire.

Despite the heat being strained through the gray cloud cover inland, it was still stifling hot. Out to sea, the sky was blue. The occasional cotton-puff cloud escaped a mile or two offshore like a clay pigeon, instantly shattered by breezes shooting up from the ocean below. We were preparing to depart by noon, moving into seaworthy mode, leaving the power hook-up that gave us air conditioning until the last possible moment.

Captain Rob spent time recharting our course from Singapore to Borneo, since we would not be visiting some places he had during the trip in reverse. He was also keeping an eye on a typhoon that was raging in the Pacific, due soon to cross over the Philippines. For this, he was relying on internet sites geared precisely to charting such storms, giving hourly movements of the big red ball on the screen. Unfortunately, in the most expensive yacht club setting in Southeast Asia, the internet was an iffy thing, messages still being sent via camel and carrier pigeon, so it seemed. It was our usual practice to tap into the yacht clubs for free, and barring that, log on to some service, like that of the three-storey condo next door. On this day, service was sporadic on the boat, so Rob shuffled back and forth to the yacht club offices for weather reports.

There was no danger of getting a direct hit at sea by a typhoon (not yet anyway), being this close to the equator. We were protected by something called the Coriolis force and beta effect, dragging storms north or south depending on what side of the equator they developed. It was the aftereffect of a storm pushing into the South China Sea, creating rough seas for hundreds of miles. The screen showed calm for our voyage to Borneo, with simulated soft blue waves on the subscription-only yachter's weather website. In the Philippines, the colours were red—bloodred, like the red that is used to torment bulls or pools across movie trailers for *Friday the 13th*... the red of death and destruction.

The entire world had been watching while the Philippines and Taiwan had been ravaged by a killer typhoon in early September. Number two since then was wreaking havoc once again in Manila with another one forming. Watching the weather website was like watching a tennis ball machine. Storm after killer storm was being lobbed from the court in the Pacific

Ocean across the network of islands that are the Philippines. Some ricocheted north towards Taiwan, while others aced their mark with such power that they carried on across the South China Sea straight into Vietnam and Cambodia. The storm of concern at the moment of our departure (lined up behind the one already in devastation mode) packed winds above 280 kilometres per hour, (over 170 mph) exceeding the highest rating of *"GET OUT OF DODGE"* storm-rating scales; so powerful, in fact, it could take down any ship on the high seas, flatten cities, or strip flesh from a man's body. The typhoon still hovered in the Pacific, which was the problem, since there was no predicting the direction it would take.

In this gathering of information on typhoons, a small tidbit of news was announced concerning an earthquake in Indonesia. It had hit a place called Padang, and was recorded at 7.9 magnitude, and there was the possibility of tsunamis in the South Pacific. News at eleven!

Should I be alarmed and spew concern or roll with the lack of concern that it seemed to be creating? I spewed as lacklustre as I could, wanting to show the highly developed sense of calm the last weeks at sea had created.

"TSUNAMI? You've gotta be kidding! I think we should stay BLOODY put." I was silenced by the speed and intensity of John's quick, eye-rolling retort.

"We are NOT in the South Pacific!" which he dismissed with the wave of a hand and a combined shrug-sneer-snort. It rained triple-idiot disdain for my *Chicken Little* response, and I backed off, realizing again that I had not done my homework. I had worried about being hit by a typhoon en route to Borneo, when I should have known they don't fly that far south. Rob had gone out of his way to calm my fears by researching to death the upcoming storm, sharing constantly the weather reports and spending time analyzing them with us. As captain, he said, it was his duty.

"Besides," Rob said, "the boats that sink from tsunamis are

not the ones at sea. That beautiful yacht club we stayed at in Phuket got wiped out during the big tsunami of 2004. All the boats ended up in a heap, destroyed. So, I think we are safer at sea." I resolved not to question again.

I had never researched places to where I was travelling. For all my experiences, Paris had been the greatest revelation since I had had no expectations. I had been a young traveller. I knew there was an Eiffel Tower and that the *Mona Lisa* hung in some gallery called the Louvre. Paris was surprising, magnificently so; all my senses poked and prodded with a myriad of sensual delights I have never forgotten. The city of Prague proved to be the same many years later. Nearly every place I had ever been in my life was viewed through the innocent eyes of a childlike traveller. I couldn't be disappointed if I didn't know what to expect, and I never was, so why should motoring in Southeast Asia be any different? Researching shifting tectonic plates would have spoiled the surprise. Ignorance is bliss when sitting on the hot coals of the Pacific Rim. Research would have told me that the most earthquakes in the world—a whopping ninety percent—happened on the forty thousand kilometres of the Pacific Rim shoreline. It only made sense, then, that the most active volcanoes in the world resided here, home to the mythologies of Krakatau and Mt. Pinatubo, and of course all this seismic belt activity created more tsunamis than anywhere else. And typhoons—well, they were a dime a dozen. On a need-to-know basis, I didn't.

John was somewhat my opposite, having left the joys of childhood ignorance back at puberty. His decrees of information, such as the statement about the tsunami, were delivered in proclamations of absolute truths; shrugged, weighted statements with hands turned up in an outward gesture to dispel any doubt—and thus given due respect. He delivered them with a Churchill scowl and a bent stance of knowledge-enhanced age (he was two months older than Rob and me) that commanded faith in what was said. He gleaned information from three newspapers daily, absorbed and filed, ready for dispensation at the drop of a hat.

In his personal life, his pursuit of a self-made fortune had left few roses to which he stooped to smell. The freedom of wealth had made him a prisoner to keeping it, and, he admitted, found little joy in spending. He had become a draught horse, industriously pulling his load, dutifully carrying his weight, blinkered to being moved by the small joys of life. Offering information and opinions, though, brought happiness.

Unfortunately, some men will be boys forever, and I was one of them. There were few Kodak moments of my childhood without contorted faces or two-finger bunny ears behind my siblings' heads. In a large family, humour saved me from getting lost in the maze. I never had to be the dutiful son. There were others older than I to carry that torch.

It was, I am sure, this childishness for which John felt the need to preach the art of the daily bowel movement or extol the benefits of using the same string of dental floss for a week. He had patted his gym bag luggage with regularity to let me know how practical he was to have such a small carbon footprint. He pointed out that he still had one pair of underwear not used, three weeks into the trip. The male bonding humour of a dropped gastric attack that cleared the decks brought the mightier-than-thou look of "Who farted?" reserved for the "We are not amused" looks from the queen. I argued if you can't drop one on the bow of a boat in the South China Sea without the incriminating jibes of a wife, then one may as well stay at home, even if it does bring tears to the eyes and leaves fish floating in the wake. But at the mature age of fifty-six, one was supposed to squeak it silently, close to the exhaust vent, and definitely never raise one cheek in pride of ownership, laugh at the ill effects, or announce the coming with a "pull my finger." It didn't mesh gentlemanly with the

Chateau Gaz Mortel Soixante-Neuf that had caused the problem in the first place.

Our captain set courses and wore blinders to our conflicting world where a familiar wound was festering like lead left in the brain. Rob and I had always been brothers in spirit, though he said he could do without the gas.

With the bills paid, power disconnected, water lines stored, and all the other small items taken care of, we motored out of the harbour sometime after noon, with the midday sun burning a path for our departure. The estimated time to Borneo was four days—ninety-six hours nonstop. It was for this crossing we had been training…sleep deprivation, now a constant in the daily routine and the short-haul routes having set our systems up for the absence of sleep and alcohol. Water was to be the only liquid for the next four days.

"You never know what can happen," Rob had said. "We need to be sharp at all times." This was a truth that foreshadowed our voyage.

13

THE ABCS FOR SURVIVAL
THE TSUNAMI HITS
A SPIRITUAL MOMENT

SAME DAY, 2 HOURS OUT

Chopping out of Singapore was a duplication of chopping in. We waited in the harbour, bobbing about as large boats jockeyed for position, assisted by tugs and shadowed by harbour police. A ship moved into the commercial lanes—four large domes of liquid natural gas under naval escort. The supercarriers of the gas ships may be carrying up to 260,000 m3 of liquefied gas (68,680,000 American gallons). It has been said by skeptics (or those in the know) that if one of these ships should collide and explode, it could flatten the entire island of Manhattan. I guess the naval escort was hoping to prevent a suicide bomber from strapping one to his waist. The ports of Halifax, Nova Scotia in 1917 and Texas City, Texas, in 1947 can tell you a lot about harbour explosions. Both ports had massive Hiroshima-type destruction, and thousands were injured or killed by exploding ships carrying munitions and fertilizer respectively. They were tiny tugboats in comparison to the ship we saw. Compressed and liquefied natural gas on boats;

even if the skeptics are wrong by half, it would seem in this case, man is playing with fire...the apocalyptic type.

We pushed off, heading east from Singapore. I snapped photos of the skyline, blocked previously by the condos and cranes surrounding the yacht club. It was impressive for its size, but from our view, it lacked the signature of trademark architecture, like the Twin Towers of Kuala Lumpur, the CN Tower of Toronto, or the Opera House in Sydney. There was no mountainous backdrop, as in Vancouver or Seattle, no statues like in New York or Copenhagen. Here, it was the glass towers of steel and concrete, magnetized to draw money from around the world. However, Singapore has since added many magnificent signature architectural marvels since our trip, including the Marina Bay Sands Hotel SkyPark Resort...three multi-story towers connecting their roofs with one giant ship-like structure. Fitting!

Our course took us through a grid of ships similar to those we saw on the way in, though it appeared these were without payloads; a floating used shipyard, moored and waiting for the redemptive call back to sea. We passed a drilling platform twenty stories high. It had boundary markers a mile or so in each direction: giant buoys with flashing lights that denoted ownership of this portion of the open seas. There were armed boats to enforce the invisible line. It was necessary, I thought, considering the threat of pirates or bombers for political causes, or simply for the amount of traffic that used this part of the sea. A collision would be catastrophic. We motored past, dwarfed by the structure, but no doubt looming large on their radar.

Some ships moving towards the Singapore port had flat bows, massive in height and width. They were the car carriers of the sea, capable of transporting thousands of vehicles. An oil boat sat beside a large tanker, pumping fuel on board. It was funny to think a boat carrying two million barrels of crude could run out of fuel. Maintenance boats were maintaining, tugboats tugging, and giant dredgers dredging. We were the only pleasure boat, doing pleasure.

An hour out, we crossed the north-south commercial lanes, dodging ships doing twenty knots (twenty-three miles per hour or forty kilometres per hour). We were doing 6.5 knots, so there was no attempt to outrun them like a Buster Keeton car chase with an oncoming train. In the battle of size, they had the most lug nuts, and we gave them lots of space. It took a while. There was a rush hour of massive ships in both directions.

Always cross shipping lanes at ninety degrees. It is a maritime law of the sea and common sense.

Heading east by northeast, our electronic compass hovered between eighty and a hundred degrees off true north, not to be confused by magnetic north, which apparently confuses everything. The earth's magnetic charm changes over time and in different places on the globe. Numbers must be added, taken away, or multiplied, I am not quite sure. Our earth positioning was counting upward from the one-degree fifteen-minute latitude of our harbour nest, gradually leaving the equator to our wake, while moving eastward from one hundred and four degrees longitude—that was Singapore. We crossed one hundred and five degrees, heading more east than north for a while, the electronic compass pumping out changing numbers with every nautical mile we went.

In life before sea travel, latitude and longitude had no relevance to my life. I lived on land. Nothing floated or moved in four directions, and destinations could not be reached moving north by northeast while your travel surface flowed south by southwest, unless you were a politician glad-handing through a crowd. I asked Rob for clarification, and he explained the relationship between hours and minutes and navigation. It was good to know in case we had to mayday for help and let someone know where we were sinking or sank and are floating in life rafts...or worse come to worse, where memorial flowers might be dropped off at sea. He took the time to explain a few other features that should have been explored before leaving shore.

There was a floating GPS PLB blinky thing hanging on the wall of the helm that activates when it hits water. PLB stands for Personal Locator Beacon. If it's zigzagging and doing a hundred miles an hour during search and rescue, it may have been swallowed by a shark. Each of the two rescue rings that are hanging on the railing has long lines with blinky lights that activate when they are turned upright. And there were other things for our consideration.

The lifeboat was strapped down, winched tight to the boat deck with nylon straps. The straps would need to be cut if we were in a hurry, so bring a knife; ditto for the canvas cover, tightly laced to hug the boat. John dismissed urgency since the dinghy sits on the top deck of the boat.

"If the boat's going down, this is the last place to take on water!" he said. The statement seemed valid and logical, again delivered in a calm tone of authority, so I relegated the importance of speed of exit to some backwater life raft in the brain. There was an inflatable raft tied to the railing. Rob was not sure how safe it was, since the sun's ultraviolet rays were eating away at the canvas cover. It was supposed to inflate when a cord was pulled. It, too, would need to be cut. The blinky GPS PLB from the cabin should be carried into the life raft. Water and rations would need to be added. A phone would be good for hailing and perhaps a couple of books. Forget the change of underwear...John would have to leave his last clean pair behind.

There were several stages of radio play on the short wave that descended towards "Mayday... Mayday... All is lost... Been good to know ya." If something were to happen and we got someone on the other end of the radio, we were to give the name of the boat, call letters, nature of the problem, and anything else that may help identify the remains. Time permitting, it is "mayday" three times, followed by *Bob-the-Boat* three times, some identifying remarks about the boat (never admit it is lemon yellow or they may let you sink), longitude and latitude coordinates along with the *Bob-the-Boat*-designated numbers and call letters. These have to be in the nautical alphabet lingo of [*B*ravo *O*scar *B*ravo] [*T*ango *H*otel *E*cho] [*B*ravo *O*scar *A*lpha *T*ango] for *Bob-the Boat*. I try committing the alphabet to memory, starting with [*A*lpha *B*ravo *C*harlie] and ending with [*O*scar *H*otel] [*S*ierra *H*otel *I*ndia *T*ango] [*W*hiskey *E*cho] [*A*lpha *R*omeo *E*cho] [*S*ierra *I*ndia *N*ovember *K*ilo *I*ndia *N*ovember *G*ol*f*]—with [**PLEASE HURRY**] thrown in. These were games I played while on the midnight shift at the helm.

If the entire boat is dog-eared shut—large levers that come four to a door to make things watertight—the boat should stay afloat if turned on its side, provided the windows don't break. There is a special door on the forward stateroom (my bedroom), with dog ears on the inside. If we collide and the bow is breached, and if this door is sealed shut, it prevents water from filling the rest of the boat. It becomes a tomb for the sleeping inhabitant—*moi*—but stops the boat from sinking. It might have been selfish, but I never closed that door. There was something about the watery tomb my brain refused to accept. The captain's stateroom has an escape hatch into the engine room, but the doors to get out lock from above. It was then that I understood the need to know, and that, had I known before we left, I might have stayed home.

⚓ ⚓ ⚓

We were in Indonesian waters, a country we had never chopped into, and, according to Rob, were not overly friendly towards Westerners. He could have been right. While we had been travelling, another Western-based hotel had been bombed in Jakarta, the capital of Indonesia. A second day underway, and we would be in Malaysian seas again anyway, so we ignored the fact that Indonesian submarines or PT boats may arrive at any moment and blow us out of the water.

Two hours out of Singapore, Rob stopped the boat, and we went for a swim. It had become a favorite pattern of the early afternoon hours. Drop the ladder off the stern, dive deep into the crystal-clear waters, taste the salt, and feel the crystals drying on our skin once we were on our way. Usually, we were in and out and motoring all within fifteen minutes, cooled and refreshed. The next ritual was to shower off, taking turns standing on the bow and using a hose set up for swabbing the deck. Hose down, shampoo up, and rinse off...all in the buff, of course. Towels were hung out to dry on the double line across the stern.

On this day, chicken had been removed from the freezer and set out to thaw on the counter. It was to be prepared on the stainless-steel barbecue that hung off the stern railing. John had already prepped for a salad, chopping and dicing fresh vegetables to marinate in rice wine and balsamic vinegar.

The seas were calm, and we were motoring at over seven knots. Not burning a trail exactly, but, as Rob jumped to his boat's defence, "try swimming to keep up." He sat at the helm. It was near three in the afternoon, quiet time before dinner preparations and clean up, and the early to bed for the early-to-rise first captain of the night. John was reading his novel he'd brought from home and I...I don't remember where I was exactly, perhaps close to the opened back doors, admiring the seas in our wake.

I heard the doors clank shut at the helm, and without warning the boat turned on a dime, perpendicularly south to the east/west course we were on. Rob shouted, "Hold on", but there wasn't time. A deafening roar enveloped the boat, which lurched as if shoved into reverse. The inertia sent me reeling, both feet lifting off the floor, but I kept from falling by clinging to the counter where chicken, left to thaw, hurled like bullets against the back wall. Glass dishes, pots, pans and cutlery rattled in unison, but held their places behind locked doors. We heard the rush, felt the air sucking, and saw the wave sliding over the boat, crashing first on the helm windshield. It rolled down the outside walkway, submersing the large windows on each side in a foamed frenzy, as if the boat had entered the high-powered jets of a car wash. When the wave hit the stern, the water was caught on the three-foot wall that enclosed the exterior deck and in its brief moment of power, sent a wave crashing through the open doors into the cabin.

And as fast it had come, the wave was gone. The water was as still and quiet as a forest pond as if nothing had ever happened. Looking in the direction the wave was heading, it was impossible to detect its presence. There was no trail of swells or breaking whitecaps. It simply vanished.

Considering what had happened, getting the unexpected bath was no big deal. From the helm, sitting in the captain's chair, Rob's eye had caught what looked to be a thin white line of thread along the south horizon. It had appeared from nowhere, he said. He had stepped out onto the deck, curious, watching the line that trailed east and west for as far as he could see, growing in size. In retrospect, he stood too long trying to make sense of what had been up to then pristine calm, but he had no way of knowing that it was a tsunami coming. He had never seen one before. The fact that tsunamis can travel faster than jet speed (depending on the depth of the water), it would not have left him much time for evasive action. He had turned the bow of the boat into the oncoming wave, rushed to close both doors to the helm, one left and one right, four dog ears each, a distance of fifteen feet apart, and then and only then considered shouting for us to hold on. It wasn't the front of the tsunami wave that brought the crash of water, since the boat climbed high up onto the crest of the wave, but the consequent dive into the trough following, driving the bow deep into the swell preceding the lesser wave being dragged in the tsunami's wake. It was a ten-second wash based on a split-second decision to turn the boat. It most likely saved us from complete disaster.

We were too busy for the next half hour cleaning up the water that had soaked the interior to even begin to consider the possibilities and what-ifs or perform the sign of the cross, spectacles, testicles, keys and wallet, to make sure nothing was lost. Every towel was wrung into action by John and me, while Rob turned the boat back on course, his eyes glued to the south...just in case.

It was Rob who suggested that it was a rogue wave. I never questioned; the warnings of tsunamis had been dismissed in my mind by the confidence in John's statement that they would appear only in the South Pacific. Rob did not venture into the realm of speculation for a couple of days, at which time he quietly submitted, had he not changed course, it may have flipped the boat. At this point, we allowed a few what-ifs to surface.

What if John or I had been at the helm, the boat not turned in time...the boat upended? What if it had been the dead of night? What if the helm doors had not been closed in time and the electronics had been hit? What if we had stopped for our midday swim an hour later and we had been playfully bobbing off the back of the boat with no eyes to the sea ahead? For whatever reason, nothing more was said. The wave was referred to as the "rogue wave" when we finally got to port in Borneo and had the opportunity to write home. It passed and held no more weight than one of the several rainstorms that we had encountered.

With the luxury of time and the internet, it has become quite clear that indeed it was a tsunami. Tsunami warnings had been issued for Indonesia, Thailand and Malaysia following an earthquake off the coast of Sumatra. Sumatra was only two hundred miles south of our location. At the speed that tsunamis travel, it would only have been a matter of minutes before it rolled over our position.

A rogue wave is slower, most often created due to a combination of storms and converging tides and other phenomena that scientists don't quite understand. They rise mysteriously from the depths of the seas, up to one hundred-foot walls of seething waters that sink, smash, kill, and destroy everything in their short path, and then somehow part and return to the surging tides as if they had never been born. They were the lore of sailors' yarns, never quite believed. Only quakes, landslides or underwater displacements like volcanoes or explosions can produce tsunamis, and unlike rogues, the tsunami with its great speed usually ends only when land stops it dead. Most tsunamis go undetected at sea, appearing like a fast-rising tide of a foot or more and hence the often-quoted tidal wave. However, the highest tsunami ever recorded was 1,720 feet (524 meters) at Lituya Bay, Alaska, on July 9, 1958. In case you think you misread that, that's a wave nearly ten times the height of Niagara Falls or one hundred feet short of Toronto's CN Tower. It was born from an earthquake-spawned rockslide on an enclosed inlet, so it is not typical of ocean tsunamis. This type of wave is referred to by scientists as a mega-tsunami (you think?). Whatever the wave was called that hit us, we were humbled by its power, saved by our captain's quick thinking, and left to contemplate our good fortune.

Research shows that same seismic shift created earthquakes elsewhere, creating seventy-foot tsunamis and ravaging the islands of Samoa and Tongo, thousands of miles east of our location. Hundreds perished.

It was sad to think that ordinary people, doing ordinary things, in ordinary lives, had vanished. The wave had been the result of an earthquake in Sumatra that killed thousands, some buried alive in mudslides, collapsed buildings, fires, and lost forever. It is possible...actually, quite likely, that some of the lone fishermen we had seen trolling in small two-seat boats with sons and daughters helping to pull in the nets had been taken, never to be known statistics by the world at large, part of humanity sucked into the chasm of anonymous death, from beaches and boats, from schools and homes, buried, forgotten, lost to time, filtered from ashes to dust to cosmic energy from whence they came. Now that we had connected with the peoples of Southeast Asia, the loss felt somewhat personal. The statistics were no longer from distant lands, announced in news blurbs that rolled across the screen.

As if the gods had called a truce, begging forgiveness for a childish prank, that evening the ocean was calm, sculpted like gray-blue slate to the horizon. A magnificent display of fire and cloud rolled into the ocean behind us, and a full moon rose over the South China Sea off the starboard bow. While snapping photos, I caught Rob in a rare moment of quiet contemplation, staring into the still waters as if giving thanks. It was not a moment to interrupt with a penny for your thoughts, not that he would have shared anyway. Catherine had given herself to spiritual contemplation a few times, even before she left terra firma in Canada, but it was not something I could imagine for Rob. If he had been giving thanks and felt he needed to do so, then I was behind it one hundred percent.

If there had ever been a reason to search for a spiritual being, it had been then and there. It took little imagination to think of oneself drifting in an open sea, clutching some flotation device with shark fins cutting ever-smaller circles. I am sure the oceans are quite used to hearing sailors' confessions, bearing witness to conversions and trading life and redemption for the promise of penitent souls. The shores of the world are littered with sailors' chapels; testaments to the oaths and vows to build, extracted through the waterboard of near death. Whatever the sentiment, I knew that Rob appreciated we had escaped a wretched moment that had had potential foreplay to an outright disaster. As for the offerings from gods, the beautiful display and pageantry of sunset clouds…I was willing to forgive, perhaps, but never forget.

14

WATER, WATER, EVERYWHERE
NAKED WITH THE GODS
LIONS, TIGERS, AND THE COMFORT OF DARK

SEPT. 30 THROUGH OCT. 3...LOTS OF TIME TO THINK

Four days...the symphony rolled on. For the first time since the trip began, we found moments, whole segments of time, where we were completely alone. The radar showed nothing. We were soloists, it appeared, which felt rather strange, considering that in the Straits of Malacca there were never fewer than a dozen ships on our radar. It was exhilarating and intimidating all at the same time. A massive rainstorm rolled over us on the second afternoon, completely enveloping us in wind and warm rain. Deploying the windshield wipers was an exercise in futility. The waves lined up like corduroy with a white piping of foam. The radar became a blur of clouds and rain pockets. If there were any ships in there, in the roil of red and blue electronic gauze moving across the screen, we never knew. It was like driving on a highway in a heavy fog or having snow coming straight at you, with the immediate road ahead being barely visible. This was the first time I detected the weakness of the electronic guide. Storms meant that you were motoring blind, and, unlike a highway, there was no place to pull over. After two hours, the calm returned but the sun did not. Cloud cover took us into darkness, and sporadic showers followed us for most of the night.

Morning sunshine crept out of the black clouds on the horizon, starting a little after six a.m. It came in monochromes of red at first, then pastels of orange and licks of yellow pushed lighter and lighter until the sun forced solo beams of white through slits in the clouds. There were no silhouettes of land, only a beam of silver reflection to a horizon that moved with the gentle swells.

The absence of visible land on the South China Sea was my first insight to the Ancient Mariner's rhyme, "Water, water, everywhere, and not a drop to drink." It didn't apply to us in that *Bob-the-Boat* was equipped with a water desalinator that produced twelve gallons of fresh water every hour, but the taste left something to be desired. The water was held in large fibreglass holding tanks, meant more for showering and toilets than for drinking. We usually stocked up on bottled water, though for this passage, Rob had taken inventory of his bottles of distilled water and decided we didn't need any more. It was tasteless and, although it was liquid, it added nothing of nourishment to our systems. Because of the heat, we each drank several litres of water a day, which we chilled in the fridge. Our need outpaced the chiller and, in the end, we had no choice but to drink lukewarm distilled water.

Two fishing lines were set up every morning, but not once since leaving Phuket had we had a bite. Two false alarms produced a long trail of seaweed and the discarded entrails of a fishing net. The fishing poles were set into special holders that Rob had mounted on the railing, one on either side of the pilot house doors, in plain view from the captain's chair. If a fish should have grabbed the lure, we had a very short time to man the pole and stop the run before a few thousand feet of line disappeared. One person was to run for the fishing pole and work the rod, while another had to throw the boat into neutral, grab the fish gaff (a monster hook on the end of a pole), run to the stern, and wait to snare the unlucky fish with the hook through the gill.

Besides the two fishing lines, Rob had set up a flutter board that skipped across the water about ten feet in front of the trailing lures. The activity of the board was supposed to simulate skittering fish on the surface of the water and trick the bigger fish into thinking that school was out, the buses were late, and the cafeteria was full. The hope was to tempt them with red or green lures crafted to look like fluorescent flying shrimp and imbedded with whale-sized hooks. Either they had seen this dog and pony show before or there were no fish left. I think it was a little of both.

I was nervous that the dolphins that visited our boat now and again would take a stab at the lures. They never did, confirming their reputation as the smartest mammal of the sea. Beautiful to watch, they appeared from somewhere in the deep in small groups of five or six and immediately lined up along either side of the boat, finding pleasure in playing with the ripples sent out by the bow. They darted in and out of the newly cut waters, conceivably getting a pleasurable sensation, like the feeling of bubbles from the jets in a hot tub. As if tempting us to play tag or catch me if you can, they would surge ahead of the boat, hold their positions like lead dogs on a sled, then loop back with lightning dips and dives and line up all over again. They never stayed for more than a few minutes, and as fast and mysterious as they came, they disappeared. We were doing eight knots and they left us in their wake. I am sure the routine was the same for all the boats, but we felt special whenever they chose to visit.

The closer we got to Borneo, the more human activity we began to see. There were pairs of fishing boats and small freighters that moved supplies from port to port, trespassing on our solitude. When they disappeared, we were left with the feeling that we again had the whole sea to ourselves. The quiet rings in your ears like standing at center field in a giant stadium after the crowd has gone home. Unlike the stadium, however, screaming at the top of your lungs brings no echo on the sea.

There was no urgency to watch the wheel, though we did out of habit. I sunbathed on the upper deck, trying to get rid of the white cheeks that hung like the cream filling of an Oreo between my darkening upper torso and the honey brown of my legs. The cheeks turned a flaming pink. I didn't dare try the other side in the extreme heat of the equatorial sun. I had seen marshmallows burn on a stick, and it wasn't pretty.

It was here that I came to appreciate idleness while watching the sun. It wasn't hard to understand why the ancients had used frothing steeds and a flaming chariot with Apollo, the god of nakedness, at the helm (there don't seem to be many statues of Apollo with clothing anywhere to be found). He is also the god of light and sunshine, health and misery, music, truth, healing, and protector from evil, to name a few. He is most famous for his antics with a large python, Trojan wars (I think it is his likeness on the packets of condoms), and the Jack of more trysts with gods and goddesses and the blessings of Zeus than all the Rolling Stones combined.

There was such raw power in the morning sun pushing up from the deep of the horizon or the end-of-day sun being sucked into the abyss; a tension between the two like an insatiable lust that is impossible to consummate but impossible to ignore. Michelangelo carved it into stone in the Medici chapel—Dusk a muscled, menacing, virile bully of gloom and enclosing darkness, while Dawn was seduction with open thighs of promised light, a temptress of voluptuous abandon. It seemed logical why naked viewing felt right.

This idle time was the kind that allowed you to sit for hours, close your eyes to slits, and pretend you were in a sea of diamonds or hold up your thumb to obliterate the sun.

mple opportunity to observe this seething love in dawn and dusk. There were theatrics involved, clouds changing, announcing like a Greek chorus antics of those same lusty gods, Apollo and Zeus, in hot pursuit of nymphs and naked water boys, Ganymede with a cockerel in hand, ending somewhere in the staged spectacle of *La Cage aux Folles*.

Each morning, the sun rose, leaving a trail of feathered clouds in pastel pinks and blues. By noon the skies cleared to a galloping high cirrus veil in shades of faded white. The heat of the midday sun gave rise to thunderheads, erect to twenty thousand feet, and spent from cooling rains, the evening skies were dragged screaming with puffs of coloured boa finales into a house of darkness. Linking both ends of the cabaret were night skies that glittered with the final acts, a chorus of hunters and masked warriors and star-crossed lovers, taut bows with arrows for the plunder of wars and love, or barring the flamboyant heroics of a classic myth, it was simply a galaxy of Tiffany jewelry set on black velour for display.

In the midnight shift...me, boat, and the ever-present music (a Filipino version of "Tie a Yellow Ribbon" sung in lounge lizard B-flat horrid rings a bell) on the last night before we arrived in Borneo, it was one such act of theatre with the rewards, for a short while, of those gazillion stars. I couldn't name any of the constellations. It didn't matter. There was such beauty in the Milky Way splashes and clusters that represented billions of twinkling galaxies. They shone in a 360 of sequined reflections in the gentle swells below.

Stargazing was done once an hour or so to keep me awake. At three a.m., when resistance to sleep required a smack to the cheeks, pinches, knuckle-biting, or head-banging on the wheel, a quick stroll to the bow of the boat, hair blowing, body caught in the wind beneath a canopy of stars cast across the heavens kept me going for another hour. It also gave me lots of time to reflect.

If I pinched myself for all that I had, the opportunities afforded, the places seen, the people met, the things done, the near-misses, my wife, my children and my extended family, I would be one giant bruise. Yes, my life had shaky beginnings, but as I've grown older—related my story to more people—I have realized that there are always those who had it worse, much worse, or so heinously terrible you wonder how they survived. One only needs to speak with Indigenous survivors of residential schools, refugees of war, or pre-oil Newfoundlanders—"Geez bye, we'ze be down to a goat's arse and a cod fin for a family of ten…dez be some tales I can tells ye"—to understand your good fortune. But everyone has a story, and my story, I have been told, is relevant, if only to me.

Sitting on the bow of the boat, watching the stars, reminded me of my childhood, sleeping in the front yard under a tarpaulin. We did this every summer until my father bought an army surplus tent to escape the oppressive summer heat of the uninsulated farmhouse. I usually shared the bed with my brother, who was kind in his stories of night-marauding, blood-sucking vampires that loved to prey on small children sleeping under tarps. I would pull the tarp over my head and find sleep for a while until the dogs came sniffing around midnight. In the quiet of the still country air, the dogs sounded like creatures of the Black Lagoon, or lions and tigers that carried off children to their lair. These were the teases of my oldest brother, who loved to see me quake. For added effect, he was known to sneak up and scream like the banshee faeries announcing death while pawing the tarp with a garden rake. It's not a phobia, I don't think, but along with Greek bouzoukis, banshee faeries still bring moments of fear in the dark. The wailing that followed might be cause for my sisters to intervene. They were my suit of armour against the minor bullying of brothers, the punishment of a father crazed at times by the lonely, black-hole loss of our mother, and the violence from the one who filled her shoes. Sometimes my sisters pulled me under their safe umbrella of gender, where my father would rarely strike, and sometimes they were not enough.

And sometimes we all watched the heavens together, waiting to make a wish on a falling star. A watched heaven never falls. You could see them back then, millions and millions of twinkling galaxies, the Milky Way, the Big and Little Dipper, Orion's Belt, and a whole host of other constellations that my siblings had studied in school. "Bunch of dead Greek guys," my brother volunteered. But it was the infinity thing I didn't get.

"So, what comes after Pluto and the stars?" I asked, never satisfied by the answer.

"More stars."

"And after that?"

"More stars, more heaven...it never ends."

"But it has to end somewhere!"

"Nope. It goes to infinity."

"What's infinity?"

"Something that never ends...like your dumb questions. Go to sleep!"

Simon and Garfunkel cooed softly in the surrounding darkness like an old friend.

So here I was, sitting on an endless sea, staring into the infinite heavens again, no wiser now than I had been as a child. Men had walked on the moon, vehicles had roamed on Mars, a telescope had peeked further into infinity than man had ever done before, and still the questions remain unanswered. It is where faith and science mingle and, in a state of muddled confusion, agree to disagree.

Pitching into the dark on relentless waves with no history of beginnings, no telling of an end, perhaps I should have been afraid. After all, there were no lights to be seen, nothing to steer towards or away from. Beyond our bow, there was not a single sign of man; no ships, no beacons, not a vapour trail above. The darkness gave up no shorelines or horizons. Instead, it wrapped me in a protective solitude, dissolving the vast space that is daytime to a cocoon of arm's-length comfort from the bow.

Simon and Garfunkel had finished, and I was left with the sound of silence. There were no lions or tigers or vampires, no sisters required to rescue me. I had never felt safer in my life.

15

THE HAIL MARY TIE-DOWN
GYM SOCKS APHRODISIAC
A HEART-TO-HEART WITH GIN

**96 HOURS OR 5,760 MINUTES LATER...
BUT WHO WAS COUNTING?**

By morning of the fourth day, Borneo loomed ahead, layers of blue hills pushing peaks into a gray wash of watercolour clouds that drooped and lumbered under the weight of rain. Mist rose from the wrinkles and hillside folds like the lingering smoulder of a forest fire. It was early morning still, but the heavy quilt of clouds masked the sunrise, which I decided, based on previous experience, was happening anyway. Autopilot gradually nudged our bow north and by noon, ninety-six hours from Singapore, we were motoring up the entrance channel to the Miri Yacht Club.

The yacht club had come into view with a black seahorse statue fifty feet high guarding the entrance channel. Closer scrutiny revealed a lighthouse beacon in its crown. It dwarfed the boat as we motored in, like a wayward chess piece that had been removed from the board of play between giants. The buildings that lined the manmade breakwater had looked like fortress walls from afar, and it appeared as we got closer that we were being channelled into the protective custody of some Knights of the Dark Sea Horse, possibly renegade soldiers with an outpost on the fringes of Poseidon's empire.

There is a code among yachters of giving help for getting help while mooring. Even though Rob had announced his arrival would be soon (he was on the radio as we entered the narrow channel to the club), no club employees were waiting to flag us in. Within moments of our arrival, however, a pair of men appeared from the depths of two moored boats and walked into position, one at either end of the pier where Rob was showing intentions of tying up. The wind that had been hard at our heels up the channel proved to be a negative factor as Rob attempted a no-point turn, side thrust, gentle-bump-the-pier mooring. John and I did our part by casting ropes to the end receivers, waiting for the two-point tie-down. The pass-off to the stern man, a wiry sloop owner, had been impeccably played if I might say so myself, but he fumbled and missed the first cleat wrap. Broadside to the wind, elements now in play, *Bob-the-Boat* pushed hard away from the pier. Rob, anxious to make the down, worked the bow thrusters hard to keep the bow tight, but the stern began to drift. The gangly six-foot, ninety-pounds-when-wet receiver holding the rope with no leverage from the dock cleat pulled with all his might, but the rope slipped quickly through his fingers. His feet slid to the edge of the pier, his body bent then bowed sharply like a swimmer waiting for the starter gun, and finally, unable to carry the pass, dropped the rope, averting a jackknife belly flop into the harbour.

For round two, Rob did a seven-point 360 turnabout, the wind constantly pushing the stern out to the harbour. The stern drifted beyond the length of the rope I cast and it fell short into the water. John and I recoiled ropes and waited once again for Rob to bring the boat around. John opened the chrome gate on the guard rail, signalling his intentions for a full-out Hail Mary once the ropes had been punted into play.

With the boat still jockeying into place, John cast his line from the bow and then ran for the gate, jumping the narrowing gap between wharf and boat, running to aid the sternman. I cast my rope from the stern and followed suit with a jump to the pier, heading for the bow. The thrusters worked their magic, keeping the bow tight to the wharf, the volunteer linesman coiling the rope around the cleat with a binding loop before I came to his aid. I turned to help John, now on rear-end defence pulling hard with Spider-Man, who had found the cleat for leverage but was still losing ground to the wind. My legs, in transition to sea legs, were heavy and rubbery at the same time, wanting to collapse. Trying to run was like a slow-motion scene with a hero sprinting away from a bomb, wearing lead shoes, moments before he was blasted into space. The blast never came, and I finally made the sprint in time to help stop the drag of the boat away from the wharf. With three bodies pulling, we gradually hauled the boat in until the fenders kissed the wharf.

While Rob worked on shutting down the engine, ninety-six hours hot, John and I introduced ourselves to the deckhand sailors nursing rope burns, and thanked them with two-handed shakes for their assistance; cursing the strong crosswinds, the gray weather, and problematic bow thrusters... avoiding any conversation regarding human error. I offered apologies for any un-sportsman-like language they may have heard coming from the wheelhouse and, since Rob was out of earshot, proffered the excuse that the captain was still getting the feel of his new boat, recently built and picked up in China... "Chinese Junk, ha-ha."

As we spoke, a tall, Buddha-round man strolled along the wharf. His chipmunk cheeks shone like burnished teak, and he was wearing a captain's hat, a white polo shirt, shorts and flip-flops and sported a Cheshire grin, suggesting he had witnessed the triple-down scrimmage with Mother Nature.

"*Bob-the-Boat?*" he asked, knowing of course who we were since we had hailed him ten minutes earlier and we were the only boat to enter the harbors that sported the large, happy lettering.

"Yes," I said, offering my hand for a shake. I assumed he was the harbor official since his shirt was embossed with the words *Miri Yacht Club, Harbour Official*. "The captain will be out in a minute. He is doing his shutdown procedures."

"Welcome back," he said, as if we had been there for lunch the week before. This was the greeting we had received at all our stops since *Bob-the-Boat* had made the rounds six months earlier. Some attendants remembered the name of the boat, fishing for the colour. "Oh yeah," they would say, "*Bob-the-Boat*...that fruity yellow...no, it's lime green, wait...I remember now, lemony lime."

"Yellow, Fighting Lady Yellow," Rob would say, and didn't mind the confusion, since it gave him an in for conversation. Many of the harbour management up to this point had been women, where Rob could shake his mane of blond hair and smile and say, "Hi Patty, or Dana, or Donna," names he had retrieved from his captain's log from six months prior, and they would melt from his genuine attention. Proceedings were usually swift with few questions. One managed to unload about her unhappy home life, with her three kids and a husband who never seemed to be around. All that happened between saying hello and filling out an information card.

"Stoning, Rob. It's death by stoning in this country. First mates too, I think, by association, so give it up," I scolded good-heartedly.

But like destinations and journeys, it was the chase for Rob, not the catch that mattered. It was all harmless play to test his virility. I wasn't sure what would have happened if the dog caught the car, but I had visions of John and me at some point camping on the pier.

It wasn't chance that brought him the attention. Rob

spent time every day doing sit-ups and leg raises, having lost nearly fifty pounds since leaving the sedentary life on Vancouver Island. There wasn't an ounce of fat to jiggle—his entire body was like a taut rope. The hair, long and flowing when he released it from the ponytail, naturally sandy blond, now had golden streaks from two years in the sun. That and the steel-blue eyes and carefully cultivated growth of a week-old beard turned heads. None of us were spring chickens, but Rob's strut was a big step closer to the hen house than either John or I could hope for. Not that I hoped to get into the henhouse. I am allergic to feathers, especially those from another rooster's yard.

"So sorry, I has bad news." It was the official, scanning the boat, squinting with a puzzled look. "What color is boat?" he said, interrupting himself, removing his hat to slowly scratch his thinning hair. "Looks like unripe banana." He laughed at his assessment. Before we could answer, he turned back to face us and again stated he had bad news, breaking into that broad smile he arrived with, seeming to like the burden of bad-news-bearer. "This spot here where he be, *Bob-the-Boat*, this be for harbour master boat... I so sorry." The "sorry" was tossed in as his smile moved towards a grimace, teeth gritting, eyes pleading as if to say *"I am just the messenger...after the video replay, the touchdown has been disallowed; you lost the game—please don't kill the messenger."*

Our volunteers took this opportunity to beg out to attend to sails on their motorboats and disappeared.

It seems we had impeccable timing. Our arrival coincided with a sailors' regatta, starting in Miri and ending in Kota Kinabalu. Not only were we moored in the harbour master's berth, empty because the harbour master boat was out setting buoys for the race, but all berths within a few days were pre-booked for the sailors amassing for the regatta. It was a small detail they had not relayed when Rob booked from Singapore. We would be allowed to stay until our berth was needed. This race posed another problem in that our destination from Miri was to be Kota Kinabalu. We had intended to hang out there for a while, our reward for pushing hard to this point, in a place Rob had described as close to Shangri-La. This meant that Kota Kinabalu would be booked solid with boats completing the race.

"No need to get our knickers in a knot," Rob explained. "We will deal with that challenge when it happens."

Our berth in Miri, once Rob wrapped his mind around moving, was two down from the harbour master's and was infinitely easier to dock into since boats moored on either side cut the wind. It was a matter of motor in and shut down the engine, no heroics required, something like climbing over a ten-foot wall covered in thorns, only to find an open door around the corner.

The harbour master of bad news delivery informed us of the good news. There was no need to go find the port authority for boat clearance. They had been informed of our arrival. An officer would come by in the morning, and customs immigration was within walking distance. Things, it seemed, were looking up.

By the time power and water were connected, we had consumed half a case of beer, our first since Singapore. Without notice, Rob disappeared, having identified a jaguar-green version of the *Sea Horse*, docked a few slips down, as one owned by Ruth and Randal. They were a couple that Rob and his wife, Catherine, had hung out with in Hong Kong while waiting for their boats on the assembly line in mainland China. Rob's disappearance left the pair of us to manage dinner preparations.

Rob, who watched every calorie and shunned good things like butter and chocolate, would have burst an artery watching his chefs at work. It was shrimp fried in garlic and butter, fish steamed in butter and wine, steamed rice topped with butter-fried almond slices, salted and peppered, a salad of crisp diced cucumber, cabbage and red bell peppers with crumbled goat cheese, all marinated in balsamic and red wine vinegar. The last of the Singapore French stick bread became bruschetta, toasted in the oven, buttered with crushed garlic, diced tomatoes, and grated Jarlsberg cheese. It wasn't for lack of trying that John and I had Buddha-esque physiques.

On the invite of cocktails, we were introduced to Ruth and Randal. They were middle-aged, American, and following Randal's dream of puttering about on a boat. Their boat was a variation on *Bob-the-Boat*'s design, with all living quarters below deck. Portal windows dropped reflected light across a living space sumptuously carpeted, teak shelving crammed with books, his and her teak computer desks and a large sectional sofa. It was all the comforts of home. Teak, by the way, is the wood of choice for boat building because it is water-, termite-, and rodent-resistant and is indigenous to these parts of the world. It is becoming rare in the monsoon forests but is grown on large plantations. The surprise was that many of the wharves and walkways we had encountered were built with teak. It's a wood that in Canada sells for the price of Gucci bangles.

Randal had once circumnavigated the globe on a bicycle with the help of a sponsor, and Ruth had joined him at some point along the way for encouragement. She was a retired head librarian from Baltimore or Boston, hence the shelves lined with books. Her real passion, however, was baseball. Her mind was an index of players past and present for teams throughout the league. I was embarrassed that she knew more about the Toronto Blue Jays than I did. I could tell she was desperate to have a fresh conversation with a new mind, especially when she found out I was a reader. We discussed books and politics...they were Democrats; Bush, of course, was an idiot, and Obama was a fresh breath of sainthood. When we begged our leave with ample thanks for the drinks and company, Ruth was reluctant to let us go, wanting to do it all again.

It gave me an insight into the at-sea loneliness felt by

those (most often wives) tempted off to sea by bored spouses with enhanced tales of probable adventure. There could be long periods of mental drought when couples ran out of things to discuss. It was a situation, I think, that may have come into play between Rob and Cathy. For Ruth and Randal, however, if they could survive a bicycle tour of the world, they would survive boating in the tropical splendor of the Far East. With books, baseball, and politics, there would always be a spark for discussion. They would need it. They spoke of plans of heading north to Thailand, crossing the Indian Ocean to Sri Lanka, visiting the Middle East and the Mediterranean via the Suez Canal, pushing west to Gibraltar, and eventually navigating to Scandinavia. It was an extremely ambitious journey to undertake, where conversations might digress to debating how many angels can jig a hornpipe on the head of a pin.

If there was regret in Ruth's voice, it was for having to watch tape-delayed games of the World Series playoffs, then in full swing and looking to be a final contest between New York and Philadelphia. It came to her, fed down the webs of the sporadic internet. As far as she was concerned, cricket and soccer, offered daily by teams in Asia, did not qualify as sports.

⚓ ⚓ ⚓

Noon arrived but port authorities didn't. We hailed a taxi and made our way to town.

In the extreme heat of the midday sun, we sought out the covered market, divided into wet and dry. Rob was familiar with many of the exotic fruits and vegetables and insisted on purchasing a little of each so that John and I could taste them. Many were covered with spikes, resembling miniature hedgehogs, and in the case of the large durian fruit, a medieval weapon of spiked ball and chain.

The durian plant has the honoured distinction of being labelled and cherished in the Far East as an aphrodisiac—"*When the durian goes down, the sarong goes up*"—though I doubt it was because of its spiny cover or fragrance. Richard Sterling, an American food and travel writer, was not impressed. He is quoted by his journalist friend, John Gottberg Anderson, referring to the durian fruit as...*odor best described as pig shit, turpentine and onions, garnished with a gym sock*. Some, I guess, familiar with gym bags and locker rooms, might find this appealing. It might be noted that the durian fruit, like kissing, is circled and banned on public transport.

As Rob bargained, my backpack began to fill. There were miniature bananas (a fruit I suspected of being the original before geneticists had their way with size), sweet potatoes, cucumber (some that were yellow when ripe), red onions, garlic, fresh tomatoes, star fruits and other spiny species I could never remember. By now, we had become accustomed to ripe oranges that were green on the outside, but sweet, succulent orange on the inside, so we bought a dozen. The wet market produced fresh quarters of chicken, an offering of fresh fish that we declined and dark, gamey water buffalo, minced by the shopkeeper for a date with a pot of chilli. On the way to the grocery store, we passed a dry goods outlet called Hung Seng Kong Piles and Acupuncture. There was a story there somewhere. Other goods we bought in the local grocery store.

It may have been the heat, or again the lack of sleep, or both, but there were signs of short tempers. John is not good with heat, a byproduct of high blood pressure, and was adamant about finding a shaded roadside tent for lunch. Rob was on a mission to find a what's-it that had all three of us walking in the noon heat. Rob ignored the rumblings of a first-mate revolt from behind. Once we found the what's-it, it was John's turn to lead at twenty paces. Rob and I were checking out the town, which John had little time for, prompting comments about not stopping to smell the roses. Rumble, rumble.

Eventually, we found lunch at an open-air eatery with assorted offerings that were hard to recognize. They could have been monkey brains or bat wings in a hot sauce; we had no way of knowing. But we were now comfortable with street meat and coconut drinks served in plastic bags.

We were informed by the bearer of bad news upon our return that we had missed the official for boat clearance. He had arrived two hours after our departure, his noon being several hours in length. With passports stamped for Borneo approval, plans were made to pull up anchor the following day and head for Labuan, Pulau Tiga, and Kota Kinabalu, each with special attractions not to be missed.

Pulau Tiga was a small island with a volcanic mud bath, and it was Rob's suggestion we should stop, venture to the centre of the island, and immerse ourselves. He and Cathy had done it and found getting mud into every orifice a not-to-be-missed life experience. John was skeptical, but Labuan held great promise. It was here that duty-free offered several large shops with badly needed supplies, a good cabernet perhaps, gin and tonic, beer of any sort and, well, an offering of chocolate. Kota Kinabalu was to be our paradise reward of five-star relaxation for a job well done thus far where Labuan's booty would be sumptuously devoured.

In the receding daylight of our last evening in Miri, we drank, starting with beer and moving into thin rations of tonic water topped with gin. It unhinged our tongues, though John could never quite find the words to express his edginess. He was unhappy but kept it bottled tightly. It had always been this way. I had known him most of my life, but sometimes I thought I barely knew him at all.

The discussions turned outwards instead, refusing introspection that may expose disquieting feelings and gin-induced thoughts better not said. It occurred to me that if three men could not be honest and forward, sitting in a boat, berthed in an oil town harbour in the wilds of Borneo, then where? It wasn't that I felt the need to bond like teenage girls at a pyjama party, but I hoped we might air our differences like mature adults. It never happened. However, prompted by the lack of sleep, the fog of Gilbey's pried loose dissertations about wives, parents and ungrateful children. It was easier, it seemed, to dissect the shortcomings of others. I ventured thoughts about my father, with whom Rob and John were familiar, having worked and lived on the farm during their teens. It touched a nerve with them both, in that it seems all our fathers, perhaps not surprisingly, had had failings in some character-building ways, setting off for us some kind of Oedipus-induced search into the shadows of childhood. No one admitted to having slept with their mother. Mothers, in fact, barely made the list, though that was no surprise either. My mother had died when I was two, John's mom had passed too recently to allow for introspective criticism (bitching), and Rob loved his mother beyond critique. I have been told that had this been three women, the conversation would have involved bottles of wine and loud, introspective critiques of their mother-daughter relationships into the wee hours of the morning.

My father had ruled with an iron fist with tendencies to sling verbal arrows of biting humiliations. Rob's father had ignored him, a position that, when I contemplated the idea, made me want to cry (something gin might induce). John's father and mother, whom I had liked, had doted on each other, which I had thought was nice, but somehow that had left John and his sister wanting for a hug. Nobody got hugs back then. It produced "sissies and light-in-the-loafers men." Rob had grown his hair long as a teenager, a proof-in-the-pudding example of too much motherly care.

And so the discussion went. My father this, John's parents that, and Rob nodded off. It had been a very long day, and the ninety-five hours of no anchors down had caught up with us all. Our family Freuding would have to wait. It was anchors up again with eyes firmly set on Kota Kinabalu.

16

WILLY WILLY WINDS
SNEAKER WAVES
SHAPE-SHIFTERS
A STARE TO SHRIVEL YOUR GRAPES

5TH, 6TH, OR 7TH DAY OF OCTOBER? NO ONE'S KEEPING TRACK

The cranky mood moved to the waves on our departure at noon the following day. The sea for the first time on this trip showed signs of irritation; whitecaps could be seen from our quiet calm in the harbour. *Bob-the-Boat* did not like waves. He did not like them one tiny bit! Unlike a sleek-hulled sloop under sail and endowed with a lead-weighted keel, *Bob-the-Boat* sported a flat bottom, like a yellow rubber duck. Technically our unripe banana was considered a full keel boat; it just didn't have any anti-rolling devices. It carried a five-foot draft, which is not a large beer, but indicates how far the boat sits beneath the surface. We were rarely in danger of hitting shallow reefs, but it meant that every ripple and wave set *Bob* rocking like a cradle.

Regardless, we dove in, wanting to head north by northeast, but soon realized that we were in a beam sea; waves crashing against the side of the boat. We would need to assume the tack position by motoring west by northwest to hit waves head-on. That would stop the rocking side to side. We also needed to get far enough west to miss the shallow reef that crossed our charted course. If viewed from above, we resembled a sidewinder rattlesnake, head moving north while its body slithered east and west. It added hours to the travel. These reversals required the skill of counting waves: waves are a tricky lot.

A captain needs to know his waves. He also needs to know the winds. Wind-water is the literal English translation of the Chinese term *Feng Shui*, the philosophy of harmonizing everything and everyone with the surroundings. The two, wind and water, are inseparable...hence gentle winds and calm seas, high winds and kiss your lunch goodbye.

Ripples caused by wind on a still pond are only a problem for water bugs. A small yacht on a vast ocean might be considered to be one. Progressive winds bring "seas," which is the name for larger, sustained waves that only gravity can calm. Long periods of sustained winds create sustained swells, creating sustained seas, separated into a crest (the top of the roll) and the trough (the bottom of the roll), which, for the layperson, is a wave. For landlubbers, the shorter the distance between crest and trough, the better. Seas can roll on swells that have ripples, much like Arnold Schwarzenegger's body.

Several things factor into the creation of waves. Wind speed is only part of the equation. The distance wind travels across open waters is important, known as the "fetch." Therefore, a wave that travels across an open sea, for instance, is perhaps far-fetched and is in no way related to the ripple on a frog pond, which is, perhaps, a white lie. The longer the fetch and the faster the wind speed, the larger and stronger the wave will be. That would seem to be a no-brainer. The width of a fetch is also important as is the duration of time the wind has blown. The depth of the water contributes. All these points factor into wave creation, but it should be noted that these are wind-generated waves as opposed to the sucking and seething of land masses that create tsunamis like the one we encountered.

Information on waves can be as relentless and unending, it seems, as waves themselves.

Waves have character defined in height and length, with periods being the time interval between getting smacked in the noggin by a wave while standing at a stationary point. The direction of a wave is defined as "wave propagation," sounding very much like some physics class I fell asleep in.

Waves have names. There are Hollywood waves, called tidal waves that turn ships ass over tea kettle. They are often cast as rogue waves, freak waves, monster waves, killer waves, or king waves (Elvis has definitely left the building). They could be the same as sneaker waves that come out of nowhere. These, like the rogue waves, can be as high as a ten-storey building, also known as hit-by-a-condo, kiss-your-ass-goodbye waves.

There are breaking waves, surfer favourites, often called surfer's waves. There are waves on waves, and, if one is caught going perpendicular to the general swell or the fetch wave, it may be called a cross sea wave. Those who pay attention to such things have named every oscillating movement of water, perhaps under the illusion that naming them is taming them. What is truly important to know, however, is that more waves on the boat or above the boat rather than under the boat, no matter what it's called, is bad.

It is interesting that in Greek mythology, the minor sea gods like Nereus and Proteus, humble servants to his mighty lordship Poseidon, have been referred to as shape-shifters and tricksters. A more appropriate description could not be found.

For all the talk of waves, their root cause, outside of changing tides and land shifts, is the winds, which should not be ignored; again, Feng Shui. For sailors, where there's a wind there's a wave.

Most winds of change and means have names. Some are

well-known, like the Trade Winds, Chinooks and the Santa Anas. Others, like the cyclonic twists of typhoons and tornados, are legendary. The Sirocco, Bora and Passat are Mediterranean Greek winds translated into cars. There are headwinds and tailwinds, ill winds and broken winds translated how you like. Every nation and language have their winds, and there are winds for all seasons: a Bora wind from Hungary might be a fall wind, while the Zephyr west wind is sometimes a wind of summer.

Australians have Willy Willies…some bigger than others. Large ones are small tropical cyclones, and small ones are large dust-devils. Argentinians and Chileans have Williwas down by the Strait of Magellan, cold blasts of mountain air that make their way out to sea. The winds come so quickly that "My Willi was…oops, now it's not."

A squall is an Abroholos off the coast of Brazil, a Brubu in the East Indies, and a Borasco in the Mediterranean. It's known as a disaster if you are sailing and not ready for it wherever you might be.

Anything that starts with "N" is usually bad news. A Nashi, Norte, Nor'easter, Nor'wester, or Norther (especially a Blue Norther, where people curse in Blue Norther streaks) are winds coming from the north and will frost your southern coconuts from Mexico to Iran. A Mistral is a cold French wind from the north, like the stare of the madame who catches the monsieur in a compromising position with the mistress. It can shrivel your grapes.

Winds that start with an "S," on the other hand, may be gentle warm breezes unless they are not. The Sirocco of the Mediterranean and the Sundowner and Santa Ana of California start warm and friendly, though the Santa Ana can turn hot like chili peppers. The Squamish of British Columbia and the often-cyclonic Suestado off the coast of Argentina and Brazil can be violent and do not qualify as warm and cozy. Nor does a Sumatra, a squall of violent thunder, lightning and rain intensified by strong mountain breezes at night, confined to the Straits of Malacca. Luckily, we missed the Sumatras while motoring down that strait.

While trade winds flow from the east to the west and have continuous flow (thus the trade winds—"We'll trade you one boat of bananas for a boat load of Eton rejects"), the Westerlies flow east and the Polar Easterlies flow west. All these winds are known as global winds. There are basically six global wind zones: the Trades, Westerlies, and Polar Easterlies with a mirror reflection of the same on the other side of the equator.

Local winds are created from the geography, like mountains and lakes and various combinations of land and sea.

Who cares about wind, you might ask, besides meteorologists and windmill makers? Balloonists, air pilots, kite fliers, wind farmers and anyone who wants to breathe fresh air in a city, for a start, but sailors, for one, care a lot. Not so much those who move with big diesel engines, but true sailors, ones who use sails, need to know this about wind and waves. Whatever you call the winds, they are not to be taken lightly or ignored.

For instance, did you know that the giant windstorms from the African Sahara feed the Amazon jungles of South America with nutrient-rich sand or the cold winds of the Antarctic that drive much of the southern hemisphere eventually affect the whole planet? And while we are at it, did you know that a cold day in hell actually exists (Vostock, Antarctica, July 21, 1983, minus 128.6 degrees F), or that there is enough hot air in Congress to heat a small city? May the shape-shifters be with you.

For the next several hours we may have met one of every wave, so I practised the goodbye wave, just in case.

It took skill to determine on which wave to make a tack correction, and John and I declined to take the helm. Rob—captain and admiral of the fleet, after all—was left in charge, as we were now under manual navigation and no longer able to chart an electronic course. Occasionally we were able to run with the wind, which meant that we surfed in the same direction the waves were blowing. It is called a "following sea." It was on one of these runs that I decided to heat the water buffalo chili made the night before.

The dark kidney-red meat of buffalo that we purchased from the wet market in Miri had been expertly cleaved from the whole by a surly saleswoman and slapped onto a spring scale that had been banned as illegal in most markets around the world. The water buffalo had dripped fresh blood from a chopping block worn deep from years of use. There was no arguing, however, about her weights and measurements, nor did we challenge the sanitation of the meat grinder that was desperately in need of a wash or the small bits of chopping block that came with the purchase. Pig heads and feet hung beside fresh lungs, tripe and plucked chickens still retaining their heads and feet to prove age and gender. Old cocks were soup birds and sold for less, though in France an old cock with wine was a prized meal. Check out any one of their dozen presidents in recent history. The buffalo chilli, to compensate, had been boiled on high for an extended period, with the hope that all microorganisms that had made the ride home would die a miserable death in the pot.

I heated individual bowls in the microwave and then passed them out with thick slabs of bread to both John and Rob. The last bowl, mine, met bad timing. It was extremely hot. As I pulled it from the microwave without mitts, I rushed it to the counter, aiming for a nonslip doily, but missed as the boat lurched (possibly a sneaker wave) and the bowl of chilli hit the floor. The crash sent a chilli wave to the ceiling, covering the teak beams, curtains, and walls in what looked to be the aftermath of a Tudor beheading. Beans slid out of the louvred doors and further inspection revealed a flat-screen TV covered in sauce. We continued to find beans for a week, one having found its way into the slotted opening of the DVD player.

As night fell, we had gained enough distance out to sea that we could turn the boat one last time and run with the wind and waves, north by northeast in a comfortable following sea, avoiding the long, shallow shoal that jutted out from the shore. John took the helm and Rob found his place on the bench behind the captain's chair and fell into a well-deserved sleep.

What should have been a solid veil of darkness was trimmed in the yellow glow of fire spewing from distant oil wells, miles out to sea. This was the beginning of the ocean oil patch feeding the economy of the country called Brunei.

Brunei—five hundred square miles smaller than the Greater Toronto Area, with 5.2 million less in population—was rated fourth in the world by the IMF for gross domestic product. They were the Beverly Hillbillies of the Pacific Rim, with the discovery of crude...oil, that is, black gold, Brunei T (Tapis Blend).

The country had a long history of occupation and changing hands, starting from the fifteenth century when Muslim explorers annexed large portions of the Borneo coast, lost most of it to the empires of Spain and Britain, the Japanese of WWII, back to post-war Britain, finally achieving independence in 1984. Oil was their ticket to freedom.

Brunei is devoutly Muslim and ruled by Islamic law. It is administered by a real live sultan complete with harems and a gaggle of princes to service their needs. The deluge of cash has been hard to spend, but the sultan's younger brother, Prince Jefri, has given it a good try by filling a football stadium-sized warehouse with the most exotic cars in the world and lost billions (with a capital B) on the American stock market. Banned from Brunei, he became a renowned playboy in New York, where he commissioned several life-sized sculptures of himself in compromising positions with numerous female conquests. He became known also for his outrageously large yacht called *Tits*, which held two speed boats called *Nipple One* and *Nipple*

Two. *Bob-the-Boat* had a dinghy called *Doug*.

Brunei's sea concession for oil drilling was six and a half thousand square kilometres, or over two thousand five hundred square miles. It was no wonder that our night skies were lit for miles or that the closest we may have come to real disaster happened here.

17

READING BOAT LIGHT ENTRAILS
A NEAR-MISS IN THE OIL FIELD JUNKYARD

HOURS LATER

Rob had charted a course across his electronic map that had dipped into Miri and then set a dotted line through the waters of the South China Sea, heading north by northeast for Labuan, Pulau Tiga (the island of bubbling mud), and Kota Kinabalu. He had projected the map a hundred miles ahead, looking for shoals and shallow reefs, oil platforms and any other obstructions that could cause general sinking mayhem. His course showed clear sailing.

My watch started somewhere around midnight, knowing that four hours of a lonely vigil lay ahead. The dragon fires, huge plumes of natural gas burning off from the oil platforms (proponents of global warming need look no further), created a distraction only for a short while, like the first hour or two of viewing mountains heading west through the Rockies. At some point, you have seen enough or the crick in your neck from looking up finally gets the better of the awe, and if you are not driving, you fall asleep. Sleep was not an option here, at one a.m., mid-South China Sea, twelve miles off the coast of Brunei.

The night sky had cleared to partially cloudy, with the nearly full moon popping out now and again, showing advancement towards a high noon placement in the heavens. The radar screen revealed the oil platforms and ships, presumably oil tankers and service boats, making their way from platform to shore and back. They appeared as moving blips, like nautical Pac-Men on the screen. Some blips came closer and turned out to be oil derricks, oil pumps, or at-sea oil storage facilities where ships could fill up with crude. When I stood on the deck of the boat, these would become visible with blinking lights of varying luminance.

Determining what's what and what's going where in darkness is a game of roulette. Each ship is required to have running lights, green for right (starboard) and red for left (port). They are situated on a high structure at the bow of the boat with a white light indicating the aft. If an electronic blip, for instance, when actualized into ship form through binoculars on the bow, has a red light but you cannot see the green, it means the boat is coming at you on your left or port side. The opposite means the boat is on the starboard or the right. If you can see green and a white light trailing, it means the boat is heading perpendicular to your course, cruising left to right and the opposite red with a white trailing light means, of course, it is moving perpendicular, right to left. If you only see white, it means the boat is moving away from you, but, perchance you can see both green and red at the same time, both boats are on a collision course, bow to bow...it is time to maneuver; do not wait to see the whites of the other captain's eyes. This carefully crafted system of red light, green light worked only as well as the crew that replaced the missing bulbs or on boats where giant working lights for dredging or fishing for squid didn't wash out any trace of red and green. It was impossible to find them on cruise liners decked out with thousands of show lights on every level, but then again, if you miss something that looks like Coney Island coming at you, you shouldn't be at the helm.

The blips that didn't move were the platforms, derricks, and storage facilities. The sea was littered with such structures. It was like sailing through an old black-and-white photo of an oil boom town somewhere in Texas.

Sometimes the radar would do some weird ghosting, catching every wave, cloud movement, or, conceivably, flying fish, and the screen would momentarily shiver with a thousand boat-sized blips that usually dissipated within seconds.

On one such encounter, one blip remained, but from the bow of the boat, when I ran to check, there was not a blinking thing to see. The blip appeared to be getting closer to starboard, opposite to the raging plume of fire on the platform, several miles west of our position. On my last run to the bow, the moon slipped out from behind a cloud, casting a weak reflection across the water. What it revealed nearly froze my blood. Within a few short boat lengths, nearly dead on to our fibreglass bow, stood an abandoned oil rig of twisted iron. There were no blinking lights or reflector tape, the only revealing detail a few silvery lines of wet moonlight rimming the steel silhouette. I immediately hit the course correction button several times, hoping to roll to port, but when I realized it would not change course in time, I hit manual override and veered wildly off the preset course. This was enough to wake Rob from his sleep (he caught himself tumbling off the bench), and together we watched the steel girders roll by.

There might have been a stifling silence had it not been for my "Fuuuuck me" stammered with every thought I had at how close we had come to disaster. Rob, dredged from a deep sleep, was mostly silent, though he managed to quickly curse the expensive electronic charts program he had been sold for this part of the journey.

"I told you these assholes have no idea what they are

doing!" The assholes were the Southeast Asian cartographers who had mapped an area of the world that had been sailed for multiple centuries. He then warned me to keep a better eye on things for fuck's sake, get back on friggin' course, and he'd see me in the morning. He fell into an exhausted sleep on the bench behind my captain's chair. He was a testy son of a bitch when he was rolled off his couch while sound asleep. John slept soundly through the whole thing, prompting me to wonder if he had succumbed to water buffalo listeriosis.

Once again, I was left with my thoughts and the unrelenting chug of the diesel engine. The "what if" terror kept ringing in my brain, and the possibility that more unmarked sea junk still lurked ahead had my frantic mind wanting to abandon ship, row *Doug-the-Dinghy* ashore, and claim refugee status in Brunei. Surely, the royal harem needed a keeper since Prince Jefri had been banned. My head was screaming with undigested bits of lunacy concerning a narrowing path of twisted, metal tombstones, leading to a final cross of no-return impalement on an invisible rack of steel. There was no nodding off as I doubled and redoubled my runs to the front bow looking for unmarked towers denoting blips that could prove hazardous to my health. There were other towers, but all of them had blinking lights in various stages of fading to black.

Once the fear subsided, the anger emerged. What kind of assholes would leave the open seas littered with junk...junk that would sink a ship? Wasn't it the oil companies' or the nations' responsibility to make the waters safe? Why was this beautiful sea teeming with incredible marine life and peppered with white-sand lagoons being abandoned to corporations and kingdoms that had no interest beyond the extraction of oil? What was wrong with this fucking world? My mind raced on until it ran out of fuel and profanity and John tapped me on the shoulder for a shift change. We had decided to do double shifts and let sleeping captains lie.

Sleep again was fitful, as I was unsure I had imparted enough of my anxiety upon John, who had shrugged with a dismissive smirk and started to give a history lesson on oil companies—the need to fill the car tanks of the world and give shareholders a good return on their capital.

"It's the price we pay so you can drive that big van of yours"—a dig that I had been too tired to refute. How does he find that black hole of sarcasm at four in the morning?

"Those blipping anomalies are not sea turtles. Be careful!" I headed down the spiral staircase into the hold, having had the last juvenile word. What was it about my tired, whacked brain that made me lash out with grade-school banter? I put an extra pillow between me and the fibreglass wall that was lined with a full-width mirror and reassured myself it would be enough of a buffer should an oil well tower skewer the boat.

18

SEA LEGS SYNDROME
PULAU TIGA
ANCHOR TROUBLES
THE RULES OF SWINGING

FIRST LIGHT, THE FOLLOWING MORNING

By morning, the towers and ships were gone and so were the waves. It was slightly after six a.m. when we arrived in Labuan, which beckoned with the temptations of duty-free goods. John longed for a bottle of good red wine, and I thought a heap of chocolate would be nice.

Rob's mind was elsewhere. It had been a very long while since he had seen Kim, and with the boat pointing harder north, he was becoming more and more like a hound on the scent of a fox (or two, since it appeared there was one in the hen house as well). Other than the few words I overheard while he was on the cell phone or computer, I knew almost nothing of the siren from Subic Bay. He had intimated that "there were problems," and raised the name "Kurt" once again, but never elaborated beyond "two-timing wench." The mice, it seemed, were playing!

Labuan proved nearly forgettable, though we did make

good on the tax-free merchandise. The harbour was dominated by a large dry dock that read *Labuan Shipyard and Engineering* and stood watch over a mess of boats, mostly large tugs and flat skiffs that belonged to an oil company. These were service boats that maintained the oil fleets and platforms we had passed in the night.

The village hugged the riverbanks on stilted piers with tin-covered warehouses side by side like the pods of a centipede. These were the shops for duty-free, Rob explained, where large tourist boats could drop their cargo of thirsty patrons into the hands of waiting vendors. It was quiet and empty when we arrived, except for the few taxi boats and ferries that moved villagers from across the bay. Since the shops would not be open for an hour or more, we dropped anchor in the harbour and brewed fresh coffee. We dozed. The quiet gave way to the harbour traffic that rocked the boat; outboard motors and ferries tooted their horns for approach. Four towers of loudspeakers called the faithful to prayer. A barge moved up the river. We held on to the dishes as *Bob* dipped and rolled with the wake. John was antsy for the *Malaysian Tribune* or the *Borneo Herald*. He eyed the watch and proclaimed it was time. We hailed a taxi and went ashore.

Stepping on the pier, my legs nearly collapsed. I had the feeling I was rolling along on a pair of beach balls, waiting for them to burst under my weight. We had been on the water for less than a day after leaving Miri, but the heavy seas had triggered my sea legs. Sea legs can be a funny lot. Not!

Sea legs are good...at sea. On land they give you the gait of a pet chimp dressed for the circus, the kind that people clear the sidewalk for, casting donations, proclaiming "Poor devil!"

Sea legs at sea act much like gimbals. Gimbals are an engineered device of rings designed to keep an object, such as a compass, level, and, on boats, can be installed into tables so that the table remains horizontal even if the floor does not. Legs will do the same thing after a while, moving with the roll of the boat while the torso stays static...in theory, anyway. To this point in travel, my legs had never quite acclimatized, and I found myself crashing into railings and walls, while Rob negotiated the walkways without hazard. On one occasion, a wave had sent me crashing against an open wall of switches. They had no more importance than all of the electrical controls for the boat. They clicked and snapped as I hit them, and I did my best to flip them on or off as I thought they should be. Within minutes things began to happen. The engine started to overheat, prompting warning horns, and John came from the dark shitter, complaining there was no power to flush. I confessed, arguing that the switches should be under a canopy of plexiglass. Rob agreed but was not amused.

"Be careful, for Christ's sake," he had said, flicking the engine vent fan on and then listening as the toilet flushed down below. "You need to get some sea legs!"

You don't grow sea legs intentionally. They simply just arrive.

Sea legs, if pushed to an extreme, hanging on for months, have the official title of *mal de debarquement,* or disembarkment sickness, coined, possibly, by a Frenchman who had problems disembarking. In keeping with the times, it has become a syndrome—the MdD syndrome. Everything, it seems, becomes a syndrome.

A man caught without his pants, in the arms of a mistress or two, may now be deemed to have a sex addiction or "sexual compulsivity" linked directly to "obsessive-compulsive disorder," OCD, or better labeled, perhaps, OPS (Overactive Penis Syndrome). This depends on how good his lawyer is. Shouting "FUCK" three times in public could mean you have Tourette's, even if you did stub your toe on the sidewalk. Not being able to sit still may qualify as ADHD (Attention Deficit Hyperactivity Disorder), or being defiant means you have ODD (Oppositional Defiance Disorder). At some phase or other in my life, I may have had all of these. To be now slammed with "the MdD syndrome" was a bummer. My wife might have embraced the ODD diagnosis asserting her theory that it was just my regular state of being. Given sway, she would have called it NS (Norm Syndrome). Part of the Norm Syndrome was my habit of uttering spoonerisms (Sorm Nyndrome), as I have already explained, but there were the forgotten words and names that my wife was expected to fill in at the drop of a hat. "What was that guy, you know, in that movie we saw?" The crazy part was, most often, she knew.

Mal de debarquement, however, was usually attributed to seafarers and some flyers, and came with the sensation of motion, like bobbing or swaying, long after one had exited the boat. The MdD syndrome is exacerbated by stress, lack of sleep, loud sounds…any one of which could have been considered fallout from our boating mission. Since I was constantly tired, wrought with anxiety (one too many tsunamis) and occasional confusion, John may have backed my wife on the theory of brain fog.

My beach ball legs took me down the pier towards duty-free.

"What the fuck is the matter with my legs?" I yelled.

"Yeah, I feel it too," John said. Even Rob had to admit he had a pair of flats.

⚓ ⚓ ⚓

By early afternoon, we could see the outline of Pulau Tiga, an island not much larger than a few football fields. Pulau Tiga, besides the attraction of a bubbling mud pit, now had the infamy of being one of the early locations of the hit TV series *Survivor*, and Rob was anxious to relive some TV history. As we moved in for closer inspection, however, we realized the island was deserted. Somewhere behind a grove of coconuts, Rob assured us, was a hotel, but hailing on the boat radio brought a hollow response. It seemed they were closed for the season, where seasons don't exist. Their seasons were determined by seasons elsewhere. There were no signs of resort canoes, Sea-Doos or yachting crews. The island was dead quiet. Of course, in horror movies, this would be ample reason to defy all senses and leave the boat where, promptly, sailors disappeared into the bubbling mud now active with fresh lava or their remains were left strewn on the beach by the Tyrannosaurus rex.

Rob was all set to drop anchor, lower *Doug-the-Dinghy*, and fashion a party of three volunteers to go ashore. The mud pit, he said, had directions on signposts all over the island. However, the wind and waves we had left the evening before caught up with us, and we realized a storm was brewing. Black clouds, flashes of lightning, and large, crashing waves are pretty good signs, adding to the perfect horror scenario. The gathering storm was pushing us ashore into a sandbar, so *Bob-the-Boat* was thrown into reverse to prevent us from getting beached. It was apparent that we needed to motor around to the opposite side of the island, where we could swing downwind, getting a break from the palms and hills that formed the island. This proved to be a smart decision, as the north side of the island was paradise calm. This was the first time for John and me to drop anchor. As with everything else, there was a system.

The bow must be pointing into the wind when dropping anchor. They are dropped from the tip of the bow so that the boats can pivot with the wind, like a windsock or a puppy pulling at the end of its leash. Sonar tells you how deep the bottom is, and the rule is for every foot of depth you should drop between four and seven times that number for anchor line, depending on how calm the water is and how solid the bottom. The anchor line is referred to as "the rode" by honest sailors. To me, it is an anchor and chain. In fifteen feet of water, nearly a hundred feet of chain needs to be dropped. This is done with the boat set in reverse, dragging the anchor to make sure it is ploughing deep past the sand and into the mud that lies below and to keep the chain away from the boat. It is easy to rake the hull. Extra chain is necessary because waves on swells on changing tides need to be anticipated. Fifteen feet of chain in the same depth of water could have a boat looking like a duck bobbing for food. Some anchors might lift and drag with rising tides, but a well-ploughed anchor should hold, though getting an anchor to hold is also an art.

It is not cool, nor legal, to drop anchor on a coral reef. It takes countless centuries (depending on the size) and millions of dead creatures to form a reef, which would be akin to dropping anchor on the House of Commons and snagging the Senate chamber. You may also lose the anchor if you snag a reef by mistake since it doesn't give things back willingly... kind of like the tax department.

When *Bob-the-Boat* chugged from the strain, Rob was confident we were hooked, and he killed the engine. The silence took me by surprise. It was the first time in a very long while that we had had complete quiet. Marinas are quiet but there are other boats and the din of town life in the distance. At sea the engine and the brush of waves on the bow were constant. It was liberating to be gently swinging in the breeze, with only the sound of breezes cutting a B-flat on the main mast. There were no water or hydro hook-ups to be done, no harbour fees to be paid, and no chopping in or out. This was maximum freedom as depicted in the glossy yachting magazines; a man's man of the Bond genre checking his Dom Pérignon while a scintillating brunette (or two) languish wantonly on a chaise lounge, wet from an afternoon swim, a coconut palm-clad island beckoning beyond. Three naked, middle-aged men, cavorting in the clear waters of the South China Sea, was not much competition for such seductive print, but the freedom... ah, the freedom—it was simply marvellous.

With the smoke of our marinated chicken and vegetables curling away from the barbecue and our first gin and tonic in two days perspiring in our hands, we relaxed, basking in the idea we had paradise all to ourselves. It lasted all of fifteen minutes. A large fishing boat motored in a hundred yards away and dropped anchor. Shortly after that, another pair showed up. Although our quiet and solitude had been broken, we realized we had made a good choice to wait out the storm if the local fishermen were seeking out the same spot. As darkness began to fall, skies to the south flashed with an unending show of lightning and we could see whitecaps forming and silver bullets of spray as the surf pounded rocks at either end of the island. We were not alone, but we were safe.

Safety, in part, was also provided by the warning presets for the anchor. In case the boat should drift and the anchor drag, the sonar had been set to wail if the depth was too shallow, indicating we were drifting into shore, and again if the depth exceeded a certain height, suggesting we had broken loose and were heading out to sea. How convenient, modern, and carefree.

The first siren let loose at a little past midnight. All hands showed up on the bridge, veins pulsing with the firehouse wail of the siren. There was an electronic visual recorded for the last hour, showing we had dragged slightly and the boat had swung in several loops. Rob reset the preset, giving slightly more tolerance to each end of the scale in shallowness and depth. All hands returned to beds, but not before we realized that we were now surrounded by an entire fishing fleet. Running lights outlined masts that seemed to stretch to an inky horizon blurred by near-horizontal sheets of rain. I listened for the A-r-r-r-s and the scurvy dogs and decided these were not the pirate hoards we had been warned of, but I slept with one eye open anyway, keeping my three-blade razor under my pillow. It was the only sharp item I owned. Shave the bastards, if all else fails!

I had never been rocked to sleep as I child, I don't think, because the rolling boat slapped by waves failed to make me sleepy. Instead, I concentrated on the patter of rain on the deck above and tried to remember my childhood, where on numerous occasions I had fallen asleep at my father's side in the car, lulled by the pings and patter of rain on the roof and the constant whir of the wipers, feeling the warmth and security of being protected while a storm raged outside. Missing, of course, was my father's protective arm. This led me to wonder how he was doing and whether I might be receiving a call on any given day that he had passed on. He was three months shy of ninety-four. His memory was failing. He knew that he knew me but seemed unable to put a finger on exactly who I was...the finger being the problem. He kept a photo by his bed in the nursing home, the three brothers and two sisters standing in a row, hovering over him and his wife. It was from his ninety-second birthday celebration. On one occasion, he lifted the photo when I had entered the room, trying to identify me as some relation of sorts, then looked dismayed and slightly troubled by this stranger who dared to call him Dad. It wasn't until I came to give him a hug that I realized he had his thumb over my head in the photo. How easy it was to disappear from someone's life.

I drove my head firmly into my pillow, trying to push out the demons of fitful sleep. My brain sent me into the deep REM of Never-Never Land where naked pixies and fairies waited for wanton souls like me. I found myself caught between a buxom pair, as siren number two unleashed a piercing wail and took me from my reverie. The fairies disappeared immediately.

It was obvious the reset of the preset had not worked and needed to be reset once again. By the time I dragged my weary ass up to the helm, Rob had started the engine, thrown the boat into reverse, and ploughed the anchor deeper.

"That will hold the mother!"

We all retired, expecting to sleep.

The third, fourth, and fifth alarms were met with meetings at the helm. John and I had suggestions as to where to put this device, but it was decided to simply turn it off. This may have seemed an obvious solution (it was to John and me, after all), but Rob knew what it could mean. He worried as John and I slept. For him, there was no sleeping. Every rock of the storm-tossed cradle sent his mind crashing ashore or drifting into the fleet of fishermen pirates. When the sun rose, the three of us had matching eyes like piss holes in the snow.

The morning rays of sunshine arrive somewhere after six a.m. in this part of the world. Those rays have a way of finding you through the pinned drapes of the tiny portals that bring daylight to the belly of the boat. They poke at vulnerable eyelids like kittens waiting for their morning scratch behind the ears. If you roll over, the rays warm a spot of skin with the childlike zeal of a bug being fried under a magnifying glass. "Get up, or I'll fry your ass!"

Rob's internal clock had been tightly wound from two years of motoring his yacht. The first sniff of daylight and he was out of bed. He rarely had to make coffee in the galley, however. John would already be reading, coffee in hand. John was an early riser and had been for years, reading a couple of newspapers before breakfast. His habits had not changed for this trip, where he longed to the point of becoming fidgety for his morning papers. The *Borneo Post* had been his last treasure, picked up in Miri and read to death.

This was not a habit honed in the safety of midlife prosperity. In our travels through Europe, living on ten dollars a day, he had always found some change to buy the *London Times*. He had set a course for being a self-made man as a teen, and it had worked.

On the boat, John's choice of bed had been the couch in the main sitting area. He could rise, drink coffee, and read his papers without disturbing a soul. He retired early and slept soundly. For this, I envied him.

My pattern of sleep, not unlike our tethered boat, was a series of twists and turns, lunges and parries at the unseen ghost, and usually ended with a sheet twisted around my neck, slightly short of a hangman's noose. For this reason, I slept commando, having too many boxer briefs twisted in serious high-C knots around my groin.

When I stepped out into the morning air, nursing my second cup of coffee, the deck was still wet. The air was tepid, charged with the salt of the storm-churned sea and the faint smell of rain, but it lacked the scent of earth and trees that came with rainstorms back home. Taking in a deep breath here, like everywhere else in this tropical heat, brought no sense of refreshment. I had made it an audible issue since we first landed in Bangkok.

"Fuck it's hot!"

The only place, it seemed, to get a breath of fresh cool air in Southeast Asia was in an air-conditioned 7-Eleven. Being hosed for a bottle of water never felt so good. At sea we never ran the AC (it took too much power), so we motored with all the doors opened to let the ocean breezes flow through. It was cooling, but not refreshing. Also, the byproduct of opened doors was brine-slicked floors and clammy linens, like waking in a tent before dawn, beads of moisture dripping from the ridge pole. In a tent, at least, you could stick your head out into the night-cooled air.

I longed for that slight autumn chill that I knew was arriving with the turning leaves at home, and for the first time I felt a small squeeze of homesickness. There was nothing as beautiful as a bright fall day in Ontario. Even rainy days had an unparalleled natural beauty, where the black veins of maple branches and the monogrammed trunks of white birch dissected gray skies like the delicate patterns on a butterfly. The colourful windfall of dropped leaves reflected a beauty that had to be seen to be appreciated...something this part of the world could never know. Homesickness, however, may have lasted all of ten seconds before I pinched myself. This was the South China Sea, after all, and I was swinging off a bubbling mud pit lagoon with white sands and palm trees. All my senses regained, I reminded myself that I had seen a lifetime of autumns in Ontario, and hopefully, there would be many more to come.

At six thirty a.m., the sea was already streaked with white reflections; those kitten rays that had poked their way into my quarters were now a full-grown pride of lions prowling with heat and pawing gaping holes through the low morning clouds. The fishing fleet was gone. The seas had calmed. *Bob-the Boat* sent gentle, cascading rings across still waters. Paradise had returned.

Reviewing the electronic history of the boat's movement throughout the night revealed a twisted pattern of lines like an Etch A Sketch. We had dragged anchor in several directions. Ploughing anchor while swinging was more complicated than the glossy ads suggested.

Precautions suggested that the anchor should have been reset, but resetting takes infinitely more time and skill than the drop. The captain must take precautions while an anchor is being drawn in to keep both the boat and the anchor in line and taut, as the boat should not be floating over the chain. A boat like *Bob*, which is fibreglass, can be badly scarred by the chain. The chain should pull perfectly straight off the bow. Angled too much right or left, the chain can slip out of the sprockets that guide it into the storage area, so care is needed via first-mate hand signals to keep the boat and anchor straight.

Currents, tides, breezes, and the wake from a passing vessel all contribute to keeping the boat in a constant motion of swing, so it takes longer than one might think to pull up the anchor. There is also the matter of mud.

The first sign of mud on the incoming chain warrants a frantic waving of arms and a "Whoa, Nelly" to stop the winch. A first mate is required to hose down the chain, preferably before it gets on deck. Anchors, having been ploughed deep, may be thick with heavy sea mud that a captain hopes to snag for a good set. The odour is eons of decayed seaweed and fish guts tempered with salt. This undoubtedly will be glued together with the shank and flukes of the anchor like a pair of teenagers in the back seat of a car. Unlike the lovers, however, the mud cannot be dislodged by a simple cry of "Your mother is coming!" The mud requires poking and prodding with something sharp to dislodge it from the shank and fluke. If it hits the deck, hard scrubbing and swabbing will be required before the guilty party is allowed inside the boat. No mud in the helm! By the time the anchor is clean and the decks are swabbed, the first mate may have the look of a chimney sweep, necessitating a jump in the sea. It was for all these reasons that resetting the anchor at midnight had not been an option.

These moments of swingers living off the hook never seem to get mentioned in the tales of South Sea Yachting.

Like many other things in life, there should be definitive rules for swinging at sea. If this was a self-help book, there would be long, droopy anchors marking these pearls of wisdom.

- ⚓ Acquaint yourself with the new harbour before dropping anchor
- ⚓ Keep nose windward, back end leeward
- ⚓ Check out bottoms
- ⚓ Use the first mate to guide your anchor
- ⚓ Drop your rode. Make sure it's long
- ⚓ Plough deep, Plough hard, hang tight, hold fast
- ⚓ If drifting occurs, plough deeper
- ⚓ In quick waters, plough faster
- ⚓ Plough faster and deeper as needed

- ⚓ If the engine screams, you are well-anchored
- ⚓ Gentle swinging side to side to be expected

NOTE: Keep anchor clean. Wash the mud off shanks and flukes. Don't let anchors dangle. Enjoy the freedom!

The idea of a mud bath hot tub had lost its charm since none of us were in the mood to drop *Doug-the-Dinghy* at the early hour, motor to shore, and walk to the abandoned mud hole. It was a late afternoon kind of activity anyway, prompted by solar flares, beers and dares and rewarded by steaks on the barbecue. In retrospect, I am glad we never landed. The island, besides hot mud and TV history, is famous for its snakes, which are up there with rats on my phobia radar. We said goodbye to Pulau Tiga with our sights on Kota Kinabalu.

19

KOTA KINABALU
SLEEP DEPRIVATION AND THE LOST MIND

HOURS LATER

We motored into Kota Kinabalu under a cover of gray, expecting clouds laboring in uncomfortable positions over a fleet of fishing boats, shoreline buildings and an oil refinery in the distance that was birthing a tanker out to sea. Occasionally, mountains inland were exposed like shy children playing hide-and-seek in the billow and folds of a mother's apron. Rob noted points of interest as we moved closer towards a thicket of masts corralled in a harbour surrounded by luxurious hotels. They were all part of the yacht club, Rob informed us. He had spent time here with Cathy, who had crowned this her favourite port. There was an island portside wrapped in a pristine white beach giving way to a lush palm forest and a small city of homes on stilts that overhung the water. It was the shady side of paradise.

"There is an amazing school in the middle of all those shacks," Rob informed us. "We'll take the dinghy out once we get settled, and do some exploring."

While I balanced the view of the luxury we were heading

into and the shantytown across the channel, John was engaged in tracking planes that were landing and taking off in a flight path over our heads.

"Must be a decent airport," he said. "There are some pretty large planes landing. I wonder what kind of connections they offer." As John loved planes, his tone and observation went without question.

"All over Southeast Asia," Rob replied. "Cat and I have flown in and out of here a few times."

I wondered, with an airport so close, would it be another distraction from sleep? The journey from Miri had taken more than fifty hours. Wrestling with the nightmares of near-misses and the demons of swinging boats and dragging anchors, I had barely slept at all, and I was hoping paradise came with quiet, silken slumber, with a fine weave of deep, dark, velvety dreams. Sleep, you would think, should come naturally, as it does for three-toed sloths, hanging bats or a croc filled with fresh gnu. But my mind and body had moved into some parallel universe where sleep—the kind of my wishful thinking—did not exist. Fashioned by several weeks at sea, I was now into a routine of fitful cat naps, the kind where the cat wakes, yawns, stretches, takes note of its surroundings, then rolls over into another position, drifting in and out of consciousness, waiting to pounce at the slightest hint of movement.

John, I think, had lived in this universe (cat naps minus the fits) for most of his retired life, but his naps, being longer, were deep, and he could rise faster and function at a higher level quicker than anyone I had ever met. He may have been the prototype for automobile airbags since he collapsed almost as quickly going off to bed. Rob moved in robotic precision of a daily schedule that never seemed to falter. When there was promise of adventure around the corner, he drew on a kryptonite source of energy that kept him going for hours. It was this energy that would push us into activity in paradise, for had I had my way, I may have crawled into the dark of the engine room and slept for a week.

With Rob tending to the wheel and John counting planes, I circled the deck, eyes to the shores of paradise. Swaying palm trees, white sands and luxurious hotels...my mind wandered again.

What had it been like, I wondered, for Columbus to leave the Bahamas, the coral sands, the warm turquoise seas and a choice of all-inclusive five-star resorts? And Amerigo Vespucci (after whom the Americas are named) leaving Brazil right in the middle of Mardi Gras? For them, captains of their fleets, there was the lure of fame, prostrated before kings and queens in the guise of loving duty for God and country. Theirs came in promises of silver and land, and continents—north, south, and central—named in their honour, or a thousand cities, towns, rivers, mountain ranges, districts and squares, a line of clothing or Hollywood rights on the four hundredth anniversary of their discoveries. But their crews...how were they able to persuade them to climb back onto their scurvy-addled boats and leave behind the Appleton's rum and native chambermaids who made lovely towel swans on their beds?

"Aye, lads, we'ze gots a choice to make. Either we'ze gets back on these boats and sails home to our loves waiting with open arms...toothless perhaps, ailing with age, balding slightly with lice infestations, and with child from the village idiots, cause they'ze be thinkin' we'ze be sailin' off the edge...but waitin' alls the same...yes, for sure...and we'ze be leaving these vixens, these moral vagrants with ample mounds of heaving flesh and lovely brown booties...and soft, warm...yes, well...as I'ze be sayin'...either yee'ze be getting back in the boat, lads, or the first mate here will be hoofin' yee'ze in the berries." And common sense must have prevailed.

"We'ze fornicates ourselves ter death in paradise or we'ze be soprano singin' eunuchs... To the boats, lads...to the boats." My mind was a treasure trove, perhaps best lost at sea, coddled by the lack of sleep.

A pair of uniformed help met our entrance to the marina, catching ropes with precision, tying us down with double cleat hitches and offering to help with water and electrical hookups. Rob declined the offer, realizing that the electrical connection would need to be changed, giving John the chore instead. I ran water hoses and, once Rob did his shutdown, began to transition *Bob-the-Boat*. Deck cushions were unearthed from several holds, and the interior was re-finessed for harbour life. Drapes were closed and the wheelhouse windows were covered for privacy. Once John gave the okay, all electrical was switched to harbour power. With doors closed, the AC chugged into cooling and dehumidifying action.

Our first night moored, we slept, or rather John and I slept, while Captain Rob rose from the after-dinner nap (John and I had taken it for bedtime) around ten in the evening and unsuccessfully tried to persuade us both to join him at ladies' night out in one of the hotel bars. I could not have joined him, even if they were naked and wrapped themselves around me in triplicate (okay...*maybe* in triplicate); my pillows had suddenly become magnetic, and my head became a large chunk of steel. I don't even remember falling asleep, but again, it must have been fitful because I woke with the sheet tied in a half-knot around my neck. This is how I am going to go, I am sure of it; headlined as **"Man Strangled While Sleeping...No Signs of Foreplay."** Some people, I've been told, hang themselves for a more intense orgasm; nothing like near-death for good sex. Maybe this is what Shakespeare's *Hamlet* meant.

> **"To die, to sleep—**
> **To sleep, perchance to dream—ay, there's the rub**
> **For in this sleep of death, what dreams may come..."**

Knowing, of course, that the Bard filled his verse with lurid double entendre.

As for actual sleep in paradise, like everywhere else we moored, fish nibbled, boats manoeuvred, and people spoke.

⚓ ⚓ ⚓

I woke to find John and Rob already into their second cups of coffee, sitting on the deck. A plane was lifting overhead, and although John noted it was a Boeing 737, it wasn't necessary. You could read the call letters and check the tire treads. I think the pilot's eyes were blue.

"It's probably one of the long-haul carriers to Hong Kong or Tokyo," John shouted, following the plane until it was lost in cloud, and then returned to reading the *Borneo Post*, *New Sabah Times*, or *Kota Kinabalu Daily Express*. There were several papers scattered about.

"I was about to come down and poke you with a stick," Rob said.

"Poke me with your what?"

"God, I don't know how anyone can sleep so long. Five hours is all I need," John offered in usual form. He didn't even look up from the paper.

"You gotta sleep when you gotta sleep...besides, I don't deflate at seven p.m. like some I know," I quibbled, knowing I had the previous night, but it was a rarity.

"As I said, it's just a matter of training the body...you've missed half the day," John replied with a shrug and Cheshire leer, failing to reply to my cranky retort. The clock was pushing ten a.m.

"Any coffee?" I asked, diverting a clogged shit valve in my brain.

Rob pointed to the jar of instant. "Help yourself."

"So, you didn't wake me with all the women you brought home. Either I am a sound sleeper, or you are fairly adept at sneaking in with consorts on your arm."

"I had a live one for a while last night. I don't know what I said, but she offered to get drinks and never came back."

"The wench! I hope you tracked her down and flogged her with a wet noodle. God, what's the world coming to?"

"I saw her later. She was with someone…maybe her boyfriend."

"Oh, well, in that case, I hope you kept your wet noodle to yourself."

The conversation degenerated into sailor talk; squeezable melons, bananas, cucumbers…at some point we had to go shopping.

Amidst the playfulness, there was a new intensity with Rob, as if this was not a game—as if the catch now was all-important. I was trying to count how long we had been at sea, and if this weeping of testosterone from the pores was some byproduct of *mal de debarquement* or salt air saturated with iodine. It could explain my dreams that culminated in sheets in a hangman's noose or Rob's alley-cat swagger. John, it seemed, remained unmoved.

20

HARBOR COMMANDMENTS
BATS AND ORANGUTANS
FILTERED BEER IN MOTHER'S KNICKERS

OCT. 8-9TH TO 15TH PERHAPS...NO TIMEKEEPERS IN PARADISE!

Paradise for us started at Sutera Harbour. It was labelled as a resort, golf and country club, spa and marina. It came with two grand hotels that had been built with views over the South China Sea and were surrounded by lush gardens and a twenty-seven-hole golf course, lit for twenty-four-hour play. There were a few acres devoted to swimming pools, waterfalls, water slides, swim-up bars and even an Olympic-sized lap pool that we were entitled to use at the unbelievably low price of twenty bucks a night, including harbour fees, for the three of us! This also included a shower area with free towel service, an area that was trimmed in the finest teak and rosewood, marble floors, a choice of soaps and perfumes and uniformed attendants to hand them out. For owners of the hundred-foot yachts that graced the harbour, such small things may have been of little worth or attraction, as I doubt such people take notice, sailing in the attended luxury of wealth.

For serious pretenders such as myself, they were worthy of a pinch or two.

One might have expected that the inexpensive harbour costs were a loss leader to lure a fleet of sailors to dine in any one of a dozen first-class restaurants, take a round of golf at midnight or frequent the waterside bars, but sailors from my short introduction (if the three of us were any indication) were cheap as pond scum. The Sutera yacht club harboured more moderate-sized boats like *Bob-the-Boat* than luxury-style cruisers and yachts, and those that were occupied seemed to make good use of their galleys and coolers; owners could be seen carting cases of liquid libations and bags of food daily. Sailors lived on boats to save money. Period! Oh, and possibly because they liked to sail.

The harbour was created perhaps as luxurious eye candy for those who paid handsomely for an ocean view from one of the two hotels. After all, what view was complete without a flotilla of three-mast sailboats with crewmen polishing chrome and teak, and bikini-clad ladies soaking up the sun? Or mystery yachts with mystery owners who had crews—some all women—or world-class racing yachts fresh from a sprint up the coast of Borneo? Not welcomed, however, was a clothesline hung with SpongeBob boxers or three sailors crushing beer cans on their foreheads or sneaking a leak at dusk or dawn. With a seven-storey hotel off the stern, our activity was a tourist fishbowl where naked viewing of sunsets would be tantamount to publishing images of Mohammed, and, for that matter, most everything else we practised on the boat would probably be punishable by the ancient laws of stoning. Paradise yacht clubs had rules.

The golden rule was simple: **Be the neighbour you would want your neighbour to be.** This is a great rule unless the neighbour has been to sea for months and drools in your presence.

Quiet decorum is rule number one among the disputed rules

of number one. There were others, beyond the commandments of helping thy neighbour moor his boat and minding your own business. Some were as follows.

> *Thou shall have no jobs before me. Keep thy vessel clean.*
>
> *Even in the shadows of darkness, thou shall not hangeth over the railing and discharge ill waters.*
>
> *Forget not to change "at-sea discharge" to holding tanks.*
>
> *Waltz not bare and have neighbours witness.*
>
> *Mind thy BBQs. Thou shall not have smoke billow off the stern.*
>
> *Though ye drink gin and tonic, ye shall not sing out of tune on the bow.*
>
> *Thou shall not ogle thy neighbour's wife whose cups runneth over in a thong bikini.*
>
> *Thou shall not steal glances*
>
> *Thou shall kill all thoughts of coveting…thy rod and thy staff shall comfort thee.*
>
> *Thou shall not kick stray cats into the harbour, though they shitteth on thy canvas covers.*
>
> *Burst not thy veins and swear like a sailor for stubbing thy toe.*

And **THE SINGAPORE RULE**…

> *Thou shall not hiss off thy neighbour!*

Our first foray from the harbour was to avail ourselves of the water park, where, between a small group of children, I tried out the water slides and cooled beneath the waterfall. Mature patrons sat in the shade of palm trees, sipping on tall, cold drinks, dabbing ultra-strength sunscreen on carefully nurtured flesh or reading glossy magazines, eyes hidden behind expensive Oakley shades, unlike my clip-on, bargain-basement eyewear. While John gleaned news from his fourth paper of the day, I hung face-down on my padded chaise lounge, knuckles dragging on the ground, and slept again. It was short-lived, as Rob was anxious to take a walk and show us the splendour of the hotels that rimmed the pools.

The Magellan Sutera five-star was impressive in that the lobby is the size of a football field. It is open to the elements from both ends in a two-storey structure, and for an explanation of style, I would say it comes close to the Native American longhouse, once particular to the indigenous Pacific people called the Haida. Massive beams vaulted a span roof that covered a luxurious floor of marble, plush matted seating areas and magnificent splays of fresh flowers hemmed by a Fifth Avenue of fine shops and restaurants.

The Pacific Sutera, in contrast, was a highly modern multi-storied building of equal luxury, and again, came with a whole new water park perk, one that gained our loyalty—a swim-up bar.

By two, we were preparing to shuffle into town to shop. Like Singapore, we were entitled to and availed ourselves of the free air-conditioned bus shuttle into the city. Rob had changed out of his SpongeBob boxers, and we were all coiffed respectably for the trip.

As we rode, Rob filled in some history, not a subject he was known to care for.

Kota Kinabalu had originally been called Jesselton under British rule, named in favor of Sir Charles Jessel, vice-chairman of the board of the British North Borneo Company. It was a monopoly, like the East India Company or the Hudson Bay Company that once claimed ownership of Canada and a percentage of all North America, but had beaver as its pursuit, not rubber, rattan, and honey, like the British North Borneo Company. One riot that led to another by local tribes and a good razing that levelled the town before the Japanese could conquer it has now left Jesselton a tidy and modern city of half a million people. As for paradise, that was in the eyes and experiences of the beholder. Rob presented a few interesting side-shows that could be accessed from Kota Kinabalu, clearly designed to enhance the reputation of this tropical Shangri-la.

"Catherine and I took an interesting trip to the east side of Borneo, which might interest you guys," he began. "You fly by plane to a small town called Sandakan and, with the aid of a guide, navigate up the Kinabatangan River and travel overland to Gomantong Cave, which has over two million bats. You can take a tour down into the cave where the bat shit is about three hundred feet deep."

John and I were not on the edge of our seats with excitement.

"Or...not," Rob concluded, noting the body language, faces skewed as if someone had dropped a freshly filled diaper in our lap.

"I think the BBC did something on that in the *Blue Planet* or *Planet Earth* or something," I added. "Aren't there a bunch of guys living in those caves with the bats? They climb the walls and retrieve the birds' nests...something to do with bird spit soup or something...very popular in China."

"Bird's nest soup," Rob corrected. "And it is saliva from the swallows that build the nest, which holds the nests together. Supposed to be an apher...afro...ah, you know, the stuff that makes you horny."

"Aphrodisiac," I offered. "Like Viagra."

"If you say so."

We spent a while mulling over how such a tradition could have begun.

"So, two Chinese guys were standing up to their asses in bat dung watching a pair of swallows build their nest... Oh, that looks tasty...let's eat that...gives me a rise just thinking of it."

"Not a lot different than some guy who decided to cut the horn off a rhino, thinking maybe it would help him get it up," John offered.

"Yeah, but nasty as that is, at least the horn is phallic-looking...something to get the brain thinking in that direction... but bird spit? What the...?"

"And while we're on the subject, who the hell watched an egg coming out of a chicken's ass and said, 'M-m-m-m, let's eat that'?" This was probably part of a George Carlin skit, I couldn't remember. The conversation turned towards other foods that would have demanded some guts and fortitude to try, like milk dripping from a cow's udder, stinky blue cheeses (how do you even know when it has gone bad?), prairie oysters (bull testicles in demi-glace or deep fried), raw fish eggs on crackers, blood soup, haggis, calf brains, fermented herring...actually fermented anything, even beer—"Let's add this wee shite together, laddies, with some honey and water, let 'er sit 'til it's so bad it's bubbling and 'ave a wee drink. Aye, that was bonnie good...next time, let's be filtering it through mother's knickers to rid it of the pieces."

"Well, I've got one for you," Rob offered amid our laughter. "How about a partially formed baby duck boiled alive in the shell? It's called balut in the Philippines. I've had it lots of times. You peel away part of the shell, suck out the juices, add some salt, and eat. Tastes like a boiled egg with a little meat thrown in."

"That's just plain sick," John and I both agreed.

"I'll get you one when we get to the Philippines." Our expressions suggested disgust. "Don't knock it until you've tried it."

The other trip suggested was to the Sepilok Orangutan Sanctuary, which was a long bus ride into the Borneo jungle and a similarly long hike along a mountain track to view these creatures in their natural habitat, often referred to as the Wild Men of Borneo. Either trip sounded exciting, but

I realized that when I had received my shots for this part of the world, the nurse had asked me if we were going into the jungle. I had said, "Not that I know of; we're motoring on a yacht," and she hadn't given me a shot for some kind of hair-falling-out, teeth-rotting, scrotum-swelling-to-the-size-of-a-basketball malaria that would have cost another two hundred and fifty bucks. I regretted not taking the shot until Rob disclosed the cost of the side trips.

"Twelve hundred bucks to stand in a cave with two million bats?" I repeated, trying to smile with sincerity. "Up a river with poisonous snakes, man-eating crocs and the high probability of being bitten by a mosquito with jungle fever that could leave me weak and vomiting, bleeding from the gums and pissing blood...sounds great!" My enthusiasm was not convincing, and Rob offered a third option.

"They have a two-hour bus ride to the base of Mount Kinabalu where you can then walk up to the peak. Depending on how fast you hike, it can take five or six hours—up and down."

The temperature inland could hover around thirty-five degrees Celsius in the shade on any given minute of any given day. Things feel hotter at ninety-five degrees Fahrenheit than thirty-five degrees Celsius, and that is cool compared to Singapore. It must be noted, though, that Mt. Kinabalu, one of the highest peaks in all of Southeast Asia, is the coolest place, temperature-wise, in all of Borneo, a refreshing mid-teen Celsius at the peak...if you make it!

"How long will it take to swim across the pool to the swim-up bar?" John asked, referring to the pool of blissful heaven back at the Pacific Sutera Hotel. Rob relented on account that he had already done these tours and wasn't particularly eager to do them again anyway. He had tried.

Our bus snaked its way along the harbor, where the city was pressed like a long sausage between the sea and the low foothills to the mountains with modern post-war structures of several stories, beautiful mosques, parks, fountains and playgrounds. Mt. Kinabalu lurked in the distant background to the smaller hills like a mother cuddling her children gathered for a group photo. Occasionally it appeared from behind the clouds that clung like a diaphanous hijab, dictating perhaps the modest morality that tempered the city.

Because the city is comprised of a large mix of Malays, Chinese, and indigenous peoples called Banjar and Dayak, with a smattering of Indians and Europeans integrated throughout, there was not the feel of a dominating Muslim presence outside the few beautiful mosques we passed on our journey. The hijab was mixed with the Western clothing of others, and once again, I felt that Malaysia was doing something right in ethnic mix and acceptance. I realized that my level of comfort was related to the fact that I lived in Toronto, possibly the most cosmopolitan city in the world, and although it wasn't perfect, Toronto was a thriving example of races and religions mostly living in harmony. Many schools, including my wife's, were a mixture of dozens of languages learning in an atmosphere of tolerance and majoring in acceptance. It crossed my mind that if the Toronto schools were looking to twin, this would be a great place to start.

We shopped. I was able to pick up the first of my Borneo souvenirs: T-shirts with Mt. Kinabalu stitched into the cotton fabric. These would be valued Christmas gifts, I thought, worn proudly by my wife and children to show the world to what lengths their husband and father would go, bearing useless gifts from distant lands that meant nothing to them. "Ahh... gee...thanks, Dad, these are...different." Gucci or Prada of New York for sure, but a Borneo mountain...a smiling orangutan... what the hell was I thinking? In my defence, I felt they would have had more use than the carved, hollow wooden frogs sold by every corner vendor that, when stroked with a stick, sounded like carved, hollow, wooden frogs stroked by a stick.

I asked Rob to pay for the goods, since from the very outset we had made Rob the banker with our joint contributions to the everyday pot for everyday living. This money was for food and other living expenses, like beer and goods in duty-free. I suggested John might like to buy a T-shirt for his kids.

"I don't buy souvenirs," he said with a pinched face of concern. He was right, after all; the shared money was to be for daily living expenses for everyone.

"I'll put some more in the pot when we get back to the boat," I offered.

John shrugged as if it didn't matter, but I knew it did. It had been nearly forty years since we backpacked Europe. Nothing had changed, but I was lost for an explanation for his assumption that I wouldn't pay. A T-shirt was perhaps five dollars tops, but, heh, things have a way of festering. Had I thought to take my eyes off the carpe diem of paradise, I might have caught the sharp current of dissent.

We ventured from the mall through the arrows of midafternoon heat to the market warehouse several blocks long. Like Miri, the market was divided into wet and dry and was the scene of moderately bustling commerce. The housewife economist had come and left early. We stocked up on fresh goods for the evening meal, stuffed them in my backpack, and then considered walking out onto the streets to nose about. I reminded Rob that fresh chicken thighs and other perishables were needing immediate refrigeration, and if we didn't want to invite Sam and Ella home to dinner, we had best return to the boat. We did and made haste for our first swim to happy hour.

Once in the water, it took approximately 5.8 seconds to cross the pool and adjust ourselves onto the barstools. The swim-up bar is possibly the most civilized side tour in all of Borneo. Natives dressed in the tribal costumes of pressed linen whites combine distilled goods with juices in units called blenders, served in all manner of available libation utilities from snifters to highballs in return for pieces of wrinkled paper with some ancient king embossed on the surface. Standing in bat dung is not required. The closest we came to the blood-sucking antics of killer mosquitoes were a pair of Bloody Marys absorbed through a straw and the only crocs was a pair worn by a maintenance man retrieving a fallen coconut from the pool. For guests lounging poolside, the sight of three sailors with the bent gait of inebriation playfully falling off their stools into coconut-infested waters may have easily doubled for a trip to meet the orangutans, except the jungle primates were better-looking. For further testaments to the savage wilds, one might have found us slithering like snakes back to our hollowed-out log called *Bob-the-Boat*, where rest was sought to slowly digest the pig, swallowed whole (pounds of wings and fries), and, for an hour or so, three ten-toed sloths napped while the jungle outside slipped into the cover of night.

It may seem a bit on the timid side...well, okay, let's call a spade a spade...downright chicken shit to have taken the road well paved with cocktails and beer over the untrodden path of the wild Borneo jungle, but let's not forget that this is Borneo, after all, and was home to the not-too-far-in-the-distant-past ritual of headhunting by the Iban tribe. *National Geographic* may still consider this virgin territory, and anthropologists cut their teeth here in the study of lost tribes. To consider as well was the Orang Mawas, the mythical version of Big Foot, possibly the original Wild Man of Borneo that roams through the jungles eating durian. Durian, you recall, is considered an aphrodisiac. No one wants to get dragged off by a Big Foot orangutan look-alike that lives on natural Viagra. Dr. Livingstone, who suffered from swollen hemorrhoids and was killed by a lion in Africa, may have gotten off easy.

And then there is Nabau, the mythical river serpent, a Borneo Nessie if you will, caught in an aerial reconnaissance photo that appears to be over a hundred feet long. The myth, it seems, until the recent photo, could not be confirmed, presumably because all previous witnesses had been eaten! If doubt clouds your mind, check out "Snakes of Borneo" or read about the "Anaconda of the Amazon." If twenty-foot crocodiles weighing one and a half tons swim out to sea in Australia, a land that is also home to eight-foot earthworms or giant squid that take on whales, this Nabau serpent might be possible, though likely is the work of a computer artist. Whatever—swim-up bars rule!

21

DOUG-THE-DINGHY
THE EGREGIOUS PLAGUE
COLOURS OF WHOVILLE
THE MORO PEOPLE AND FAST BOATS

DAY THREE IN PARADISE

The next morning, we were back on the water again, only this time we were in *Doug-the-Dinghy*. We were heading for the white sands of Pulau Gaya, across the channel from the yacht club. Getting *Doug* waterborne was a whole matter and a half.

In his usual hang-out, *Doug* was found sitting on the half deck, midway between the flying bridge (the upper deck) and the quarter deck of the bow (over my stateroom), which in turn sat halfway up from the mini deck that serviced the stern. The design of the boat was such that no one operated with a full deck. The first item of work was to get *Doug* undressed of his special UV-protected raincoat. It was a matter of unclasping string ties and bungee cords and rolling back the canvas to expose *Doug*'s naked interior. There was also a separate cover for his outboard motor, hung like a codpiece, which needed to be unzipped of Velcro ties, removed, folded, and stored. Next, there were a series of nylon straps that held *Doug* fast to the crescent-moon perch that was built solidly into the fibreglass deck. Remove them and *Doug* was free to be moved, but, since he sat on the second-tier half deck like a baby loon on its mother's back, a winch had to be brought into play. Before the winch, chains needed to be attached both front and back, left and right, and drawn into two "U" shapes to the center of the dinghy. A single winch hook would hold the chain from both ends together. Canvas covers for the electric winch controls needed to be untied and removed.

With the cable attached to the center clasp, *Doug* needed to be lifted high enough to swivel the crane arm over the railing, leaving *Doug* free to be lowered to the water. With a single center point of attachment, it was important to keep *Doug* parallel to the boat. Captain Rob, balancing on one foot and hanging precariously by one arm with a control rope in hand, stood on the first-tier railing to make sure *Doug* did not pivot. A pivoting *Doug* on descent might catch the railings, sending *Doug* off in an embarrassing, un-nautical nosedive into the harbour. Deployment went without a hitch, textbook in fact, and *Doug* cut a handsome swath of ripples as he was pulled up and tethered to the ladder of his proud Papa *Bob*, caught, perhaps, measuring the size of his boy.

It occurred to me somewhere in this process that the only way we would be able to save our lives at sea via the use of the lifeboat was if we were hit by a wayward coconut, took on water slowly, and waited, as John had said, for the water to float us off the top deck. In the black of night, waves pounding, *Bob-the-Boat* straining from the impalement of an abandoned oil well, taking on a tilt to dive straight to the bottom, we would be helpless to launch. With this kind of fastidious deployment for a lifeboat, it's a wonder that the *Titanic* had any survivors at all. But then, *Doug* was not actually considered the lifeboat. Hanging on the opposite railing, waiting for such a challenge, was an uninflated dinghy. All it required were straps to be removed and a hand toss overboard. It self-inflates.

Finally underway, we left the Sutera marina harbour and *Doug* made a beeline for the island, pulling onto what looked to be a pristine beach of white coral sand, and we headed for a palm-shaded log to eat lunch. In a cooler, we had packed a Pulau picnic...beer and some other stuff.

Unfortunately, Pulau Gaya soon revealed itself to have succumbed to a virus threatening the entire world...plastic garbage. Bags and water bottles were seeded into the sand and tree roots, a plague we had encountered on many of the beaches and islands we had visited since leaving Thailand. What I had originally thought to be seaweed brushing against my legs in Phuket were revealed as strips of plastic so plentiful that you could not swim more than a few strokes in any direction before crossing the path of more.

To return to a theme lightly touched on before, this egregious plague is truly maddening since it would seem easy to prevent; recycle, reuse, and make all plastics biodegradable. The saddest part is the amount of sea life found with this killing junk in their systems, but with the world producing hundreds of millions of metric tons of plastic garbage each year and dumping thousands of truckloads a day into the oceans, it is not hard to make a connection.

It is said that somewhere in the Pacific there are trash vortexes, mostly plastic, held together by circling currents that are twice the size of the continental USA. Read that again if you must! Even if you believe the oceanographer who dared voice this notion is a bald-faced motherless liar and in truth it is only the size of Texas, this is an abomination so foul that man, I think, has lost the right to claim the title of most intelligent species on earth. We can send a man to the moon and map the contours of Mars and planets beyond, but we have yet to learn not to foul the birth waters of all life here on earth. Sad beyond words. But then, I digress again.

Rob was hard-pressed to sit still, even while eating, and it wasn't long before he was pointing to buildings at the far end of the island and suggesting we go look. He was up and moving, towards pushing *Doug* into the water without the voting "Yeas" or "Nays" of the plebeian crew. It made me wonder why we had landed here in the first place, though first mates must assume the plight of the gladiator in Caesar's arena.

Then again, three grown men on a deserted beach having a picnic was not all that exciting anyway. Missing were the orbs of heavenly bodies to which string bikinis clung for dear life, tried by coconut oil, beads of perfumed perspiration, and the pressures of expanding silicone in a noonday sun. Missing also were the playful dog-whistle shrieks of children caught in breaking waves, indicating a good time is being had by all. There were no frisbees in the potato salad, airless kites dropped on unsuspecting sleepers, or muscled men kicking sand in the faces of the likes of me, so it was no real day at the beach. Quiet, absolute solitude with the promise of twenty minutes of sleep in the sun where the horizon stands still is highly overrated, I've been told.

Before mutiny erupted, we were puttering through that stilted neighbourhood over water. Homes were attached to their neighbours and connected with planks. They stood high off the water; each dwelling no larger than a single room, some sporting balconies, but few had the luxury of railings. We were motoring through their basements, a vast thicket of supporting poles. The first appearance had been that of a small community along the beaches, but as we continued to motor it opened to a sprawl of thousands of connected shacks and shanties pushing offshore in all directions. It was mostly a sea of weathered gray plywood shacks, but I counted five brightly painted buildings with the trademark domes of the mosque.

We were met by enthusiastic waves of children, many of them infants, standing precariously at the edge of their doorways and balconies. They seemed thrilled that three white men in a dinghy were in their neck of the woods. John felt we were intruding, especially by taking photos (he was probably right), but the children scrambled to watch, waving with extra energy toward the lens.

In memorable shots, six boys were pushing and scrambling to pose, hanging dangerously close to the edge of the wharf. They flashed peace signs, not unlike ten-year-old boys in any neighbourhood, anywhere, hamming it up for the camera. Another caught a solitary boy no older than five or six, sitting in a tiny skiff, fishing with the intensity of a cat watching a cornered mouse. He had a fishing line, no pole, and there were no adults in sight. A smiling mother held her baby up for the camera, while another photo revealed a naked infant barely able to walk standing at the very edge of a ten-foot drop to the water, unattended, wondering what the excitement was all about.

A pattern revealed itself, though I was too busy snapping photos to see it.

There were so many happy faces, young and old, waves of enthusiasm, genuine smiles, squeals of childish glee that I had felt in my naivety, viewing things from afar, could not be possible in an assumed place of such privation and need. If I look back, there is one photo that is emblematic of this unique city over the water. It reveals half a dozen colorful kites hovering above the gray mass of corrugated tin and plywood homes. The kites perforated the blue sky like tiny united voices from some Dr. Seuss book.

> "Where some persons are persons,
> No matter how small,
> And were clambering to be heard,
> Beyond the gray walls."

And I truly wondered how it could be,

> "In this Whoville of poverty,
> They had happiness too,

Though the rich Grinches had everything,
In Kota Kinabalu."

The further we travelled, weaving through the forest of pylon structures, the more colour began to show; colour not obvious from a distance where the main theme was gray. Some shacks were painted in bright yellows, reds and blues, all on the same surface. The laundry that fluttered and billowed in the breezes and hung between buildings were bright hues of the rainbow. I knew that this laundry had been washed and wrung by hand, but somehow the colours, sparkling in the sunshine, seemed to counter the drudgery I knew it would have taken to get it hung on the lines.

Most of these people, I guessed, were fishermen, or at least fished for food, as many structures had fishnets and boats tied to their bases. Boats came in all sizes, but there was a large collection of powerful boats with expensive outboards, and, considering the survey of poverty, these appeared quite out of place, leaving me to wonder what kind of fish paid so handsomely. Some boats sported the native Malay design, looking like the dugouts of the Haida of the Pacific Northwest. A boat, painted with the phrase *2 Long Life* in large, colourful lettering bobbed quietly in our wake and stood out like a beacon of defiance to the surrounding habitat.

In juxtaposition to the city across the bay, this village was a massive slum, but somehow in the pattern slowly revealed, it took energy from the life-giving waters below, the blue sky above creating charged smiles connecting them both. The flashes of colour were not unlike the lone hand of defiance to the death tanks in Tiananmen Square. It didn't stop the problem, it simply showed the world that it refused to succumb.

It turns out that this village is relatively new and most of the people, called the Moros, are refugees from the Philippines. *Moro* is Spanish for "Moors," which the colonial Spanish of the 1500s called those who were Islamic followers and had similar beliefs to the Moors back in Spain. In typical colonial fashion, they had tried to convert the locals, against the strong objections of the Moro people. Like the history of colonization everywhere, long-term discontent had been the legacy. The Moro were pushed to the fringes of the Philippines by Spanish Catholicism. Even today in the hinterland provinces, battles rage on between the Philippine Christian militia and the Islamic Moro National Liberation Front. We would cross their paths, if only in a very remote way, on our journey to Subic after leaving Kota Kinabalu. The Moro, we came to understand, fight against the religious intolerance of the Philippines (which is predominantly Catholic) and to correct the corruption of the Philippine government. When one considers the likes of Ferdinand Marcos and his legacy of graft and absolute corruption, one might be tempted to join their cause.

I knew I was probably overly naive in my sweeping benediction of this Borneo Whoville. One had to assume that these refugees of a guerrilla war in the Philippines were not completely innocent, as there have been crimes against humanity committed by both sides of the Philippine equation. Allowing for this realization, it was quite probable that militants were living among the cluster of homes, and that the sleek, fast boats we saw were more than the product of fishing, as in gunrunning perhaps, drugs or kidnapping for ransom, whatever freedom fighters might need for their struggle.

But I liked my first assessment best, and we found no such discontent as we motored under and through the web of stilted housing. *Doug-the-Dinghy* was not fired upon, and no one aimed with yellow streams overhead.

The best was yet to come. As we rounded the bend and entered a large bay, we could see an oil supertanker moving out to sea, the proceeds from which could have changed the fortunes of every villager for life. We pushed past a large mosque that stood alone, meaning it was only accessible by those with boats. It was well maintained with a cheerful coat of Van-Gogh-yellow, suggesting it was well attended by the flock. Rob pointed deep into the bay and gave notice of our next destination. From our distance, it looked like a long, tidy warehouse hugging the shore. What we found, however, was a shining diamond in what some might consider to be a pit of coal.

22

HARVARD, OXFORD, AND THIS SCHOOL OF NOTE
PEACE, LOVE, RESPECT...A NOVEL IDEA

AFTERNOON OF THE SAME DAY

The roof of the building was painted with large letters—*SMK PULAU GAYA*, denoting it was a public junior and secondary school. The fact that this side tour excited Rob in turn excited me, because schools had never excited Rob, or, come to think of it, John either. There must have been something magical to their lack of school excitement because to harp on a dead horse flogging, they were millionaires both, and I was not.

This school met us long before we could dock, with two piers that pushed well out into the bay. One pier, it was obvious, was a loading zone for boats, some of which were tied at its base, also marked *SMK Pulau Gaya*. These were the water buses for the children of the stilted suburb of Kota Kinabalu. The other pier was a covered walkway and spawned a dozen perpendicular pods along the way, like a chemistry experiment growing oblong crystals left and right of a causeway link.

"Those are classrooms," Rob explained, telling us that he

and Cathy had toured this place before. "They are areas for quiet study. The wind blows through them and keeps them cool."

I didn't expect that we would be stopping, let alone going ashore. It appeared that school was out and the buildings were mostly vacant except for a few children who were waiting for rides. They waved enthusiastically at our approach. The first thing I noted was the lack of uniforms. These children were dressed in jeans, skirts and T-shirts, looking like students from any school back home. All the children I had observed in Thailand and other parts of Malaysia had been in uniforms, looking very much like the kids of the distinguished UCC or Branksome Hall back in Toronto. I had read how Oprah Winfrey had donated millions to African children, with a big part towards uniforms; their ticket for going to school. It was bureaucratic nonsense at the highest levels of some countries trying to abscond from their duties of education. Borneo Malaysia, it appeared, once the home of the Iban headhunters, was miles ahead.

Rob pulled up, cut the motor, and stepped out of the boat as if this was his usual routine, so we followed, though John lightly protested about private property, trespassing and the possibility of being shot on sight. We were barely docked before we were met by a man, requesting to know our mission. John looked for a flak jacket. Rob explained that he had been here once before with his wife and that he now wanted to show his good friends from America—more pointedly, Canada—this fabulous school. The man's approach softened immediately, and, as it turned out, we were in the knowledgeable and friendly hands of the school custodian, now puffed with pride at Rob's flattery, and he would be only too glad to show us around. He introduced himself, but unfortunately, I have forgotten his name, though it may have been Mike. Ben also rings a bell, as does Marco…sorry. It was probably none of these.

"In Canada? Where come from you in Canada?" Michael Benjamin Marco asked as he ushered us along.

"Toronto," I said, ignoring the fact that Rob was from Vancouver Island and John was from Edmonton, since initially we had all started in the same place.

"Toronto? I have cousin in Toronto." He beamed with pride, and for a moment I thought he might ask if we knew a so-and-so who worked at such-and-such, but he didn't.

The world is a small place, I thought, and getting smaller every day, but this was not my first encounter with a shrinking planet. I remembered similar experiences with my wife when we had travelled in Europe. There was Jimmy the Greek who rescued us in Greece when our van blew a piston out through the engine block (I am no mechanic, but I knew this was a problem). He had lived in Toronto at some time or other, and so we became "family" while we were hosed for a new engine. Jimmy made the hosing easier by negotiating the hosing rate. In Holland, every Dutchman knew a Canadian; either they or their parents had been saved by a Canadian soldier; and in Paris, every Parisian knew a Quebecois, "*qui parle merde francais,*" they didn't like. Canada takes in nearly three hundred thousand immigrants a year, so I should not have been surprised. They come from all corners of the world, but from East Asia especially, where everyone knows someone who fled from the terrors of communism to Canada.

"Well, my good friends from Canada, let me show you school."

He took us first along the pier with the connecting pods, lovingly appointed with dozens of colourful pots filled with palm plants and flowers set precariously on the handrail. The walk took us about the length of a football field out over the bay. There was a roof that covered the walkway and hanging from the support beams were banners in both Malaysian Jawi (a Sanskrit-styled writing) and English, with single words like *Love, Patience, Cooperation,* and *Diligence*...words to inspire, encourage and teach. It gave the walk a special feel, knowing that someone had decided to make this school a genuine place of higher learning, like the Latin motto of *Veritas*, for "Truth," carved into Harvard stone, or Oxford's *Dominus Illuminato Mea*, for the Lord is My Light. Here, it possibly should have been *Sic Educari*, for Education is the Way, but instead, it was *Love* and *Patience* and all the other words that were necessary to let these children know that neither Latin nor hallowed halls were necessary to succeed.

We poked our heads into the different pods that were offset left and right of the walk, I assumed to minimize the noise between them. They had no doors, were tightly intimate, maybe ten by twenty feet, and were made of lattice in the style of a Muskoka gazebo, without mosquito netting. Believe it or not, in a place where one might think it should be swarming, there were no mosquitoes or flies to be had. An island cave with a gazillion bats will do that, I guess. Each pod looked as if it might hold a dozen students, at most. Some were plainly accommodating, while others had posters or explanatory charts; parts and functions of the body for health, notations for science and chemistry, or maps for geography, creating a link of warm and fuzzy familiarity to my childhood classes, where teachers wrote words that rhymed or were synonyms or antonyms, or perhaps more recently, my not-so-warm-and-fuzzy proctologist who had intricate diagrams of the long and winding road of his dedication, in relief, all over the wall. Here in the afternoon breezes, strained through the painted red lattice, the charts fluttered aimlessly, giving the rooms a cottage veranda-like comfort where one might snooze or thumb through magazines on a hot August afternoon. Since school was out, the pods were quiet, with only the sound of the lapping waves on the pylons below.

The main structure of the school followed the shoreline, hanging on hefty stilts, where I suppose it had been easier to build over water than to deforest the island. We walked along wide corridors, some carpeted, with classrooms on either side. Except for the planked floors, burnished teak walls, three paddle fans hanging from the ceilings, and windows of Venetian blind glass, they may have looked like old-fashioned school rooms anywhere; neat rows of desks, chalkboards, student projects hanging on the walls, with a large teacher's desk at the front. The difference, however, was always the sound of water, the brackish smell and those breezes, gently nibbling at the pinned-up work on the corkboards, to remind you of where you were.

We entered a large auditorium via a short causeway that was hung with large banners on opposing walls—*Success Depends on What You Do with You* and *The Secret of Success is to Try Harder* (there were no Malay translations). They were hung to be in-your-face-can't-miss-them-read-them-twenty-times-a-day, and like elsewhere in the school, these banners of encouragement had not been defaced, something I thought would be their probable fate in most schools back home. These students had read and understood the banner called RESPECT. It was clear that the students of SMK Pulau Gaya were not being allowed to wallow in the brine of self-pity that, given the economic circumstances, might have been their right to claim.

By the time the tour was finished, however, for reasons I could never quite pin down, the school took on the quiet whispering respectfulness I had felt in the great cathedrals of Europe where there was always someone telling you, "Quiet down and whisper... This is a house of God...have some respect." It was, perhaps, like passing the stages of the cross in a cathedral, if you are Catholic, which I am not, but with the greater importance of expanding minds rather than capturing souls.

The auditorium/gymnasium/all-purpose great room was covered, but the walls were partially open to the elements, allowing air to flow through, giving respite from the sun. With a stage at one end, it had the feel of a band shell in the park.

This openness might suggest that there were rarely, if ever, driving rains or windstorms. We knew from damages at the marina that this was not the case, as a tail end of some tropical storm had pulled apart a portion of the concrete wharf at the harbor marina. This was a rarity, we were told, but it appeared that this auditorium structure—the whole school, in fact—was fragile, as was the entire Moro village. The monster winds that had torn apart the harbour pier, a pier protected by massive stone breakwaters, must have been terrifying to the people of the stilted village and the children of this school. Every storm, it would seem, brought the possibility of massive destruction and death, like blowing on pick-up sticks, but there were no signs of storm trauma in this sheltered cove where SMK Pulau Gaya resided.

As we left, saying goodbye to our kind host Michael Benjamin Marco (though Stefanos now rings a bell), I began to wonder again what it was that intrigued me about this school. The school, we had been told, was home to over two and a half thousand students from grade one to grade twelve. In any country, by any standards, this was a very large school. It was exquisitely clean, cheerfully coated in bright colours and hung with colourful posters and potted plants, and every inch screamed pride of ownership by students and teachers alike.

My wife, once a teacher, was a vice principal of a public school at the time of this trip. For years I had listened to the stories of students, parents and teachers, many unflattering and some outrageous; tales of arrogance, indifference and unfounded entitlement. In fairness, these would be the stories of a vice principal, but I also knew, based on my schooling encounters, that much of it wasn't entirely her perception, but endemic to teaching the world over...the Western world, anyway. What was it about our systems that saw the fiery expectations in the eyes of kindergarten disappear long before high school? Watching students on their way to school back home, you'd think you were witnessing a trip to the gallows.

It was a different story on the way home; animated skip in the gait and the fox-in-the-hen-house cackles of laughter and joy. Did education entitlement breed indifference? Or have we lost the ability to engage our young people in learning?

Many schools have become battlegrounds for gangs and drugs and the buildings themselves, broken-down vestiges of what once was a proud moment in the community's history; a school, with the promise of bright futures for all who attended. Whatever the reasons, they were not evident here, and this was at the heart of my surprise and joy at seeing this school shining in the middle of destitution and poverty. It was the proud heart of the village, a revered golden ticket to cross the bay and leave this life behind.

23

THANK GOOGLE IN JAVA'S NAME
DOWN BY ONE
EVERYTHING = MIRACLES × CHOICES
SQUARED

OCT. 12. CANADIAN THANKSGIVING, EH!

We were barely settled in the marina with gin and tonics in the cooled air of the boat before Rob was itching to go back into town and meet up with the Aussie owners of a bar called the Pirate's Den. He had been a frequent flyer on his last stay in Kota Kinabalu. There was also the matter of shopping for our Canadian Thanksgiving (the first drumstick weekend in October). It's not a holiday in Borneo, of course: the black-wool Puritan of the early Americas would have perished in the heat. If the Iban headhunters—naked with bone-pierced penises and nipples—didn't shrink their heads, they may have caused ungodly swelling to the pantaloons.

The matter of cooking a turkey had been raised only to be deflated by the news that turkey did not exist in the Far East.

"A fat ferkin' chicken will do," it was noted, and an FFC was put on the list of groceries.

"What about pumpkin pie? Nothing says Thanksgiving like pumpkin pie."

"Not a chance in hell of finding a pumpkin here," Rob had said with an authority that neither John nor I needed to challenge.

"You don't need a pumpkin," John had added with such a weighted tone that neither Rob nor I answered. "Any squash will do. It's all about the spices," and he opened the computer to Google pumpkin pie. Several spices were added to the list.

"Pie crust?"

"No problem. I've made tons of them," John, our pie expert, vowed. He Googled pie crust. Shortening and sifted white flour were added to the list.

"Stuffing?" Google moments passed before celery, sage, bread, and raisins were added. It was becoming obvious we would have had to bow our heads and thank Google in Java's name for the meal.

"H-m-m-m, so what are we missing?"

"Family!"

There was a silence as each of us gave a moment of thought to our families back home. Rob was feasibly torn between home at Qualicum Beach on Vancouver Island, where Cathy and their two grown children would be getting together with a real turkey, and Subic, where he knew Kim was waiting for him to return. John said little about what the family was doing as he had made little effort to e-mail and communicate. Ann, his wife, would send messages occasionally, usually to Rob or me or through his sister Judy, who might forward a Facebook message or text to me, wanting to know what her brother was doing. Rob or I would send e-mails with photo attachments. John's excuse was that he didn't want to be bothered, that "All this electronic shit cluttered the voyage." He would be home soon enough, he felt, and why do we need to check in like children on a school trip, or something to that effect. I tended to agree since I had never sent postcards, when postcards were in fashion, on one- or two-week outings, and in truth, all this "electronic shit" did clutter things. It's hard to feel you are having a South Seas adventure of pirate proportions when "You've Got Mail" keeps popping up. John had been given a new camera as a parting gift from his neighbourhood gang, a retired group that celebrated happy hour at a local hall or in John's home every Friday. They wanted all the gory details: pixel moments held in Canon digitations, maximized, resized, photoshopped, encapsulated and sent with a diary of explanations. It was hard to disagree with John's resentment since all this electronic clutter was giving some wankers back home a free ride. We agreed. Get your own bloody adventures!

However, we had been gone a month now. With the barrage of typhoons, the earthquake and the length of time away, it was important to let people know back home that we had not succumbed to the sharks and pirates and that news of our probable demise was greatly exaggerated.

For reasons unexplained, John had said he would not take more than three photos a day, as if he owned an old-fashioned camera from before the turn of the century (2000, that is), where costs were accrued for film and processing. But this was a digital camera. He didn't stick to his guns; he one-upped it. He didn't take any photos at all.

I knew there would be a big gathering for my family back home with maybe thirty-plus turkey eaters all vying for seconds. Dad would be brought from the home to take the ceremonial head chair. My sister would cut his meat into bird-size morsels that he would suck on and then return to the plate. I could only hope he would still be there when I returned home.

Thanksgiving is my wife's favorite holiday, even though she had never grown up with it. Europeans don't have Thanksgiving, as they were happy to see the backside of the Puritans as they left for the New World. For my wife, it's all about the brilliant colours—vermilions, ochre yellows, and kumquat oranges they don't get in Sweden—and the bounty of fresh vegetables at the roadside stands. But best of all, she loves the gathering of families without the inane pressure of gifts and trees and brainless commercials that started... well, right about now for the Christmas rush. There was a lot she had found in Canada that she would gladly give up, but Thanksgiving was not one of them. I loved shuffling through the leaves, that rustling sound that nothing in the world can imitate, and the smell of their decay, the wet earth and the fresh air and...wait...is that dog shi— Sheesh, why me? Giving thanks had its challenges.

"We are family," one of us noted, and there were snorts and embarrassed smiles as we acknowledged the truth, but, wanting to make sure that this melancholy lapse didn't mean we were a suspect bowl of mixed nuts, we playfully exchanged a round of punches to the arm.

I am not sure when the crack opened and sank the cast of captain and crew, but it seemed to come quickly. Rob and I slipped into town looking for immigration, customs, or port authority, I don't recall which, but it was far and required buses and walking at noon, and, as usual, it was found on the second floor with a dry goods business below. By the time we returned, John had made plans to leave in two days, having bought tickets online. Needless to say, we were shocked, surprised, but looking back, it was obvious all the signs had been there.

Rob admitted that John had only committed to thirty days, and thirty days were up, but Rob had thought he would relent. It was a statement made before having experienced paradise. This was a once-in-a-lifetime opportunity, Rob argued, and we weren't spring chickens, so quite likely there would never be a second chance. There was still so much to see with the Philippines and the Great Wall of China ahead. Unfortunately for John, the concept of carpe diem never seemed to catch. He had found a "not-to-be-missed deal" on the internet, Hong Kong to Edmonton, that he couldn't refuse and jokingly said he was needed at home since his family couldn't organize a two-car parade without him.

My mind bounced between shock and relief; gone would be the edge of sarcasm and constant rebukes, real or imagined, but nervous at the new turn of events pitting Rob and me against the coming voyage. We still had over a thousand kilometres to go. If the long hauls through the night had been difficult to manage with three people, they would now be daunting tasks with only two.

It had been no secret that we had all sniped about the third person not on deck; I had heard them have a go about my lack of computer savvy; I constantly asked for help. Before that, it had been a deodorant problem (stress-related and made worse by our dip in Langkawi harbour), which had abated with the new Dettol antiseptic, germicidal powder purchased in Singapore. It is a product usually reserved for eliminating the smell of death, is poisonous, must not be ingested, and has been used to kill cane toads in Australia. Both sides weighed, I couldn't help feeling that the absence of non-plussed enthusiasm and negativity would lighten the load.

While planning for Thanksgiving dinner, we had also been making plans for the final legs of the journey home. Our flights had been one-way, not knowing how long it would take to cruise from Thailand to the Philippines. First, there were the trips that needed to be arranged to fly from the Philippines to Hong Kong. Rob was anxious to accompany us on this portion of the journey home since he and Cathy had stayed in Hong Kong for several months while the boat was being built. He suggested we stay a week, and he would show us the city from his familiar perspective. There was no talk of having to leave Kim again or bringing her along, but then again there had been rumbles in that area, so I had no idea where this relationship stood. I assumed it was still on, since he mentioned her frequently, even if it was through gritted teeth.

Rob had been promised the loan of a very large yacht at the Hebe Haven Yacht Club in Hong Kong, which would give us a free place to stay. He and Cathy had lived at the marina for a month or more while getting familiar with their new yacht and had made a good number of friends. The owner of the yacht in promise was a pilot for Air Asia and lived in Sydney, Australia, but kept the boat for long layovers or several short-haul flights out of Hong Kong. Who could refuse?

Other planning needed to be fixed. From Hong Kong, John and I had both planned to fly to Dalian in mainland China, where we were to stay with my nephew Michael. He was the acting assistant dean of the Missouri State University Branch Campus, where he taught higher mathematics.

Higher or lower, mathematics was never my thing; the simple conjugation of 1 + 1 had equaled 3, times twice was a family of four, the rest being multipliers of upkeep and divisions in savings that never seemed to add up above a red line of more month than money. My simple math had befuddled my giant bear hug of a nephew, keeping him single; that, and a social-defying brilliance that had him creating scores of music, building scale models of dodecahedrons, or becoming completely fluent in Cantonese. Having this connection in China, with a promise to see the Great Wall, was an opportunity I was not going to miss.

Both John and I had spent a great deal of time securing travel visas for China before leaving Canada, efforts that garnered us full-page visas pasted into our passports. Now we needed flights to both Dalian and Beijing before we flew home to Canada. All of these flights and connections needed to be put together before we left Kota Kinabalu. Many transactions were iffy in the Philippines, Rob said, unless large sums were submitted and might require expeditions to Manila.

"You don't want to go to Manila. It is dirty, congested and full of thieves. The Philippines is a throwback to the Wild West. McDonald's even has armed guards at their front doors."

"Tell me why we're heading there again?"

"Aw, don't worry. We'll be fine in Subic. There aren't many shootings there."

"That makes me feel a whole lot better."

"The governor says Olongapo is crime-free."

"So, the guys meeting you at the doors with sawed-off shotguns are simply the Philippine version of Walmart greeters?"

"You could say that. Just don't stare at their guns or make eye contact. It makes their fingers itchy."

This banter had rolled through the helm as we all tinkered at securing workable links to cut-rate travel vendors online such as Expedia, Kayak, or something like Cheap-as-hell.com, something I had never done before, but in which John, who had travelled many times in recent years, was well-versed. The whole process was foreign to me and frustrating beyond words. My experience had always been calling a travel agency and waiting for results. Recently, they were things my wife had done. She understood computers. But, since I was aware that my lack of computer savvy irritated the other two, I surfed, slowly drowning as I went.

"Cebu Airlines is your best choice out of the Philippines," Rob had said, "departing from Clark Air Force Base, direct to Hong Kong. Start with that."

"While you are at it," John piped in with interest, "get two tickets."

The provided site seemed simple enough; a matter of typing in required info, which I did, but I was unceremoniously kicked out try after try. It was annoying.

"Fuck...it kicked me out again." The frustration rose from the fact that nothing was retained. Every single piece of info had to be reentered, down to, it seemed, underwear size. Name, address, postal code, date of birth, sex (yes please), date of departure, date of return (none), spouse, name and address, e-mail, passport number, expiry date, citizenship, place of birth, number of tickets required ("1" entered automatically), credit card number, expiry date, name of second passenger, name, address (if different to first address), postal code, e-mail—

"John, what's your passport number again?"

"And expiry?"

"FUUUUCK, I just lost the signal again! Fuck! Fuck! Fuck!"

"Let me try on my computer," Rob had said, "but I need to finish what I am doing first," said not without a hint of "Oh bloody bother," since this had been the irritating rub from the first day I had tried e-mailing home from Phuket. Most of the time my complaints were legit, since signals had varied and were weak to near-death-rattles quite often. This, again, is what happens when you steal unsecured signals from fellow yachters who in turn have plugged in through trench-coated sources that step out of the bandwidths of darkness whispering, "Psst, want a signal? Marrakesh Two Humps! Alice the Camel is the carrier." Rob's laptop was hardwired to an aerial that shared the mast with the radar and other important electronics, like a fat-banded multi-channelled Marine VHF Radio. Mine shared the ghosts of wireless castoffs, left to haunt Middle Earth.

This story could be endless and, in truth, would have been shorter and ended happier had I left the job to Rob and waited patiently. I didn't and it's not.

"Wahoo, I finally got a ticket."

"A ticket?"

"Oh damn, I forgot to change the number required to two."

Several tries later to secure the second ticket, I bellowed, "I give up," and then asked John if I could use his credit card to see if it made any difference. There was an instant polar shift in the winds with an icy reply.

"Forget it," followed by looks to kill.

It happened something like that, though I may have asked for the card sooner than later, but the crack had been wedged. Though never articulated, the feeling was that I had avoided buying him a ticket. In lieu of the fact that he had paid my way to Thailand on saved travel miles, it would have been an inexpensive gesture of thanks for which, in retrospect, I am deeply sorry I failed. However, when it comes to computers, I am truly roadkill on the internet highway. Rob offered to try on his computer but was met with a cold "Don't bother!" There were no comfortable retreats that apologies could buy, even offering to pay cash for the ticket once it was bought. This was an insult added to injury since it was not the money but a free-will gesture that counted. I could be wrong, as John never confided.

It was this, that and a litany of other things that in hindsight sound like children on a playground, but these paled in comparison to the dangling noose.

Captain Rob, in an exhausted, insensitive, non-retractable manner, had informed his crew on entering the harbour of Kota Kinabalu that they would need to scrub the decks and wax the chrome. I had allowed a loud guffaw, then realized he wasn't joking, swallowed a profane retort, and said nothing, still pinching myself as the freeloader in paradise. On our second day in the harbour, buckets were unveiled, cans of polish revealed, method displayed, and then we—I—was left to clean, since Rob tinkered in the engine room and John mutinied a few keel-haul lengths away in a leather sofa of the yacht club reading room.

It was wrong, crassly conveyed as an order instead of a request, which indeed it was, and again I could only chalk it up to Rob's complete exhaustion. I don't believe he had slept a deep, invigorating sleep since he had purchased the boat two years prior to this voyage. He suffered from sleep deprivation. It's a condition that can interfere with your ability to function socially, making it difficult to judge people's emotions and reactions. It can even ruin your health. It was Captain Rob in a nutshell.

I have said that boaters love their crafts to a distraction, and Rob was no different. It may seem excessive, but it was evident that salt was already starting to cause patches of pitted chrome and brown tarnish, and the doors to the helm showed signs of bubbling under the paint, much like North American cars of the 1970s two weeks after purchase. We had been at sea for nearly a month, and everything was covered in a brine wash. It needed to be done.

Unfortunately for John and me, Rob had been spoiled by his Filipino first mate on his trip to Phuket. Besides tending to his assigned duties of navigating the boat, he had cooked and cleaned and fished (gutting and preparing), tended to mechanical repairs, bargained for food in ports, dealt with harbour officials, taught Rob laws of the open seas and, on his downtime, had played guitar with Rob, adding a harmonic voice, teaching chord method instrumentation and introducing Rob to ballads and folk songs of the Philippines. In short, the sun shone out of his nether regions.

"Filipino sailors are the best in the world," Rob had said while recounting some story of his adventures in reverse. "They are in high demand. I wasn't surprised he got his green card to the States."

I found out later that there are more than seven hundred thousand Filipino sailors, making them the largest group of seafarers in the world. It was obvious John and I paled in comparison, but I knew he had not said these things to goad us. He was not prone to layering thoughts in innuendo to catch his drift.

Rob's failure was that he had forgotten we were friends and not the hired help. Hindsight, being what it is, suggests that I should have stood with John and voiced my displeasure at being treated like a menial worker. As the friend between, I should have taken Rob aside and had a chat; explained the rules of friendship and discussed the fate of Captain Bligh (leaving out the minor detail that Bligh had hunted down most of the mutineers of the Bounty and had them hung).

Though surprised by the request and slighted by the tone,

I was not daunted by the task at hand, and work progressed in a *Karate Kid* wax-on, wax-off monotony. I was surrounded by the beauty of Sutera harbour complete with the view of yachts and sailboats and palms that dropped coconuts on occasion, like bombs from a B-52. Let's face it, I was waxing chrome in paradise. Life could have been worse.

And sometimes memorable moments come from the simplest of things.

It may have been the hallucinatory effects of excessive wax vapours or the Tiger beer, but it was a magical treat to watch thousands of tropical fish biting at the soap bubbles and wax bits as they fell from the boat. Fish, schools and singles, dashed in and out of the shadows of the wharf. Some fish came dressed in black and orange Nemo pyjamas or bars of gold foil, and others were painted blue, solid yellow or Darth Vader black. There were brassy singles, shimmering schools of silver and more in shades of pink and purple and stripes of neon glow, jailbirds in black and white, sleek bullets of steely grays and speeding darts of florescent mother-of-pearl. Others paraded in pageantries of silk, flagellating fins, a Mardi Gras of costumes, masked and multi-banded angels and devils, kings, queens and a full house of jacks, dancing, swirling, migrating with each great splash of suds to the shadowed protection of wharf and boat, and then, moments later, the canvas was painted anew as they filtered out, living, shifting Kandinsky compositions, untitled to infinity.

Einstein suggested that there are only two ways to live your life; as if nothing is a miracle, or choosing to treat the world and everything in it as truly what it is—a total miracle... *Everything = Miracles × Choices Squared*...don't add plutonium. This was one of those moments and an answer perhaps to understanding man's elusive search for happiness and meaning in this cogwheel of life. We should choose to accept that everything in life is a miracle, considering the not-so-insignificant fact that man's entire evolutionary existence thrives on a crust of cooled rock over a ball of fire. That we don't exist at the wave of a magic wand of a maker is the greatest miracle of life. Saint Augustine, a theologian and philosopher, perhaps stated it best. "Men go abroad to wonder at the height of mountains, at the huge waves of the sea, at the long courses of the rivers, at the vast compass of the ocean, at the circular motions of the stars, and they pass themselves without wondering." Listen, look, feel, taste, smell and wonder at your miraculous existence, but stop to smell the roses and watch the colourful fish.

I realized that something in me...the curious child or simpleton...was a reflection of that very equation and had been most of my life. My sister Marion, who taught school for forty years, embodied this idea in its purest form. It was her that I was thinking of while watching the fish. She would want to take pictures, paint them in acrylics or watercolours, or carve them into wood, thinking of ways to teach patterns or colours or species in groupings of ten...because the world is truly a magical place.

"Hey boat boy, how's the cleaning coming?"

He had caught me mid-polish, mesmerized by the show. This might have been the moment to hurl invectives, paste him with expletives, then tie him to *Doug-the-Dinghy* and set him adrift since I had been publicly branded and vocally demoted to the lowliest common denominator of the sailing trade.

"That's Mr. Boat Boy to you, Captain." I remained hanging over the railing, not wanting to disturb the fish. "These fish are amazing...every colour of the rainbow," thinking to myself that I sounded like someone tripping on vapours.

"That's nothing. Wait 'til we get to Busuanga in the Philippines. We'll throw on the diving gear. The reefs there are spectacular." He described the colourful schools of fish, then moved on to the three-foot fruit bats that hung in the trees and the floating forest of mangrove trees, all whetting my appetite to see Busuanga. "Reminds me I've gotta call Tequila Mike and find out what's happing there in Busuanga. He's my typhoon watch as we head north. A couple of tethered boats sank there last year during one of the storms."

"Really? Sank? Anyone die?"

"Nah, I think it just scared the shit out of them."

"Gee, I can't imagine why," I remarked, priding myself on swallowing a lump of anxiety, putting pressure on a sphincter that did not know whether to tighten or explode.

"The problem is there's no protected harbour with a yacht club. We have to swing."

Swing? *Good God*, I thought, remembering Pulau Tiga. I couldn't imagine trying to swing in a typhoon.

"So, who's this Tequila Mike guy anyway?"

"He's an American that sort of lives at the resort in Busuanga."

"Sort of...he doesn't own it?"

"Don't think so. Christ, he was always too hammered when I met him to run a resort. He has tequila for breakfast, I think."

"Hence the name, I am guessing."

"He knows everyone in this part of the world...sailors, anyway. Cat and I spent quite a while with him the last time we came through. He's quite a character." I was imagining a Humphrey Bogart sort, with an *African Queen* sitting on makeshift lifts that kept him scraping, painting or tinkering with salvaged motors, chain-smoking with an endless glass of booze. "You'll meet him when we get to Busuanga."

As Rob turned to leave, he stopped to look around at the boat, pulling his shades down from the top of his head, giving a hollow whistle. "Wow, this boat hasn't looked like this since it came out of the factory. Good job! This has got to be worth a trip to the Pirate's Den."

We made it to the Pirate's Den. Surprisingly, John came along, and as usual, he kept his thoughts and emotions to himself. We drank enough Foster's beer to become honorary Aussies and toasted to John's bon voyage a few days down the road. He never expressed regrets in his decision to leave.

Over the remaining days, Busuanga, with its promise of fruit bats, magnificent coral reefs and the infamous Tequila Mike, looked to becoming further out of our reach. Typhoons have a way of changing everything.

24

THE BIG FISH STORY
CEREMONIAL WAR BUBBLES AND THE
BRAZILIAN FRUIT BASKET

DAY WHATEVER, MAYBE THE 15TH OF OCT.

It had only been an hour or so since we had parted ways, John carrying his single bag of launder-in-the-sink, non-wrinkle wardrobe, heading for the harbour exit and towards a waiting cab to the airport. The departure had been cordial, man hugs and a back slap, and John was gone.

Rob and I had not talked it over, and now we were slated to depart the marina by noon. We fell into the chores of leaving port and not a moment too soon. The first racing boats from the Borneo International Yachting Challenge that had followed us from Miri and Labuan were starting to make their way into the harbour of Kota Kinabalu.

We motored north out of the channel separating the Moro island village and Kota Kinabalu. A plane announced its departure like a fat, pollinating bee lifting into the midday heat. Standing on the stern of *Bob-the-Boat* looking back towards the harbour, my mind began to digest the events of the past week, hoping to make sense of what happened to our "three men in a tub."

I looked skyward and gave a two-armed wave from the flying bridge. I thought John might be scanning the bay, looking for our boat. It was ridiculous to wave, of course. Harbour patrol might think we were sinking.

I wished we had a banner that read *Goodbye John*. Despite my wavering thoughts to the contrary, I wanted him to know he would be missed, but I knew he was happier on his way home to the familiar. Years of conditioning had made him a slave to routine, something that could be routinely discounted at sea.

In Singapore, he had suggested perhaps we forgo the two squares of the hypotenuse for a straight run to the Philippines across the South China Sea. Deliver the boat and go home. But the squares, Rob explained, east to Borneo and north through the islands and ports of Indonesia, Brunei, Malaysia and the Philippines were all the colours of the rainbow. The hypotenuse was like *National Geographic* in black and white. Rob and I, caught in the preparation to leave the harbour, had both silently reflected on the turn of events, knowing there would be ample time to check the rearview mirror and study reflections in a glass.

While I watched over the controls, Rob had gone about setting up both fishing lines and the flutter board, a daily chore that, to this point in the journey, had produced nothing but empty hooks and fish stories.

"On the journey down," Rob offered, referring to south as down, where up was north and east and west were simply that, "we snagged a marlin."

"What's a marlin?"

"Swordfish...big mothers with sail-like fins. Sometimes they're called sailfish."

"You caught one of those suckers?"

"Hooked one, momentarily... I'm not sure who caught who, but it was pretty exciting." He checked the tension on the lines and let out the flutter board another few feet. "I caught the line with about a hundred feet left before it would have disappeared into the ocean. I knew it was something big because the pole was bent in half. As soon as I grabbed it, I could feel it was no ordinary fish... I thought it was a shark or a dolphin or something. Never even crossed my mind it might be a marlin, but then, all the fish here are pretty big, so there is always some sort of a fight."

I had a photo saved in my e-mail exchanges, downloaded while Rob was still motoring with Cathy. It was the first fish he caught off *Bob-the-Boat*. You could see he was struggling to hold it for the camera. Other than the size, it was notable for its distinctive looks. It had an almost human-like face. This may have been the fish whose ancestors had walked ashore, declared all lands in the name of King Charlie the Tuna, begat an ape line and then returned to the deep.

"The marlin jumped out of the water, and then I knew I was in trouble. It was huge!"

"Okay, here we go...the big fish that got away story," I said, even though I knew Rob was not prone to exaggeration. "What...forty...fifty pounds?" I said, thinking I was pushing the large end of the envelope.

"Maybe his left fin! You don't know jack about marlins, do you? These fish can be huge, like five hundred to a thousand pounds huge."

"No way, you're pulling my leg," I laughed, thinking the salt air was rusting his mechanics.

"I'm not! They don't tend to get as big in Southeast Asia as they do in the Atlantic, possibly because they get over-fished here, but the largest marlin recorded, if it is to be believed, was somewhere around eighteen hundred pounds."

"That's not a marlin; that's a friggin' whale."

"Whales are measured in tons! Anyway, you can see why I wasn't too sad it got away. What the hell was I going to do with five hundred pounds of marlin? And many of them are

otected, so it's not like you can pull into
...our trophy. They are liable to clap you in
...ped you from showing off your trophy in
... no clap."

"...are still talking fish here, aren't we?"

"Of course, what else?"

"Even if I had managed to reel the bugger in, how would I have gotten it on the boat? If I threw it on the stern, I'd've been popping wheelies. I would have been stuck dragging a quarter ton of marlin behind the boat!"

"Aha!"

"What's 'Aha'?"

"I had a flashback to a novel I read years ago, called *The Old Man and the Sea* by Ernest Hemingway. That's exactly what his story was all about."

"Ernest who?"

"Ernest Heming...aw, never mind, he's not important, but the story was about this old fisherman who caught a huge marlin...I knew I heard that name before. The old man was by himself in a small fishing boat and had a hell of a time reeling it in, and when he did, he had to pull it behind the boat. Long story short, he died, and the sharks ate his fish. It's a classic fish whopper!"

"Well, mine's for real and it's not over."

"I thought you said it got away."

"It did, but a short while after it broke free, it popped up right behind the stern, standing on its tail...its whole body out of the water like a trained dolphin, and it started screeching something awful. I had no idea, other than dolphins, that fish could make a sound. It still had some line attached so it must have been royally pissed. I think if I had been on the stern deck, it would have taken a lunge at me with its sword."

"Whoa...Moby Marlin Dick," I said, thinking this fish story was getting away and needed a little reeling in.

"What?"

"Moby Dick! The whale? It takes down the entire sh the end of the book!"

"You read too much."

"Okay, well how about Marlin T. Jaws? You remember in the movie, the shark bites the back end of the boat off, eats the captain just before he gets blown up by an oxygen tank shot with a flare gun or something."

"That's one way to make sushi. I'll have to remember to bring the tanks up out of the hold," he replied.

"Well, how about a marlin that turns the boat into a pin cushion and shish-kebabs the crew?"

"I am going to take a shower." Rob eyed me suspiciously, grabbing his towel and shampoo. He went off to the bow of the boat, stripped down and lathered up.

I let my mind wander toward what surely would be a multi-million-dollar series of thrillers, promising to turn marlin into the new villains of the sea. *Death Sword from the Deep*, *The Revenge of the Mad Marlin*, and *Marlin Does Debbie and Mrs. Jones* (something for the adult crowd), all in 3D, of course, about a pissed-off marlin that stalks its prey, starting with four guys out for a weekend of deep-sea fishing and male bonding. On route there will be a musical duel between a banjo catfish and a harp seal. The marlin, a legend that has drawn the fishermen to sea, picks off his targets one by one as they hang off the stern or take afternoon dips in the sea. The victims are skewered through the heart, like martini olives. Somewhere along the way, a Ned Beatty-type character will squeal like a pig and the theme music will be from *Jaws*, played backwards to disguise the rip-off.

"The shower is all yours." Rob passed me by, giving a short sniff to suggest that the cane toads were not dead yet. He was naked except for a towel wrapped around his head, stacked higher than a fruit basket on a Brazilian nightclub singer.

I strode to the bow, where he had left the hose and shampoo waiting.

If naked dips are refreshing, a shower on the bow of the boat—wind blowing, sunshine catching the sea spray with a 360 panorama of the passing world—is slightly naughtily exhilarating. Because it is necessary to stand spread-eagle to maximize one's holding power on the increasingly soapy deck and the rocking from the waves, the angle of the dangle begins to change with the breeze, held in check by the cool water from the hose. Standing in a Shiva-like pose, soaping appendages, hair filled with suds, eyes closed, might compare favourably with some *Kama Sutra*-like move for the single man. I was in such a state, lathered and billowing with suds, when I thought I heard the faint sound of a whir, confirmed by the bellow of "Fish! Man the controls."

I had been briefed on the imperative of quick action, so there was no time to rinse off...not even to turn off the water hose. The fish line was running out at x number of feet per second, enhanced by a power factor of the forward motion of the boat. I ran in a dangerous slip-slide for the wheelhouse to set the boat in neutral, did a quick slide back to the bow to shut off the water and got a visual on Rob, who had grabbed the rod and stopped the run. I held tight to the railing, soap running into my eyes.

"Grab the gaff," Rob shouted as *Bob-the-Boat* finally stopped. I could see that he was posed with his feet pushing against the rail, pole bent in a struggle with weight. I pushed suds out of my eyes, grabbed the razor-barbed hook from its perch, ran for the stern, opened the gate and stepped out onto the swim platform. It was a vision, I suspect if viewed from afar, of an aboriginal dressed in ceremonial war bubbles with a Brazilian fruit basket manning the rod. I checked for signs of swords or sails or water surging ahead of a half-ton of charging fish, but there was only a taut line dipping and diving, a whirring castor as the line was let out, followed by the ratchet of the line being spooled in. Feet braced, back bent, the rod curled to the water, Rob spooled hard. There was the sighting of a silver streak, pulling hard to port, gone, then a half-reveal as the fish attempted to jump skyward and plunged deep, causing more line to be released, followed by a quick ratchet as the pull softened slightly. Whatever it was, it was larger than the average sunfish I had pulled out of Lake Muskoka.

"Get the gaff ready. It's coming closer," Rob shouted from the above deck.

I stood poised like a tribesman, caught wide-angle, waiting to harpoon a piranha.

"You're not going to club the bugger. Put the gaff in the water. When it gets close, hook him behind the gill." Rob pulled hard, and I could hear the ratcheting of some hard-fought line.

There was another whir and ratchet combination, so I kept my eyes sharp on the travelling line in the water. It moved in a zigzag pattern, a streak visible now and again of something fairly large. And then, there it was, a long, sleek polish of silver and black zebra striping, squirming in its ever-decreasing circle of freedom with Rob ratcheting tighter and tighter. I was slightly in awe, with a twinge of pity and remorse at having caught such a beautiful creature.

"Hook him! Hook him now," Rob yelled, bent like a man pinned in stocks and gasping for air. He knew this was a crucial moment where lines break or snag, and the fish miraculously squirms off the hook. I slid the gaff further into the water and attempted a quick snag. The fish moved. I missed.

Rob howled. "Hook him, for Christ's sake. I can't hold him for much longer."

The next jerk found its mark...the gaff hook sank deep into the gill. Instantly the power and weight were transferred to me, a writhing weight of frantic fish caught in a last-ditch effort to save its life. I lifted with both hands, my back muscles straining like ABS brakes on black ice, left-right-bottom-top until a three-foot silvery something or other was fully revealed and quickly dropped to the floor. The gaff detached itself, leaving the fish to buckle and bend a death dance that lasted for a few minutes. From my limited knowledge of fish, it looked like a twenty-pound sardine.

"Hang tight," Rob said, catching his breath while moving down from the top deck. "I'll get the camera. We need a photo."

"No way in bloody hell you are taking a photo of me like this." I knew he wouldn't hesitate to post it with the caption "*Norm and his Sardine.*"

Rob was anxious to start the sushi/sashimi/ceviche process, so when the camera was set aside, he attacked with a large filleting knife, tossing removed parts overboard. I was silently hoping that this was not the prized son of some larger lethal momma who would stalk us in revenge for the rest of the trip. Over the next two days, this fish story was repeated twice more, suds not included, with all three fish being vastly different in shapes and sizes.

It was day whatever. There was no place we had to be. I think John might have been swayed by this palette of colour. We had the square of a fish tale with steaks on the barbecue, and a gold sequined sea in the afternoon sun.

25

SQUID: THE GOD MATTER OF CREATION
PIRATES IN UNIFORM
THE MR. ZULU SEA

EVENING, THAT SAME DAY

With the sun setting to our backs, we finally entered the Balabac Strait, a body of water that runs east-west at the northernmost tip of Borneo. If you check your atlas, you will find a red line mid-strait denoting the separation of Malaysian Borneo and the Philippines. It is here the waters make a strong current flowing between the Sulu Sea and the South China Sea, a current so strong it was like being caught in a charge of students released for the summer break, preceded, of course, by the stampede of staff. We felt it instantly as we left the protection of the Borneo coastline. It was so strong I thought *Bob-the-Boat* might stall. The engine whined and coughed as we were tossed about, forcing us to hold on tight to railings.

It had been six hours since John had left the boat, but it seemed a lot of water had passed beneath our bridge. The dynamics would be different now with only two of us, but how that would play out had not been verbalized. I think we both felt we had failed John in some way—at least I did, since he had paid my way with travel points, making the trip possible. Rob was not the look-back-with-regrets kind of guy, but I knew he had enjoyed John's company. He didn't share our vintage of sour grapes. In addition, John had a mechanical mind and understood the workings of the boat. As for me, I understood that engine running made the propeller go round and made the boat go forward. In a mechanical breakdown, I would be as useless as that bit on our family bull when I was a kid. It never produced an offspring, so baloney was his end.

Under his father's tutelage, John had rebuilt engines. Both he and Rob had taken shop mechanics at school. John had even challenged Rob on the rpm of the boat for maximum fuel efficiency, a number that Rob had established over two years of use. His encyclopedic mind could always be useful. He understood fuel injection thingies, propeller rotation thrusty stuff, crankshaft what's-its, fuel pump how's-its, coolant flows, pressure flaws, desalination water creation and beyond; current movements, tidal shifts, moon rotations, solar flares, planet orbits, and had a sound theory on the big bang of beginning. I knew for a mechanical fact, however, "The wheels on the bus go round and round, round and round, round and round…"

The coming night would be our first without him, the first where night watch would be double duty. Rob was unfazed since he had done double duty to Thailand. Suck it up, sailor!

I was sure John would have enjoyed catching the fish and sharing the sashimi, conceivably conjuring up a few good recipes. His acumen as a cook was truly going to be missed. He had worked in the galley as if he was born to bake, chopping, mincing and flavouring with the flair of a practiced chef. Our Thanksgiving bird had been a true delight.

To buoy my spirits, catching me biting a nail, Rob informed me that the best of the voyage was yet to come. Busuanga bats were still being held up as a prized reward. Subic and Barretto had great promise. Hong Kong, Beijing and the Great

Wall would be highlights of the three-month trip. These were promises, I think, he wished he had rolled out for John before he abandoned ship.

It was nearing dusk, a time in this part of the world that goes from daylight to total darkness like a midnight cabin when the candle is blown out. On the very edge of this darkness, before our sight was limited to a few feet, we witnessed something that is a common occurrence on seas around the world. A bright light from a ship came on as if a wall switch had been flicked. Then, as if that switch was a catalyst, a precise row of lights appeared in rapid succession, like a highway with streetlights wired in series, slave to an electric eye. It went to and presumably beyond the horizon. I lost count somewhere around thirty. It was, Rob explained, a fleet of squid ships and the lights were bright fluorescent torches designed to bring the squid to the surface. The lights came on in such precision that they could only have been ignited by a single hand via satellite control. We had not spotted these ships on radar, though in truth we had not been looking. Our radar had been set on a short six-mile radius.

The thought occurred to me that these numerous squid boats must be dangerously close to overfishing the species and in all probability still are. We had encountered other squid fleets along the Straits of Malacca, but none so large. Once I was able to research the squid, I understood why fleets were huge.

There are around three hundred species of squid, ranging in size from twenty-plus inches to the giant squid, made famous by Hollywood (of course) in *Twenty Thousand Leagues Under the Sea*. Some come in large packages, however, fifty to sixty feet long, weighing in at over six hundred pounds—almost enough calamari to feed an entire Greek wedding. Some reports have them even larger, but not scientifically proven, though one supposedly left large circular sucker marks on an American naval ship. When they want to mate, look out.

Males in some species have penises about the same length as the overall body, giving them the second-longest penis in the mobile animal kingdom next to sessile barnacles and Harry Rheams. This is a fact I thought one needs to know in case you are wrapped in a battle to the death in squid tentacles and, upon counting, there is one appendage too many. If you win but wake up carrying twenty thousand squid eggs, you lost. They take nine months to hatch. That gestation period alone may make squid the hidden God Matter of man's creation. And those who brag of royalty might want to consider their humble beginnings. Squid, octopi, spiders and all crustaceans—like lobster and horseshoe crabs—have blue blood. Already I can smell a bestseller; *ArachnaRoyalty*, in which an unhappily married prince gets his toe pinched on the beach... okay, essentially *Spider-Man* with crabs...and spends his life lodged up the reproductive channel of a mermaid from where he does good deeds for mankind. Oh, the possibilities.

However, the real story on squid is the fact that most females can lay as many as thirty million eggs in their lifetime. That's a lot of calamari, no matter how you slice it. Hence, the squid fleet twenty miles long.

⚓ ⚓ ⚓

Rob had been in radio contact with our next destination, a marina on Balabac Island, which was to be our first island encounter with the Philippines. There were complications.

Rob, the social being that he is, had recently spoken with someone who had heard something about the fact that Moro guerillas were active in Balabac, supposedly. We were lucky to be so well informed.

The Islamic Moro National Liberation Front was militarily active in the hinterland provinces of the Philippines, trying to remove Catholic Christian power, dictated from far-off Manila. There were stories of murdered nuns, hand grenades tossed into crowds, hostages, ransoms and beheadings, all tragic, but common atrocities to struggles of power. Nothing more needs to be said. Rob and I decided to keep moving and avoid the middleman position of collateral damage. His initial conversation had been with the Philippine Coast Guard, an organization for which he had little trust. There was good reason.

On the trip in reverse to Thailand, he had been stopped at sea by that very same marine constabulary, which had turned into an attempted shakedown. They were looking for smugglers, pirates, gunrunners, marlin poachers...anything, in fact, that would allow them to board the boat. Who could say no? The problem, it seemed, was that some members of the coast guard were not above board.

The vast majority of our fellow Canadians, born and raised in Canada, have probably never been subject to petty graft and bribery, though I may be wrong. The "You need protection" style of organized crime is a player everywhere. But we pay our fines and bills, sometimes standing in lines at official government offices; passports, driver's licenses, road fines, water, heat, electric bills, transfer taxes for homes and automobiles—in fact a whole host of payments we begrudge, but never worry as far as graft is concerned. Not so in some of the darker economies of the world. Cash is expected: the more, the faster you are served. Do you want your mail unopened before it arrives? Do you want it to arrive at all? Do you need a travel visa? Would you like your car back after it was impounded for doing twenty kilometers over? Do you want protection? Do you need a clean bill of health from the doctor? Official documents required, customs? Immigration? Port authority? The universal thumb and finger slide, a nudge, raised eyebrow, documents pushed back and forth, opened and closed, and off you go on your merry way. Thankfully, up to this point in the trip, I had not been part of any of it.

Rob, having been forewarned and thus forearmed, had

stocked up on cartons of cigarettes, bottles of booze and extra food. His encounter had only cost some cigarettes and a case of liquid libation. Others he had heard of were not so lucky, losing all their cash and anything else that could not be traced. Pirates are one thing, but men dressed in the official uniforms of their country, flying their flags, manning their boats, was a whole other ball of wax. Denial would be their first defence, feasibly followed by recriminations. This may not happen, but officials of the Coast Guard Navy, the very few who stoop to piracy, would do anything, I am sure, to save their jobs. A wandering mind could imagine the subtle act of boarding and finding a bag of planted drugs to the not-so-subtle sinking of "An uncooperative ship at sea, suspected of harbouring terrorists." But, again, these may be the meanderings of a spring-fed, overactive mind.

It was for this reason that Rob had shown me his stash of American money, hidden in the cavity of a light. He also pointed out something I had taken for a TV remote. It was a taser gun, totally illegal, of course.

Private boats are not allowed to carry weapons like guns or ground-to-air missiles. If boarded and found, there is the very real threat of heavy fines, confiscations and even craft seizure, depending on the number of weapons. This might allow one to assume that private boaters are sitting ducks for pirates. They are, but the other option, that of carrying weapons, is even worse. What could you possibly arm yourself with to fend off an experienced band of pirates? If you have a revolver, they have a rifle. If you have a machine gun, they have a grenade launcher trained at your head. Sleeping in a vest of explosives controlled by a hand trigger is lethal when you nod off. Larger ships, the kind owned by mega-billionaires, have torpedoes, armed helicopters, amphibious assault boats, missiles, have I forgotten anything...oh, and maybe a small armed camp to deploy them—but regular boaters would have little hope in defending themselves, no matter what they carried. Pictures of large supertankers captured by pirates come to mind, especially the *Maersk Alabama*, the one captained by Captain Phillips and immortalized in celluloid with Tom Hanks. That attack had happened in April 2009, five months before our journey began. Although that act of piracy took place midday, pirates—understandably, for pleasure craft like ours—like to attack when the crew is asleep, swinging in quiet, out-of-the-way waters. They don't announce themselves with the traditional "A-r-r-r-r ye scurvy dogs," flying the skull and crossbones. If they do approach in daylight, they may come pretending to be fishermen, offering to sell you the daily catch and thus getting close enough to board. If they are ten and you are two, and you two are not Schwarzenegger and Stallone, the best rule is to give them what they want. For most pirates, it's money.

In defence of my lack of research towards travelling, I found out—but only after returning home to Canada—that the Straits of Malacca, through which 40% of the world's shipping trade moves, is one of the most pirate-infested waterways in the world. The highest number of recorded attacks came only one year before our travels, and this was after Malaysia, Singapore and Indonesia created a joint navy to deal specifically with piracy in 2004. It isn't working! But why would I need to worry when most recorded assaults were against commercial boats? The word "most," however, is troubling. Ignorance, I guess, is bliss.

There is a difference, however, between pirates and beheading freedom fighters. Pirates want to stay off the radar of attention; guerilla fighters do not. Pirates have no political agenda, considered scumbags by all, while liberationists who wrap themselves in the promises of new democracies, champions of the oppressed, lights at the end of dictatorial tunnels gain more notoriety and authority with every act of terror.

A story close to the heart of Canadians arose in 2016 when John Ridsdel and Robert Hall, both Canadian sailors, were kidnapped by these same Moro freedom fighters extremists from a yacht club on the island of Mindanao. Both were executed after ransom money was not paid. They had been held for several months on the island of Jolo, a short jaunt from where Rob and I entered the Sulu Sea. It was for these reasons that we pressed on past Balabac Island and found refuge, swinging free to all the possibilities that fear could conjure, in a cove a few hours north. We were visited only by the peaceful sounds of fishermen casting nets at the first glimmer of dawn.

⚓ ⚓ ⚓

The Sulu Sea is bordered in the south by Borneo and a loosely scattered horseshoe of Philippine islands—seven thousand, one hundred and seven, to be exact. What defines seas is their size; they are smaller than oceans and hang on their edge like aunties and third cousins to the royal throne. Seas are partially surrounded by land, whereas oceans surround the seven continents. Gulfs are minor seas, and there are seas within seas like peas in a pod. Channels are short straits, and both can connect seas and oceans. If you don't like what you seas, change the channel.

As seas go, the Sulu is small in comparison to the numerous seas for this part of the world, including the Celebes Sea, the Banda Sea, the Java Sea and, of course, the great South China Sea. The Sulu Sea, however, is larger than all the great lakes of North America put together, though it would fit fourteen times into the South China Sea and ten times into the Mediterranean. What's the big deal? The Sulu waters that connect most points of the Philippines have rare fish and fauna. There are nearly twenty-five active volcanoes on the islands that surround it. Anything with smoke in the last few hundred years is considered active. However, the name is the Sulu Sea's real claim to modern fame. Gene Roddenberry, creator of *Star Trek*, wanted a character and a name to represent all of Asia (Hikaru Sulu). He pointed to a map, saw the name, and

Sulu's-your-Uncle, Mr. Hikaru Sulu...Mr. Sulu to you, Lou...was born. Mr. Sulu could easily have been called Mr. Bali, Banda, or Java.

We lifted anchor at six a.m. and chugged north along Mr. Sulu's western leg, a long, bony extremity called the island of Palawan. I wondered as to what we might find at the top of Sulu's leg, but Rob assured me there was nothing more than the hanging fruit bats of Busuanga. Our midday goal was a place called Puerto Princesa, where Rob had made reservations at the Abanico Yacht Club. This was the beginning of my Philippine experience.

26

DWARF TOSSING AND A DEAD GOAT
PHILIPPINE HISTORY
MUD BALLS FROM HEAVEN
GIFTING A DEAD FISH

NOON THE SAME DAY

The Philippines, I was forewarned, existed in a time warp, stalled in poverty with a reputation for Wild West lawlessness. It hasn't helped that nations have fought over and controlled this scattering of islands for hundreds of years—thousands, if you count the ancient tribes that settled the islands, though no one seems to count history before the arrival of the Spanish. It also doesn't help that typhoons rage across its landscape several times a year (sometimes thirty a year develop off its coast), or that there have been several active volcanoes and earthquakes, centuries of plundering both religious and political, years of guerilla warfare, six months of rain, six months of drought, leaving huge portions of the one hundred million Filipinos on the edge of daily survival.

Philippine history, I have discovered, was so fast, furious and violent that it might be compared to an unending seventh game of Stanley Cup hockey, where rules are tossed out the window and officiating is nonexistent. In their game, the rubber puck of theocracy had been slammed into the native nets with nothing more than their life and liberty on the line. Mixed in was the push-and-shove-in-the-mud of a rugby scrum, bone-crunching football tackles, caber-throwing, dwarf-tossing, a demolition derby smash-up, wrestling throw-downs, Afghani polo with a dead goat, rough 'em up, fuck 'em over, fight to the finish, and you might have an inkling of the Philippine historic timeline. Or perhaps that is world history in a nutshell.

Ferdinand Magellan, the first European credited with circumnavigating the world, claimed the Philippines in the name of Spain in 1521. Four hundred and thirty-five years later, they claimed independence. During that time, most of the world fell to brutal colonialism, but in comparison to its Southeast Asian neighbours, Malaysia and Singapore, politically and economically the Philippines might be called a travesty, caught still trying to lace up its skates.

As mentioned, the Philippines has several typhoons a year. Earthquakes, volcanoes and tsunamis plague the islands. And sometimes they all ride in tandem.

When Mt. Pinatubo blew up in 1991, sending ash a hundred thousand feet into the air, it killed eight hundred and left one hundred thousand homeless. This explosion coincided with Typhoon Yunya, which came blasting in from the Pacific. The thick ash that was blown into the stratosphere got caught in the winds and rain of the typhoon. The ash turned into giant mud-balls mixed with volcanic pumice and rained down on parts of the Philippines like meteorites without fire. The mud-balls pummelled villages, flattening cars and homes, shredding forests and stripping foliage until there was nothing left but sticks. This was on top of the meters of ash that had already accumulated. If this wasn't enough, the monsoon rains mixed with the ash sent floods of mud and volcanic rock—called lahars (rivers of debris that flowed extremely fast and were hundreds of feet deep)—that covered whole towns and villages. You know it is a regular and serious problem, like avalanches for snow, when it has a name. North Americans are no strangers to the devastation of hurricanes and tornados. Most of the world has some sort of natural pestilence to deal with in devastation form, but volcanic mud-balls delivered by a typhoon, I think, takes the sodden cake. Most of North America has a network of emergency services to help them flee. There is no place to run in the Philippines and probably never will be. You will see distressing videos of families swept away in floods, mudslides and whatever else nature can toss their way, forever. If the hot spice of politics can't defeat the Filipino people, then let Mother Nature throw in her recipe of blow down the house, lash with rain, cover in mud, dust with ash, shake, bake, boil or fry. And this short dissertation was included simply to let you know what kind of a potential fuster cluck we were heading for.

This same Mother Nature, however, has blessed the Philippines with a natural beauty; azure blues in the sea and sky, lush greens of the tropical vegetation, fish that cover the spectrums of species and colour, and the pearly whites in the smiles of its people, contrasting the warmth of their caramel skin.

Our first encounter with that smile came after we caught fish number three, wondering where to put it. The galley freezer was nearly full.

Bob-the-Boat, under the spell of automatic pilot, had automatically piloted, changing course from north to west, into the harbour mouth for Puerto Princesa, the capital of Palawan and our first stop in the Philippines.

Rob had spotted a small *bangka*. That's Filipino for "outrigger canoe," a traditional Southeast Asian watercraft rigged with a bamboo pontoon that hangs several feet off the gunnels on one side or the other and quite often both. In it was a fisherman, eyes glued to a fishing line that hung from his bare hands. There was no pole. Rob went to the pilot house and steered *Bob* off course, tucking us in close to the fisherman's boat. The fisherman's look could only be described as *"What the fuck...find your own fishing hole."* It is expressed with shrugged shoulders, hands turned up, furrowed eyebrows, wrinkled nose, sucked-in cheeks, and lips miming in the local dialect. Rob hollered a few words that caught me by surprise since I had no idea what he was saying.

"You speak Filipino?"

"Tagalog. It's called Tagalog, and I only speak about enough to get me a beer in the bar," he fibbed, as I found out later that he could order pizza as well. He lifted the fish, turned to the fisherman and held it like a giant submarine sandwich with both hands as if he was ready to take a bite.

"This guy doesn't look like a bartender," I said as the boats edged closer together.

He ignored me, as probably he should have. The fisherman had pulled up his line and was now paddling toward us.

"Directions? Beer? What?" I thought I was witnessing some strange ritual between fishermen.

"No, I want to give him this fish."

My second surprise. Rob was not known to be a philanthropist, even if the gift was a dead fish, recently murdered by yours truly.

"We don't have room for it in the freezer, and this fish could probably feed his family for a whole week."

Rob shouted a few more words. I was happily surprised, suddenly envisioning the Grinch, with Rob's face, carving the Christmas tuna.

It was obvious that Rob's Tagalog was intermittent. There was a lot of repetition, miming of eating the fish, complete with gnashing teeth, pretending to tear it apart and, finally, holding it out in front of him like a biblical figure offering his son for sacrifice. Who would have thought that giving away a fish could be so difficult?

The fisherman had moved beyond his first look to a gentler facial expression of *"What's this asshole idiot up to anyway?"* You know the look...half smile, half frown, eyes dancing about, looking for a quick escape. It's the kind of look you get when you meet the Jehovah's Witnesses at the front door, stark naked. And, of course, who could blame him? If a yacht pulled up beside your dinghy and offered you a dead fish, would you take it? The fisherman, thinking possibly we would steal his bait and have our way with him, looked concerned.

At some point, the fish was accepted, and despite the big smiles, the fisherman did some rapid back-paddling, while *Bob-the-Boat* continued on course for Puerto Princesa Yacht Club, called Abanico. Even with reservations having been booked well in advance, the maneuver of getting to and settling into port took some time.

⚓ ⚓ ⚓

"Hello, Abanico Yacht Club...this is *Bob-the-Boat*. Over."

Silence.

"Hello, Abanico Yacht Club...this is *Bob-the-Boat*...looking for directions to your club. Over."

Silence.

"Hello, Abanico Yacht—"

"Forsh the love of gods, mate, I heard you the firscht friggin' time. Jusch trying to find my... Cissy? C-i-s-s-sssy? You see my fricken glasses? Bloody hell...I left the mic on...sorry about that *B-a-a-w-b-the-Boat*... Just trying to get myself organized here." There was the sound of shuffling papers, clinking glasses, and heavy breath exhaled into the mic.

"S-o-o-o-o-o... Welcome to Puerto Princesa, *Bob-the—* Sorry, Cissy, what was that? Where... On top of my head? Shit...not again...ah...yes, that's better. So...*Bob-the-Boat*...you're fucking early. Over?"

There was banter to and fro, with an introduction from

the other end of the mic, and it was established that he, John, the owner of the Abanico Yacht Club, was waiting for his boat boy to get back from picking up a pack of smokes.

"Shouldn't be too long now," he assured us, then asked us to motor to the west end of the harbour entrance at the dog leg that veers off to the right and wait. "He'll be arriving in a small dinghy, and you need to follow him back here to the moorings since the tide's out and we wouldn't want you pranging up your boat, would we? See you when you get here. Over."

So, we waited.

From the harbour, Puerto Princesa didn't present much of a profile. The shore was a stilted neighbourhood in the fashion of Kota Kinabalu, except here the only visible structure above the shoreline village and palm trees was a pair of church spires, the first Christian church I had seen during the trip.

The bay opened into what appeared to be a small sea like an inflated balloon (we had entered via the balloon nozzle), and it extended deep into the island, with a backdrop of mountains that climbed quickly from the water's edge. Black clouds rained on the foothills to our west, held in place by the moist winds pushing in from the east. Hitting the mountainside, those same winds curled back off the hills, pushing the storm clouds into a heavy semicircle of darkness around the highest peak. This in turn allowed the sun to send fingers of light through the pelting rain.

It reminded me of those paintings on the vaulted ceilings of cathedrals where celestial rings of dark clouds surrounded a host of sun-baked angels in diaphanous robes with naked cherubs and the apostles. They gaze down upon us, the wretched parishioners, while witnessing either the delivery of the Christ child or the ascension of the resurgent via a single shaft of light. If I was witnessing this from the vantage of hell, the view was beautiful.

A ray of sunshine moved across the water, catching the

outline of a large navy vessel for the first time. It was flying the American flag. Security patrol boats skirted the perimeter. Along with the usual appointment of gun turrets, it carried several domed units, which I assumed housed radar. There was also a full complement of satellite dishes and tall radio antennas. If I could guess that this was a "fact-gathering" ship, I guess the enemy, whoever they were, could as well. *Bob-the-Boat* sat far enough away to be on the radar of interest, but an eyeball on the Canadian flag would, one hoped, take us out of the crosshairs of concern.

The sound of a small outboard approaching alerted us to the fact that our boat boy pilot guide was arriving.

Twenty minutes later, with *Bob-the-Boat* hitched to a mooring a hundred meters offshore and *Doug-the-Dinghy* ceremoniously moved mid-deck to the glass calm of the bay, we were ready to move ashore. There would be no electrical hookups or water supply. We would be swinging, but, with the bonus of the mooring chain, we couldn't drift shallow or deep, so there would be no need for the electronic night knockers that drove fear into the hearts of knickerless sleepers like me.

There seemed to be a touch of self-importance in *Doug*'s bobbing and weaving as we tried to board, since it was obvious that, without him, it was a long swim to shore.

27

COCKLEDOODLES IN THE JUNGLE
THE REAL SOUTH SEAS EXPERIENCE
BAKLA, NOT GREEK DESSERT

OCT. 16TH...IF THE 15TH WAS CORRECT

If Kota Kinabalu was the Ying of fine harbour yacht clubbing, Abanico Yacht Club appeared to be the poor cousin Yang. From our approach, the club had the look of a Polynesian palm hut resort, minus the white-sand beaches, swimming pools, white-gloved attendants, fine restaurants, welcome signs or even a place to tether a dinghy. The buildings hung out over the water; the gray weathered poles in the harbour supported honey-lacquered bamboo structures that had settled over time to a comfortable tilt towards the bay. A hand-painted sign read *Abanico Yacht Club* on a salvaged piece of lumber cut into the shape of a small boat and hung in a contrary slant to the railings.

Pushing out from the huts was a twenty-foot wharf, built from used lumber and bamboo poles that served as an "at-sea" entrance to the facilities. The ladder hung straight down from the wharf, and at low tide, several steps needed to be negotiated with both hands to help pull yourself up, much like those New York steel ladder escapes that drop into back alleys, though these steps were fixed and made of wood. The steps were slick with algae and barnacles, a test, I would venture to say, even for a Navy Seal. Disembarking involved tying *Doug* on a long leash to the closest possible pole, pulling ourselves towards the ladder and carefully stepping out to the rungs so as not to push the dinghy away, lest we found ourselves negotiating an expanding gap between gunnel and wharf. *Doug* was left to float about on his leash, looking somewhat the cock-of-the-walk, sharing space with another pair of small boats that had seen better times.

Once on the wharf, I surveyed the surroundings. Looking out to the water I could see a small flock of swallows dancing around a catamaran and a steel-hulled boat styled like a Chinese junk. They both shared the bay with *Bob-the-Boat*, giving *Bob*, at last, the advantage of being best-dressed at the party.

The rainstorms that had pestered the far-off mountains were now pushing back in our direction, and, I assumed, it would be a few short moments before the rain was upon us. Close to the thick vegetation at the water's edge, I watched a pair of young boys, maybe five or six years old, in fits of laughter, splashing about in water up to their waists. There were no attending adults. But it was the sound of birds that caught my attention. They were not, as one might suspect, the chatter of budgies, cockatiels, parrots, or other tropical birds. Somewhere in the thickets of jungle vines, there were thousands of chickens betrayed by the cock-a-doodle-doos of the roosters and the cackle of contented hens. But, for all the sounds of the chicken coops, there were no sounds of their keepers.

John, our host from the earlier call-in show, was found in the office/bar/dining room, sitting at a small table with his packet of Marlboro smokes, one lit in hand while a stub smouldered in an ashtray. It was early afternoon, but a few bottles and a half-full glass of beer sat by an empty trio of coffee cups.

With glasses tucked into his unkempt hair, he was the vision I had conjured, though leaner and taller, of Tequila Mike in Busuanga. Glassy eyes and his rough complexion betrayed the lazy weave of drinks and cigarettes that surrounded him on the table. In an attempt, I think, to make up for the radio call, he was gracious and very thorough in his explanations of fees, rules, times for meals if desired, a Sunday brunch if we would like to attend and directions to the city and bars. His accent was British with a slur of upper crust. Cissy, John's wife, was Filipino, and she threw in corrections occasionally from the kitchen window, but for the most part kept to her business of minding the store along with a pair of young girls, who were now hustling to bring John his lunch and two beers and snacks for Rob and myself. It was obvious from Cissy's attention to everything around her who captained this end of the ship.

My initial assessment of a second-class Polynesian hut melted as I assessed the room. It was, I fancied (never having been there), South Seas homey, with everything made of or trimmed in bamboo and rattan. An antique, six-spoke captain's wheel stood in the centre of the room. Bamboo supports on the conical ceiling that held the high-reaching thatched roof were hung with pieces retrieved from boats over the years; brass horns, bells, whistles, atmospheric gauges and clocks that complimented the array of nautical lamps and lanterns to light the room. The lights were off, since the wicker screens that served as walls were rolled up, letting in the cloud-diffused daylight. There were charts on the walls, with the names and pictures of Southeast Asian fish (three of which I recognized from our fishing excursions), and proudly hanging front and centre on a ceiling beam was a set of jawbones that had belonged to some unlucky shark.

Except for the jawbones, the whole place exuded warmth and years of personality (giving extra merit to the saying "You can't tell a book by its cover") and whether Cissy's or John's, it said, "Finally you've arrived in the real contrivance of the South Seas." Real, of course, as opposed to the make-believe such as that of the Rum Jungle Polynesian bar and restaurant in Kuala Lumpur, where the money traders went to unwind with umbrella drinks at the foot of steel and glass towers. For all the supporting cast of decors, this place felt genuine. It was a place where one could imagine Somerset Maugham sorting notes and two finger-pecking chapters of *The Moon and Sixpence*, which took him in search of the Gauguin experience in the South Pacific or any number of short stories wound around the jungles of Borneo and Malaysia. It was a pinch-me moment, not totally for the ambiance of the present surroundings, but for the connections it stirred through literature and movies in my past; *Robinson Crusoe, Treasure Island*, Michener's tales from the South Pacific and Hawaii, to all the romance and adventure of Hollywood like *Swiss Family Robinson* (my childhood favorite), to *Paradise Lagoon, Lost Lagoon, Blue Lagoon* and all *Lagoons* revisited, which were inspirations of fantasy in the lost-and-found department of deserted islands. We were in the South Pacific in all but the geography of the few thousand miles that divided the two.

I could have stayed here for hours, pondering native adventure, pirates, and buccaneer skullduggery—the kind, again, that came with full brass orchestrations after some Captain Swarthy or his swarthiest first-mate call: "Prepare to make sail, ye scurvy dogs," men scrambling aloft, sails unfurling in pursuit of the skull and crossbones or a big white whale. "A-r-r-r lads, a keg o' rum to the first man to spot the whale," and a "thar she blows," bits of Hollywood lore that I had lapped up as a child. Of course, guys were being roasted on a spit or being fed to the volcano, but for the most part, my South Seas reminiscing had good Hollywood endings. All this in a wandering mind, sparked by rattan chairs, woven palm rugs and bamboo pillars holding up a thatched roof hut.

While Captain Rob chatted with Captain John, discussing

minor things like hidden shoals and the typhoon brewing, I slipped over to the open window blind and took in the view. It was, again, pinch-me beautiful. The rain had now reached us and was creating a soft, pattering hum on the roof. Water fell like a glittering veil from the eaves. The bay was consumed by what appeared to be the same black cloud we had witnessed upon arrival. It had come around for the second or third time. Those same winds from the east continued to push the cloud towards the mountains in the west. The same winds curled back off the mountain, pushing the cloud back to the east. It, we found out, was a daily occurrence of the recycled cloud. In between, rays of light continued to cut slices on the hillside, revealing wisps of clouds tucked into the folds as if the mountain was cooking in steam, waiting for a cherub or two to fall into the pot. It was a storm of warm rains that never seemed to end, but so quiet you barely knew it was happening. I was hooked watching this unfolding nature channel. Faced with that same cloud for six months, however, and I am sure I would fall upon Cato's sword.

Rob questioned Captain John on the status of Palawan nightlife.

"What exactly are you looking for?" he answered, starting with, "There's a quiet American bar..." but Rob must have given a look that prompted "Right then, just ask the trike drivers." That was short for "tricycles," which were poor cousins of tuk-tuks in Thailand. "They know all the bars and can take you where you want." This was after we had signed in, paid up and returned to the boat to change into something bar-worthy; longer shorts, flip-flops to sandals, and something fresh from the rumpled pile of T-shirts.

⚓ ⚓ ⚓

This was to be my introduction to the Philippine bar scene, a perusal primer for Subic, where Rob was an expert. We had not been to any "real" bars on this trip, according to Rob, who, in his mind, had definitions as to what that meant.

"Music, beer and bar girls...that about sums it up," dropped with a hint of playful urgency after weeks on the boat. I hadn't bothered briefing him on John's (the departed one) and my soirée into the Bangkok bar scene. It wouldn't count, technically, I guess, by his definition.

"Although there are a lot of he-she's here in the Philippines that tend to be part of the bar scene; must be something in the water," he added. Maybe I was too quick to judge. "They call them bakla here," he added. The word "transgender" was not part of his vocabulary. I thought it interesting that the name was probably derived from the Greek god Dionysus, known as Bacchus in Roman times, ambiguously depicted as androgynous male, God of Wine, theatre, merry-making, and the ecstasy of making Mary. His procession was normally depicted with women and satyrs with large erections, and he was often cast as the protectorate of those who did not belong to the conventional society. As much as that fit, it has been suggested that "bakla" came from the ancient Philippine alphabet, where *Ba* meant "female" and *La* stood for "male."

"Interesting," I said, thinking "bakla" sounded like a sticky Greek dessert.

"Cat and I caught a cabaret show in Phuket. It was amazing. It was impossible to tell they were guys...well, technically they were both, I guess, so I don't know what you call them."

"I am not sure," I said, "but I think they go by the term 'transgender' now...a part of the LGBT family."

"Yeah? Toasted or plain?"

It was no use adding the "Q" for "Queer" or "Questioning," or the "I" for "Intersex," "H" for "Hijra"—third gender (Indian eunuchs)—or, given a discussion with any of the above, a whole alphabet of variations to the list. I could never quickly configure those initials in proper order myself. It normally came out sounding like a quick lunch.

"They used to be transvestites, I think. I heard my dad call them hermaphrodites or eunuchs once, though his generation also called them fruit cakes and pansies."

"I am not sure that his assessments were technically correct. Many fruit cakes don't have nuts. Hermaphrodites tend to have both genitalia for reproduction from birth, but eunuchs have none due to a large dull axe. They might fall under a bunch of categories like homosexual, bisexual, pansexual, asexu—"

"Hold the lettuce and mayo, professor! There just seem to be a lot of them."

"Hey, you brought it up."

We were talking as we walked. Cissy had shown us the exit gate that led from the club to the street.

"If you walk up to the main road, flag down a trike. When you are coming home, tell them you're at the yacht club. They all know where it is," Cissy had said, telling us to ring the bell when we returned, then, with a resonating click of hardware, locked us out.

28

THE CIA AND SALT PETRE
THE PYGMALION SURPRISE
THE MAMA-SAN SURPRISE
ICK-SNAY HOME-SAY

LATER THAT EVENING

We left our delivery to a local bar in the hands of our trike driver, ambushed from out of the dark. He nearly drove off the road. Since we had no names or locations to give him, Rob only insisted that it have "girls," throwing in some animation for "large zuzus," which made the young driver laugh.

"I take you, nice place...no locals," he said.

Rob explained that "We" did not frequent the same bars as the local men. The locals, he said, resented "Us," because "We" had money and could afford to buy the ladies' drinks, the ping-pong balls, and all the bar fines that to "Us" was pocket change, relative to the meagre pesos earned by "Them," the locals. He had also been told by Kim that the girls preferred "Us," not only because "We" had money, but because, as a general rule, "We" were kinder.

"Lots of girls are driven to work in the bars because of the violence that goes on at home," Rob added over the wheezing cough of the two-stroke cycle coping with the stress of weight. There was a trail of blue smoke that followed us and every vehicle that passed left a hover of fumes in the air. It was ironic, I thought, since a large sign on the dash advised us that *The Office of The City Mayor of Puerto Princesa, through Ordinance No. 278, prohibited smoking in these vehicles.* Before we were dropped at our destination, I had inhaled half a carton of Diesel Fume Lights, non-filtered. Rob gave up a small, hacked cough before continuing.

"There are even wives in the bar, encouraged to make money by their husbands." His brows lifted slightly as if to say even he was surprised.

"Everything but the bar fine, I presume," I said, remembering Rob's explanation about paying a fine to the bars for taking the girls home.

"You presume wrong, as usual. As you might recall from our conversation a while back, the most money to be made is in the bar fine."

As the driver skirted another pothole, I could feel the hair rising on my neck. Husbands pushing wives into the arms of strangers. Shit! I simply wanted to have a beer in the bar…no politics of the hanky-panky. What the hell are "We" getting into? How far does this rabbit hole go? Or perhaps I was so naive about the world of bar joints and how they worked that these indignities I sensed, like the Bangkok sex shows, were the common rules of play. On the other hand, as far as I was concerned, the girls could work their patrons in the quiet of the dark corners of the bar. It would have nothing to do with me.

"You've gotta be kidding me," I mumbled when our driver stopped and notified us that we had arrived. A cement block building, slung low like a Western saloon, stood in a clearing of vegetation, and, if not for the yellow glow of light coming from a pair of whitewashed windows, might have appeared abandoned. Peeled paint disfigured a mural of a tipping martini beneath a sign flashing *BAR*. The logo of a girl was bent back, breasts pushed high in a Marilyn Monroe pose, with a G-string alternating between half-lit and off. The entrance faced towards the side street, an unpaved, drive-at-your-own-risk pox of potholes. The street continued down a hill, where I could see the outlines of other buildings, but no lights denoting active life. There was life, I guessed, but no electricity. A second building, sitting in the shadows of the first, was flashing a lethargic *BAR* light that, after three flashes, slowly illuminated one letter at a time, to, I suspect, create suspense.

We entered the first. There were no greeters at the front door. Except for the sound of Lady Gaga pumping loudly from a speaker somewhere and rotating shafts of sparkle from a disco ball filtering through a bead curtain, there seemed to be no sign of bar life period. We thought to leave and make our way next door when a hand parted the beads, swishing them aside where they were left to hang over the arm like a waiter's napkin. The second arm made a large sweeping motion, inviting us through in tandem with a booming voice, bidding us welcome.

"Hello, my name is Wendy. I am Mama-san here. Please come in," she said, jerking her head, bowing slightly in a humble invitation, towards the inside for quick instructions on where to proceed. We stepped through the beaded wall of in and out and I heard them clatter as they were dropped behind us without ceremony like the clanking of iron and keys rattling the sounds of committed.

We followed Wendy, who from the back resembled a stocky schoolmarm. Her black hair was pulled back into a severe bun over wide shoulders and hips filling a white waitress blouse, legs covered to the knees by a pleated blue plaid skirt and white knee socks pulled high from practical black pumps, suggesting girls' field hockey, perhaps, or coach of the wrestling team.

"Have a seat here," she commanded, pointing to a sparse cafeteria-style table with four chairs, which we accepted without hesitation, fearing a command to get down and do twenty.

The room was a naked mausoleum of cement block walls. The floor was polished concrete, and the ceiling, held by rusty iron trusses, broke up the monotone of gray decor. It evoked thoughts of a creek without water in a canoe without paddles. Tables lined the outside walls, leaving the center of the room for dancing. One wall had a hand-painted sign listing drinks signed with capital Ps for Pesos: two horizontal lines through the pregnant head. It came into view now and again with reflections from the disco ball. This, and a long, gray counter across the back, mostly hidden in shadows, which may have been the bar, was the total interior décor.

Strip joints back home—or the few that I have seen—were usually near-naked adventures with thongs revealing cheeks, tassels and nipples among tables of boisterous patrons, stages with poles, shower cabinets for lesbian slip-and-slides, clinking glasses, frantic bartenders, and whiskey baritones on mics asking for a round of applause. This joint had been stripped of it all.

When my eyes adjusted to the room, I realized we were not alone; a table, two tables over, was occupied by three men with a pair standing who wandered in and out of the disco-ball sparkle. They were a group, it seemed, as they bantered and swaggered back and forth into each other's space, young (early thirties would be a stretch), clean-cut, tall, fit Americans, overdressed in fashionably casual cords and open-neck shirts, almost campus prep, Harvard or Yale. Besides Mama-san and us, they were the only other occupants in the bar. They seemed to eye us suspiciously, giving us the once-over CIA; curt smiles quickly set to serious tones, acknowledging our presence without the courtesy of a "Hello" or even a "How's it hangin'," almost in a state of training. *WHO is in the room? At WHAT positions? And, in case of terrorist activity, WHEN these two idiots may need to be dispatched with "extreme prejudice," WHERE are the exits?* However, they could have been best buddies out for a good time bachelor stag, which wasn't happening.

"Beer, please, San Miguel, if you have it," was Rob's reply to what we would like to drink, and I followed suit, giving Wendy a two-finger signal to make it double. One is never enough. As if reading my mind, Rob verbalized the fact that he thought the place sucked the big one, whispered in case the CIA was in league with the coach. "This is crap...even for the Philippines." It was thrown out in defence and meant to comfort me; he had praised Philippine bars since the trip began.

"We're early," I said. "Maybe things will pick up later." We chatted over a boom box of sound in a series of grunts to acknowledge that the other was speaking, but the conversation had no direction or current. We could do this, not needing to fill silent moments between us. As best friends, we could not talk for years. Men are funny that way, I guess. I had been with my wife for nearly forty years, and there were always things to be said...and heard! But Rob never asked if I liked his hair up or down, or if his new shorts made him look fat, so we could sit in silence at times, simply sniffing the air.

"You like girlies?" Coach Wendy threw out the question in a matter-of-fact tone as if she was offering a side order of nuts to go with the platter of beers she delivered, thrust onto the table in a referee-style smack on the mats, declaring a winner. A weighted response should have been calculated, something to the effect of "Women...we like women," or "What exactly do you mean by girlies?" in the hope that she wasn't talking about children, or that if our response was "no," meaning that we didn't like children, she wouldn't automatically peg us to be playing for the home team...not that there is anything wrong with playing for the home team.

"Good... Okay, I get some." She disappeared as if heading out to change the side order from nuts to a platter of hot girlies. I silently wondered if they, "the girlies," were kept neatly pressed and hung in the closet. It was all so matter-of-fact.

No Bangkok menus? No warm-up acts of Great Danes and Chihuahuas? Where were the perfumed boas, stilettos and series of warm-up acts to create the mood?

It occurred to me that these men who had gathered in this forsaken hole before our appearance had no girlies attending either, and if rambling about in such a place was their idea of a little R and R, then the spy ship must be a vessel straight from hell. Unlike the tankers and container ships where I had seen men top deck stripped to shorts in a full court press of basketball or soccer, jogging or merely hanging with a buddy for a smoke (the waiting games of off-loading or picking up merchandise in industrial ports), the Navy vessel we had seen upon arrival had been a cold gray void of humanity. Even the security boats that had hovered a measured distance from the mother ship were absent of visible crews. I guessed this was a response to successful suicide attempts on American Navy ships, which feasibly explained these guarded revellers who were constantly aware of the possibilities of letting down their hair. There was no life like it.

With my mind wandering elsewhere, I missed the girlies' entrance and the lining up at our table; four turned to the left and three to the right with Wendy standing in the middle. I felt a rush of panic. Rob had warned me, preparing me in advance possibly for a future meeting with Kim, that Filipino girls all looked young due to their tiny physiques of short and thin, even those who were married and had children. It didn't matter that they were "all of a certified age," "government-sanctioned," "city hall approved," "publicly inspected" and "medically certified," like a sign hanging in a pet shop window. What I saw were tittering young teenagers (though supposedly all in their twenties)—bashful, nervous smiles, fidgety hands and darting eyes, betraying the fear of what I guessed would be their daily state of mind. These girls were my daughter, her young university friends, the girl next door, groups of unnamed chatter and laughter passing on the sidewalk, best friends in lineups to bars, sequined assemblies of gaiety flush with their first drinks, taking a group walk to the ladies' room. But, if I naively saw young girls, they were not wrong in seeing old men, a pair conceivably sexy to cougars, but to girls in their twenties, where mid-thirties is pushing envelopes of age, we would have appeared as ancient.

If I had notions of entertainment, stirred by desires in needs unmet, it was deflated with my first glance of the girls.

"You like?" Wendy asked with hesitation, suggesting she had caught my look of anxious disapproval. Even Rob sported a frown, though he had managed to maintain the smile. Again, this should have called for a thoughtful, combined, weighted answer, though I realized as the hole was getting deeper with quicksand sucking me in that only a yes would suffice. Anything less would be an insult. The girls were pretty; even a "Yes, but" would diminish the girl's esteem. Each would take personally what to me was an obvious truth, that yes, but they were all much too young for us. But then who goes to a "girlie" show and gives a damn about what they think or how they feel?

This had been my problem from the first strip club I entered…some Puritan seed preaching about the temptations of the flesh sparking doubt from somewhere in a lost corridor of the brain. The problem was it was a near-endless corridor that involved most of the brain. I knew it stemmed from the fact I had never had a one-night stand with a paid stranger and the mind was invoking fear of the unknown. It didn't involve questions of cheating. My wife and I had agreed that there was no ownership in our marriage. If things happened… something of releasing a hound or fox and if it returns, it was yours, but without a deer or hen…shoot it. No wait, that's wrong…the gist, however, was no cages. The freedom has kept us together; best friends, confidantes and soul mates, loves of our lives for life.

No matter what my judgement was to be in this situation, if Bangkok was an indication, we might expect an assault of wet tongues anyway.

The young men from the ship would have been the three-bear perfection. A glance, however, revealed the group to be without interest. Perhaps it was true what my father had told me years ago, that the army laced the food of its troops with saltpetre to decrease sexual appetite (also widely used to promote rot in tree stumps)—that, or all the microwave dishes on the boat had zapped their gonads and shrivelled their "drive" to "park."

And what exactly would "yes" mean? I had no intention of bar-fining these girls. It was unthinkable. It was one thing to stand on tsunami beach in Phuket, determined to experience as much earthly infinity as finite longevity would allow, to end the moralizing judgement, to taste the unknown, but this felt wrong, no matter how it was parsed. They were not children, as my daughter was not a child, though always a child to me. Children or not, somehow, I began to feel I would be safer at sea with a ten-meter sneaker wave moments off the bow.

"Yes," Rob offered to Wendy's "Do you like?" My telepathy of concern had never reached the tip of my tongue.

"They are all so pretty and cute, like my young daughter at home, with my wife," I quickly added, feeling events moving faster than my mind could absorb, hoping they caught my drift. It was an assumption that they understood the morality implied, that I was married and off-limits, but it seemed to float on another current. And of course, why wouldn't it? I was on their turf, like Patpong Bangkok or the canal district of Amsterdam or Vegas, which in their mind meant only one thing...business. We were looking for entertainment. They were open for business. Leave your baggage at the door.

The girls blushed with appreciation, shy laughter hidden behind excited hands, clutching arms and twisting hair like schoolgirls. Wendy joined in and raised her arms, stretching to embrace as many girls in her reach as she could, like a mother hen gathering her chicks to the nest. I could see there was genuine affection, with each girl vying to attract Wendy's proud smile for having passed the test of approval. My words had not been interpreted as a red-flag warning by the group to back off, this man's got a headache...not tonight, honey! Instead, they may have viewed me as a fish out of water; hook him with the gaff and get a skillet.

"Okay, you choose now...one each. More if you like!" Wendy drew her arms out with magician-style theatrics, as if on the drop of a wand there may be darts fired or a room full of birds.

"Excuse me?" My voice was a little stretched, bordering on falsetto panic as I searched for high ground; quicksand filling my shorts. I stared at Rob with that look. Panic!

"You choose one! They all pretty. You choose one for take home, yes?" Wendy's smile stretched to reveal a full set of smoky teeth. The girls giggled in unison.

"Ex-cu-u-u-s-e me," upping the panic in my voice to a scratchy hip-hop needle pulled heavily in reverse across vinyl.

"Relax, Norm. Don't get your knickers in a knot."

"Too late, they're full of sand."

"They're what?"

"Never mind! Ick-snay, girly home-say," I said, slowly shaking my head to clarify my point.

"No problem," Rob assured me. "We'll just choose a couple of girls and buy them a drink." I was about to open my mouth in protest, but Rob had already turned to the lineup. Perhaps he was right. I needed to relax. *What's the harm?* I thought. I was an adult with the power to take control, to say no to whatever part of the process I didn't like. Mature adults, my wife had said.

"Okay," I said, intending, perhaps, to let chips fall where they may. "But I decide when to cash out."

Rob had started a chat with the girls, conversing in Filipino, which I assumed was slightly off-colour, judging by the way the girls giggled and covered their faces. Wendy had them turn around, which they did, with shy reluctance.

There was no seductive batting of big eyelashes, playful pouting of swallow-you-whole lips, or breasts pressed forward and shaken with pasties spinning. They sported none of the "experienced skank" factors that allowed men to forget their mothers or Aunt Erma with her holy book or the baby sisters they swore to protect to the ends of the earth while Dad was receiving the last rites. Nor could I imagine fantasies of being whipped, paddled, tied or, God forbid, having sex in positions that defied the antics of the Cirque du Soleil.

It's not that these were my usual fantasies. I don't have usual fantasies. This is not to say I have unusual fantasies...I mean, I don't usually have unusual fantasies at all. Occasionally my brain feeds me vicarious acts that only after the fact I recognize as my own, arriving in fading sepia, and the film breaks or fades to black before the monster is slain. Let's say I was suggesting that these might be the fantasies of frequent flyers to such establishments.

"And you?" It was Wendy addressing me.

It seemed that Rob had chosen. A girl stepped forward and began massaging his shoulders. He may have asked how old she was since she made a point of flipping her name tag to show her age.

"I can't decide," I said. "You are all so...so—" I wanted to say *young, childlike, babies...* "Pretty! You are all so pretty...too pretty to choose between." I averted my gaze to look at Rob, hoping he would understand my saucer eyes. He wasn't good at interpreting saucers.

"The one on the far left. Geena, is it? Forgive my friend here. He is very shy." Rob laughed. The girls laughed along. Geena stepped out of line. Wendy clapped her hands and held them clasped at her breast as if someone had announced a long-overdue engagement.

"Okay, you buy girls drink," Wendy bellowed like a proud mother-in-law-to-be.

"Whatever they want," Rob replied.

I thought milk and cookies. The girls tittered. Wendy addressed them in Filipino. They nodded with two fingers raised, as I had done for double beers. Wendy sent a girl to the bar. I raised my hand with four fingers and shouted "Beer." A second girl rushed off to the bar. The log jam had been moved. The remaining girls left. Wendy hugged the chosen and ushered each of them towards us, a ritual I had witnessed by a mother whose new bride was heading off to the marriage bed. The chips were falling.

Rob was on the receiving end of a head massage. Geena, my chosen bar girl, took up a chair beside me, attempting to make small talk.

"Where from you come?" she asked shyly, shrugging her shoulders with a smile. She leaned forward and laid a tentative hand on my knee. The palm was moist.

"Toronto," I said. She gave me a blank stare. "In Canada." The eyebrows furrowed. "We are close to the United States... near New York City."

"O-h-h ho, you come from New York City." Her voice rose and there was a new flux of excitement in her eyes, as if a celebrity had been dropped in her lap. Rob eyed me with the *"What kind of crap are you feeding her?"* look. She immediately softened her approach, dropping her other hand onto my thigh, clutching my leg as if she had got a hold of the last Ferragamo handbag in a blowout sale.

"No, but very close," I said, holding my fingers up in a pinch motion, knowing that on my globe back home, the two cities were merely a thumb's width apart.

"New York City...I like New York City." Her voice climbed. "I want to go someday. Big city...no?"

"Very big," I edged in, wondering if I should try to explain about Toronto and Canada, the two different countries, or that actually I had never been to New York.

"Big building...lots of people...lots of money. I like to go someday?" The last statement was pulled into a question. She was asking me.

I smiled to myself, realizing the American dream was alive and well, bigger than ever, images of hedonist success a minute-by-minute tweet around the world. There was no use trying to explain that not all Americans were wealthy, that there were lots of poor people and lots of problems, since she had moments before stood in a lineup of seven girls to be picked over like vegetables in the morning market. The ladies' drinks might be all the money she would make over the three dollars a day she was paid if, indeed, she was paid at all. Her only hope and fear was to screw this old man (the thought of which probably reviled her) to earn more than she made in a week. *Don't talk to her about poverty and hard times!*

Many of these girls were sent, sold or pushed by their parents, Rob had said, and, unbelievably, husbands as well. Often, they were the only providers to the family. Why would I dash her hopes about going to America? Hope, I would think, was all they had. In all probability, it was like hanging onto a life preserver in that swirling mass of refuse in the Pacific that became larger and denser every day with the cast-offs of junk—an analogy, perhaps, that only someone caught in a massive grid of poverty could relate to.

"You have good president too...Obama...I like Obama."

The *Audacity of Hope* had reached the psyche of the poor around the world. I didn't bother trying to correct her geography, history or politics. I liked him too, and, like many Canadians, lamented the sorry state of Canadian politics with the auditor-approved balanced ledgers swimming in the inky void of inspiration or vision. It worked, I guess, but I sought the dream that Obama had brought to America. I was impressed that Geena had mentioned his name, raising herself, in my estimation, above the status quo of bar girl workers.

"He very sexy. I like very sexy," she said, sliding a hand into my shorts, short of its intended destination or, more likely, the intended destination far short of the hand. She had very small hands. Whoa...then again, perhaps not. I quickly moved my hand to hers and pushed back into my chair. There was more experienced girlie here than met the eye.

"Naughty, naughty," I laughed, lifting the hand with a playful smack, but I continued to hold it to avoid embarrassment...for her. She giggled, but like clockwork, the second hand moved into action.

Thankfully a tray of beer was dropped on the table along with a second tray of four martinis. Martinis? Whoa again...I had envisioned Shirley Temples for the ladies' drinks. My brain reserved martinis for elegant uptown hairdos on *Sex in the City* cougar adults. Then again, I realized it was an image that was all about New York.

The arrival of the drinks had both ladies excited. Their hands went for the glasses, and Rob and I reached for the brews. I could relax for a while...saved momentarily by the beer.

Sipping their drinks, the girls aged immensely—early twenties maybe? Geena drew a packet of cigarettes from a hand clutch, offering one to me before taking one herself. I took it. It's not my habit unless I am drinking in bars; something to do with the hands, a trick, possibly, I could teach Geena. She snapped a lighter, lighting us both, then took a long, luxurious drag on her slim menthol ladies, holding the on-screen moment, before tilting her head back to blow Lauren Bacall smoke from pursed lips, surveying the ceiling. In a soft, elegant movement, she reached again for her martini, hooking two fingers around the stem, allowing the glass to rest in her palm, cigarette clamped between fingers with manicured nails, and held them with perfect, practised form, suggesting, perhaps, she had nursed in this manner. I inhaled and stifled a cough.

When she caught me staring, she shyly shrugged and giggled and pulled a wayward strand of hair behind her ear, exposing a long, slender neck. It was then I realized she wasn't pretty. She was beautiful. She had a delicate perfection, an

Audrey Hepburn elegance, especially when she smiled. I hadn't taken the time to survey the girls, branding them all in one negative sweep. As a race, these girls were exquisite. Suddenly I saw the huge attraction some men had to the women of the Far East. I had never paid attention. I had left my lusting mind for those out of reach like Monroe and Audrey Hepburn or, more recently, the girl next door in Meg Ryan. Hepburn, however, could still make me wanton in a biblical way.

Hepburn had been about the age of these girls, all of twenty-four, when she shone hugely desirable from the big screen, already a seasoned actress by the time she bedazzled the world in *Roman Holiday*. The world had loved her; couldn't get enough. She had been the idle of every aspiring actress, the lust of every desiring male.

My mind shifted and I realized that there wasn't much—if any—difference at all in the age of these girls and their relative position of interest to me and that of a whole legitimate industry of movie fantasy or Hugh Hefner titillations wrapped in multi-billion dollar gloss or centuries of odes to beautiful young women taught as great literature. Hefner bedded and married them three-quarters his age. A former Prime Minister of Canada at fifty had married a young bride of twenty-one. Sultans had filled their harems with the voluptuous peaches of youth for centuries. Was it wrong or was it human nature to crave the beauty of youth? Could I justify my rising interest with my views on women? I wasn't against sex, in or out of marriage, paid for or given freely. It was sexual violence that was disturbing, and rape was not sex. It was violence in the same way as shooting semi-automatic rifles was not hunting. It was power taken violently. My mind knew how to put the damper on a good time.

Geena, I was betting, would never be discovered. Not by those who counted, anyway. I imagined her hair pulled up, dressed in Dior, a diamond tiara in her silky black hair. It wouldn't take much, I felt, to turn this Pygmalion beauty into a queen.

As I gulped beer, she gently leaned forward and whispered, "You like I suck your cock?"

I snorted beer from my nostrils, causing my eyes to tear up. Well, Enry Iggins, you just might 'afta wait!

Wendy was at the table in a flash, having noticed perhaps the long mucous tendrils hanging from my nose or the subsequent drying of my face with my shirt. There were no napkins. I had no sleeves.

"Washroom? Where is the washroom?"

Geena was too horrified by the splatter of beer and mucus on her knee to answer. Wendy started to give me instructions but then motioned for me to follow her. I left Geena focused on her knee, tears welling in her eyes.

"I am so sorry," I began, but Wendy had strolled off with a mission. I followed as she disappeared around the corner, somewhere into the shadows.

She was waiting behind the wall that housed the bar to the big room, hands lifted in a kind of *"Welcome to the shitter,"* similar to the welcome we had received to the bar...a little less pomp; a little less maître d' ceremony, though it would take an expert to tell the difference. She again used a shift of the head to indicate the washroom. There were no doors with *Herr* or *Damen*, *Signor*, *Signoras*, or the little boys peeing in a pot. When my eyes adapted to the dim lighting, I saw a long trough on a perpendicular wall. I looked at Wendy, using my best Marcel Marceau grimace. Her hands shifted in *voila* unison, pointing to the trough. She smiled as if proudly unveiling a modern French pissoir. I wanted to wash my hands before the mucous fingers found my fly. She pointed to a sink at the end of the trough then stepped back into the shadows. A hot water tap was sitting in parts, handles and nuts side by side. Cold water trickled from a corroded spout where I rinsed my hands, and with no paper to dry myself, I wiped my hands on my shorts in desperation. The beer was working. My head was spinning, and I had to pee.

I tried pulling down my zipper until I remembered I didn't have one. In a stall, of course, I would have dropped my shorts, but this arrangement was open for all to see. There was no way I was going to stand bare-assed at the trough, so I pulled up the loose leg of my shorts and waited. It took a while to begin streaming. Feet were approaching so I kept my head down in concentration to avoid a conversation. The newcomer was sounding like a mountain waterfall, so I glanced over at the shoes. White socks stood out from black pumps and bare legs. I glanced up. It was Wendy, but it didn't register immediately that Mama-san Wendy was standing beside me, skirt hiked up to her waist. I was feeling the beer. When it finally clicked, another wave of mucous headed for the nostrils. It wasn't simply the fact that she—he, Mama-san—was hung like a man (was a man?)...but that Mama-san was hung like that horse that made sailors cry, and that if one believed in such things as God and his/her omniscient powers, that it was bloody unfair. I think I wet my foot as I sidestepped in disbelief.

I'm a big boy; I won't cry. Grown adults for Christ's sake! Let chips fall where they may. Infinity, ad-infinitum! Blah-blah-blah. The yin-yang colluded with a pageantry of mocking reminders, screened through a tired haze of beer.

"You bar fine Geena? She nice girl. You bar fine tonight," Wendy said, giving herself three shakes and dropping her skirt. He? She? They strolled out of the room, not waiting for an answer like any kilted man who has hiked up his skirt to take a leak. What the hell...a real-life Mrs. Doubtfire! That had been funny at the movies. Here, I wasn't at all sure.

Back at the table, Rob was preoccupied, his girl Colleen having moved to his lap. There was shy tittering followed by whispers to the ear. Geena was on her second martini and smiled when I returned. I apologized again. I didn't sit down but stood holding the back of my chair in hopes that the wet stain on my shorts was hidden.

"You piss yourself?" Rob missed nothing.

"Ick-snay girlie home-say," I said again. Without turning my head, I rolled my eyes three times towards Wendy, who now stood a few feet back from the table, flashing my brows like wig-wag warnings for an oncoming train. "Ick-snay! Ick-snay!" Rob was laughing, barely listening, trying to battle off hands that threatened his belt, zipper, and manhood.

"Ick-snay girlie-say! Possibl-ay big dick-snay!"

Rob had no idea. We had never spoken in Latin or pig.

It had occurred to me earlier, in a desperate act of thought (before my trip to the washroom), that if I needed to extricate myself with dignity, I could bar fine Wendy, negating the thought and/or seeming act of pedophilia, real or imagined. Now, I only wanted to cash in the chips and make tracks for home.

"Rob, I'm going to be sick," I half lied, feigning dry heaves. Geena immediately sprang from her chair, feeling possibly she had suffered enough indignity for one evening. "I think I have the shits as well," I added—a very real possibility for my sensitive stomach. I had been battling loose bowel syndrome for most of the trip. I hadn't seen a toilet in the back anywhere, and my shock had, luckily, tightened the sphincter. I thought it was wise to take advantage of the moment.

"God, you're a mess," he said, trying to rise from the chair while pulling a hand out of the leg of his shorts. He looked at Wendy and called for the bill. She was not happy. The coach was not used to ceding the game.

"You bar fine girls. They nice girls. You have good time. Take home tonight," Wendy pleaded. There was desperation mixed with anger. I stood ready to fend off a Full Nelson. At stake here was enough money to possibly feed two families for a week...or more. Wendy stood to take a sizeable share as well.

"Tomorrow, Wendy," I lied. "I feel sick," I continued with less dishonesty. My insides were beginning to grumble.

"No problem...you go outside. Toss cookies. Come back... You bar fine Geena. She nice girl. Make you very happy." Wendy had Geena turn around. She pulled up her skirt and pinched both of her cheeks. I felt terrible. Was that a burble in the bowel?

"Tomorrow," I repeated. "We come back tomorrow," I lied, knowing I had no intention of setting foot here again.

Both girls were now standing by Wendy's side with long faces. Colleen managed to squeeze a tear. Geena looked relieved. Wendy cradled them both with her arms and spoke softly in Filipino. I could only imagine what was being said... *"The old man has dick like choirboy."* She used the index-thumb measurement denoting *tiny*. *"Maybe they gay...better you stay with Mama-san."* The girls seemed convinced and settled. Wendy did not.

"You say you like girlies. I go get. I ask if you like. You say yes. Now you don't want. They good girls...nice girls. Make you very happy." Wendy threw her arms upward, palms spread in the universal sign of *"you-dumb-dickless-motherless-swine-can't-get-it-up-fuck-off-now-before-I-pin-you-to-the-mat-scumbag."* So much for lying to protect feelings...all we had done was foster expectations and then poisoned the well of hope. *What a pair of shits!* Even my yin-yang were revolted.

Rob pulled some large peso notes from his pocket and dropped them on the table. There was something about the Philippines that turned this man into Mother Teresa. I patted my pockets, looking for more. They were empty. Rob still carried all the cash. I now looked like a *CHEAP*, dickless, motherless swine, to boot.

"That should cover all the drinks and leave extra for the girls," Rob explained for all to hear.

"What about poor Mama-san?" Wendy pouted. "Mama-san work hard all night. Bring you nice girlies...bring you beer...work hard. You no like Mama-san? Mama-san have to eat too."

Rob rolled his eyes and pushed a couple of hundred-peso bills into my hands. It amounted to less than five dollars. I folded them and walked over to Wendy, stuffing pesos mid-cleavage while giving her a hug. There were real breasts in there. This was no Mrs. Doubtfire.

Wendy beamed from ear to ear. "You best guys ever. Let me call you ride."

The girls seemed wildly relieved.

29

BALLERINAS ON THE BAY
MAGIC IN THE WATER
HITCHCOCK REVISITED
PUERTO PRINCESA

AFTER MIDNIGHT, OCT. 17

"Norm...wake up!" Rob was tugging at my arm. I opened my eyes into a blackness that didn't suggest I was awake.

"It can't be morning yet."

"It's not. You fell asleep on the deck. You need to go to bed."

The air was a warm quilt of soft wind and humidity. I could feel the hair on my body moving with the breezes. The boomerang cloud had shifted elsewhere for the time being.

I sat up, trying to remember how I came to be there. A loud splash from a fish jumping by the boat caused me to turn my head quickly, and instantly I had the urge to puke. The whirlies...again. The reason I had laid down on the deck in the first place.

Had the whole night been a dream? With the spin cycle returning, I guessed it wasn't. The beer. The girls. Christ, Mama-san. Wendy was a Wendell. Good God! Rob had been less than sympathetic to my bolt-and-run. He had laughed so hard on the way home that he had to get the trike driver to pull over to avert wetting his pants. The driver had nearly swerved out of control when Rob repeated the story. It would probably be tweeted old-fashioned style around the island. Gossip at trike dispatch!

We had practically fallen through the gate on our return to the yacht club, pulling the rope attached to a bell somewhere distant with too much vigour. The young girl that Cissy had left to deal with gate service was not amused. She didn't acknowledge our drunken "Good evening" or drunken "Good night." The gate opened, we entered, it closed, and she was gone, leaving us to stumble through the darkened premises out to the wharf. There wasn't a light to be found anywhere.

We were poster idiots for potential disaster: two drunken sailors hoping to negotiate the return to ship past curfew, unable to distinguish our butts from a porthole window. That we made it back to the boat was due only to Rob's built-in radar.

The harbor had a full ballet of misting dancers rising off the water. It was, I thought, the most magical thing I had ever seen. Once in *Doug-the-Dinghy*, Rob handed me a lamp pulled from his supplies. In a bigger boat, higher up from the water, it would not have been a problem, but in *Doug*, where the flashlight turned everything into a diffused white fog, we were running blind, as if the ballet swan had been spun into a thousand plies of dancing ballerinas. When I turned the lamp off, the bow, ploughing through the water, left a trail of colour that hung like Christmas lights, in every shade of the rainbow. It's a rare wonder offered up by the sea, called bioluminescent plankton or algae. It was like a tide of glow sticks revealed at a rock concert to a chorus of "Oh wow, man... Cool colours," though probably forgotten in the search for munchies. I draped myself over the bow, let my hand drag, and revelled in this small, unexpected wonder of the world, like a young boy who has recently discovered the wonders of penile growth.

"Would you stop messing around? I need some light!" Rob was standing in the back of *Doug-the-Dinghy* like a Rubicon admiral begging to take a late-night dip. I turned the lamp back on and put my hand over it to dampen the intensity, thinking it might help.

"That's about as useful as a tit on a bull." The admiral was unusually testy. "Move the light back and forth like a quick searchlight. I don't want to run into a mooring ball or one of those frigging boats." Our positions should have been reversed, since he had to hunch over slightly to hold the outboard motor arm, looking more like the defeated Napoleon on his way to Elba rather than Nelson making a Trafalgar victory lap in a dinghy named *Doug*.

"I am pretty sure we are heading in the right direction," Rob assured himself, since I had returned to making rainbows in the waves. The admiral called for more light just as our dinghy emerged into a no-fog zone.

The lamp revealed *Bob-the-Boat* dead ahead, like the HMS *Victory* awaiting Horatio's return. *Doug* reunited with *Bob*; a gentle nudge and we were home.

⚓ ⚓ ⚓

Oh, sleep. Deep, glorious sleep. Not even four hours' worth.

A screech-owl of horror from on deck woke me up and had me running without time for shorts or a single sock. Pirates?

"F-U-U-U-U-C-K!" Was that an order? It was repeated in staccato forte.

I arrived at the wheelhouse door at the top of the spiral stairs, steps from my berth in the bow. Rob stood outside the door, frozen. His language was a convoluted twist of expletives not deleted. I poked my head out.

Based on the fact that what I was looking at was biblical in scope, my mind should have been thinking, "Dear Lord what plague and pestilence hath thou wrought upon the land," but "WHAT-THE-FUCK" was all I could muster, since Rob seemed to have a monopoly on the rest. Locust? Harpies? I pinched myself to confirm I was awake. What I was watching suggested otherwise; a nightmare, possibly, with chilling sound effects and a 3D staging.

My exclamation was lost in the squealing and twittering of hundreds of thousands of birds, barn swallows to be exact, darting and diving around the boat and all across the bay. Patches of the sky were darkened with their presence. It was Hitchcock horror, but the flying birds were a minor shadow on the screen. Sometime between Rob waking me and his alarm-clock cry, this swarming mass of migrating swallows had arrived in the harbour, fresh from some beginning in northern China, en route to Singapore, Indonesia, or northern Australia. Upon arrival, they had perched on every available horizontal railing, spar, and guide wire as if these were the ancient luxuries they sought from their million years of instinctual flight. They had flown four thousand miles (take or leave a thousand or two), evading what barn swallows evade, and, fresh from feasting on millions of mosquitoes and whatever else hovers over the tropics, they had shat a massive storm over *Bob-the-Boat*, a kind of *"Hi honey, I'm home"* salutation. There wasn't an inch of boat that had been spared; vertical rises dripping from the horizontal perches, the large, flat decks having been the targets of shitter flybys. The boat looked like a Jackson Pollock, potentially titled *Migratory Swallows: Number Twos*. The swallows had been nesting quietly when Rob had flung open the door to greet the day. The howl of horror when he stepped barefoot into a slithery mess of bird dung had set them off; that, and similar cries from half a dozen fishermen waking to the same graffiti.

My instincts were to shrug it off and go back to sleep—

"Just one bloody morning...please, just one"—but Rob understood the chemistry that would be required if we left it to a hot morning sun. Not only would it need to be scrubbed with serious elbow grease, but quickly, since the acid might mark the lacquer glaze that covered the paint.

The sun was beginning to lift itself out of bed, having caroused the night away giving life around the world. It appeared as well that the boomerang cloud had caught something and left town. High above the frenzied smoke cluster of birds, the sky was a brilliant blue. A few wisps of shredded cloud over the western hills caught the first morning rays, announcing that the daily special—sunshine with heat basted in a layer of humidity—was coming. I dressed appropriately with only a pair of light cotton briefs and flip-flops to protect the early morning fishermen from straining their eyeballs.

Cleaning supplies were retrieved from the hold; buckets, scrubbers, and soap. Starting on the flying bridge, we worked our way down. Over three hours we scrubbed and rinsed, and Rob had been wise to proceed early. By the time we got to the bottom rails, with the sun now over the trees, the droppings were semi-glued. What the hell was in mosquitoes anyway? We stood back and admired our work, shooting water cannons at tired swallows wanting to land and happy that Canada geese didn't migrate here or perch on boats and ecstatic that cows didn't fly. Over the next few days, we would repeat this procedure two more times.

By midafternoon, Rob and I found ourselves back at the tryke intersection, looking for a way into town. We needed groceries and a place to get away from the swallows that still swarmed like darting missiles over the bay. Rob had never been to Puerto Princesa before, so this was also exploration time. He had decided to leave the chopping business of immigration and customs to another day. We probably could have waited until we made it to Subic, but that meant travelling a couple of hours to Manila, a city of millions, to get what this small town afforded at our fingertips.

We soon found ourselves bumper to bumper in a metropolis of bikes, scooters, taxis, jeepneys, trikes and trucks of daily commerce. Trails of blue smoke followed everything. It was an image of Asia that had dominated the scene two generations ago, like rickshaws that had been the demarcation of China. The modern world, I thought, had all but erased those clusters of mayhem and confusion. It was alive and thriving in Puerto Princesa.

The main thoroughfare was two lanes wide and a hustle of busy in either direction. There were no buildings of prominent height or architecture; one- and two-storey structures, like many small towns back home. It was a picture of panic, however, with hydro wires looped in knots of spaghetti tangle from pole to pole, palm trees leaning heavily in all directions, clusters of bamboo swaying over the frantic and seeming unorganized mayhem of beehive activity. There were a thousand tin-roofed shops with open gates and doors to mechanics, tire sales, gas bars, salons for hair, nails, tattoos and massage; repair shops for small appliances; trikes and bicycles; taxi, bus and jeepney stands; and, as we crept closer to the centre, banks, fast food emporiums, a fine hotel and lesser buildings with cheaper accommodation. The hum and buzz of coming and going met us as we stepped from the tryke and paid the fare; one hundred and fifty pesos for two. A Mastercard advertisement: a four-dollar charge for a fifty-buck ride through a priceless landscape of visual activity.

Our first order of business was to get money, so we lined up at an ATM hung on the wall in a marketplace between a hawker of colourful dresses and a cell phone booth. An old woman carried plastic bags of coconut water, pedalling them down the line of bankers. Rob and I each purchased one. It was essential to keep the body lubricated, as walking—or even simply standing still—caused the body to sweat. The coconut was refreshing, as it did not come with added sugar.

Our turn at the money machine proved fruitful. It felt out-of-world to receive money out of a wall machine in a decrepit hovel punched out of a lean-to shack. It was bills in exchange for plastic in a country in which—except for the luxuriant growth of tropical plants, the noisy drone of mechanization, and pesos instead of Roman denarii—Christ on a donkey might have found himself at home, raising the dead or curing the lepers. And if Christ were here, he would be on a cell phone, of course. Everyone, it seemed, was—even the elderly beggars.

With wallets bulging, we ventured out into the town and spent the next couple of days wending our way through the sights. They were few and far between, but a few things stood out.

Rob had not exaggerated the Wild West. A fried chicken franchise had not one but two security guards standing at the front door. They carried sawed-off shotguns and a crosshatch of bullets hung from cartridge bandoliers dripping menace from their torsos; torsos, I might add, that stood out for their hulking size like an anorexic body turns heads at a Midwestern fair. I didn't see any guards standing in front of the banks, making me wonder what was in the secret recipe for the chicken and what one might expect on entering a bank.

There was a giant banner that hung across the main street with a personal happy birthday wish from the mayor of Puerto Princesa to the governor of Palawan. It was important to know on which side the bread was buttered and to let the populace know who was buttering it. Back-room politics was spelled on public banners. It shouldn't have struck me as onerous, but it did.

Most public buildings like hospitals and schools bore the name of the mayor or governor, either senior or junior. Politics was a family business...and lethal. It turns out, three years after we visited Palawan, that same governor celebrating his settled. Whole cities vaporized never took away the anger. It never could and it never will. You want to say "Never again," knowing very well that it is happening every day, by all sides of the equation. It will happen again tomorrow. But the fact that I write about it here is perhaps why the monument was necessary. Lest! We! Forget!

We moved on through the back streets of Puerto Princesa, locating the quiet American bar that John from the yacht club had suggested. Unfortunately, the cemetery had more action. Either the spy ship had left town, or this place was too far off the beaten track. No one else showed up in the hour we stayed.

The next bar was quite the opposite, a Canadian-run enterprise called Jess Billiard Bar (perhaps an apostrophe "s" after Jess's name had cost too much to insert on the flashing sign that stood by the road). It was small, lively, and on the main strip. The owner was French Canadian, and his wife was Filipino. They were a happy couple. The bar was testimony to the joy they had in running it.

It was here we found out about our next great adventure before returning to the boat for the evening. Throughout the night, the swallows continued to swarm and twitter, casting shadows through the porthole as they came into land, shadows that prompted memories of Hitchcock's *The Birds* that chewed through boarded windows, came down chimneys, and dined on the eyeballs of more than a few movie extras. Sleep—oh, glorious sleep. My brain forgot what it was, and we were committed to an early morning call.

30

ROCKIN' THROUGH RICE
A MORAL CONUNDRUM
KAMA SUTRA OF SAILING
THE PROCTOLOGIST AND THE CAVE

THE FOLLOWING DAY

"You must travel to see the Great Puerto Princesa Subterranean River National Park," someone in the know at Jess's bar advised on a named destination as long as the voyage. The journey was worth the destination.

The tourist bus was at the yacht club by a quarter to eight in the morning. This, of course, had meant getting up early (why start with sleep now?), and luckily most of the birds had moved on or found other Johnnies to spot. The van already had passengers who looked as whacked by the early hour as we did. In truth, it would not have been overly early if we had not gone to bed overly late and had been sober. However, who could tell, since up to this point on our trip, early and late shared the same sweep of the hand. We drove into the heart of Puerto Princesa and picked up more passengers, ensuring the small bus was full. It was now an international cast: Germans, Americans, Filipinos from Manila and us, two Canadians. The trip was to take an hour and a half, which by my map was half an hour's drive as the crow flies, ten minutes by swallow, if swallows could figure out how to fly straight. I am not sure, but I think a four-thousand-mile migration for a swallow runs about eight thousand and change.

It was soon obvious that the road was a swallow's design, climbing to hilltops, dropping into valleys, left and right zigs following a constant northerly zag. All that added time, of course, along with the rice paddies.

Rice growing is nothing new to the Philippines. The UNESCO Heritage site of Banaue Rice Terraces North of Manila, for example, had been created out of mountain tops over two thousand years ago. Here in Palawan, some paddies were in the process of being flooded for replanting, while others were in mid-growth or harvest. Rice was a year-round project, it appeared, in the heat of the tropics. Since the terrain was hilly with no real flat spaces, the rice paddies had been etched out of hillsides and terraced in small ascending fields (or descending, depending on where we were on the road). This meant flat land not occupied in some form of growth or harvest was in scarce supply.

Flat land is required to spread out the harvested rice to dry. In Palawan, most paddies are surrounded by palms and banana trees, leaving little room for direct sun. No room for sun? No problem. The paddy owners dropped tarps on the road—our road, a busy two-lane highway and the only road between Puerto Princesa and the subterranean river. There were tarps on the left and tarps on the right, each about eight by ten in size, with a thin layer of rice spread atop them in the process of drying. This left a narrow path for traffic, both north and south, on which to drive in a serpentine rock and roll, right-left-right that would give most theme parks a run for their money. The road was a ribbon of sunshine and the... oh my God...I am going to be sick. The sea had nothing on this scenic tour! If we were lucky, there might be a long stretch of straight driving (as straight as a zigzag road can be) and then another paddy attack.

Some tarps were attended to by young children or elderly women raking the rice, which allowed the sun to dry everything down to the bottom. Occasionally they had help. I noticed that more than one chicken was scratching about, feasting on this ready meal, and in one spot an image that had the potential to put me off rice for life: a dog hunched in a bowel evacuation in the middle of the canvas. A note to all: wash rice before cooking! One might be put off by the thought of such flagrant disregard for the food chain, but having grown up on a farm I knew that in the billions of tons of grains harvested around the world, there were the entrails of something or other—locust, grasshoppers, snakes, spiders, mice, or rats—though I guess you don't need to know this. It is enough to make a vegetarian long for the ass end of a cow.

If the tarps had been cleared from the road, there might be hundred-pound bags of rice piled like burlap pylons waiting to be picked up for market. Sometimes the pylons were moving; bags loaded on trikes or pickups, piled so high that it was impossible to see past them, though it did not seem to be a visible hazard to our driver, who treated all visual impairments with disdain. What you can't see coming won't hurt you, will it? Our pee break coffee stop couldn't have come too soon.

The stop afforded us a fabulous view looking westward out over the South China Sea. It appeared to be arm's length away, though we were informed it would be three-quarters of an hour's drive before we hit the beach. It wasn't the view or the rice paddies or even the anticipated adventure to come that had our small group animatedly chatting.

A while back, in a spurt of acceleration around a trike to outrun an oncoming bus, our eyes had been diverted to an image that we were now trying to confirm. It had caused a few of us to stand up and shout, "Holy shit, did you see that?"

What we thought we saw, confirmed now by most, was a small boy lying on the roadside, arms and legs splayed in such a manner of unconscious abandon that we felt it could only be one thing. The boy had been hit. The cruel realization was not only that he had been hit, but that there were adults within view of his body, working at their rice paddies and tarps, and seemingly didn't care.

"He could have been sleeping."

"He was half on the road. He'd get run over!"

"There was no way he was sleeping...that boy was hit!"

"Hey, driver? Did you see the small boy lying on the road?"

No answer. He had a serious pained look suggesting he had, and that perhaps this was life, Palawan-style, denoted by the quick flash of his eyebrows and hands spread in a "*C'est la vie; not my monkey, not my circus*" manner. Had he...had we been morally responsible to stop and investigate? This was our question, for which there seemed to be two answers. We, the tourists, mostly agreed yes, that a child's life was in danger, even if it would be gross interference, since there were adults—parents, we assumed—nearby. Maybe he was sleeping, but all the same, it was a child. However, a story was floated, offered by someone, the German I believe, who had heard of or possibly experienced children in almost identical situations in other countries, on other continents, used as bait to suck in the tourist for begging or selling trinkets, and, sometimes, to rob the bus.

"Oh! Oh my god...really?" Our doubting compassionate minds became divided and twisted in the not-so-black-and-white of rainbows of possibilities. We climbed back in the bus, silent, each in our own solitude of contemplation. I wanted to believe that the boy had been asleep, possibly hit (but not dead), a terrible position given the scenario, but preferable, I felt, over the sinister alternative; however, that would have left me complicit in the gross negligence of moral duty to help. My yin-yang mind spun in a battle of righteousness in my mind.

How could people be so ruthless as to use children in such a ploy?

Really? You ask this question having watched the sodomized man in Bangkok...most likely sold into sexual slavery? Children are tortured and twisted into blind and crippled waifs to be beggars. Remember Slum Dog Millionaire? Have you forgotten your near-miss in Greece? Sometimes I can't believe I share a brain with you. You're so naive about the nature of mankind...always thinking the best. Grow up! Stay sharp...man's a beast in a lamb's wool suit. These people are desperately poor...anything goes for survival!

But...we bring much-needed tourism, money, and work for the people. This business will all dry up if word gets out.

Really? There are desperately poor nations rife with violence all over the world filled with tourists. Mexico and Jamaica come to mind.

Yes, but...

Yes, but nothing! Stay focussed or we are a dead man.

My mind was jolted back to the here and now when the driver stopped next to a wharf, announcing arrival. A small fleet of bangkas outfitted to hold a dozen people tossed in the surf not far off shore. They were festooned with colourful banners and flags, and the shading canvases carried the names of assorted tour companies or individual owners, all part of the park ferry service. The cave was a few kilometres down the coast, we were told, and we would have to be ferried by bangka to its mouth. Other buses arrived and the boats were dragged to shore. It was single-file loading via the nose since the out-rigging pontoons on either side prevented the boats from being tied broadside to a wharf.

In short order, we were a flotilla of bangkas heading north, hugging the shore.

⚓ ⚓ ⚓

Although it had only been a couple of days, I realized that already I missed being on the water; the undulation of waves, periods of heart-ticking quiet, and the curious seduction of sea spray that dried in white pearls of salt on our skin. I began to understand Herman Melville's fascination for the sea, though I had no hankering for his pistol-and-ball drive to fall on swords. I had not yet met my Moby Dick and I was pretty confident I never would.

It might have been the bar scene which had ended badly, but I had to admit, once I entertained what could have been, had the women not been young girls, I felt a stirring of desire.

Perhaps it had been the fantasy of seduction, the tendered notion of a bawdy encounter, the crossed lines of raw sexuality, and their absence of judgement that had primed my pump and exposed some ageless drive. Was I wrong to think that being at sea was like being part of a primordial sex act where existence was an infinite circle of temptations, submissions, and the endless giving of life? After all, what was the sea to Mother Earth if not the womb and the birthing canal to all life on the planet? Maybe my mind was overreaching in its tired wandering state, but it was tossing about the possibilities anyway.

Before the birthing, of course, there was the affair, the wanton seduction, the coupling and the spent calm, begun, as it had, since man first set eyes on the sea. And then the call.

"Hey, sailor, lookin' for a good time?" offered in a bourbon exhale through a smoky nightfall of gossamer mist.

Eyes rolled right, then left, head turned to look for others, wondering what a sailor was and who was behind that voice from the fog offshore. Our first sailor may have gingerly replied with a De Niro grimace. "You talkin' to me?"

"Yeah, you, handsome, wanna play?"

And before he knew it, there was the touch; toes caressing the melting shores, shivers of invitation to immerse the whole body into the waters of naked want and desire. Stripped down, modesty left to the view of cockles beneath, nature's seduction began.

And before man knew it, he was riding high, plunging

deep, the silken waters lubricant to the oblong hulls of invention. Every wave entered was parted and ploughed, like the fervour of a couple's first passionate connection, unaware of the endless conquests to be yet fought and won. They pierced the seas like a prying tongue, folds parting, inviting them in as they performed the act of exploration again and again. And the sea was the perfect mistress; the strong forward insertions were met with a bucking sensation of untold pleasure, deep thrusts rewarded with the pushback, wanting more. But, like the sea's land-based counterpart, hell hath no fury like a lover scorned. For survivors, there were the final triumphs: maiden islands inviting the touch, plump with tufts of palm forests surrounded by the rippled sands of the virgin beach. Not to be tempted was to ignore...and no one could ignore the sea for long.

It occurred to me that there had to be a *Kama Sutra* for sailing in there somewhere; those endless postures and positions with invitations by androgynous seas that man could not resist...inverted, ascending, embracing, encircling, splitting, thrusting, tossing...basic postures of lovemaking motion, aptly named Swallows in Love, Seagulls on the Wing, a Huge Bird above a Dark Sea.

It's crazy what comes to mind, watching the bow thrust through a wave.

It didn't help, of course, that a young couple, newlyweds (Rob had already inquired), sat facing me, the stimulation all around them ignored in their gentle caresses of one another.

And I needed to pee. Men are pretty basic.

We passed a magnificent white shoreline that anywhere else on earth would have been littered with exclusive hotels and palm sunshades, but here were left natural, surf rolling across sands hemmed with thick groves of lush palms and tropical fronds. These shores, I surmised, were in the same untamed state as they had been when windjammers of empires past scoured the seas for new places to plunder. Aside from birthday in 2009 was fleeing the law with his brother in 2012, both accused of murder. It is situations like this where mayors might want to rethink their showy displays of endorsement.

The cathedral we had seen upon arrival was Catholic, and on our visit, was filled with parishioners mourning a small white casket, the rhythm of healing incantations from pulpit and pew floating through open doors.

The church cemetery came with a plaque informing the curious that it was one of the oldest in the Philippines. It adjoined a park of sorts where we found a monument with a large brass plaque. It turned out it had only been erected two months before our visit in the first week of September 2009. The plaque read:

> "I WILL MAKE YOUR DREAM COME TRUE"
> Mayor S. Hagedorn's promise
> Made to former WWII American POW Don Schloat,
> Creator of the Palawan Massacre Monument
> September 15, 2009

There was a short statement giving tribute to others who helped via donations for the monument, including the mayor's wife and the mayor himself. It continued:

> American WWII POWs were massacred in this place
>
> On December 14, 1944
>
> On that day Japanese guards stationed here in Palawan
>
> Ordered the American POWs under their control into the
>
> air raid shelters.
>
> Japanese soldiers suddenly poured gasoline on and into the

American POW shelters and set them on fire with
flaming torches, followed by hand grenades.

As the American POWs, engulfed in flames broke out of the

fiery deathtraps, their Japanese guards machine-gunned, bayoneted,

Decapitated and clubbed them to death.

Of the American POWs, only 11 survived the massacre.

This memorial is by artist Don Schloat, a former POW

of the Japanese at Palawan.

September 26, 2009

Puerto Princesa City

Sixty-five years had passed since this atrocity had been committed, but the inscribed emotion was as raw as if it happened yesterday. The monument was not even two months old. Sixty-five years of bitter hatred etched into bronze, Lest We Forget.

It was the villainous deed that was memorialized, not the fallen. There were no names of the dead or of the eleven survivors, except Don Schloat, a man, I can only assume, who has survived on hatred and vengeance for sixty-five years. In Canada, war memorials praised the valiant soldiers who gave up their lives, honored the dead with names and regiments, praised the victors, and seldom mentioned the vanquished. There was nothing tidy or sanitized about this message, each word chiselled with venom. I understood the hatred and where it came from, but it was hard to imagine someone carrying the weight of this carnage for so long, with so much vitriol, and surviving. And somehow, I do not believe the monument has been cathartic or settled the score. Scores like these are never the *tic-tic-tic* of the small motor on our boat and the gathering of a modern crew of humanity, we could have been native fishermen, a dugout of tribal warriors, or Indonesian tradesmen from any time in the last thousand or so years.

The bangka is so primitive in design yet so efficient in skirting the waves that it was most likely the model for the modern catamaran design that has revolutionized the sailboat industry. It is also the inspiration for the stabilizer systems used on small yachts such as *Bob-the-Boat*, though not employed on *Bob-the-Boat* due to huge expense and mechanical difficulties like being torn off during rough seas. There was no swaying or undue rocking in the waves with the bangka, however; the single pole pontoons of bamboo worked in some unique fashion of physics to keep the boats steady. They are the perfect modes of transport, though here, their Achilles' heel is the ancient outboard motors.

I was busy taking photos of the approaching islands, carved structures of monolithic rock eaten at their base by millenniums of waves, unrelenting in their quest to find comfort in an ending that proved to be their demise. One large rock was splitting the surf and casting the recoiling waves into a show of silver bullets that caught the sun, forming a small rainbow of activity. I kept my camera trained, waiting for the perfect splash, the defining wave that would say in one upward crash and explosion what a thousand words could only hope to create: raw, powerful, untamed beauty with no two waves ever the same. I was mesmerized by the brute force, squared through the lens of my camera, when it occurred to me that something in our rhythm had changed. The motor sound had stopped.

Our navigator in the engine room (the back end of the boat) was a tall, rake-thin, middle-aged man, scarf tied around the head like a Ho Chi Minh henchman who caught bullets in his teeth. He finessed the mechanics of the motor as a harpist would tune strings. He pulled a rope without result. He tinkered again, wrapped the rope on the flywheel, and pulled. Nothing happened beyond a sputter that died quickly. I watched with interest as he adjusted a knob, turned a screw, moved a lever, nothing done in a hurry or with the building panic I felt and thought was starting to move through the rest of the patrons on the boat. The rock that had so captured my attention for its beauty was now on my radar for making us one with the sea. We were moving closer with every surfing roller to the point where I could see barnacle clusters that had avoided my view before. One hundred feet had shortened to fifty and I knew it wouldn't take long to halve that distance. I took Rob's lead and pretended not to be concerned, though I felt the sphincter and facial muscles pursed in a mirror image. A couple more waves and we would be on the rock. With a long, deliberate pull, the flywheel spun, sputtered, coughed, and, caught in mid-mucus spatter, came back to life. We moved forward twenty feet and it died, but we were now out of danger of colliding with the rock. A half-tweak of the worn mechanics and the motor was back in action. If the captain had been worried, he never showed a blink of concern. He looked out over our heads as if all this was in the scope of a normal voyage, rocks-smocks, death at the doorstep be damned. Was that shrapnel or a gold tooth he sported?

We rounded into a cove and rode the surf to shore, where this time the motor was cut intentionally. Our boat boy, who had ridden at the nose of the boat, jumped into the pristine water and pulled us ashore. I jumped into a roller and my bladder let loose. Not the best idea, since the caves proved to be cold.

⚓ ⚓ ⚓

The caves…h-m-m-m…well, what can one say about being ferried into a twelve-mile colon? Jungle growth hung like hair to the entrance, and once in, it was darker than the Black Hole of Calcutta.

We were grouped into small boats like those of amusement park rides that ferried young couples through tunnels of love, minus the groping, petting, and saliva exchange, though I might be wrong. I sat single in the nose, and for this honour, I was given the twelve-volt lamp to light the way. It was our only salvation between hitting prostatic outgrowths on the wall or polyp stalactites hanging from above and smooth sailing around bends and elbows that took us further up the digestive tract. It was déjà vu Dr. Proctology.

A couple of years before this trip, my doctor had sent me for a colonoscopy. The specialist looked to be way past retirement and much too happy about wielding his tool.

"Would you like to watch?" he asked, turning the fifty-five-inch color flat-screen 1080 HD monitor in my direction while pumping my anus with air. All that was missing were 3D glasses. His Coke-bottle lenses magnified a sparkle of glee, and I thought I saw him dabbing drool from his bottom lip. Perhaps the invitation to watch was an attempt to divert my attention while a metal probe and tube about the size of a gas pump hose, but twice as long, were inserted. He didn't divert my attention! If you haven't seen your colon in colour, you don't know what you're missing.

"Those small black things moving about are bats," our guide explained, having pointed out the spaghetti stalactite and a few other growths. I was invited to sweep the beam like a searchlight to point out the huddles of bats. For the most, the light was held at boat height, getting reflection off the water and walls. It was important to know where the walls were. I had the very strong urge to hold the light under my chin, turn to the back of our boat, and scream, "H-E-E-E-E-R-S JOHNNY." I was afraid I would have to clean up the mess, so I resisted my infantile urge.

Occasionally we were met by oncoming boats returning

from the large intestine. They were on their way downstream, back to the opening where they would be deposited into the catch basin before the river made its way to the sea. It was a constant flush, and it wasn't long before we were also returned to the daylight. I don't wish to undermine the experience, but other than the sensation of movement in pitch-black surroundings, outgrowths like fat tissues with given names on the cave walls, a slight chill (wet shorts don't help), and things dripping from above (Borneo bat droppings came to mind, though it was condensation...I hope), the ride was anti-climactic in comparison to the journey by bangka and bus.

There was the customary tourist shakedown before disembarking as we were offered photos of ourselves moments before cave insertion, and, as the tourist guides had risked life and limb to motor us in and out, perhaps a small tip would be nice. I had taken plenty of photos, so we only contributed once.

While waiting for other boats to empty, we were informed that this subterranean river park was vying with several other natural wonders around the world to become recognized as a United Nations Natural Wonder in the same manner as Niagara Falls, the Grand Canyon, and Dolly Parton, and naturally I wondered if this was an attempt to qualify for UN handouts to preserve it. If it meant helping the people and bringing badly needed tourist dollars, I was all for it. Despite my unfortunate flashback, it was truly worth the day's adventure.

Oh, and my doctor found nothing worthy of UN recognition, even if I believed it was a natural wonder.

31

MAD HATTERS IN THE RABBIT HOLE
THE CIA
MARGARITAVILLE MADNESS

LATER THAT EVENING

That evening, we found ourselves back at Jess Billiard Bar.

Such a day should be rewarded at its end with a quiet evening, dining in the luxury of the boat and the beauty that were the surroundings of our harbour. Alcoholic drinks should be involved. Rob had other plans.

"I told Jess I would be at the bar by five thirty," he informed me, stepping out of the bus at 4:45. We had made better time home. The rice, tarps and bags had vanished by late afternoon.

"What's happening at the bar?"

"Jess wants to jam with me before things get too busy." It was to be a quick jaunt to the boat and back to retrieve the guitar, fresh underwear and cologne.

Over our stay in Puerto Princesa, we had made numerous runs to Jess Billiard Bar, but none faster than the one following our return from the caves. On this trip, we arrived in quick order, since the trike operated by a young teen and his girlfriend was in a hurry. The girlfriend, dressed in jeans, tight like a vacuum-sealed ham, rode sidesaddle behind the driver since there wasn't room for Rob, me, the large guitar case, and one leg of ham. She had her arms wrapped around her boyfriend's waist; hands tucked quietly into his groin. While he ran the throttle, she handled the stick. There was a method to the mad driving, I think, since with each pothole averted, a corner taken too fast, or if the bike was throttled too quickly, the grip tightened, then relaxed. If there was a stable, this horse was fast-tracking to have his oats and sow them too.

There was more to this mad scurry than the jam I knew; a tart or two at the bar, for starters.

Somehow Rob had convinced himself that Kim, back in Subic, was history. Kurt, his nemesis in courtship, had won Kim back. It wasn't exactly a win; Rob had cut Kim off from finances when he found out she had been moonlighting burning candles at both ends in the department of romance.

I wish I had kept notes because there was a tragi-comic love-hate harlot romance in there somewhere. At the moment Kim was "out," leaving Rob with a free conscience to dally with the dillies at Jess Billiard Bar, even though this was not "that" kind of a bar.

As for the bar, imagine falling down the rabbit hole and meeting all the players buzzing around the cuckoo's nest. On any given visit it was a tea party—Mad Hatters United.

As has been noted, the Philippines was a high-noon haven for the expats of past wars such as Korea and Vietnam and, as the war memorial suggested, leftovers of WWII as well. Palawan and its capital city of Puerto Princesa was a magnet for these and the runners from ugly divorce, unsavory deals, leaky bank accounts and paternity suits. These, I think, were the good guys.

On our last day before departure, we were sitting at a long row of assembled tables adjacent to the front walk to the bar.

The "We" had grown from Rob and myself to a familiar entourage of faces. Familiar, yes, but I'll be damned if I can remember a single name.

There were two men about my age, mid-fifties, looking older due to hair loss, paunchy midriffs and cigars chewed, shortened and not lit. They drank bourbon, neat. Their clothing was southern—American Southern, not South American. The look was gentlemen CIA, the contrived Hollywood version; smarmy subversive types continually sent by Hollywood producers to represent the American government, white cotton or linen shirts, sleeves rolled, vests tightly buttoned to reveal the capon rolls, and though they should have had long, matching cuffed trousers, wardrobe outfitted them with cuffed shorts instead. Both wore sandals and dark aviator glasses...I'll admit, I saw conspiracy everywhere. They moved as a pair, Hatter and Hare. Rob and I had verbally sparred with them a few nights before. They had been unfriendly, to say the least.

"Do you live here on the island?" I had asked one of them, with the same innocent tone as my inquiry into what the man on the boat did for a living in Singapore. There was a guarded, chewed-back reply.

"Got a farm across the other side of the bay."

"A farm?" It perhaps had too much question mixed with surprised exclamation. I could see his eyes darting, as if searching for incoming. Farmer was not what I was expecting. "What kind of farm? What do you grow?"

"Who the fuck wants to know?"

I flushed several shades of red in the chill of the open and closed fridge. His darting eyes looked at me, through me and scanned all corners around me.

"Norm didn't mean anything by it. He used to live on a farm back in Canada," Rob was quick to add, feeling, as I had, a cold polar wind in bilateral relations.

"Sorry, I didn't mean to pry...I was merely interested in what you might be farming." I thought maybe digging the hole deeper might help. My subconscious was silent, thinking, perhaps, death was coming. If I had thought pigs, cows and chickens or golden fields of wheat, sinister minds may have envisioned Palawan Gold, Subterranean Meth or White Pulau Coke. Persons with a sense of the dark intrigue of the underworld might have expected the farm was a B&B for S&M or that the word "farm" was short for "firearm" or an acronym for Freedom / Anarchy / the Right is / Might. I simply thought a dozen fresh eggs for the boat would have been nice.

"A little bit of this…a little bit of that" was shunted like coupling boxcars, and then the conversation ended. His eyes returned to his partner in silence. Thankfully there had been others within conversation distance. I had sipped on a beer and left the rest of the opening lines to Rob. Mine had produced a can of worms to date.

There was another Canadian, affable but forgettable. On a previous evening, I had bumped him while leaving the washroom, and he apologized twice. It's one of those things Americans found endearing about Canadians but hard to understand. Some Americans may have eyeballed me, offered me a warning and sprawled me on the floor—not necessarily in that order.

The young Spanish father had shown up and brought his boys. I saw a game of tag going on in and out the front door of the bar. Jess had small boys as well. It seemed they all knew each other. The Spanish father looked more Middle Eastern, sporting a ragged black beard and an open-necked button-up shirt, smokes tucked in one hand like worry beads with the other making some points of flapping denunciations in a heated discussion. I had conversed with him before, though his English was as fresh as my non-Italian.

The Italian line was introduced by another fellow, for whom communication in any language was all Greek to me. He attempted to negotiate translations from Spanish, which he barely knew, through his Italian, which I hoped he knew, to broken French and English, which, if he knew, were guarded state secrets. His explanations for all things, when short for words (and he always was), degenerated to bebop. I had asked him about his wife and children and he had answered, "Auch (as if clearing his throat)... Na-nana-na, ne-na-na...ze vife (simulating cutting the throat), de meestrees (simulated castration), de na-nana-na, geerlfreend, ne-nana (simulated hanging, complete with a swollen tongue out the side)." He spat into a barrel of flowers. Before I sat with the gathering, a beautiful Filipina woman came out to the patio with bottles of wine and beer, kissed the Spaniard, hugged the Italian and called to one of the children in Tagalog, who yelled back in perfect English that he was playing tag. Apparently, this troop performed together regularly.

Beers and nuts were served up by her sister Josie and two girls, for whom I also have no names, hence, Dilly and Dally. One was a niece to Jess and Josie and friend to the other girl who seemed to be a friend but may have been related—it was never established. The two girls and sister-aunt were there because, on a previous visit, Rob might have made ingenuous inquiries as to availabilities, ventured interest beyond how old they were, and made flattering comments as to physiques. A family portrait had already been taken with Rob, Aunt, Niece and Friend, arms over shoulders; the kind sent from engagement parties announcing wedding dates. Someone may have told a story about sailing into the harbour on a private yacht, milked and enlarged to arrival on the S.S. *Britannia*. Someone might have assumed that Easy Street was coming into view. Not once were those assumptions made about me. I drank in the sunshine but noticed Rob breaking hearts in the shadows of the bar. The friend left with hugs all around, and the niece and aunt followed not long after. The aunt had the look of "*off with his head.*" Josie, her smiling sister, didn't seem to harbor any ill will, for which I was glad, not wishing anyone to spit into my beer by association.

At some point, Rob and Jess set up a pair of chairs and poured their souls into Neil Young, Dylan, and "Margaritaville." It was obvious that Jess was an accomplished musician, playing and singing with ease; the kind of playing that had probably inspired him to buy a bar to have a permanent gig. It never fazed Rob to be outgunned, since he admitted later it was the first time he got to jam with anyone. While they played, a tea party of conversations continued on the patio like an orchestral accompaniment of castanets, cowbells and woodblocks.

The CIA was there, speaking again in code. I don't remember much of anything, since I was reluctant to look at them or even be caught listening, thinking maybe the farm was a collection of waterboards waiting to be tested. The conversation sounded something toward, "Are the pigs flying?" followed by, "If pigs could fly, they might be" or "That will happen when pigs can fly." I might have had a few beers by then. It had me thinking, though, that fresh bacon would be nice with those dozen eggs.

Between sets, Rob stopped to talk to someone who must have asked about our intended voyage ahead. I was eavesdropping in broken Spanglish and Franco-Calabressi elsewhere, so I only heard a few bits that seemed irrelevant. "Busuanga fruit bats... Pearl farms...consider reprogramming course... Dumaran Island...armed to the teeth." Rob defended staying the course, I think, speaking of time-saving and pending typhoons. There were kids weaving in and out playing tag, beers being delivered, finger food arriving and codes to be cracked. Rob went back to playing with Jess, who closed the world out in song with a second round of "Margaritaville."

"Tag! You it!" A cluster, then an explosion of fleeing kids. Someone knocked over a tray of nuts and shakers of salt.

"Not fair! Papa? Papa? PAPA-A-A-A, tell Francois to play fair. Papa? PAPA-A-A-A!"

"She says, I'ze the blame! She's not, how says...na...nana na ne nana (simulated gun to head)...happies!"

"It's nobody's fault...*mon petit chou*..." A child sent back into play.

"There's no reason for all this. What the fuck?"

"Excuse, please. Sorry, mister."

"Is this a fucking daycare or a bar? Piss off, you little bastards!" A special forces tattoo bulged on his forearm when he made a fist.

"I so sorry, I no mean to bump you." The cute curly-haired daughter of the Spanish or Italian father (I never established whose was whom) threw up her arms and hunched her shoulders when asked what happened.

"Jess, I didn't come here to be harassed by bloody kids! Are you going to control these brats or—"

"Margaritaville" wafted through the air without an answer.

The Hatter and Hare rose as a pair, clutching their bottles of beer.

"TAXI—"

"Blame! Blame! Blame! I says...na, ne-nana... *Ciao, Señorita.*"

"The last time I am coming here. Goddamn romper room!" Taxi doors slammed.

"Jess, what happened out here? I was serving at the bar."

Jess shrugged and shook his head as if to say "*It's not my fault.*"

⚓ ⚓ ⚓

Back to sea and not a moment too soon. "With a philosophical flourish Cato throws himself upon his sword; I quietly take to the ship." Melville understood!

32

THE ABCS OF ENCS: AUTO PILOT EVEREST VS MARIANA: CRY OF HELP FROM THE PIZZA BUSUANGA BUST

…OCT. 18-19…STILL 2009

Cruising north again off the coast of Palawan, the sea sparkled and shimmered, each ray caught, bent, and refracted into a million points of light like a city through a windshield of rain. It was now mid-October, and I knew the autumn rains would be descending on Toronto, with a few early snow flurries, nature's way in Canada of gently announcing "Bend over." Here, it is six months hot and six months hot and wet. One day it stops raining and that's it, a change of season.

I was hanging through the railings on the bow once again, thinking to myself that I must be one of the luckiest bastards in the world, next to all those other lucky ones born with golden halos and silver spoons—though, unlike their luck, mine ran out at the treasury. But here I was, salt spray splashing up from the Sulu Sea, dried by the tropical sun while sitting on a private yacht, watching the tinted hills of Palawan as we motored by.

Pinch me again. Pinch me for all the things that could have been and all the things that were, for two great kids and a wife that I have pinched myself many times before. She was the lucky fate of light that came into my life when I had no other plans. Happily ever after didn't happen to people like me.

And now here I am, another golden day in paradise. Pinch me black and blue. I would have loved to share this experience with my wife, except she hated boats...gagged at the thought of rolling seas.

Rob decided to take his on-deck shower, so I moved to the helm and sat in the captain's chair.

The automatic pilot was extremely capable of keeping the boat on course. If it looked to be straying off the red dotted line that the program followed, it was simply a matter of hitting the button left or right and the boat adjusted to a satellite correction. Because of the simplicity, I can never boast that I know how to navigate. I was good at watching the boat do it for me. Rob had shelves filled with all the appropriate charts that only he knew how to read. God forbid that we should lose our electronic guide, but if that happened, it meant pulling out the appropriate charts and reading; longitude, latitude, and minutes, using a compass, some earth magnetism, and mixing them through the brain. Other than the compass, everything was electronic, so I am not sure what we would do, but Rob was surely capable, having taken the Power Squadron course back in Canada. One then needs only add currents, winds and visible landmarks, if at all possible, to navigate. Daytime was easier if you could read the sun. Reading stars would be another matter, and what one would do in a storm, fog or on an overcast day is beyond me. I know there are methods, but I never needed to know anything beyond watching the electronic display.

It died momentarily that afternoon. Alarms went off, and Rob removed a small chip and inserted a new one. In a matter of seconds, everything was fixed. The first chip was electronic charts covering our voyage from close to India (we started further east in Thailand) to our present location. The new chip would take us north to Hong Kong or Japan and I am not sure how far east.

This was the world of automatic pilot, driven by electronic navigation charts (ENCs), used by electronic charting display information services (ECDIS), which we had. These charts were supposed to conform to the International Hydrographic Organization's (IHO) high standards to be included in a special publication (S-57) before getting recognition as an ENC and meet the even higher standards of the International Maritime Organization (IMO). ENCs were available from RENCs (Regional Electronic Navigational Chart Coordinating Centers). Numerous companies are competing with both the hard- and software.

Imagine being invited to a convention for electronic cartographers. If you don't speak acronyms and don't know the ABCs of your ENCs, you are pretty much at a loss.

"HI. Looking for an ENC."

"NOAA ENC or NOAA from USACE?"

"DOA from NGA."

"You have the ECDIS?"

"RC435i."

"PC?"

"MS XP."

"DOD?"

"ASAP!"

"ID?"

"E.T."

A dive into the world of ENCs and ECDISs revealed more than I cared to know and share. And a man who would read up on ENCs for ECDISs for pleasure might go to hell for a pastime, though he won't have any trouble finding it. However, let it be known that there are dozens of manufacturers that all promise the world in the palm of your hand, which technically, I guess, they deliver.

I am so un-tech-savvy that most all of this info flew over my head, but I am assured that it is a sophisticated GPS for ship navigation and is a multi-billion-dollar business. The electronic charts come in various forms, from a series of chips the size of those used in cell phones and they cover specific geographical areas and navigation functions. There are more than 90,000 merchant vessels at sea at any given time. Add to that ferry boats and the thousands of pleasure craft like *Bob-the-Boat* and there may be a few hundred thousand watercraft out at sea—and even that may be a conservative number. This doesn't include inland waterways (covered by IENCs). The charted waters comprise hundreds, maybe thousands of different zones, for which you can buy specific electronic charts. All boats of a certain size now have to carry ENCs, regulations decreed by GODs at the IMO. It makes sense, but at several hundred dollars per chip times the number of ships and zones, and you can see the beginning of a large bank huddled around marine navigation alone.

Navigation chips can also carry information on currents, tides and weather patterns with some programs downloading new information daily. It helps to know if there is a new sunken hazard, like an oil rig or a cruise ship lying on its side. To this end, and to add weighted merit to the download, in 2003 a collision of two ships, the MV *Tricolor* and the *Kariba*, in the English Channel ended with the *Tricolor* lying on its side, with nearly three thousand BMWs, Volvos, and Saabs destroyed. (When I read this story, I cried—for the vehicles, not the boat. As Colonel Kurtz would have said, "The horror... The horror.") Within two days, two large ships, the *Nicola* and the *Vicky*, crashed into the sunken ship, even with French police boats and others standing guard to warn and reroute shipping. It was not revealed if Captain Clouseau was in charge, but a third indignity followed when a salvage tug ruptured a safety valve on the submersed wreck, spilling massive amounts of oil. I realize that "ship" happens, but it is easy to see how an up-to-the-minute satellite download would have helped in preventing this complete disaster.

Other programs assist with boat security, such as anchor drag. We got a firsthand look at how well that works from swinging in Pulau Tiga. The program can't fail if the unit fails to let you sleep. If there is a point of warning, it may be that navigation is too reliant on things that go beep in the night, but, given the choice of ENCs over paper charts, reading constellations and chicken-blood spatter, I vote electronics: most boats carry both ENCs and paper charts. Electronics do fail occasionally…okay, a lot, but—knock on fibreglass—except for the near-miss of the unmarked oil derrick off the shores of Borneo, it had not failed us yet.

While sitting in the captain's chair, I watched the navigation screen, which was set in a three-way split. One was a display with sonar depths via ENC and the GPS tracking of our route, and it was paired opposite the actual on-board electronic sonar reading that gave us the "real" profile of the sea bottom with instant depth readings. The third was the radar that scanned the boats around us. At that moment there were no boats within twelve miles.

Most often the ocean depth varied from fifteen to two hundred feet, changing constantly as it detected coral reef shoals and flat beds of sand or mud. At one point as I was watching, the live sonar went blank, unable to scan the depth. What appeared on the electronic navigation chart was a little scary. It showed a dark blue pit (everything was colour-coded; the darker the blue the deeper the water), and the numbers had me checking them twice. The depth below us was now somewhere around twenty-five thousand feet, almost five miles or eight kilometres. Mt. Everest would still have projected over four thousand feet above this, which, I guess, would make it a lot easier to climb. The deepest spot in the world's oceans is the Mariana Trench in the Pacific at 36,201 feet, which could vary slightly if you got carried upward on a sneaker wave while measuring. Mt. Everest this time would be over seven thousand feet short of the surface. This got my mind wandering a little.

People climb mountains, some say, because they are there. Do we venture into valleys because they are *not* there? Why do we put such value on climbing the highest peak? How many bucket lists include the Mariana Trench with the bragging rights to hitting the lowest point in your life? Can we reprogram children to come down from the top of a snowbank, singing, "I'm at the bottom of the castle and you're a dirty rascal"? Are valleys getting a bum rap? These are the things that idleness on a boat allows you to contemplate. However, one thing was for sure. This was one valley (usually called "rifts" underwater) I wasn't interested in seeing. I wasn't sure why it should have bothered me because you can drown in a foot of water, but I felt that if the boat decided to sink here it would be a greater tragedy since *Bob-the-Boat* would be crushed by the weight into something the size of a sardine can by the time it hit the bottom. We would disappear off the face of the earth, closer to hell than its opposite pole, about the size of an anchovy. Remember that the next time the anchovy calls for help from your pizza.

Almost as quickly as the rift appeared, it was gone, and the depth returned to a more manageable expiry level of a little over fifty feet. The thought of drowning had never preoccupied my mind in the same way I had never given much thought to falling from the sky while flying. I knew I had a greater chance of survival if the boat sank than if a plane crashed, though there is possibly something to be said for a sure death from the sky over a few hours or weeks as probable shark bait. It was hard to sustain such thoughts and to be afraid of the sea when the waters were sparkling from a radiant sun in a sky of cotton-puff clouds. It was like thinking about one's diabetes in a chocolate factory. If you are going to go, this is the place!

Rob finished his shower, completely unaware we had crossed a Sulu sinkhole, not that I believe it would have tweaked a contemplative moment for him. He had both feet firmly planted on the bobbing deck, with all thoughts focused on things to the north.

By now Rob had confirmed with Tequila Mike that we would not be visiting Busuanga with promises of four-foot fruit bats, a real live tunnel of mangroves, the amazing Calauit Game Reserve that included transplanted wildlife such as free-roaming zebras and giraffes or the greatest underwater reef of sea life outside of the Great Barrier. This was the island paradise I had waited for, and now we were going to pass it by. We simply could not trust the next typhoon to wreak havoc to the north and leave us alone.

If it has not already been made clear, one does not play games with typhoons. There were no natural coves that could protect us if the typhoons (another of which was brewing in the Pacific) decided to head south (not unusual) and spank the middle to northern tip of Palawan, then carry through to South Vietnam and possibly Thailand. We were not into sea spankings, apparently, which I heartily agreed with. Those could come with waves at over fifty feet high. Even at a quarter of that height, you were bound to get an enema, which, if nurtured properly, might produce a giant pearl in a few years' time. Unlucky souls, however, might be found to have sea urchins. Death was possible and possibly probable in any case. And on the subject of pearls, we were about to learn something new.

33

HERDING CLAMS AT THE PEARL FARM
THE BIG PEARLS LEFT INTACT

AFTER MIDNIGHT, OCT.19

I gave up the reins of the midnight watch, promising to return in a few hours. There was to be no swinging since it had been determined that time was of the essence toward the goal of reaching Subic. Every hour wasted could be an hour closer to getting caught at sea by the typhoon. It was moving very slowly, still far east of the Philippines, waiting like that breath of air that finally sets off an avalanche to wreak havoc on the world in its path.

Rob had studied his route north, and, given a pair of options, decided to take the inside channel between the mainland of Palawan and its northern island of Dumaran. Dumaran pushed eastward out into the Sulu Sea like a large proboscis on the northern groin of the Palawan leg. It would have grown the voyage by precious hours if we navigated around the far eastern tip. Dumaran rang a bell of familiarity but not loud enough to warn the brain that danger was imminent.

I heard the smacking and crunching of the fibreglass hull, and I was immediately propelled out of bed. With my head pressed up against the very nose of the hull, it didn't take much. There was a distress call from above. In the Morse code of distress, it was the triple "fuck" followed by a long "fuck" followed by my name. I didn't stop for shorts as the code became more frantic. In seconds I was at Rob's side by the wheel. The crunching continued. Even though Rob had put the boat in neutral, the boat was still thrusting forward. *Thwack*, a sound like a wet towel on a bare ass in a locker room. A few seconds later it was *Thwack* again. We assembled the crew on the bow, both of us waiting for the sound of gushing water. It never came. We hung over the bow, looking for logs or a whole jimmy of coconuts. No coconuts, no logs. Sonar had shown plenty of depth. Rob retrieved his large lamp and shone it over the water.

"Oh my God," he shouted. That was twisted around some protracted Morse made famous by troopers and sailors.

As far as the eye could see (which was getting farther as my eyes adjusted to the night) there were small floats holding nets that went off in diagonal strands to the projection of our charted course, spaced like yardage on a football field. They ran beyond our beam of light. It was like floating through a submersed vineyard of trellised vines that went to the horizon.

"Fishing nets? What the fuck!"

"Not fishing nets," Rob said. "This is a pearl farm."

"A pearl farm? You've gotta be shitting me!" And then it clicked, slowly unwinding in my head. That conversation I had caught bits and pieces of back at Jess Billiard Bar in Puerto Princesa was all about this predicament pickle we were in.

"So, this is what they meant," Rob muttered out loud. "I didn't think it would stretch across the entire bloody channel." We took turns swearing a blue streak, and then Rob went suddenly quiet, indicating I should as well. He began looking wildly in all directions, darted for the wheelhouse and returned with the binoculars.

"What's happening?" I asked as mildly as I could, not wanting to add my rising hysteria to a seemingly tense moment.

"Let's motor slowly ahead," I added, hoping to bring Rob back to earth.

"This is the place they were warning me about," Rob said, suddenly clueing into that conversation, culling for worthy information. "Avoid the pearl farm, they said. I didn't pay a lot of attention. Apparently, they have armed patrols."

"Armed to the teeth" resonated in my mind. The conversation had been about pearl farms somewhere or other and, like Rob, I hadn't paid much attention, as I was busy eavesdropping while deciphering Franco-Italian-Spanglish. I thought he was taking notes and I would get a copy later.

"A small fleet of floating artillery is how they put it, I think," Rob said.

Midnight pearl theft, like cattle rustling, is a big hazard of the industry, but frustrating, I would presume, since clams, like cats, were difficult to herd. Serious poachers would require underwater equipment; scuba gear, lights, sharp sheers, and a very fast getaway boat. These were not your gentle thieving cowpokes; most were pirates who came well-armed. A fine quality pearl can be worth thousands of dollars, depending on its size, shape, lustre, and colour, so pirates would certainly need to know what they were looking for—specifically, willing subjects that wouldn't clam up and inside info as to where the big boys hung out. In anticipation, the security crews in boats and on guard towers were most likely authorized to ready, fire, aim at any suspects. We were possibly in someone's crosshairs as we spoke. That took the situation from a "what-the-hell" to a triple "eff me" like American Homeland Security moving from code yellow to flashing red.

We decided to turn on all the lights in the boat, including the floodlight for the bow.

"Security has to know that thieves would not be stupid enough to floodlight their boat," Rob reassured himself, "and we have a Canadian flag."

"That could be reason enough for them to start shooting.

Canada does share the same continent with the Americans," I reminded Rob, "and everybody, it seems, wants to shoot the Americans."

A red and green light revealed itself in the distance, but it didn't appear to be moving. It could have been a boat approaching or moving away or a bobbing marker buoy; it was difficult to see anything in the dark beyond our bright lights. Maybe they hadn't noticed us, though that somehow seemed unlikely. I suspected they had night goggles and were watching our every move. There were probably underwater cameras, wired alarms, mines and S.P.E.C.T.R.E. submarines that opened fire or ate small boats with countdowns from five minutes to zero, for total destruction. Bond would only arrive after we had been fed to a tank of hungry sharks. And all I wanted was a few hours of sleep.

If someone did take a shot, it would be out of kindness, to put me out of my misery.

I was busy giving arm signals, left, right and full steam ahead, in the same manner as I had approached dropping and pulling up anchor, only this time I was trying to avoid floating markers, cables and netting while the boat was moving forward as fast as we could go. Rob had trained the floodlight on me, and, as usual, having been roused from sleep, I was as naked as a pole dancer, with about as many moves. Every *thwack* and *bang* sent me into a new flurry of hand signals that, through a high-powered scope, may have viewed like a full moon over the cuckoo nest of the hokey pokey ballet.

We were trying to zigzag through several miles of nets that were set out in a herringbone pattern, next to impossible to navigate by night. In the daytime, it would have been relatively simple, since there were wide-spaced channels that had been left as working areas for boats used for harvesting or setting new lines, but not for the efficient straight-through traffic such as ours.

The pearl nets were strong lines of rope or wire that ran

horizontally across the water or slightly below. Hanging from each wire that ran hundreds of feet were thousands of vertical wires to which millions of oyster and clam shells were suspended. These had been tied on and impregnated by hand (I hope) with a grain of sand irritant. There were feasibly twenty or more shells hanging on each vertical wire. What we navigated through represented hundreds of millions of pearls, one per shell.

This farming operation was no small deal—millions of invested dollars—so the surprise was that it had not been included in the ENCs we followed. Well, it was a surprise to me, but Rob only shrugged again about the incompetent cartographers who charted these waters, as if finding an unmarked pearl farm was simply par for the course. A wayward frigate could have destroyed the entire operation. *Bob-the-Boat* had a special metal protector around the propeller area and thus we were spared chewing up the nets and winding hundreds of feet of netting around the prop. This experience did, however, scrape paint off the hull of the boat, which had been given a brand-new paint job a few weeks prior in Phuket. Rob was not a happy captain. I had made noise concerning what we were doing to the pearl nets.

"Fuck their pearls. What about my boat?"

"Fuck your boat, what about my pearls? They probably have a gun trained on them right now. Let's get the hell out of here before someone starts shooting."

"And what about that bloody navigation program? No warning whatsoever," Rob said. I was not required to answer. This was the continued rant that echoed the "we nearly hit the abandoned oil well" off the coast of Brunei, only this time it hadn't been me at the wheel. Rob was not prone to berating himself; the electronic cartographers were still assholes, the whole Asian quadrant damned to hell. Nothing was to be gained by admonishing oneself for ignoring drunken advice in a bar. A couple of hours later, the thwacking stopped, and

Bob-the-Boat's rhythm returned. No shots were fired, and the big pearls were left intact.

Though I hadn't slept, I couldn't sleep, so I took over at the helm. Rob had us back on course and to show his complete faith that there would be no more problems, he retired to his stateroom below.

Shortly after, a few fingers of daylight stroked along the naked clouds, probing for a morning rendezvous. Covers of darkness, giving way to veils of dawn, hung in crumpled sheets over the distant hills that were the northern tip of Dumaran, suggesting it had already been an active night. The clouds, teased by the warmth, rolled ever so gently, and thighs parted, allowing a solitary beam to penetrate the depths below. I was envious of these ribald heavens sleeping in satisfied pleasure. Somewhere, though, in a rhythm close to my own, the typhoon was creating havoc.

34

THE VITRUVIAN MAN
ZERO PLUS AND ZERO MINUS

A FEW HOURS LATER. PAUSE FOR THOUGHTS...

Late midmorning, Rob tapped my shoulder, and I went below to sleep, but it never came. My mind was still adrift in a Bond-type Thunderball of pearl rustlers and a platoon of aquanauts armed to the teeth. The yin-yang duo screamed in unison that I nearly got them killed. I returned to the deck, where we had coffee and then stopped to swim. It had been nearly twenty-four hours since we had awakened in Puerto Princesa, made ready, waited for high tide and then motored out to the Sulu Sea for the final leg of the journey. The pearl farm debacle had left us with barely a moment of recharging sleep, and there were another thirty-five hours yet to come of no-anchors-down steady-as-she-goes. Before diving in, we quickly checked the horizon for waves—the kind that, like sharks and poisoned jelly masses, tend to disrupt an otherwise fabulous day. The swim was a welcomed break.

The water was refreshing and pristine. We could see the outlines of a reef below. Rob grabbed his snorkel and took the opportunity to inspect the damage from the night before.

There were multiple scratches and scrapes, but most were below the waterline. He talked of getting it repainted in Subic. I thought it was a waste of money since, like notches on a belt, the marked hull was proof positive that we had battled some unknown creature in the night and that, like a tiger in the boat, most people would rather hear of our heroic efforts to thwart a multi-limbed giant squid than hear the truth. And the truth, unfortunately, did not particularly work in our favour. As we found out later, the whole sailing world in these parts knew about the pearl farm, though that did not get the ENC cartographers off the hook. Rob inspected and I continued swimming, rolling and dipping like a sea otter in the gentle swells of the blue-green Sulu Sea.

When I became tired, I floated on my back, ears submerged slightly below the surface. There is something about floating this way…the Vitruvian man meets snow angels in the sea… which allows you to think and rejuvenate the soul.

⚓ ⚓ ⚓

The Vitruvian design is of the perfect man, encapsulated in a circle and squared by Leonardo da Vinci. This perfect man appears to be exercising, with four legs and four arms in the process of jumping jacks, a form of exercise I had mastered floating on my back in the water, including chin-ups while holding a floating rope. I didn't fit the perfect structure, although after several weeks at sea, eating rice salads and fruits, I was shrinking in the Vitruvian direction.

For a few moments I indulged in thoughts of Leonardo and his creation, my arms pointed east-west, legs testing the compass to the south. Da Vinci's man is supposedly the consummate model, the union of man with the divine, a perfect body with perfect soul to a union of masculine and feminine. Perhaps Wendy of Puerto Princesa was what he had in mind.

Of body and soul, I found it easier to work on the former.

I had nicely finished doing three sets each of fingertip push-offs from the side of the boat, knee bends on my back and ball scrunches to work on the wrists. I pondered on a winning video of Jane Fonda-style workouts; sea calisthenics called Walrus to Seal without Effort.

As for my soul, I had never spent much time thinking about it or working on its formation. I had rejected all arguments for the incorporeal-stuffed incarnate god that demanded the faith of wait-and-see, so, compared to the billions who defined their souls by such matters, it might have been fair to compare mine to a train wreck in that bridging of material and spiritual worlds. Occasionally I was envious of those who could give everything over without question, no matter how ridiculous the sumptuous coach on the train ride to the expiration date. They seemed to float with ease through life, where black and white had no shades of gray. And who wouldn't be tempted by the quiet solitude of the monasteries of Mt. Athos or Tibet; the courage to give over all thoughts and questions of our beginnings to the simplistic explanations of churches for the spiritual mind? But my yearning never lasted long.

Believing in something firmly meant rejecting so many huge possibilities in life and was the reason I had refused to sign on to big capital anything politically and shunned religious organizations like the plague. For me, there was no salvation in a soul carved and chinked in the stones of rigid beliefs that ignored half of humanity that had dissimilar views. The three big religions that share the same Jerusalem rock of creation is my case in point, but could truly extend to all spiritual dissension, east or west, that spills blood in dogmatic disagreement. It is beyond my comprehension as to why we draw ourselves into strict corners of behaviour and unwavering belief; the five pillars of Islam, the ten commandments of Christianity, the six hundred and thirteen laws of Moses and Judaism or the infinite legislated laws of social and civil human connections. Wouldn't the golden rule suffice? Naive, I know, but there seems to be no end to the barriers we will build between ourselves. Why create spiritual roads toward eternal life only to mine it with ugly rules of death and everlasting damnation? I have heard all the answers...like chutes culling lambs for soup or cutlets. Some would say that a person who believes in nothing will fall for anything, but I think those who believe rationally in the possibilities of everything—the likes of Gandhi, Galileo, Einstein or those who put men on the moon—will fall for nothing short of the truth, though I might be off in left field with a fly ball heading for right. We owe the disbelievers—the first sailors who didn't fall off the edge or scientists who were not burned as heretics—a huge debt of gratitude for refusing to be bound by dominant thought. I would rather wallow in the darkness of unproved truths than sit on a sandcastle of possible certainties in the sunshine of faith, waves of change crashing all around. Admitting to not knowing all the answers has been the impetus of change and growth for all of mankind. We seek, like Galileo, to understand and find truths along the way. Unwavering faith, however, leaves the believers scrambling to defend the unknown, wrapped in the myths of the ignorant. Can you truly defend a god, an all-powerful and loving one who is given credit for all life as we know it, but would shun women, bind them in the chains of second-class servitude, covered in veils and hoods, or allow his gay creations to be despised and murdered? The learned men of spiritual philosophies will invoke the dictums of Free Will bestowed upon mankind by God, to be atoned for on the Day of Judgement... *Man is responsible for all the humane and inhumanities given to him by God.* Knowing what we are capable of, can you truly defend such a god for this creation?

Leonardo, I think, may have had like thoughts. This is not to say that we are in the same league of minds. I am an idiot. He was a genius. After that, all comparison pales. But what we are allowed to think openly, engage willfully, take for granted, ponder over with no more thought than taking a breath, Leonardo da Vinci had to conceal or display through secret symbols like his Vitruvian man so as not to be burned as a Floridian or stretched on the rack of degenerate science. His Vitruvian man was a link, squared by the solid physical world and circled by the spiritual and eternal. I understood the circle. I simply couldn't hang one on me.

I stretched and paddled around the boat, returning to the stern and holding secret formation. Little did I know, based on ancient symbols, that I was proclaiming a sinister connection with hell.

Where all these thoughts came from, I really couldn't say. Who would think that floating in Vitruvian form, absorbing the warmth of the sun and enjoying the quiet of the moment, was justification for the proselytizing, sad sack of a tired mind to hijack my spiritual vacuums that existed within? That vacuum was too large to fill, but it swarmed with thoughts of my immediate surroundings; surroundings that reduced me to the size of a gnat's arse, a mite in that dust in the wind of Kansas. Maybe my mind was striving to make up for lost time, making connections with things much larger than I was capable of comprehending. Without invitations to do so, can the mind do this on its own? It was as if my sleep-deprived brain had been abducted by those aliens of the two minds, the type that perched on my shoulders, battling with opposite advice.

I pulled my head up from the water and listened, but the yin-yang were silent. The silence was unlike anything I had never heard before! No waves were breaking, no shrill cries of gulls or swarms of frantic swallows, no breezes cutting resonating notes in the stay wires of the mast. The cloudless sky, the heat and the warm ripples of water like silk threads on my skin made me take pause and wonder. I did a squid-like jet propulsion fifty feet out and back to the boat, then resumed my floating posture. I was an imperfect man in the perfect universe of the Sulu Sea contemplating questions most might not care to waste time pondering. The size of my manhood never came up.

However, sea levels did.

I was floating on the ocean, and the ocean was our comparative measurement for height the world over. Starting at zero, the ocean's surface was the beginning. But floating at zero was not as simple as one might think. Sometimes I was at zero, sometimes I was three feet above or several feet below, and wherever I was floating I was higher than I would have been a hundred years ago...eight inches and counting. Height matters with sea level and it was a tricky zero to nail down on any given day. So, what determines sea level zero?

Daily storms, currents, and tides move massive amounts of water around the globe. The greatest influence is the moon and its gravitational pull. The moon pulls up, the earth pulls down, the moon wins, and voila, tides happen. Align the earth, moon, and sun, and the extra gravitational pull from the sun gives maximum tides. There are volumes written on tides as related to moons and suns, with Sir Isaac Newton getting credit for putting things together.

One must wait for several changes of the tides to get the MSL (Mean Sea Level), which is the midpoint between the mean low tide and the mean high tide. This, at one time, might have required several cases of beer, sunglasses and a good book, possibly *War and Peace* in Farsi, while waiting to take the measurements, but it is now done from satellites in the care of NOAA, the National Oceanic and Atmospheric Administration. Several factors add weight to this mean, short-term and long.

Short-term can be anywhere from twelve hours to a year and a half. Lunar tides, referred to as semidiurnal cycles, happen every twelve hours and twenty-five minutes, and in the card game of earth life, one rotation spawns a trade of one diurnal cycle for a sunrise, two tides, and a sunset. Hearts (for life) are trump. Short-term factors include things like atmospheric pressure, winds that create surges (a typhoon can create a five-meter or sixteen-and-a-half-foot tidal surge), evaporation and its opposite, precipitation. Even El Niño gets in the act in duels with its lesser half, La Niña. This club-and-spade duo creates battles in warming and cooling, causing high and low air surface pressures, which somehow affect the sea level. The jury is still out on the exact cause of life and death. El Niño, "The Boy" and the "Christ child" (things tend to heat up around Christmas), get the bad press when warm waters with hot winds create fires in Hollywood...special effects nobody seems to want. Even the ocean's surface, called "ocean topography," changes like drifting dunes in a desert, due to the density of the water. Add heat, and it swells and rises. This is more fuel for the Vitruvian wisdom from da Vinci.

I was still doing jumping jacks to stay afloat, and the brain's vacuum was swirling out of control.

Without conspiracy, da Vinci believed that how the perfect man's anatomy worked—everything from the heat of the blood flow to the magic of muscle and rising mechanics—was a pretty good analogy for the technicalities of the universe; tides rising, nuts falling, moons circling Uranus, though Uranus wouldn't be discovered for more than two hundred years after da Vinci's death. All this, of course, was considering the anatomy worked. He certainly did lots of studies on fulcrums and getting things up though his Vitruvian man did not appear to be someone in need of such help. I am not sure if da Vinci had ever been in an old men's locker room (almost definitely in a few younger ones), but his anatomy drawings of male corpses suggest he had been somewhere. Perchance noticing the sagging, flaccid and wrinkled remains, he felt the world was going to hell in a handbag. Either way, perhaps there was some truth to his assertions on anatomy, the perfect man and the universe. Other comparative insights might have been included.

- The universe, for a large part, is a swirling mass of gases—a fact any wife, mine specifically, could verify.

- There are reasonable theories about the existence of parallel universes...any husband will validate the fact.

- Everything revolves around the sun, including Uranus. Insert wife or woman for sun: add heat, life-giving, sparkle and diamonds. Insert husband for Uranus. It's the law of the happy marriage universe. Assert any laws to the contrary and watch the quarks fly.

- Death and destruction from natural disasters are the work of God. Blue skies and butterflies are the work of Mother Nature.

- Full moons cause things to rise.

Where were we? Right—things that make the tides swell.

Tide movements also happen because of the salt. If water salinity changes, due to extra fresh water, for instance, water density changes, which affects tidal flow. Sea levels change. Who knew?

And did you know that the earth has a wobble, noticed by some guy on the way home from the pub? Actually, he was sober, named Chandler, and he determined the earth has a small wobble in rotation occasionally, which lasts for a while and causes short-term changes in tides and long-term things like ice ages. If you thought the earth moved for you one night, possibly it did.

Add to short-term changes things like earthquakes, tsunamis, occasional lands falling into water, ice calving, penguins and walruses returning to the sea, New Yorkers swimming at Coney Island, spring runoff, fall runaway, winter freeze and summer drought, and you have most everything that may cause short-term changes in sea level.

Long-term? Well, aye kurumba, as Bart Simpson might say, ice caps melting, tectonic plates shifting, volcanos growing in the deep...there is no rest for those with a measuring stick.

So, while doing my jumping jacks at zero, if the earth's plates move or a few dozen volcanoes grow under the ocean, this makes a difference. Up I go. If there is a cold snap (a few hundred years) and more snow gets dropped on the Antarctic than melts, down I go. Earthquakes and tsunamis will drive me up temporarily and drown me permanently. Inland erosion sending silt to the sea might push things up a little, but very hot weather that heats up the water, making it expand, will push it up a lot—that, and a hefty inclusion of new melted ice from the Antarctic and Greenland and dozens of glaciers around the world. The Arctic will not lift the zero level since most of the ice is already in the water. Finding zero is like nailing jelly to the wall. And don't even attempt it in the Bay of Fundy, between Nova Scotia and New Brunswick. Tidal changes are regularly around forty-five feet with storm surges as high as, well, most of Hollywood.

If there should happen to be a perfect storm of one of Chandler's wobbles, an earth tilt change of about one and a half degrees away from the sun, and a rare alignment on the outside edge of the earth's eccentricity (an elliptical orbit of the sun, in this case, pushing earth further from the heat of the sun), an ice age will return. Since there is an ice age once every hundred thousand years or so and the last one finished ten to twelve thousand years ago, there is probably no need to buy extra snow shovels yet. The oceans will probably drop by a couple of hundred feet or more, leaving Manhattan on the mount, under an ice cover several miles thick. Unfortunately, the last guy to take measurements while it happened was a politician with legislation for change who got run over by a moving glacier, so this may be all speculation in terms of years.

If the ice caps melt, feasibly sooner than later, a penguin might sit, on a calm day, somewhere around the bosom of the Statue of Liberty. Manhattan towers will still protrude above the ocean, walruses will lounge on the Brooklyn Bridge, and whales will play up and down the new rifts called Manhattan Trenches, maybe two hundred and fifty feet below sea level. But this theme has been touched on before...*Waterworld* and webbed feet. It has been suggested if everything melts, Antarctica, Greenland, the whole enchilada, the dark oceans—rather than reflect the sun's heat (jobs performed now by the snows of both poles), they will absorb the heat, turning everything into a hot soup. Maybe there will be no life at all, though I doubt it. There are shrimp that thrive by the boiling waters of deep-sea fissures already, so they may take over the seas. Reptiles that live in today's hot deserts may rule the land. Man, if he survives, will be a delicacy in their diets or a casual observer from an overcrowded colony on Mars.

You see, floating on your back at zero, mid-ocean, staring up into the blue, is more complicated than you might have thought, but it makes the contemplations of life seem fairly simple. However, it is not the kind of contemplation that one can do in the harbours of New York or Hong Kong. Horizons must be flat, unencumbered of the trappings of civilizations, so as not to muddle the naive musings of an idiot.

My zero was the raw natural entity, the naked sailor of conjugation minus the sheaths of circle and square. At my zero, give or take a foot or two, there are no boundaries or borders, no countries or flags, no language of control; creed, colour, race, religion, gender and sexual orientation have no meaning. The equations of inequality seem to disappear. These are the same things that are noticed from space by astronauts; the world is ocean blue and not a coloured map of barbed and wired ownerships, the things that, if one believes in a creator, were possibly part of the grand design. If that said creator had to do it all over again, would we—man—be included?

At my zero, where the world was flat, there were no spires or minarets, domes or arches with Holy Sees and scholars paralyzing the joy of life with the ugly fear of death. There were no towers of steel and glass that harboured corporate greed. From my perspective, zero plus and zero minus, everything seemed to have an equal, running chance: zero pockets of zero advantage, zero books from zero gods of law, except, perhaps, the law of gravity. Of course, my zero was a bit of a lie. To sustain my zero contemplations, I floated by a boat, valued by several zeroes pushing close to a million. If John was here, he would have lectured me on the futility of adding zeroes against the advantage of adding numbers that count. He might have won had he been there to defend his probable point.

At zero, if one is in tune with its rhythms, one might hear the songs of whales and all life in the sea; songs that tell of our beginnings, overtures of where we are going and whole symphonies about a chartered course to hell if we don't stop and listen.

The sea, you see, has seen it all before—boiling, bubbling, frozen, seething, calm—over a few billion years. It might be worth listening if the sea could only get our ears. It might say "Stop feeding me your filth. Stop emptying your bilges, dumping your barges, pouring raw sewage into my body. I am not a sewer. Ignore me and abuse me at your peril. I am willing to be as long and hard as you want, but to save our planet, it's naked sailor no more. For humanity, it's time to practice safe cruising...and cover up!"

If I, the naive sailor, first time to sea, could understand this cry for help and how the spirit and nature of oceans and man should be the perfect Vitruvian fit, why couldn't all the world see it as well?

As for our beginnings, well, the sea might graciously finger the moon, noting that it, the sea, solely went along for the tide; if you're looking for big bangs of creation, look up, far out, or deep to the core of the planet. But there was always something crawling from the ocean's deep to implicate its complicity in our being. It slithered up and skittered away, returning after ample time on fours or twos in fear and awe of their watery beginnings. These things answered and unlocked, perhaps, the universal questions, things that pointed to the great blue masses of this planet and shouted, "Look no further."

If you are looking for your maker, swim the perfect man at zero seas. If you want to meet him, dither down below.

"**Shark!**"

I blinked my eyes open, treading water. It was Rob, staring down from the stern, half playful grin, half disheartened I had not panicked into a frenzy. We had not seen one shark on the whole trip, though this didn't mean they weren't there.

"What the hell are you nattering about? I called your name three times. We gotta get going." Persnickety captains were always worrying about typhoons and fifty-foot waves.

At my zero, it is good to have a captain with two feet on the ground.

35

THE SUNSET MASTERPIECE
ENGINE TROUBLE
SHIPWRECKS
RATS ON THE RUN

OCT. 20-21, 2009, OUR LAST NIGHT AT SEA

Partially cloudy skies covered our journey as we pushed past the island of Culion, with the bleak nicknames of "Island of the Living Dead" and "Island of No Return." Believe it or not, Hollywood had no hand in the names. It's one of the oldest leper colonies in the world, dating back to the Spanish invasion of the 1500s. Leprosy is still a vile affliction to many in Southeast Asia, though it is curable and it now goes by the civilized name of "Hansen's Disease." There were no signs of its dark history as a leper colony (Easter Island-type sculptures missing parts)—in fact, from our perspective there was no sign of habitation at all.

Culion was surrounded by stone sentinels off the eastern coast, bald rock, a result of being open to winds across the Sulu Sea where typhoons could gather speed and strip vegetation like a hungry goat. But we knew inhabitants lived there since there were online ads for exotic resorts and dive centers tucked in on the northwestern tip where there were sheltered coves and inlets. These would be important in a part of the world where typhoons are endless. The brochures we had seen showed lush, leafy retreats. We were not aware of Culion's museum of history if we had wanted to stop, but Culion was a neighbor to Busuanga, and Tequila Mike, fruit bats and leprosy museums were all on the back burner of "another time, perhaps."

⚓ ⚓ ⚓

The collective islands of northern Palawan are ruggedly beautiful from the sea. They stand out because of their barren and rocky remoteness, much larger than the carved mushroom islands that cluttered the archipelago waters near Phuket hanging with lush growth. These islands looked like photos I had seen of the Orkney archipelago of Northern Scotland, minus the slate-gray villages, castle ruins and bagpipers. I had never been that far north in Scotland, but from what I remember, much of Scotland resembles the back-view topography of a windblown kilt. Some of the Palawan islands grew straight up from the water, colourless slivers of rock like hundred-year-old men, tangled wisps of vegetation on craggy, wrinkled faces, topped by baldness. The waters surrounding them were sparkling blue and green, and some had white-sand beaches stretched like welcome mats. It made sense that the Scottish hills were barren due to how far north they were and the cold, unrelenting winds, but here it seemed so out of place, as if they had been skinned. Conceivably they had. We were now far enough north in the Sulu Sea to take direct hits from storms, and it only took one typhoon to kill everything.

A late afternoon rainstorm found us as we were leaving the protection of the islands, a junction of the Sulu and the South China Sea before the large island of Mindoro created another dividing wall. The storm passed quickly, but left a moody presence of clouds and mists that changed the look again. The islands and dark hills became long, gangly profiles of sleeping crocodiles...jagged armored coats hovering close to the water's surface. Some of the small singular outcrops of rock floated like the last remnants of an unlucky wildebeest caught in the river crossing. Again, the rain had the warmth of an indoor shower, so I stood on the bow and let the wind and rain drench me and blow me dry through patterns of dripping clouds and patches of almost-blue. The waters remained mirror-calm between rainfalls; the bow cutting glass, the stern smoothing edges in our wake. At one point an aerial perspective through mists and drooping clouds was an oriental fusion of floating worlds; hillsides with black islands in the foreground to distant reptilian shapes, and pointillist shadows in shades of Prussian blue and gray. Other than one small fishing boat setting out nets, the sea was all ours, a fresh canvas for miles. It is the kind of beauty and tranquillity—like setting suns, new dawns and a fresh carpet of pristine snow—that you want to last forever. Only a Canadian might wish for snow to last forever.

As much as I loved the brilliant blue and yellow of the perfect tropical day, I enjoyed the advance of storms with their mile-high thunderheads, sometimes glowing with sheets of lightning. You could watch clouds form, innocent puffs to mushrooming nimbus in very short order. As the tops billowed and climbed, bottoms flattened, sending gray and blue veils to connect with the sea. When the front wall of rain hit, it was like being drawn into a live rock concert, thunderous applause of anticipation on the bow and windshield, full metal acoustics on the wheelhouse roof, and a standing ovation for several minutes until we pierced the storm's trailing edge with the nose into the calm of the emptied stadium. In the city, dogs, babies and smart cars were hurled like missiles before the cleansing rain. Bent trees and structures that gave resistance were the alarm bells of the coming storm. Here, like the boomerang cloud of Puerto Princesa, the rains were warm and almost eerily quiet in their stealth approach and departure. I knew that a typhoon would be a horse of a different colour.

By five in the afternoon, we were preparing for our final night at sea. Perhaps this should have been a moment of quiet reflections or high-five celebrations between us—after all, this was a once-in-a-lifetime journey, for me anyway—and what's next, perhaps, should have been rolling through my mind, but the lack of sleep and the real threat of the new typhoon dominated my thoughts. Thoughtful reflection would have to wait.

By Rob's estimation, we should arrive in Subic by noon of the following day. Earlier, he had spoken with Tequila Mike, toying last minute with making a sojourn to Busuanga, but, in reality, was only an excuse to quiz "The Tequila" about his perceptions and gut feelings on the typhoon's movement. Our onboard ENC package did not allow for automatic up-to-the-minute weather feeds or shipwrecks, a package I daresay was probably worth its weight in digital download at moments such as these. The next best solution was Tequila Mike, who was surrounded by electronic gadgetry, though often Rob remembered him saying they had to shut everything down, as they worked off sun and wind power, charging batteries to run the resort. His advice was...well, friendly, I guess, though not overly helpful in making up our minds.

"Probably you will be okay, but one never knows with these things. I'm no psychic when it comes to storms. Best make up your own mind...I can't say one way or the other."

The storm was still east of the Philippine mainland, he had informed us, which meant it still had the option of traveling south, but it would be "A couple of days probably, a week maybe...one thing for certain, it's coming." I thought Rob might have saved money on phone calls and invested in a crystal ball instead.

"I think we'll push on for Subic," Rob had said to Mike,

along with farewell goodbyes. It was too late in the day to get a straight answer from Tequila Mike, where perhaps the bottle had had the advantage. However, it was noted in his defence that typhoons were very unpredictable, and, of course, he was protecting his interest. If our boat sank, like a pair had a year earlier, he might feel responsible. He didn't want to turn business away, but when business sank, the stories hung like albatross lore for years.

The western horizon was taking on a watercolor luminance, a Turner masterpiece minus the steam, speed, smoke and smog of nineteenth-century London skies, which, come to think of it, was almost everything a great Turner boasted. The grays and blues of the rainstorm that were moving south as we headed north surrounded a fusion of colors that had burned through an open patch of clouds. One almost expected the prow of some monolithic warship to push through, awash in the glow of a battle won or seething with smoke and fire, raging beauty in the death throes of its final battle, to be named and hung on the gallery wall. Instead, a simple canvas-topped fishing boat cut a black silhouette against the diffused palette of orange and yellow tranquillity. For a final night at sea, one could hardly ask for more.

It was less than an hour to darkness. With *Bob-the-Boat* powering forward in his usual form, we sat down for a salad of cucumber, diced red onions, red peppers and rice sprinkled with balsamic vinegar and olive oil, doors opened wide...it was the setting for a perfect meal.

If it had been a dropped note, no one may have noticed. However, the entire brass section caved while the winds and strings were resting. *Bob-the-Boat* was suddenly in trouble.

There was the sound of a high, whirring spin, the engine chugging, and we had stopped moving. Rob raced for the controls and threw the boat in neutral. The unusual noises stopped. Everything seemed fine. Gauges read normal. There were no blinking lights for countdown destruction or ENC flashing admissions of "O-o-p-s, sorry, there is a sunken ship skewered on a hidden reef, available on version 2.0."

Rob was worried. It was a sound he had not yet encountered on any boat. Gently, he shifted the boat back into forward and gave it some throttle. The sound returned. Back to neutral. Rob called on the Gods of Fuck.

"What the fuck do I do now?" It was, probably, the most disconcerting question I had ever heard him pose. I was expecting knowledgeable statements of diagnosis—"It sounds like a fuel line is clogged" or "It needs oil" or "A piston has left the building"—anything but "What the fuck do I do now?" That was a question one could ask on dry land, in a garage where those same gods are often tested (usually without success) with a ball-peen hammer. At the end of the day, lights could be doused because there was always tomorrow. The situation did, however, trigger a pair of thoughts.

The first had no use whatsoever. It was from another life when I worked in television.

I was first assistant director on a film shoot. I informed the producer we had a problem.

"Norm," he said smugly, "we don't have problems…only solutions!"

"Well, your lead actor is nowhere to be found and shooting begins in ten minutes!"

"Oh, fuck. Houston, we have a problem."

I didn't tell him his lead had been hijacked by an extra who had locked herself into his trailer, stripped naked and tied herself to his bed.

This thought was discarded for some future happy hour.

The other thought, however, was triggered by a sound that stirred a memory filed under [**Childhood**], sub-section {**Outboard motor loses propeller**}.

My brother had built a barge for our cottage on Lake Muskoka, a community of stuffed-shirt millionaires who puttered around in shapely wooden boats that burbled breeding like their Rolls Royce owners who sported titles that had been passed through generations. Even the Canadian geese honked heritage like Eider Duvet the 3rd. A barge on this lake was prized like a Walmart on the Champs-Élysées, unless, of course, it was carrying second-floor extensions to their island retreats.

The day was a colourful affair. Everything was in place after several days of assembling the pontoons, decking, wheelhouse, and, lastly, hanging the outboard motor on the moveable transom. The outboard motor started, wailed in neutral, then settled to a contented burble as it was backed off the beach, but when thrown into forward, there was a clunk, thump and whir, and we watched as a spinning propeller headed like a gold Rolex watch to the bottom of the lake. My brother let go with a colourful streak of blue.

The similarities in sound were too depressing, and I was reluctant to say anything, lest those same gods be called on me. I sure as hell didn't want to be right.

"Maybe we should check the propeller," I offered, stifling the urge to add, "if there is one."

"Great idea, get the snorkeling equipment, quick," Rob commanded. "It's already getting dark."

I scrambled into a bunker on the stern that housed the hoses and pump. Rob's system had two hoses for two divers, one hundred feet each, attached to an electric pump on the deck. We had tried the system out in Langkawi when the boat's side thrusters had failed. I had no problem breaching, but I had been unable to get my body to stay under the water.

While I set up, Rob dove into the water with his snorkel and checked things out. He was back in seconds. "Good call! There is a huge piece of rope wrapped around the propeller. I will need a knife."

I returned quickly with a box knife (all I could find), but there wasn't much blade left. Rob had already changed into the air mask. Knife in hand, he disappeared.

The sun was now sitting on the horizon, testing the water

for its nightly dip. Darkness, I knew, would follow swiftly behind. I waited. I pulled out the large flashlight we had used while navigating the pearl farm. It was dead. The discipline of fixing, repairing and recharging during downtime had been ignored, though, in my defence, it had power when I returned it to the bunker. The switch may have been pressed to "on" in the clutter of the storage. If there was luck involved, it was that some daylight remained and it was not the middle of the night. I waited. Rob had not resurfaced, so I had no idea of his progress, but bubbles were still surfacing, the hose tugged now and again, so I was quite sure he had not been eaten. There would have been a floating flipper at least. Dusk would be all of a minute and a half when it came, and then night would swallow us whole. I waited. The sun set and within moments, a contented darkness chased it into the pre-warmed bed.

Thump! A large piece of gnawed rope landed on the deck. It was followed by a lagoon-like creature, a pair of yellow webbed feet tossed from the darkness, wrinkled, pasty white flesh crouched menacingly in a steady movement, rung by rung, up the ladder. It was a hybrid sea-land concoction with a raccoon imprint, mask askew over knotted tentacles of hair, all wrapped in a tangle of yellow tubing, dripping water and exhaustion. The faint glow of the stern light did not show Rob well at all.

There was no time to congratulate. Rob hurried to the console and restarted the engine. It purred. He gently eased it out of neutral and listened. The high-pitched whir was gone; the boat moved forward, accelerating as Rob cranked the engine speed. At 1,400 rpm, *Bob-the-Boat* pushed forward as if nothing had happened, content with its twenty-minute pause from the thirty-six-hour push to our final goal. Only eighteen or twenty left to go.

With everything stored, the offending rope hanging from the bow as a warning to other would-be rope assassins, we stopped to consider our luck—and, most of all, our quick action that had saved the day. We high-fived, man-hugged, then finished our meal. I took the first watch, thinking Rob might like some rest. My mind wandered, knowing another potential disaster had been averted.

In the overall scheme of things, it was a non-issue blip on the radar of boating disasters. This had been child's play, but, like everything else we had encountered, it had the potential of turning ugly. At midnight with tossing seas, this boat could have had another end, drifting onto rocks or wandering into shipping lanes, or, had we called in distress on an open channel, we could have been wounded game for pirates. There was no chance to drop anchor when it happened. The depth was over two hundred feet. It was easy to dismiss the simple problem when it was quickly fixed, but it was a reminder that, at sea, disaster was only a moment's rush away.

⚓ ⚓ ⚓

UNESCO estimates that there are over three million shipwrecks on the ocean floors, but gives no timeline as to when counting started. On average, I read, two large ships sink every week in this century, and these are not including inland statistics for the Great Lakes or other freshwater channels.

My first reaction was, "Nonsense, it can't be possible"—exclaimed to whom, I don't remember—but, after a little digging, I realized I was wrong! We hear about wrecks of high drama, the ferries with huge loss of life, cruise ships on their sides and the oil tankers spewing crude into sensitive wildlife habitats, yet for the rest they are statistics for insurance companies and the shipping news, as per the aforementioned, the MV *Tricolor* and its load of luxury cars. Pardon me while I pause for a memorial service.

We gather today to remember the Volvo S80s, SAAB 9-3s and BMW X1 through 8. May God deliver a new one to my door. Amen.

There are no estimates for lost sailors, but if we consider

battles from the ancient Phoenicians to modern times, knowing the crews and size of battleships and all the navies and merchant vessels around the world, over a billion would not be an outlandish guess. May all their souls rest in peace.

Our tiny incident had developed into nothing more than momentary high blood pressure. We had dealt with it quickly and without panic. Therein was the secret to a good captain.

Rob may have left the impression on others of a distant, cool, bull-headed, tenacious, self-centred, single-minded man, which some days would have been accurate assessments, but these same character traits were the merits one required in their captain at sea. It was cold, calculating precision that was needed to lead men to war or to captain ships. On fine days of calm, it was easy to second-guess, but in crisis, at sea especially, there is little time for consensus-building amongst the tribal elders. The talking stick and the tomahawk stay with the captain. Hopefully, you can pass the peace pipe later.

It was sad but understandable how his marriage had faltered. For a captain, especially a novice, a wife on board, I apologize to say, can rank down the list of prominent distractions, after motors and sails, fuel pumps, bilges, propellers, flagging rudders, drifting anchors, tides coming and going, a crew if he is lucky to have one, destinations, safe arrivals, rocky shoals, coral reefs, unexpected waves and abandoned oil wells. Throw in rough seas, the threat of typhoons, the possible boarding by pirates, and, well, relationships suffer badly—and, oh, maybe temptations in warm, dark groves of pleasure offered on a platter.

Bob-the-Boat plugged on through the night with Rob and me taking turns at three-to-four-hour intervals. I slept so lightly, I wondered if I slept at all, not wanting to sleep past my shifts. I woke every twenty minutes or so and checked my watch. Morning's unveiling found us pushing past the northern tip of Mindoro or one of its smaller islands. This would be the last land we would see until we entered Subic Bay.

Still several hours from our final destination, we witnessed a disconcerting view, one that made us stop and wonder about our decision to push toward Subic.

There were still no signs of a storm; the waters were calm, and the skies were un-shaded blue; no clouds to protect us from the heat. It was Rob who pointed out that the shipping lanes, off the port side to our west, were a bit of a traffic jam. Indeed, there was a long line of frigates, tankers, containers and warships, all heading south, like rats single-file down the ropes of a plague ship. It was customary, Rob said, that ships—especially navy warships like aircraft carriers that have up to five thousand sailors on board—be given instructions to find quiet pastures in the event of a pending typhoon. Ship after ship, bow to stern, heading south, and we were heading north. Did Rob know something these guys didn't?

He caught my doubting looks, a twitching nose caught between furrowed brows and a tight pucker of concern.

"I hear you. Trust me!" Rob said. "Where we are going is as safe as anywhere we could be." He thought for a few moments and continued, "Unless we were at home, of course...which we're not."

36

B.O.A.K.Y.A.G.BY
TYPHOONS: THE ART OF TURNING A PIG INSIDE OUT

TIMELESS INFO

The Philippine word for typhoon is "bagyo," which may be a shortened version of the English acronym, BOAKYAGBY—Bend Over and Kiss Your Ass Goodbye.

Apparently, "Safe Harbour" does not apply to hurricanes and typhoons, or any storm that can turn a pig inside out. The most dangerous place for a ship is in the eye of the hurricane. The second worst place is in a harbour. If moorings give way in the harbour, a ship becomes a loose cannon wrecking ball, like an uncontrolled pinball, each double D-I-N-G racking up a potential hundred-million-dollar loss. If a bunch of ships become unpegged, look out. Big ships are built to weather large storms at sea. Cyclonic storms are the exceptions. Ignore them at your peril.

The eye of the storm, though sunny and momentarily calm above, can be a death trap for ships. High winds circling a vortex send waves crashing in from all directions. They meet, join forces and can become rogue waves; ten-storey condos seeking lifetime tenants, no maintenance fees included. A ship caught in this for long is on borrowed time. Ships need to avoid the eye at all costs.

Storms with eyes are special and get a lot of attention. It means they are full-fledged hurricanes, (Spanish, from Mayan Caribbean *Haracan*), typhoons (*Typhos*, the most deadly monster of Greek mythology or from the Chinese *ty-fung*, for "large wind"), or cyclones (Greek origin *kyklon*...moving in a circle, not Cyclops for the single-eyed monster, though it fits)...different words for the same type of storm, except for one difference. Cyclones, depending on the information resource, are said to spin clockwise since they are south of the equator—however, most resources tend to label them all cyclones with sub-species hurricanes, typhoons, and tornadoes. They all have the potential to be real killers, both on land and at sea, so all maritime countries pay close attention when they begin to develop. With satellites and a space station, it is now easier than ever to monitor their development.

But where do these storms come from? My explanation is for heat-generated storms only, since these things can develop via other means in the Poles as well and have been captured via the Hubble Telescope on Mars. The Mars thing is probably a whole book of speculation on its own and better left to others for explanation. Routine earth is still a big mystery to me.

Heat-driven cyclones start with very warm water, which gets that way due to long periods of hot sun over large, open bodies of water. The Pacific, mid-Atlantic, and the Indian Ocean qualify as such. They form in waters from five to thirty degrees latitude north or south of the equator. These latitudes north and south of the equator are also referred to as the "horse latitudes." This area is often so calm that, without winds, sailing ships could sit for weeks, while precious supplies ran low. Thirsty horses were often sacrificed to the deep.

For storms to begin brewing, the water needs to be warm, bathtub warm, no less than twenty-seven degrees Celsius or eighty Fahrenheit, and, not reserved for surface water, but down to a depth of a hundred and sixty feet or fifty meters. Canadians may have a hard time comprehending this idea since Canadian lake water warms the neck and positively shrivels the gonads at the same time. By any measurement, fifty at twenty-seven degrees Celsius over the vastness of the Pacific, Atlantic, or Indian Ocean is a tremendous amount of heat over a vast amount of water and qualifies quite nicely for one of those things that changes sea level zero. This is possible since the daytime air temperatures in the latitudes mentioned rarely venture below the ideal warmth for creating storms. Think Mexico, sunburns and jalapeño peppers. With this much warmth to such a depth, the overlaying atmosphere can become unstable, since there is a great deal of convection happening (heat rising via gas or liquid, evaporating at a cooler location), which eventually leads to cooling condensation called rain. It's like a lidded pasta pot on its way to boil. A big thunderhead would qualify as unstable, but in the cyclonic process it's not one but lots of thunderheads; thousands all forming at the same time. The hotter, the higher the vapors go, but the critical height seems to be around thirty-three hundred feet to set things in motion.

If a bunch of thunderheads form at close range, they start to communicate. This happens since what goes up must come down, and all that vaporized water that rises eventually recondenses and begins to fall as rain. The rise and fall of these vapors are important, but without clouds working together, it is only a rainstorm.

As vapors condense to form rain in a single cloud, it begins to fall, and that fall creates a breeze. In the formation of a typhoon, however, we are talking about vast amounts of water being involved in thousands of clouds, from over a few thousand square miles of ocean surface. One typical thunderhead cloud might hold upward of two hundred and seventy-five million gallons or one billion litres. Read that again!

That amount of water is the equivalent of nearly six minutes of water flow over Niagara Falls (though there does not seem to be any consensus on that number) and is nearly one-third of the one billion gallons or nearly four billion litres of drinking water consumed by New York City every day. One gallon of water weighs 8.34 pounds, which means there are nearly 2.3 billion pounds of water in that one cloud alone, falling or waiting to fall. That weight is comparable to a freight train with six hundred and thirty boxcars (if you need a visual, that's a train approximately six miles or 9.7 kilometres long), so that amount of weight falling is going to create an enormous amount of air movement. If things get derailed during typhoons and hurricanes, now you know why. Now multiply all this by hundreds, even thousands of thunderheads being created at the same time, and, well, my calculator can't generate enough zeros to figure this out, but we are talking heavy in whatever measurements you want to use. Thankfully, it doesn't all fall at the same time. The rise and fall is a continuous process.

When the water falls after condensing, it doesn't drop straight down like the ACME anvil from Wile E. Coyote, but shifts slightly off-center, which is due to the world spinning and gravitational forces. The movement thus creates a ball of wind and rain rolling from the center to the outside of the cloud while falling into the ocean. One thunderhead is a local rain shower, but a group of thunderheads all doing the same thing start to create heavy-duty winds, which, in turn, begin to connect them. Again, the winds are being moved by gravity and the spin of the earth, so at some point, like connecting the dots, the clouds begin to merge their energies.

There is something in the spin of the wind from these clouds (if I remember correctly from my cartoon days, it was the Tasmanian Devil) that creates the "eye," which in turn forms ideal conditions for a low barometric pressure. Low barometric pressure is the necessary defibrillator to start the whole process happening. The low pressure, while making soft, joyous breezes and light clouds directly above it, creates a connectivity for the whirlwind of spin at the ocean surface, much like the spin cycle of your washing machine that leaves your socks pinned to the drain holes of the tub. And yes, socks go missing in typhoons. The low-pressure system causes air to flow towards it. In a major typhoon, the eye can be at fifteen percent less pressure than the surroundings, so there is little wonder that air flows in that direction, sucking you out of your best pair of boxer shorts as well. Because of the heat and something called the Coriolis effect (winds and earth rotation that help pull the storms towards the Poles...get someone like Stephen Hawking to explain the mathematics), those winds begin to move outward, away from the equator. They move to the north in the northern hemisphere and opposite in the south and get sucked upward with all the air that is already being channelled in that direction. High up—again, about three and a half thousand feet—some winds start to siphon off, cooling into something called the cirrus effect, giving that smooth, flat spinning cap of air that we see from space (like the pizza guy making his dough, thick crust), and this cap in turn helps to unite the rogue thunderheads beneath (birds of a feather flocking together) into organized circular rain bands. Again, think gravity, the spinning earth and the Coriolis effect adding to the mix. Beneath the calm flat cap of air are these circles of thundercloud rain bands, still sucking up heat and water, but since the heat from the rain bands can no longer escape due to the pizza cap, the air cooling beneath falls, creating spaces between each rain band called moats. For a visual, these could be compared to the round red and white circles of a shooting target—the red are the rain bands, and the white are the moats. These moats allow the cooling air—thousands of six-mile freight trains' worth of weight and energy—to flow downward, as the center of the rain band is drawing more heat and moisture up. This energy gets sucked toward the spinning eye, feeding the monster.

Now let me take this opportunity to apologize for this explanation. It's boring and disruptive to my story, I know. But had I known what I now know, I would never have accepted (long distance) that call of the sea.

There is something called "positive feedback" happening and has been compared to the squeal created by a sound system known as electronic feedback. This is where the system catches its amplification output from the speakers, sending it back through more amplification, creating an ear-piercing screech. Energy adds to more energy, which feeds off itself, and *voila*, you have a big noise or, in this case, a huge rotating storm. As the turbine starts to rotate, it sucks in more and more heat and humidity, which adds energy and speed and so on and so on, until Dorothy and Toto arrive in Oz. Oh wait, that's a whole different set of airbags.

Around the eye—unlike a tornado, which is a single spinning funnel—are those numerous rain bands sucking up heat, driving cold air to the ocean surface, creating one of the most efficient heat engines in our universe.

Occasionally, two or more tropical storms will develop at the same time, and they can merge to create one large superstorm. It is called the Fujiwhara effect after the Japanese fellow who studied this atmospheric phenomenon. While we were on *Bob-the-Boat*, this collusion of winds happened twice, once while we were heading from Singapore to Borneo and once again while we were in the Philippines, though we were none the wiser, and, on both occasions, this probably saved us a lot of grief. The larger of the two and sometimes three storms tends to hold gravitational sway over the smaller ones. In our case, it dragged the typhoons north.

With an understanding of the conditions for creation and the mechanics of typhoons, you might ask yourself, what is stopping typhoons from developing every day? Nothing, it would seem, as the season for typhoons can go from January

1st through to December 31st in this part of the world, which by my calculation is pretty much a full year. 1964 holds the record for storms, thirty-nine in all, of which thirteen were tropical storms, nineteen were typhoons, and seven were super typhoons. From the day in June when Rob had dropped by to make his case until the time we left the Philippines for Hong Kong—a period of five months—there had been no less than fifteen tropical depressions, storms or outright typhoons that had formed, dissipated, or gone on to wreak havoc throughout the region, each with a lifespan of a week or two. One typhoon in particular, Typhoon Quedan, started as two—Tropical Storm Parma and Typhoon Melor. Names don't matter, but this combination was viewed from space and captured the Fujiwhara effect as it happened. The swirling winds of Parma could be seen unraveling like cotton candy off its paper core and winding itself into Typhoon Melor, which then became the second Category 5 typhoon to hit the Philippines that year, renamed Typhoon Quedan. This typhoon dropped nearly eighteen inches of rain in twenty-four hours in Manila, the most of any storm in forty-two years. Nearly eight hundred people were known to have died.

Viewing online montages and news footage of the storm now, a few years later, it is heartbreaking, to say the least, as it is with any natural disaster anywhere in the world, to watch videos of bodies floating in swollen rivers and streets through towns and cities, or limbs protruding from mud, families trapped on bus tops and balconies, children orphaned in an instant, crying in the debris where their homes once stood. One week after Quedan, another typhoon followed, and two storms within two weeks followed that one. This was all happening as we calmly navigated from Singapore to Borneo and north to the Philippines. Somewhere, someone needs to build a monument to the resilience of the Filipino people.

Like I said, had I known what I know now about typhoons, I may have never ventured out of bed in Toronto.

A large Northwest Pacific typhoon, the largest on earth (the very same location we were heading for) can have a radius of up to nearly nine hundred kilometres or five hundred and fifty miles. This is the radius! Imagine a giant hoover machine moving along and gathering heat and speed that is over one thousand miles wide. This is the distance between New York and Kansas City or London, England, and Naples, Italy. Hurricanes of the Atlantic, by comparison, are roughly half the size. Neither type can sustain strength over land, since they need to feed off the ocean's heat, but this doesn't mean they can't do damage by sending high winds and massive rain fronts over entire continents. As global warming takes effect, we can only expect there will be more and conceivably larger storms in the future.

Scientists estimate that a full-blown cyclone can release heat energy equivalent to two hundred times the world's electrical generating capacity, which, they point out, is like exploding a ten-megaton nuclear bomb every twenty minutes. Say "typhoon" to a seasoned sailor and expect him to fill his pants!

Into this potential, we plugged along at 1,400 rpm, while some of the world's largest ships were beating a trail to the south.

37

SUBIC PHILIPPINES
THE FINAL HOUR OF THE VOYAGE
CATHARSIS IN THE QUIET

A WEEK BEFORE THE TYPHOON HITS

My thoughts were temporarily hijacked by *Bob-the-Boat*. He made a large starboard manoeuvre, like a hound that had sniffed the waters and recognized the trail. There were no hands at the wheel. Rob adjusted fishing lines, and I hung at the bow, letting the spray from parting waves cool my feet. *Bob-the-Boat* with Rob as captain had now successfully crossed the South China Sea twice, finding their way back to Subic Bay once again. Thankfully, *Bob-the-Boat* was programmed to hunt and flush out the rewards of exotic ports and, in this case, a port to shelter us from the coming storm.

We were now pushing eastward, following an invisible line of sea toward the treasured protection of Subic Bay. Two typhoons had merged into one, and it was now a thousand miles wide, winds pushing darkened skies with lethal possibilities at over two hundred and fifty kilometres an hour. We were aiming for the safety of a harbour where we could tie up, hoping that, like many typhoons, it would veer north or lapse into a tropical storm before it found our hideout. No one plays chicken with typhoons. Even the gods leave town.

As boats went, *Bob* was probably man's best friend. He had been relentless, almost unfailing and dutiful in his task to this point, but, like all hounds, stubborn and single-minded of intent. If we had fallen overboard, there would have been no hope of him stopping or even looking back—such was the obsession of the ENC implanted in his core.

If he had noticed that Subic and Olongapo were close at hand, he showed no excitement. There was no baying gallop to the finish line. He maintained vigilant attention to his vital signs; heartbeats counted in rpms, a huffing burble from the stern. A flexing needle monitored his PSIs of cooling oil, and 20/20 vision was maintained by a satellite far above the clouds. *Bob-the-Boat*, it seemed, was as content and dutiful as any boat could be.

In this final hour, I drank it all in; heat, salt, the tropical vegetation. The air was hot, even by Philippine standards, though paled in comparison to the heat we had experienced in Singapore. A breeze stirred by our movement, eight knots per hour, helped to keep us cool, and the silver linings that rimmed the afternoon clouds helped filter the stifling noonday sun. The bay danced in a sequined sparkle from rays that pushed through ever-churning clouds, up where the winds called the tune.

Those silver linings, I thought, reflected my good luck to have had a friend who owned a yacht—a yacht that was favourably floating in the sun and pristine waters of Southeast Asia and not trolling for Alaskan crab. I felt privileged that he had thought enough of our lifetime friendship to allow me to share the journey, even knighting me as his first mate. It was silver linings, trimmed with paradise gold. There had been no swearing-in. It had been an acclamation by default: Catherine, first mate of nearly forty years, returned home, and his trusted first choice, a Filipino navigator of first-class standing, gone to America, so I, without class, was chosen.

It had been a token appointment, I knew, allowing me to share split shifts of four-hour naps between navigation duties and cooking meals with an opportunity to wax and polish railings until they gleamed, but who could complain of line-ups at the bank while waiting to cash the winning lottery cheque? I had stopped pinching myself to see if it was for real (it was now six weeks real), but I refused to blink in case it all disappeared too quickly. The changing view of distant shores—palms, sand and breaking surf—continued to excite me as if it was our first day out.

Rob had moved inside to fix a sandwich in the galley, while I continued to dangle limbs to the spray of the parting waves. The captain's wheel in the helm moved in small, quiet corrections. I could feel the change of direction, the western sun now applying licks of heat to my back until a shadow moved in, interrupting the tan I had been working on for weeks. Rob stood behind me, holding the last of his ham and cheese, clad in his captain's attire...SpongeBob boxers and sunglasses, his sun-bleached ponytail catching in the breeze.

"We're almost there," he said, pulling his arms back in a long stretch above his head, betraying the exhaustion we both felt. Neither of us had slept with any substance for a full fifty-six hours and counting.

"It's been a good trip, all considered," Rob offered, devouring the last corner of his sandwich. "Best of all, we're going to beat this bloody typhoon."

I nodded agreement, shuddering at the thought that we had raced full tilt like thrill junkies into the middle of a coming typhoon...a storm with the terrifying reputation of being the largest on earth. We could see the tail end of those large ships fleeing to the south.

"It doesn't get safer than Subic, Norm," Rob added again for reassurance, a refrain I guess my face told him needed to be repeated from time to time. "We might get lucky...the storm may change direction." He laughed, guessing, I think, that it wouldn't. Nearly all the Pacific typhoons were aimed at the Philippines.

I said nothing. There is nothing like complete exhaustion to calm the nerves or coerce the mind into casual acceptance of inevitable death; if you are going to go, this is as good a place as any. I let my mind wander as it wanted to do, to focus on the beauty of the shoreline.

From our entrance into Subic Bay, we continued heading east, with windrowed clouds chasing the sun to the west and casting shadows of animation across a scene of tropical bliss. The north shore was a tangle of palms—coconut, banana, mango—swaying over pristine white sands and even a gnat-like jet ski that cut a swath of zigzag destruction on the bay could not diminish the view.

Subic Bay may have once been a volcano. It is surrounded by layers of steep hills. They climb from close to the water's edge and intersect hundreds of feet above with the gray-sharpened ridges that once were the volcano's edge. Experts would tell you the volcano had either pushed up from the sea or had been worn down to it, thus covering both ends of the bay's creation. At some point, before continents knew their place, Australia drifted toward Asia, tectonic plates shifted, and volcanic islands appeared like a bad case of acne. The Philippines was born. This predated Spanish invasion, of course, by about thirty million years. Our view was pretty much the early Spanish vista except for the small fleet of tankers anchored with an American warship, the Jet Ski, a jet's vapour trail high above and, oh—if you listened hard, a fleet of diesel trucks mid-mountain climb.

The ships, waiting for repairs I assumed, dwarfed us as we passed. They sat close to a shipyard, a blight of orange cranes and bright blue buildings etched out of that jungle green, distraction from the colourful line of structures tumbled like craps dice onto the beach. They were mostly single-storey and also qualified post-Ferdinand Magellan's Spanish exploration.

"That's Barretto," Rob said, pointing toward the shore. "That's where the bars are." He pointed out that patch of tumbled buildings along the sandy shore. There were no signs of welcome...flashing neon signs denoting hotels, bars or casinos...the stuff of adult playgrounds. From a mile out, the huddle appeared deserted.

That's where the bars are. It should have tweaked my memory or at least my curiosity—after all, we had spent plenty of time talking about them during the weeks of our voyage, but the long hours of motoring and my desperate need for sleep had clouded my thinking.

Through the heat and silent sway of vegetation, Barretto revealed nothing of the shadow that cloaked its reputation as we passed it by. The deck air and our conversation were keeping my mind somewhat in focus, and I returned to the view.

"It's that beach-town getaway for expats I've been talking about," Rob reminded me, holding the railing, port side, beside my perch on the bow. "Most of the guys are American or Australian, and I guess, except for the bar girls, the town is pretty much all men."

Some of the men, he explained, were soldiers of the last wars of Indochina, namely Korea and Vietnam, and this had been an American soldier's paradise when given leave for a little R and R. Others, it seemed, were from board rooms and bedrooms...burned-out and then spat out when "the systems" had spent their last ounce of usefulness. These men had heard the sirens' call in Barretto and willingly submitted.

"That red building on the waterfront," Rob said, pointing at the buildings huddled between thick patches of green, "that's Midnight Rambler."

The town and building melded with others that stretched along a road not visible. I knew it was there because Rob said so. He had been here before—Subic, Olongapo, Barretto of the Philippines.

"Midnight Rambler," he said. "You know, where I met Kim."

Kim...yes, of course...she was the reason this voyage for me had begun. Rob and Catherine had bought the boat with intentions of sailing the seven seas...and then the ship hit the sand. Issues never resolved bubbled like a volcanic mud bath, and the slinging began. There had been no place to hide on *Bob-the-Boat* in the South China Sea. The irritants of the cramped space were too small to be ignored and grew too large to wait for mediation. Their thirty-seven years of marriage lost out to the heat of the monsoon days, the screaming silence of the night, and the port with a black-hole pull on loneliness and pleasure. And lucky me, I had been the collateral damage recipient of it all.

I continued to hang from the bow, assessing our last miles of entry to Subic and Olongapo, the final port of call, our final waypoint. That's a terminology of navigation of the ENC, denoting landmarks and destinations. Unlike some journeys, where the going trumped the getting there, this sheltered destination mattered. Here we could strip off the canvas covers, remove any items that may catch the typhoon winds, tie up between cement piers and cross-tie and double-knot everything. Then wait!

At some point, Olongapo showed its face, and it appeared, on first sighting, that the city slept on the edge of Subic Bay like that three-headed hound of mythology, Cerberus, guarding Hades. One head was a neat, sprawling complex of military structures, mostly abandoned, though at the moment home to a pair of American Navy ships. There was a flutter of activity; preparations, I assumed, for heading south with all the rest of the fleeing ships. The other pair of heads guarded humanity, and for all the nourishment that centuries of Spanish and American naval establishment should have provided, some points revealed themselves as a bleak assembly of tin shacks clinging to life on the hillsides of a paradise hell.

On the white beach of an abandoned container yard, giant cranes waited like hungry vultures, unaware that trade had moved to Shanghai and Singapore.

Rob had begun manually piloting the boat. We moved past a pair of ships bleeding wounds of rust and a cavernous dry dock busy with ship repairs, grinders and cutting torches spewing showers of sparks. A magnificent craft called the *Archimedes*, a billionaire's toy of over two hundred feet, was chained and anchored to a wharf. Its presence lifted my spirits. If they were staying, something was right about this location.

We moved down a narrowing throat of channel markers, cracked cement piers and breakwaters, the bow pointing towards a pair of dock hands waving us in.

Our slowing approach was overseen by an imposing clubhouse with large, tinted windows and doors of smoked glass. Once, possibly, it had been a proud community structure. Now, it kept vigil, sporting repaired patches of hot pink stucco on a façade of faded color like a pasty-hued Englishman on the second day of a Greek beach.

Masts of sailboats swayed as we motored by. They sang the mizzen wind song...breezes of long solo notes pulled across stay wires, taut as a bass violin. Somewhere, a loose line drummed a slow, incessant beat like a melancholy dirge. If it had truly tapped my brain for feelings, it might have hissed like the tired scratching of a vinyl LP left turning.

Rob eased the nose of *Bob-the-Boat* into its berth. The deckhands took the ropes I cast and slowed our approach.

And then we stopped. The engine ceased to revolve. The burble of exhaust was quiet. The parting swish of waves was no more, yet my mind still swayed in a fog of relentless white noise, hammering a silent rpm rhythm in my head. In those first silent moments, it was as if the heart monitor flatlined. My mind should have been rejoicing for a job well done. Our final waypoint had been met with pinpoint accuracy. We had travelled over two thousand miles at a steamy nine miles per hour and beat the storm. But my mind refused to accept that my life—a life that had been transplanted to a higher existence in this mind-blowing journey—would be returned to its beige existence in this pin-drop quiet of an ending. With this milestone achieved, what could be next?

The last time I had felt this way was my last day of high school and, to some degree, university; the free rides of youth slammed to a halt and the multiple variables of adulthood, like a black hole in space, drawing me in. Youth, I don't believe, have a monopoly over the anxiety of future plans. It was a feeling that had crept in during the last hour of the journey; the euphoria of accomplishment and the sensation of loss in the same breath, ready to tip an anxious domino, with no predetermined course.

Thankfully, this trip had more to come: Hong Kong, Beijing and the Great Wall. And on our doorstep, there was Olongapo to be explored, Barretto to touch and other lives to intersect. And sleep—bloody hell, please let there be sleep.

38

THE TYPHOON HITS
MEETING KIM
THE JEEPNEY EXPERIENCE
FAXES FROM A TOASTER

OCT. 26, 2009

It was more than a week before Typhoon Mirinae hit. It started as a Category 2 typhoon, but as soon as it hit land, it lost speed and was downgraded to a severe tropical storm. This was no reason, however, to ignore it by setting up the lawn furniture to watch. It crossed the Philippines, leaving destruction in its wake, then headed north, stopping mid-South China Sea churning itself into Typhoon 5 status. Wind gusts exceeded one hundred and sixty-five miles per hour. It sat like an angry Medusa, within a serpent's strike of Taiwan to the north, the Philippines back to the south, and the Vietnam-Cambodia land mass straight west. There was no turning back to the east. Typhoon Tino, the ninth since September the first, was busy spawning in its wake. Mirinae, thankfully for us, decided to take out Vietnam instead.

But for all the buildup and hoo-ha and the missed opportunities of places not visited, Typhoon Mirinae was a bit of a dud in Subic, a flaccid Dali of melted expectations sent out by Mother Nature's anger management coach. For that, I guess, we should have been thankful. In Vietnam, the hum of nature turned into the roar of a Category 5 universe; floods and mudslides took a hundred and sixty lives.

The worst that we experienced in our Subic harbour was the arrival of a pair of bangka canoes, delivered in the middle of the night. It hadn't started that way. The locals were told to prepare for the worst. Somewhere before dark, I had seen the ominous clouds to the east, so high they looked like Himalayan mountains, the peaks rimmed by the shimmer of silver and gold from the setting sun to the west. Winds had picked up between midnight and two, and by three it was a deafening roar. When I climbed up to the wheelhouse, I could see palm trees stretched like inverted umbrellas, parallel to the ground. The first light that should have been dawn was thwarted by pelting rain and cannons of explosions on the fibreglass roof. Alongside the marina, the bay was a white-foam frenzy, but other than the surprise canoes, nothing flew out of control. It rained all day, justification to bake muffins and brownies and drink copious amounts of gin and tonic as if it was our last day on earth. The day was followed by glorious sunshine, a whole week's worth in fact, justification to drink copious amounts of beer to celebrate survival. A week or so later, Typhoon Tino, downgraded to a tropical depression, sent in more rain. By this time, we were settled into Subic, where I had met some key players in what was to be Rob's new life.

It was soon evident that being a sailor was a lot more than bringing the ship safely to the harbour. The antics that bring many sailors fame—excluding Drake, Nelson, Ahab, Bligh or Billy Budd—are often those that happen on shore.

Shore leave for me had been deferred by a day upon arrival, in pursuit of nod, that broken-record pursuit of Never-Never Land, never achieved until now. I slept so deeply that Rob suspected I had been taken by the cold steel of the grim reaper.

Seventeen hours after I said good night, I opened my eyes, wondering where I was. Outside I could hear the city in a state of hungry growl—the deep-throated pull of motorcycles straining on hillsides, the wheeze of air brakes and squeal of no brakes and the double-beep warnings of angry horns. In the haze of overslept, I wondered about that three-headed guard dog that waited beyond the tamed walls of the yacht club. It was so easy to think of settling into the comfort of a Kota Kinabalu-type setting, avoiding what sounded like chaos on the streets.

I heard giggles coming from the master en suite, a shower running and, best of all, a long, uninhibited laugh from Rob, something I had not heard for quite a while. There was also the smell of baked goods in the air.

I climbed the stairs and made my way to the galley. The curtains had been pulled back, and a full chorus of sunlight bathed the interior, forcing my eyeballs into a squinting retreat. I looked out over a tranquil harbour, boats rocking gently to a motor launch moving out, masts tilting in a tick-tock rhythm of waves finding calm. Sometime during the night, a large yacht, something over a hundred feet, had moved in to share our pier. There was no movement on board, nor did it sway in the wake of the moving boat. Other boats were caught in chores of cleaning and maintenance; suds rinsing into the harbour, uniting the boats in a trail of bubbles. Voices, a chatter of dialogue I couldn't understand, grounded me with a small surge of excitement of things yet to see and do; the emotions that had crashed like a carpet pulled from under my feet hours earlier now began to rise with the possibilities of the coming adventure.

The oven was hot, and a quick peek revealed a dozen muffins rising. They were oatmeal banana raisin, a treat Rob created at every port, eaten before the oven had a chance to cool. I set the kettle to boil and dished some instant coffee into my cup in anticipation, opening the fridge to retrieve cream, and when I closed the door, I got a shocking surprise.

"Hi. You must be Norm. I'm Kim."

"Hi," I said, too high or too fast or barely audible, I'm not sure, but it obviously spoke volumes.

"I look younger than you were expecting? You don't approve?" I had no idea I was so transparent; that my first impression, betrayed by a stray brainwave, flashed a neon judgement in a blink.

"No...well, yes to the first, but no...actually, I have no thoughts. I am not quite awake." I was being forced into backtracking to a petite young woman with a stacked towel on her head. Her eyes beamed with playful mischief and her forward English delivered with nuanced understanding threw me off my guard. Her nose and cheeks, fresh from the shower, shone like polished newels on a teak staircase, but it was those sparkling dark eyes and a smile with a hint of a girlish titter that won me instantly. A second head of towel appeared before I could further dazzle her with my words of wisdom.

"Well, the dead has risen," Rob said. He slipped behind Kim, wrapping her in his arms, resting his chin on her towelled head. "I thought I might have to call the morgue." His large smile revealed a freshly shorn face, giving him a domesticity I had not seen for years. He moved his hands down to Kim's behind and gently squeezed both cheeks, eliciting a giggle and a gentle recriminating slap as she moved out of his grasp.

"Just checking the muffins," he laughed, then stepped into my space and pulled the oven door ajar. "M-m-m-m, they look good enough to eat...and these too."

"You bad. You very bad," Kim giggled and smacked him on the behind. It was the play of new lovers, testing the limits of shared intimacy beyond the confines of privacy, a test Rob knew he would pass in my presence.

Upon arrival, he had pushed for me to come along to the bars, without hinting at the fact that he was going to surprise

Kim. I thought she was on the "out," remembering that Kim had made moves back to Kurt, the village had moved into Rob's hillside apartment and there was a plethora of prospects lining up. Girls seemed to fall easily at his feet, but when you own a yacht and are single in a land of poverty, it wasn't hard to see why. In the land of bar-girl candy stores, Rob was a special catch.

Kim left us shortly after we were introduced. She was heading for the bar eventually (her shift began at seven p.m.), but first there was shopping at the market, groceries for her granny (and the village), and visiting friends. As the crow flew (they fly in convoluted circles in the Philippines), it was still an hour by walking and jeepney, a vehicle of the local bus system, with a transfer to Barretto where she worked.

Rob and I followed shortly after. From Subic Harbour on my first foray into Olongapo, we exited through the cooling of tinted glass, polished marble and wood of the yacht club to a busy street that hummed with moving economies; truckloads of produce, taxis, buses and motorcycles. If not for the palm trees, it had the calculated squaring of small-town America.

The city of Olongapo is separated from the Subic America that had been, by a sixteenth-century Spanish moat. It was built to keep the natives at bay. A pair of bridges, fenced and gated with Checkpoint Charlies, still exist, where once American MP guards used sniffer dogs on the nearly fifteen thousand Filipino labourers that flowed in from Olongapo daily. These were service personnel to the four and a half thousand military and civilian Americans who lived in the Subic compound. During the Vietnam War, dozens of ships arrived and departed daily, and in one year, nearly four and a half million sailors visited the port, making it possibly the largest penis colony on earth. They left millions in revenue. There was no reflection of such boom times now.

A walk through Subic revealed bits of America left dangling in the street names…Dewey Avenue, Washington and

Pershing Streets and Waterfront Road linking places like Times Square and Boardwalk. A fifties-style burger joint, a few hotel nightclubs flashing rooms by the hour and one grand hotel in the style of New Orleans might be all that remains of American history in an architectural print. Many streets were missing buildings altogether. The Quonset huts had been removed, leaving driveways and a few tufts of landscaping like a trailer park ghost town after a tornado had spun through.

In the chess game, nature made the first move; black queen took the entire board. The combination of Mt. Pinatubo volcanic ash and Typhoon Yunya rains created first those giant mud balls like Roman catapults from hell, followed by a fall of wet ash several feet deep crushing most remaining buildings under the weight. By the end of 1991, the Philippine government did the rest...checkmate to the Americans' continued use of the base. The base was stripped of anything of value and handed back to the Philippine people. Olongapo was the recipient of said rewards.

Olongapo, not unlike Puerto Princesa, had the unkempt feel of hair raised in the hackled manner of a guard dog in a perpetual state of watch. Olongapo was a different world from the once-American Subic, starting with crossing the bridge. We were surrounded by children, elderly, blind and crippled beggars who begged for pesos. Rob advised me not to indulge them since it would set off an avalanche. It did, unfortunately...he was right. We beat a hasty path off the bridge into the streets filled with the industry of life. A big part of that industry was centred around the jeepney.

Parked curbside in the first busy square we entered was a long line of squat, squared buses, sporting Jeep grills and canvas-covered boxes on the back. The first jeepneys we met were painted yellow. This was the yellow line.

Jeepneys had their beginning after the Second World War. The Americans had imported thousands of Jeeps for the Philippine assault, the favourite chariot for General

MacArthur and his corncob pipe. When the war was finished, the military didn't want to repatriate used Jeeps, especially if they were filled with bullet holes…it made them hard to sell. They were left or sold to the Filipinos. Some enterprising fellow turned his Jeep into a bus and one thing led to another and history was made. Several companies continue to build jeepneys in different assembly-line styles, most maintaining the squared Jeep grill. Like a ride on the San Francisco trams, no visit to the Philippines is complete without at least one trip in a jeepney—but not, as you might think, for a scenic ride.

We approached the line of jeepneys from the last vehicle parked. There were a dozen waiting. Two pulled away, leaving us in a fog of diesel fumes. A man stood roadside beside the third, barking at some unseen person sitting inside. He poked a stick in the form of a riding crop through the canvas wall, shouting a command I didn't understand.

"He's telling the riders inside to move forward," Rob said, hopping on the back bumper and pulling himself through the canvas door. I followed.

It was cramped inside, less than the box interior of a dump truck and about as comfortable. Benches lined the canvas walls, partially opened to filter the stifling heat. Patrons sat shoulder to shoulder, facing inward. Children, wives, and girlfriends were perched on knees with parcels underneath. We found seats while two more climbed aboard. It was full, I thought, but a stick appeared through the side wall, prodding passengers and shouting the command "Move up, move up," English this time, since he had seen us enter. I was appalled that someone would prod riders like cattle, but no one objected. Riders moved, spaces were created, and the new couple sat.

Our seats were close enough to the front that I could watch the driver at work. Two girls in school uniforms had parked themselves beside the driver in the most civilized part of the vehicle. One sat with her feet on the dashboard, skirt drooping toward her waist, lost temporarily in the art of texting.

A man tapped me on the shoulder, dropping twenty pesos in my hand, and with two pointed fingers, he nudged his head toward the front, suggesting I pass it forward. Rob took it and leaned toward the driver, speaking Tagalog, holding up two fingers. The driver, already underway, shifting through the gears, took the money, signalled, turned left, shifted again, dropped the money in a pot, shifted, handed Rob change, then shifted once again, pulling from the side street into the main hemorrhage of mass congestion. He also found time to honk, whereby a loose wire on his dash was held on a metal bar to make an electrical connection, and he waved at a driver going the opposite way. Rob handed the change to its rightful owner. This was the process of payment, and we, sitting in the middle, handled pesos forward and back for the entire ride.

Knocking twice lets the driver know you want to get out. Knock, knock when you are out, letting the driver know all is clear, and off he goes. We knock-knocked ourselves out to the open-air market for food supplies, and for our weeks of stay, this was our mode of transport.

Like Puerto Princesa, and perhaps like open-air markets around the world, there was beauty in the chaos and colour of the produce and the people going about their shopping. I snapped a photo or two. This in turn was a cue for all those who suspected they had been photographed to turn up their palms for payment. A nodded gesture with a facial twitch and open palm towards my camera asking permission prompted not one- but two-handed begging instead. Playing stupid, which took little effort, got me off the hook. I tapped the camera as if it was broken, gave a disappointed look and tucked the camera back into the case. In the end, I couldn't blame them for trying to make some money.

"Up those stairs," Rob said, pointing to a hillside of cluttered tin shacks, "is my apartment." The stairs ascended in a steep ladder-like climb with no handrails visible, disappearing into a growth of banana palms. "We can go up tomorrow when Kim's off from work. We might need to clear out some freeloaders." It wasn't said with malice.

With knapsacks loaded, we stepped back onto the main road, thinking we might flag a jeepney, but Rob balked at the idea of waiting when none were in sight and asked if I minded walking. After weeks on the boat, we needed the exercise. It was fine by me as long as the fresh fish and chicken could handle the heat. He picked up his pace, a cantor that demanded my occasional gallop to keep pace since I had reopened my camera, stopping occasionally to read signs and absorb the culture in the street.

It was a busy mixture of trucks, taxis, jeepneys, motorcycles and trikes. Trikes, Rob informed me, had been banned from using the main roads. To get from A in the north to B in the south, trikes were forced to zigzag east and west, tacking like a sailor into the wind in a crisscrossing of the main drag via intersecting streets. This turned a one-kilometre ride into twenty in a side-street-and-back-alley adventure. It also added to the excitement of the walk, as we now had to watch out for trikes gunning out of side streets, ignoring stop signs to take advantage of opening breaks in traffic. It was impossible to think that tryke drivers could make money when jeepneys cost less than a quarter, but trykes came without the cattle prods, long lineups, constant stops for pickup and delivery, and overcrowding. There was a thriving business of trikes weaving a crosshatch of activity over the main esplanade jammed with jeepneys. It was only a matter of time, I thought to myself, before there would be a trike prang-up at a jeepney knock-knock. We stepped lively, keeping eyes peeled to the side streets.

Like Puerto Princesa, Olongapo was a visual smorgasbord of post-war construction worn from tropic rains, humidity, heat, an onslaught of typhoon destructions never repaired or repaired badly and the poverty that feeds it all. Electricity is a special problem—most power lines can't be buried due to typhoon flooding, but stringing them between poles leaves them vulnerable to the high winds of the same cyclonic storms.

For the stringing of wires, the words "rat nests" came to mind, but it wasn't something unique to the Philippines as I had noticed the same spaghetti lack of concern in Bangkok as well. Wires were strung along buildings, occasionally to poles in a Rastafarian tangle that sometimes met at hubs where thousands of wires intersected and hung in precarious knots. God help anyone trying to trace an intermittent feed. Some snake pits might have had the original wiring of Edison's creation along with several upgrades since, and all the new wiring requirements that included telephone; cable; satellite TV; low-, medium- and high-speed internet; and several repairs and additions of each. One might envisage someone receiving a fax through their toaster if such things still exist.

Adding to the feel of decay was the stench of sewage. It emanated from the squared concrete ditches that formed part of the sidewalk. The sewers were covered with a slatted concrete top for rainwater to enter and where tops had broken, the ditch water and road sewage were visible, still and fermenting in the tropical heat. The system did not appear to have a sloped destination, but I assumed it all made its way to the river and, eventually, the white sands of Subic Bay. Unlike the modern sophistication of Singapore or what we saw in Kuala Lumpur, it was truly third-world. In the Philippines, the sanitation crisis is nationwide; of the more than a hundred million residents, nearly sixty percent lack clean water and over forty million have no safe toilets. In the vein of the electric cables, these problems, I suspect, stem from the thirty-plus typhoons a year. What do you do with sewage in a land of constant flooding?

I thought I could smell barbecued chicken, and thinking mine was cooking in the backpack, we made a beeline for home. Subic Yacht Club did not support exclusive air-conditioned buses, so getting home was all footwork.

That evening, I made my first foray into Barretto and its dingy street of bars and bar girls, a bit like stepping into the Lion's wardrobe and being swallowed whole.

39

BARRETTO BAR GIRLS
T-BONED TO STEAK TARTAR
COMPLIMENTARY BEER. AM I IN HEAVEN?

A FEW DAYS BEFORE UNDRAS (HALLOWEEN)

Barretto was a two-jeepney ride from the yacht club. The Red Line started in the east at the city limit and dropped us midtown while a Blue Line took us out of the city, westward to the beachside resort. Each ride was seven and a half pesos, approximately twenty cents, and the ride was nearly half an hour. I am not sure a person can ride a free bicycle for that amount.

Our ride began when most riders in a civilized world should have been at home tucking children into beds, but the jeepneys were filled with workers, nodding in fitful bouts of exhaustion merely to carry their heads.

The knock-knock for disembarking the jeepney was a voiced call to the driver to stop, both by Rob and another pair of patrons, who found the tarped roof and loud diesel engine immune to knock-knock strategies. The vehicle swerved onto the sandy roadside. Four of us disembarked. There was a rattle of grinding gears and diesel fumes as the jeepney carried on.

Barretto was nothing of what I had expected.

First, it was dark—not a huge surprise, since the sun had turned in at its usual hour and was off carousing somewhere further west—but there were sporadic streetlights to fill the absence. It was not a Vegas strip of Marquis neon; in fact, *strip*, implying an assembly of flash and buzz and a strobe of chase wattage, was much too kind. I had been spoiled by Patpong and Phuket, where everything pulsed, throbbed and palpitated like a snorted ecstasy that never quit. Here, there were soft cushions of front-stoop lighting peeking out from doorways and a few fluorescent signs. It was like a hovel of dying businesses in a near-deserted downtown, where the strip malls had made the town core obsolete.

For all the build-up, I had expected a whole summer Centerville of activity, fast foods, hotels, bars, strip joints and marts for all the needs. I was also disappointed to find the non-strip was short. There was a cluster of a few dozen buildings a block or two long facing the highway, with a quiet and darkened village behind. The highway was a main artery for trucks and other late-night traffic whizzing through. I could see from where we stood that there was another group of buildings, up the road on the opposite side. Mecca, I thought, was a bust, but people were moving about, a large improvement over our first outing in Puerto Princesa.

We strolled past a bar hung with girls on the front walk, steps and stoops as if there had been a pressure leak at the door. They were decked in glittery cowgirl tassels and hats with white boots to match.

"Hey, handsome," they called in our direction, forcing me to turn to see if we were being followed. "You buy me nice drink? You come in...relax...we give you goooood time!" It was the Yogi Berra déjà vu all over again, but this time I was mentally prepared.

"Not tonight, girls," Rob replied. We were heading for the Rum Jungle, the bar that shared the name with the Kuala

Lumpur oasis and had prompted a lesson in Far East girls. "Hey, Mandi...cowgirls tonight, I see. Maybe we come by later," Rob added, obviously familiar with the entourage.

"You come for ride later," shouted after us, was followed by collective giggles and a "Giddy up, baby."

We traveled through a few gauntlets, each extending gracious invitations for a good time. It reminded me of that famous photo of an American girl walking down the sidewalk in Florence, Italy, ogled, visually stripped and verbally abused by fifteen men to a bloodied carnal steak. With each catcall and whistle as we walked, I felt I had been T-boned a dozen times, and the night had barely begun. Of course, we were here by choice, "looking for action," unlike the populace of women who are peeled and processed daily, walking sidewalks, stepping through doorways, climbing stairs, in and out of taxis, minding their own on their way to work. For some it worked, stilettos and silks and fragrances, foreplay to an office orgy. For others, I believe, there are not enough showers in a day. I might have begun to understand how some ladies felt, but again, we had put ourselves here by choice, and men seem to like this kind of attention...objects of desire, reduced to steak tartar and an empty wallet from pleasure.

Barretto, however, was more personal than Bangkok or Phuket had been, because it was infinitely smaller and we were closer to being the sole focus of attention. The feel of small and personal, colourfully lit doorways and verandas with girls in scanty costumes had the festive gaiety of trick-or-treating as a kid, with the bonus of doors that never closed and never-ending treats.

The Rum Jungle was a party. Rob embraced a pair of hostesses outside the door and received hugs and lifted mugs of welcome from several others, like an opening scene from *Cheers*. I received residual hugs and patted cheeks as his friend and the bar manager shouted my name—"NOR-R-RM" (scene two from *Cheers*)—shook my hand in welcome and gave Rob a friendly slap on the back, and we were barely settled before complimentary beers were set before us.

Complimentary beer. I had never heard those two words together in my life. Was I in heaven? Music pulsed. A dozen girls pulsed in unison, as if they were wired to the beat. They clicked their heels, turned 360s, clapped hands, and sang choruses. A few girls danced with patrons, some of whom were my age or older. Girls at the bar shook martinis, and waitresses wove orders through the patrons, platters lofted one-handed over their heads. They delivered to tables with laughter and chatter, where cigarettes were lit in every hand not holding a drink.

This was Rob's promise fulfilled, and this was the landscape for the next few weeks while I waited to fly from Subic to Hong Kong and Dalian, China. There were a few memorable times and people who filtered through that space. Christina was one of them.

40

THE TEQUILA GIRL: CHRISTINA

IDLE TIME BEFORE NOV. 9, 2009

I met Christina in the Rum Jungle. She was the Tequila Girl. There were no rum girls or gin and tonic girls. She was the only designated drink. The Tequila Girl was dressed in a cowgirl outfit; hat and fringes, plus a tequila belt. A tequila belt (not a belt of tequila) was a work belt of shot glasses, a shaker of salt, fresh fruit, and a bottle of tequila. Buying a shot of tequila at inflated prices entitled one to moisten the Tequila Girl's breast with a wedge of lime, salt it, take a belt of tequila, and lick off the chaser of salt. This was a favourite routine in many bars—including Bangkok gay bars, I was told, where breasts were not the option.

Christina caught my eye for a couple of reasons. First, I am a sucker for smiles and laughter, and Christina had them both in spades. She truly seemed to enjoy her role as Tequila Girl, and she rewarded the patrons with laughter straight from the midway.

I am guessing that most men in Western bars don't find smiles and laughter sexy, since women who strip, play the pole or serve shooters refuse to smile. Like runway models, they sulk with pouty lips, playing the role of damsel in distress. Smiles, apparently, detract from the runway items worn by models or the disappearing clothing of strippers, clothing designed to sell garments or the body inside. If the clothing is gone (and G-strings don't qualify), exotic dancers can't be that wholesome girl next door with a smile. That doesn't sell forbidden fruit. This was not a strip joint, but, among the display of serious pout, Christina's laughter was a breath of minted air.

Secondly, there were moments when I thought she looked quite familiar. I realized, between smiles, that she resembled the dark-haired, full-bodied temptress in a painting of a Spanish girl hung by my in-laws in Sweden. They had bought the painting in the Canary Islands from a painter who turned them out in droves. My father-in-law hung it up, and my mother-in-law found attic space to hide it. It always found its way out, hung front and centre, the first thing you saw as you entered the Fine Room—the room where all the sewing bee ladies sat for coffee, nibbled and sipped, gossiped and sometimes sewed, admiring the artwork. The painting essentially said, "I am open for business."

Christina was a younger version of that Picasso. She had a raspy, rolling laugh like Janice Joplin—a laugh that melted me like Bobby McGee's butter. That laugh made her seem older and wiser, and it pierced the din of the bar when salt was being removed from her body. She also liked to dance when she wasn't pushing shots. It appeared she was Miss Congeniality, setting a tempo for the rest...a friend and go-to for most of the other girls in the bar.

She caught me watching her one night, my head loosely propped on a faltering elbow, threatening to collapse into my beer. She refused to let go of my stare. *Oh no*, I thought, *I've done it now; I am being super-sized for a meal.* When there was a break in the music, she floated toward my table, sporting a shy smile that rolled into a large grin and then that laugh with a saucy rasp that had me hooked.

"Buy me a drink?"

"Of course," I said without hesitation, having no idea where that would lead, her black Spanish eyes and laughter working me like a serpent's stare. If you had heard that offer from Marilyn Monroe, Angelina Jolie or, for the ladies, George Clooney, would you have hesitated to say yes? Joplin was asking to enter my world. It might have been the beer.

She sat with practised savvy, catching the eye of the waitress with a gentle nod that signalled, I guess, the eagle had landed, and without anything more being said, drinks arrived at our table.

"I takes liberty of ordering beer, okay, yes?" She laughed a riff of raspy notes that melted my look of surprise. She still wore the tequila hat, but the belt of glasses and half-empty bottle had disappeared. It might have been half full, I am not sure; my optimism was searching for some safe ground from the Palawan quicksand that had dragged me into defensive mode.

"Well, thank you, I think. Are you buying, or am I?" I laughed and put out my hand for one of the menthol cigarettes she was pulling from her purse. She lighted mine first, taking her time with hers, and then blew smoke in my direction.

"Youze buy. I drink. That how things work. When you gets me drunk maybe youze gets lucky." Another long laugh, suggesting she didn't take herself too seriously, or that I shouldn't, or it was all a playful act, I am not sure. The laugh kind of muddied the waters of where this conversation was supposed to go.

"My name is Norm. And what should I call you?" I thought a formal introduction would be best to get things moving on a drink she had bought at my expense before a blessed consent.

"Christina. No bulla bulla."

"No bulla bulla?" I laughed, wondering where she was taking this. "What's bulla bulla?"

"No bullshit. No bulla bulla." She laughed again with a quizzical look, wondering, perchance, if she had landed a complete dumbass. "Lots of girls use bar names," she said, pointing to a girl sitting in a guy's lap a couple of tables over. "Shees calls herself Cherry because she eez cherry girl. But my name really Christina."

"Okay, no bulla bulla—really, Christina, what is a cherry girl?"

"Youze don't know cherry girl?" She blew some hasty smoke, laughed, and rolled her eyes...possibly "dumbass" was too light of an assessment. Her eyes narrowed over a wrinkled nose. "Shees no...youze know," inserting an index finger into a circled thumb and finger on the other hand, "shees, how youze say..."

"Virgin? We say virgin," I suggested, hoping to regain some stature off the idiot list.

"Like Mary."

I searched the room. "And which one exactly is Mary?"

"The Virgin Mary," Christina laughed, crossing herself to make the point. "Shees no here, that for damn sure." Her laughter rose above the din of everything in the bar and scratched its way pleasantly under my skin. It rolled out uninhibited, natural as exhaling air. It was the real her, I had no doubt...no bulla bulla. Alcohol or not, I am a pushover for easy laughter. It had been what initially attracted me to my wife (not that my wife was easy) and was the two-second litmus test I used for liking strangers. And like some barbiturate of addiction, I craved the kind of high that free and easy laughter gave me.

I heard a loud squeal of excitement, and my head spun in time to watch a mad dash of girls chasing ping-pong balls across the floor. Christina cheered them on as balls rolled and bounced under tables and chairs and out onto the dance floor. It was, I had to admit, funny to watch, and I was buoyed by Christina's laugh, which had me laughing as well. She kicked a ball that rolled in our direction and watched a pair of girls squeal with delight as they tried to pin it down. I remembered that conversation Rob, John, and I had had about the humiliation of patrons casting balls to watch girls do a scramble and chase, all for entertainment and a few pennies' worth of extra cash. I was tempted to ask Christina about her views. I was pretty sure, however, based on her level of excitement, that she wouldn't see it badly, since she spent her working hours selling chasers of tequila, where patrons salted her breasts and licked them clean. Chasing a few balls was probably the least humiliating thing she had ever done. Her story unravelled over the next couple of weeks, proving this to be an understatement.

Her world, at fourteen, had come crashing down when her father was murdered with an ice pick.

"I no for sure, if theese be true," she said one night, stopping for a break, needing to refresh her bottle of tequila, while adding salt to the shaker, "but some say the man who kill my father was jealous husband. They says my father was fucking hees wife. They all lies. My father was good man...good man who love hees children." She stopped for a moment, eyes rimmed with tears. I had reason to doubt this was true since I had met her older half-sister from another village, who also worked the bar. She had helped Christina get the job in Barretto. It appeared that if Christina had done her genealogical tracking, half-sisters were not irrelevant in the calculation of the family whole.

"It was all my fault...heez no be dead, if I...if I no bad girl... heez still be alive. I disobey him. Now heez be dead. I very bad girl."

Perhaps I should have changed the subject since it seemed obvious that it was a painful, dark moment best avoided, but I was hooked. I simply couldn't leave a jealous murderer with an ice pick and an admission of guilt alone.

"I no listen to my father. Heez say I not to go in the house, but I want to go in the house. I was very hungry. I just do what

I wants." The words trailed off, and I waited for an explanation. There was none.

"Whose house?" I asked. "What happened in the house?"

She started putting on her cowboy hat and hitching up the tequila belt as if the mud had cleared. "Maybies later," she said, nodding toward the Mama-san, who was watching Christina's every move. She was expected to move the merchandise. "I work now."

"You are working. I am talking to you, and you are chatting up the customer."

"I Tequila Girl. You want tequila? Three hundred pesos..." She reached in, about to unpack a breast.

"Okay, I understand...we can talk another time," I said quickly before a contract got started that I had no intention of honouring, and I didn't want her to lose face, so to speak, unpacking the merchandise only to have it rejected. I knew it was something a person probably could not have done back home in a strip club had a person back home ever been in the mood for salted areola...not in the public forum of the bar, anyway.

She patted my hand before she left the table and grimaced. I understood. Business first.

She returned later, and somehow it didn't matter that the story picked up elsewhere. I didn't attempt to guide her back to the house...I had filled in the blanks. Her father was murdered by a jealous husband or lover, despite Christina's protestations to the contrary. He was murdered in front of her eyes with an ice pick, an axe, or a knife, she wasn't exactly sure.

"It's no matters what it be. Heez die."

She came from a town in the mountains called Bongabon on the island of Mindoro.

"Eez very beautiful, you must go see my village sometime."

At fourteen, with her father dead, her mother sold her into domestic slavery to the village crone to help make money to survive. Her mother then took on a young lover, hoping he would bring along with him the other benefit...money. It turned out he was a vicious predator. Christina was raped, forcing her to flee her home. In any other world, the rapists flee. She was a vulnerable and frightened girl from a small mountain village, undereducated with no salable skills. Hunger and tears drove her into the arms of the bar scene where Mama-san offered handouts of motherly care. It was care twisted around loyalty from the girls in return for protection inside the doors of the bar. Beyond those doors from which the Mama-san pushed every girl eventually was the trade of sex.

To make things worse, in very short order, Christina found herself in charge of her two young sisters, eleven and nine years old, sent by their mother for protection. Both had been molested by the boyfriend who remained in their mother's bed. Christina had been barely eighteen when her sisters arrived in her care, and even though she carried herself with a maturity beyond her years, she was, she confessed, still shy of twenty-one when we met.

Christina had matched me beer for beer one evening (why not? I was paying), and I shared her filtered menthol smokes. I let her lead the conversation, which started all about me. I had set the boundaries early in my visits to the bar, realizing that I was being sized for future husbandry. Still, she was curious... like a fisherman was curious about hooks.

"You has wife, no?" It was more of a wishful statement towards the word "no" than a question. Nearly all the men she met had wives, she explained, or had had wives, or were being had by wives. She said she knew all the wife stories, where the phrase "doesn't understand me" meant they weren't getting laid. I was determined not to fall into the usual pattern of wife stories, though, as you might expect, some of it fit. Men never seem to get enough no matter what our age. Women are different. After twenty years of marriage, most women (it's been studied) have had enough. Men, it seems, go to their graves ready for sex.

Nature is kinder to men. Not having to birth a ten-pound turkey through a keyhole is all the argument needed.

"Yes, I do have a wife and two children, a girl and a boy." I pulled out my wallet with the small photo gallery inside. The pictures were not current; a wedding photo thirty years old, some toddler shots of both kids and a graduation photo of each. She politely flipped through them with appropriate comments—"So cute" and what I thought was a grudging "Pretty"—while I filled her in on brothers and sisters and friends. I put names to the pictures, making sure she understood they were my family; a family I was returning to in a few weeks. I wanted her to understand that I was not "husband" available—that, if I had the financial means, I would have helped her out of this horror story of life, but unfortunately, I couldn't be her ticket to freedom. I expected her to find another table with a real prospect, but she didn't.

"Youse nice guy," she said. "Youse no ask for...you know." Again, she used the universal animation of the inserted finger to make her point, though her teasing smile had the yin-yang wondering.

She thinks you can't get it up!
No, she thinks you're gay!
A gay guy who can't get it up!

I let the conversation die, quashing the idiots in my head, confident I had deflected her unspoken intentions. I wanted to keep things honest.

It never occurred to me that it might all be an act, that the story, "Christina's story" could have been fabricated with a theatrical flutter board of tragedy to catch a fat marlin with money bags. It wasn't until weeks later while Rob and I were touring Hong Kong that we met an American veteran from Colorado. His wife was Filipino. I am not sure how the conversation arose or flowed, but a few well-intended pearls of wisdom were dropped our way from the wife.

"Beware the bar girls" was tossed out like the three-witch

concoction from *Macbeth*. "They weave the best stories of woe you've ever heard. It's big business, you know...lonely American sugar daddies getting hooked with a few bar-fined nights of pleasure. Before you know it, you are sending money to help the girl stay out of the bar. What they want is marriage and sponsorship to freedom. Take me home to Mother and apple pie. Most of them run off before the sheets are folded back. Sponsoring girls is very big business, very big."

Her story, I've come to understand, was not dissimilar to a plague of millions of others. Borrowed or true, the Christina bar-girl story, I found out later, was the driving engine behind a massive shadow economy in the Philippines; bar girls to girl-friends to wives of foreigners around the world, all sending home money for those left behind. In the year of a recent report by a reliable news source, Filipinos living abroad sent home more than thirty-three billion dollars...that's Billion with a capital B as in Big Business.

Our self-help moderator confessed she had met her husband when he was on leave from the Vietnam War, but never said how or where they met. She seemed to have little sympathy for her own. Her statement caught me by surprise and jolted my senses. Had I been played with a pack of lies? It did occur to me that most of the girls Christina had pointed out had "stories," but they never seemed out of line with the work. Who would sell themselves if their lives were any less tragic?

But I was glad I had met Christina in a cloud of possible ignorance. As the smiling children, coloured kites and the Moro school of Kota Kinabalu had put faces to their poverty, Christina, with her rose-coloured world of glass-filled optimism, was the hope in a rainbow over flooded devastation. It wasn't the kind of hope that, somehow, the world of bar girls, Mama-sans, and bar fines would all disappear—I doubt it ever will—but the simple hope and faith that she would rise above it and leave it all behind. And I couldn't deny I was fond of her. Her large laugh had sucked me in.

We had visited Rob and Kim's hillside shantytown that perched precariously a few hundred feet up from the open-air market. It wasn't paradise; there was no running water for toilets or showers. Bathing took place at a communal spring where residents gathered water, lathered in soap and showered and washed dishes, but with its order (there was a small store built into a footpath), the tropical vegetation and the feel of a community, the shantytown seemed more like a *Swiss Family Robinson* tree house than a slum gathering of tin shacks.

Christina's rented space, an easy jog from the Barretto beach, paled in comparison. She had asked me if I would like to see her room, a short walk from the bar into that dark huddle of buildings I had noticed on my first visit to Barretto. I said I would. First, however, she wished to visit a small store that sold skewered street meats braised on a barbecue, bags of coconut water, steamed rice and balut. Everyone, it seemed, sold balut. Balut, you might recall, was that delicacy of boiled duck eggs, with partial growth of baby ducks inside, a delicacy that fell into those wonder foods like bird's nest soup and monkey brains of which Westerners wondered, "Who eats that shit?" In this case, it seems, everyone does. Street hawkers peddled balut like vendors pushing cotton candy at the fair. Christina bought a half dozen, determined to get me to try one.

"Ah-h, no thanks."

"You try. Eest very good... Really, eest taste good," she said as she sucked the juice from an egg, where I could see yellow, fuzzy down and a beak. I had to look away, hoping my stomach would settle.

She also bought a whole cooked chicken. It was for her sisters, now thirteen and eleven, whom, if I had been party to my future conversation in Hong Kong sometime in my past, I might have been prompted to believe were fictional characters, fabricated deceit designed to gain a sympathetic ear or hopefully a paying patron, here in my present.

Her sisters were very real, however, though rather elusive.

Christina had admitted that she had not been home for a few days. She had been bar fined twice, which meant sleeping wherever that took her. Often, she stayed with her girlfriend, a friend, she admitted somewhat shyly, with benefits. Though Christina defended the fact, it wasn't necessary. I understood long before she declared that all men were "peegs," stopping to apologize, "I nos mean youse," that most men took what they wanted and never cared a damn about giving pleasure in return. The fact that an average sexual act in the heterosexual world has been averaged to about three minutes I think makes my point. Together, Christina and her friend found the pleasure that men denied them. She admitted that between bar fines, she had spent a lot of time in her friend's apartment.

"What about your sisters?" I asked.

"My seesters?" She stopped to look at me with disbelief. "My seesters...theys go to school." She shrugged and cast her hands out as if this should be self-explanatory.

"But who looks after them...gets them up, sends them off to school? Who feeds them?" I asked with the same shrug of disbelief. She had stopped and eyeballed me as if I was mad.

"Theys be my seesters. Ize no their mommy."

We stood in her bedroom, a single, windowless, cement-block room, ten feet square. A solitary light bulb hung from a wire. The room was empty except for the small piles of clothing sitting in the corners and an interlocking, coloured foam puzzle covering the floor. This was her bed. There were no pillows. A rumpled comforter was pushed up against the wall. This was everything she owned. She and her sisters shared the room with another woman who worked at the bar. The woman had been beaten into the streets by an abusive husband, and Christina had taken her in. The four of them shared a kitchen with two other rooms of tenants; like the bedroom, it was a dingy, colourless space, the single light bulb dulled by a layer of grease. Cabinet doors hung from broken hinges, a tap dripped water into a brown-stained sink, countertops were peeling layers of plywood and the floor was a checkerboard of missing and broken tiles. A communal toilet sent a wafting gag of odour from a dark room that I assumed housed a shower or bath.

The invitation home had been to meet her sisters. They were nowhere to be found. It was very late…midweek…meaning there was school tomorrow, sending Christina into a panicked rant that, as a parent, I understood without translation; a few expletives wrapped around the possibilities of desired neck-wringing or one week without cell phones. I was startled, of course, considering a few minutes prior she had seemed indifferent to their survival.

Outside, Christina spoke with two men hanging by the entrance. They pointed down the street. She handed me the chicken and disappeared in that direction, leaving me kicking sand while the two men smoked a shared cigarette. Three dogs, rakes of skin and bone, sniffed shorter and shorter circles around me, noses lifted toward a possible prize of a whole chicken if I capitulated and bones of my carcass if I didn't. The pit bull bared its teeth when I shifted my weight in its direction. One man shouted with an added boot to the ribs, and all three retreated, eyes focused on the prize.

From the shadows beyond the dim pool of the streetlight, I could hear the shrill voices, a banter in Tagalog that again needed no explanation. It was the cry of teenagers called home against their will. There was a charge of animated arms and quick steps making their way toward us, one girl leading, chased by Christina, who in turn was followed by a disgruntled dragging of feet. When they finally arrived, the girls brushed past me without introduction, and Christina took the chicken and disappeared inside.

My heart was tugged in both directions, having now seen the room, and, I must admit, I was sister-sympathetic. The room had nothing, not a poster or family photo to connect with. Fairness should have dictated that the mother's boyfriend be shot or, better, his raping genitals offered to the crows in a regenerative daily Promethean ritual...and then everyone returned to their mountain village for a happy ever after.

I also understood Christina's frustrations. These were the sisters she had rescued from the terror of rape. They were the lives thrust upon her that she nurtured to the best of her childhood ability rushed to adulthood. She had saved them with bar fines, tequila shots and every humiliating ping-pong ball she chased. They were the frayed threads of her family, threads expected to be mended and woven by her into a cloth of meaningful existence. She played mother, teacher and mentor, but was barely one step ahead. Her cloth was torn and tattered, badly in need of repair, too thin and frayed, perhaps, to ever be repaired itself.

But she battled and fought for her sisters and sent money to her mother and brothers, and I had no doubt she would survive. She cared, and that, I determined, made her worthy of a chapter or two.

41

THERE BEEZ TWO BIG SHIPS
THE ONE-NIGHT FLU
DANCING
THE REALITIES OF SAILOR SEX
MONEY!

THE FIRST WEEK OF NOVEMBER

"**Y**ouze like dance?" Christina asked one afternoon while sitting with Rob, Kim and me at a beach diner in Barretto. Both Kim and Christina loved the invitation to dine out since it afforded them a respectable status off the grid of the bar girl's vulnerability.

It was Kim and Christina's day off from the bar, and Christina had announced, "Sheez like to go for dinner and maybies dance too." The four of us had fallen into a comfortable routine. Kim and Christina would join us at our nightly table in the bar during their breaks, where they pointed out who was who, doing what with whom, sometimes where and even why.

"Heez be from California," Christina said at one point, nodding to a newcomer through the door. "Heez maybe sponsor Carla to America," nodding in the opposite direction to a girl who had left the dance lineup and was already making a move toward massaging his shoulders. You could see a genuine glow of affection that flowed between them. It was not long before they were leaving the bar. She had bounded from her stool and disappeared to change into street clothes, while "Heez be from California" paid up with the Mama-san and was given a receipt complete with a voucher for a free drink the following day, similar to my Mr. Lube voucher back home for a free filter on the next oil change.

On another occasion, a fellow wearing a long coat and leather Aussie hat stood out because the rest of us were dressed in T-shirts and shorts. He was surrounded by girls, and Christina and Kim went into a fit of giggles when one of them sized both hands as if measuring a large fish. Further explanations were not necessary. For everyone who came through the door, there was a not-so-subtle measurement, scanning like a barcode for possibilities of sale.

In the beachside diner, conversations were more relaxed. No Mama-san was peering over the shoulder.

"Dancing? I love dancing," I replied, shuffling both arms in the air from my chair. "That's the way, uh-huh, uh-huh, I like it, uh-huh, uh-huh..."

"Okay, weez dance tonight. Pier One, big place, haz live bands. There beez two big American ships come in today. Lots of party, party!"

Both girls had to be escorted across the bridge of no-man's-land; security was heightened since American Navy ships were in port. This meant the Filipino officer on the footbridge randomly checked the credentials of the Filipinos. Christina caught his attention, dressed in a short cotton party dress and sequined sandals. He held her ID longer than required, comparing photo to cleavage. I don't think he looked at her face.

We followed her into and through the maze of the deserted streets, crossing Dewey Avenue until we hit Waterfront Road.

The road was a crush of sailors in a steady, mile-long stream back to the wharf entrance where the ships were berthed. They scrambled out of the gate like ants downwind of a picnic basket. Filing into the movement, it could have been the cheap side of Vegas on a warm Nevada night; rooms with hourly rates, lights chasing toward hotel entrances, revolving doors carrying couples in and out and voices booming for cabs. Music filtered from several establishments where lineups pushed down the street.

This was my first introduction to sailor mythologies in action, or at least the one of a girl in every port. My simple-minded perception of sailor mischief was the *On the Town* shore leave antics of Frank Sinatra, Gene Kelly and a whole cast of others singing, "*Gotta pick up a date, perhaps seven or eight.*" Those memories were hemmed by the prosceniums of Hollywood through our black-and-white TV when I was a kid. It mostly ghosted images through a fog of snow, but sometimes a crow landed on the antenna and *voila*. Sailors, if they were not being sunk by U-boats or skittering through the halyards between pirate attacks, were on shore leave, and they were dancing as part of TV's Afternoon Playhouse Theater. Hollywood forbade bald-faced nudity or anything looking like copulation, which, in reality, would have been wartime shore leave, so dancing was the next best thing.

Modern aircraft carriers have crews of five and a half thousand with some maintaining twelve percent women. With an average age of twenty-eight, all of the hormone mentality of "get laid or die," sex, not dancing, has got to be an issue. To temper this discourse on sailors, some mention, of course, will have to be made of the sailor with a woman in every port. Lest anyone be tempted off to sea based on this idea alone, one should again be reminded of the amount of time ships spend at sea. Nuclear aircraft carriers can go for twenty-five years without ever coming ashore for fuel and repairs. Some at-sea deployments can go as long as eight months. Sex on board is prohibited. Sex while dancing on board will have you shot. Like it or not, I think the priesthood might see more action.

At one time, affairs and pregnancy came with dishonourable discharges, demotions, large pay cuts and even two years in prison. Sex on shore leave, however, is not penalized, as long as it's between equal rank—no stars of command bedding the lonely stripes—and only if no pregnancy is involved, though shore leave conceptions carry no legal penalty. On the beach or on board can be the question. If sexual misconduct is suspected, enter the NCIS to determine what happened where and when, though what happened should be no mystery at all. In the end, however, the women are usually sent home regardless. So, on board, you are allowed to date, but hey, no touchy-feely: at some point, you would have to think, the back pressure is going to blow the wax out of their ears.

Talk about sexual frustration might prompt discussion toward other myths and stories; San Francisco and those gay sailors…or is the caricature assessment of a lisped "Hey there, sailor, is that a tuna in your pocket?" uttered in drag for laughs accurate or fair? It would appear not, since according to studies, less than five percent of active and retired military of the United States claim to be gay, which is approximately equal in percentage to the general population.

Judging by the frenetic scurrying of the other ninety-five percent heading for the dance halls of Subic, however, I think the "person" in every port may have a semblance of truth.

This was not a juvenile script with song and dance and love-struck couples facing the angst of war. The hot night air seemed driven by testosterone so thick it would impregnate a cat in heat on a cold tin roof. And, of course, all things considered, why wouldn't it be?

Enter the bar girls of Barretto, Olongapo, and all the harbour towns of the world.

Pier One; music sucked us in with our escort to a table for four. A tented structure covered a skeleton of metal frames, sides open to the tropic air, giving the feeling of an opulent circus tent. Our table had a great sight line to the dance floor and the extremely large bar, though the lines were hemmed in by a crush of sailors and bar girls. Christina seemed to know them all...the girls, that is. She wandered off to socialize and perform ladies' room activities. I could follow her progress through the crowd by her sonic wave of laughter. I was surprised by how many faces I recognized myself. News travelled fast when a boatload of sailors arrived and, it seemed, so did a one-night contagion of the flu. Barretto bars, like bars from Olongapo, would be nearly empty if it was anything like the last time the fleet had arrived; a mass quarantine of sailors required bar girl inoculations down on Waterfront Road, especially at Pier One. Scoring here meant taking home all the loot...no Mama-sans, no owners, but also no bar protection. It was here, Christina had informed me, she had met the sailor who sadistically raped her. That had been a late-night revelation when I asked her about her life in the bars, a story so brutal it's best left in her summation: "Ize nearly die, no bulla," followed by a rare moment of silence as she kissed her silver cross. "Maybies God sees all and heez dick shrivel up and fall off," followed by a quick correction, "No God's dick..." which was followed by that laugh; her cure for the woes of the world.

Five musicians and a pair of female vocalists navigated through a nonstop medley of pop. It wasn't long before we were lost in the tight weave of dancers, pushed closer as each new couple joined the fray until we were a mosh pit of jumping jacks. In the heat, bodies glistened with sweat. Dancers whooped appreciation with every new tune. The medleys picked up the tempo, groups clapped hands over their heads as individuals gyrated through circles of friends, and some couples hung tight and slowly danced, oblivious to the beat. Everyone joined in. "If you can't be with the one you love, love the one you're with." That, possibly, is the sailor's anthem.

It was a dance hall, like anywhere on a Friday night, with

one exception. Here, there was a curfew of twenty-three hundred hours.

In the frenzy of short time given to the sailors on shore leave, matches needed to be met, small-talked through an order of drinks, danced into comfortable persuasion, chatted out the door, waltzed into a room, consumed until passions were spent, showered back to respectability and standing on the deck of the ship before 23:01. Pier One peaked and skidded to an empty halt before most weekend partiers not of the sailor's world would have decided what to wear.

And not all sailors found a room with partners to share.

During a break for air, I ducked out a back entrance and found myself standing on the beach separating the dance hall and Subic Harbour. The night air was warm with barely a cooling breeze. As my eyes adjusted, I could see others in the dark—sailors and girls, I guessed (it was very dark), who had not been able to obtain a room. Those on bended knee, I surmised, were not proposing marriage. There were others; I was soon surrounded by beggars pushing handfuls of condoms or crushed cartons of Viagra, arm and fist raised in the universal sign of hard virility. A woman's face popped up close to mine, pushing her tongue into her cheek to suggest sexual favours. It was a mad scramble back into the safety of the hall, but not before I was pawed and groped in desperate, not-so-subtle advances. There had been a strong muscled attempt to pick my pockets. I realized that for the first time in my life, I had narrowly escaped being mugged.

Back inside, Christina had met her girlfriend and departed quickly. She told me later that she saw the "Ize nearly dies, no bulla" man who had raped her...sat near him at the bar, and, of course, he hadn't recognized her. Who could call him out? "Heez big captains, I thinks." Who could accuse him of rape? She was an invisible bar girl, an economy of one who had no face.

It was down to a few locals with no agendas other than to

dine and dance, or so I thought.

Rob and Kim were making tracks for the marina as I was invited to dance by an elegant Filipino woman, aged closer to me than most of the sailors who had come and gone. She was dressed in a tight red gown, a long slit allowing her perfectly formed legs to step out, carve circles around me and, as often as possible, push a naked hip into my groin and grind. After two dances she leaned in and gently whispered, "I am yours for the night…three thousand pesos." I thanked her kindly for thinking I was worthy, told her how beautiful she was (because she was) and revealed I was happily married. She patted my cheek and said, "What a waste." The feeling was mutual. Had she scored, it would have been more than an entire month's pay for a woman from the bar.

If each of those sailors, male or female, spent a hundred dollars, they would have left no less than a cool half million in the Subic economy. The Americans run a fleet of nineteen aircraft carriers and have 472 ships overall in service. If there are half a million personnel in the United States Navy, with a hundred and twenty-five thousand in ready reserve, of which eighty percent are enlisted sailors and fifteen percent are commissioned officers (who also have needs), how many millions get left in port economies around the world, whenever the fleets pull in? Now add Britain (117 ships), France (128 ships), Russia (781 ships), China (730 ships), Canada (67 ships…plus 2 canoes filled with tomahawks…the real McCoys, not those missile thingies), or any one of the more than a hundred other navies around the world, from Abkhazia to Yemen, and, well, there are more needy sailors than you can shake a whole plantation of rubber trees at. We might pardon sailors and bar girls the world over if they are caught dancing the *Mambo*, straight up or flat out, wherever the two might meet.

42

THE LAST SWING AT PARADISE
THE SEA: THE DEEP END OF THE POOL
LEAVING: OFF LIKE A BAND-AID

NOV. 6-9: LAST WEEK IN SUBIC, PHILIPPINES

Rob had preordered well in advance the local taxi driver to get us to Clark Air Force Base, where our Cebu Philippines flight would take us to Hong Kong. Our flight booking, to refresh the memory, was the straw that broke the camel's back between Rob, John and me in Kota Kinabalu, moving us from a three-hump crew to only two. Rob had decided to follow me to Hong Kong before my departure for Dalian, China, to meet my nephew, at which time Rob would return to Subic to settle into a whole new life. He had lived in Hong Kong for months attending to the details of *Bob-the-Boat* while it was being crafted on the mainland and then stayed for a few months learning the ropes of operation. Hong Kong and the Hebe Haven Yacht Club were like his second home, but Hong Kong was still a week away, and he was determined to keep the Subic adventures happening.

A few days preceding, we had moved *Bob-the-Boat* to swing off the sandy beaches of Barretto and, more pointedly, to swing close to the Blue Lagoon Floating Bar, owned and operated by the multi-bar owner of the Rum Jungle. A yacht swinging in its presence added some attractive value, like a Ferrari outside of a burger joint. It also entitled us to a few free beers and a fun backdrop all day long to the antics within; ping-pong balls cast into the waters and a whole throng of girls diving in to retrieve them, followed by wet T-shirts or no shirts at all the rest of the afternoon. It was hard work, but Rob and I decided we should man up and shoulder the load.

A day or so before the move, we had received our first communication from John Don of Edmonton since he had left us in Kota Kinabalu. It was a photo of him and a couple of his female neighbors, dressed in Victorian hats and scarves. They were having a themed Friday night wine and cheese gathering, befitting the first or second snowfall since he had arrived home. There were no hellos or inquiries as to our health or the state of our security since the raging typhoon was making international news for its destruction, albeit north of the Philippines. The e-mail caption with the photo simply stated *"The benefits of returning home early."* I dismissed it with an exasperated "Good grief" and rolling eyes, but Rob took it as a personal challenge, I think, wondering, like me, how that could match this, as we were sitting drinking gin and tonic watching the sun set over the beauty of Subic Bay, palm trees wafting in the breezes, surrounded by naked women. Well, okay, there were no naked women (not sitting on our deck anyway), but discussions of such launched a plan that required immediate action.

Christina, Kim and a pair of Kim's friends were invited to the boat for an afternoon of drinks and a swim party, common to yachts moored within a short distance of a floating bar. Two other boats had already dropped anchor since we arrived.

It was only after I was perilously close to drowning with Christina's frantic arms locked around my throat that she informed me she could not swim. She had never waded into water deeper than her waist. Jumping off the boat, following my cannonball, she suddenly realized there was nothing to stand on, specifically a sandy-bottomed beach, and who would have thought to tell her she was jumping into the deep end of the pool? It was lucky for her that I was a mere arm's length of strangulation away, and lucky for me we were close to the swim platform ladder. It saved my life. With one hand on the small of her back, I enticed her to roll on her back and float, gently waving her arms...good for a few seconds until her feet sank like stones. This was followed by screams, splashing and an attempt to drown the motherless dung heap who dared teach her to swim. Rob was oblivious to my near-death experiences, having found a crowd of viewers on the floating bar watching his dives from the highest point of the boat.

Back on board as everyone dried off, the girls posed and photos were snapped, innocent wet portraits of the South Seas at play. One with Kim and Christine hugging and sporting two-finger peace signs and not much else was downloaded and sent to John in Edmonton. There were no inquiries as to his health or his state of security; winter was howling from out of the north. The caption simply read "*The benefits of staying behind.*" John had the last word, however. "*Touché!*"

This state of bliss, swinging and partying until all hours of the night, lasted the better part of the week. *Doug-the-Dinghy* was employed to run us to the floating bar or to shore where we could walk to all the bars or get a few groceries, and one could not want for a more bohemian week of fun. It came without a care in the world.

Each morning, we were greeted by the sparkle and glitter on the bay. Sand white as snow served as a measured swim to the beach and back, and the water was always clear and warm. Hawkers of large seashells or fishermen with fresh catch sometimes paddled boats out to greet us. Some of the shell collections were magnificent, but unfortunately did not fall into my "if it folds or rolls into a ball" parameters for souvenirs. And always some gentle breezes and palms that caught them in a rhythm and sway like the slow-motion seduction of naked hula hips hung with grass. Now I understood the lure for the army expats that populated Barretto. This was a slice of paradise. And this voyage was threatening to steal my heart for good. My brain, usually a trust of common sense, was tempting me with multiple scenarios of how to stay in a yin-yang battle of dumb and dumber.

Go AWOL.

From who, idiot? He's not enlisted.

He can tell his wife he needs a year to find himself!

We know his wife. She'll tell him when he finds himself, to keep himself where he is.

Go fuck himself, you mean?

How indelicate of you…but, yes. And then, how would he survive?

He could manage a bar.

A slave owner to bar girls? You're in his head; have you not heard a thing he's said?

Ah yes, but he has two heads and he only thinks with one. What a dick!

Home is where his heart is. The rest of him will follow…eventually!

If you own such a pair as these, request electric shock therapy and have them murdered.

But as the yin-yang duo knew quite rightly, this once-in-a-lifetime experience did not exist in a vacuum. The end of the trip loomed large for me; the flights were booked to Hong Kong, Dalian, Beijing, and home to Canada. My wife and kids were waiting for my return while friends and extended family wanted to see a shark-induced peg leg and the scars of battles with pirates.

Within a week we were like that Band-Aid quickly removed, a last gasp infused with the balm of sea salt, wet vegetation and jet fumes. The exhale found us in the cold geometries of the circled and squared called Hong Kong.

43

HONG KONG
SAD DEPARTURES
THE GREAT WALL OF CHINA
YIN-YANG AGREE
THAT'S A WRAP

NOV. 9-22, 2009, HONG KONG, DALIAN, BEIJING / VANCOUVER / TORONTO...HOME

The taxi picked us up at four thirty a.m. outside the marina. Luggage was quietly placed in the trunk, clicked shut without noise as if stealing off for an early round of golf. I looked back to where *Bob-the-Boat* sat in the shadows of other boats, catching winds in the guide wires. I combined them into an imaginary moan of "Goodbye, old friend. 'Til we meet again," a wish I was quite sure would never happen. With an hour's ride to the Clark International Airport ahead of us, we nodded off. There was nothing more to see in the dark for last goodbyes.

    The naked sailor may have started to fade before landing in Hong Kong, but Hong Kong proved to have more than enough distractions to divert my addled minds. The yin-yang duo was still going strong.

Woo hoo, Hong Kong!
So, what's in Hong Kong?
No idea. I thought you knew.
I haven't got the foggiest idea.

Hong Kong pushes up from the sea like a nuclear experiment in crystalline growth. From the air, it was hard to find a horizon not given over to towers of glass and steel. The first sight caught me oohing and aahing because, again, I had failed to do my homework. It's not that I had lived in a cave of ignorance (James Bond had been here a few times), but a first glimpse from the air is simply awe-inspiring.

The harbour is the key. It cuts a wide swath through the city like an emerald serpent, depending on a skin of changing patterns from boats, crystal suns and clouds fractured into thousands of towering reflections. It was hard to distinguish where land and water met.

Like the city of ships in Singapore, the towers of Hong Kong demonstrated wealth beyond the wildest of expectations. But hey, you might get a sense of all that by Googling *WWW.org//Whazoos and Yin Yangs*, or *The smell of money @ WickiHolySmokes.org/Wicki-what-the-hell-happened/Hong Kong fragrance/Minted Money/leaving the world behind in a hubris of contentment and apathy/While the West spanked the monkey/HSBC builds bigger silos for loot*...or look at a few online photos and decide for yourself.

We entered the city of Hong Kong from the airport on a train that moved at over two hundred kilometres per hour, which is about a hundred and ninety kilometres faster than the fastest Canadian VIA Trains on a cold day in hell. One day I suspect that Bombardier, which builds HSR (High Speed Rail) trains for the world, will get a contract for one in its home country of Canada. Two subways and a bus ride and we eventually arrived at the Hebe Haven Yacht Club.

It was here that Rob and Cathy had lived for several months, learning the ropes of their new yacht, *Bob-the-Boat*.

I was returning with Rob to the yacht club to stay on another yacht, compliments of Rob's friend, an Air Asia pilot who lived in Sydney, Australia, but was job-based in Hong Kong. He was on leave in Sydney to be with his wife and children, so we had the yacht all to ourselves.

By the time we had settled in, it was nearly a full twelve hours since we had uprooted in the middle of the night with sad farewells to *Bob-the-Boat* in Subic. Our new home came with a view through yachts in the harbour of low-rise hills and islands floating in the South China Sea.

Yacht club life in Hong Kong came with invitations for wine and cheese. On one such occasion, we were made aware of the greatest scourges of the Philippines and its surrounding seas. They were thrown into the conversation with robust bite, hoping to elicit a like response.

"Palawan? The leprosy capital of the world?" That was in response to some story about our week's stay in Puerto Princesa and had followed a similar outburst.

"You swam in the ocean? One touch of a box jellyfish and you are dead in thirty seconds!"

"Puerto Princesa! That crime-infested hole?" This was followed by stories of mayhem and murder.

"Abanico Yacht Club? They call that a yacht club? I've never been there, but I hear it's a real piece of work."

These pearls of happiness were delivered from the yacht owners on whose boat we wined and cheesed. They were Australian and found joy in dropping poison on the world. They had a vineyard back home where they planted, plucked, stomped and bottled their creation, "*A hemorrhage red, hemlock cured, hints of vitriol, underscored by acid, venom and bile...goes well with vented spleen.*" It may have been called **POISON PEE of TWO THIN BASTARDS ON A GOOD TIME**. Canadian ice wine took a hit, as did many of the Australian wines from their compatriots. Everything, it seemed, was handed down in clay-tablet proclamations, weighted with the authority of elegant age, surrounded by the trappings of luxury from knowledgeable gain.

The yacht club's bar and restaurant proved to be more amenable to a good time. We joined for Crazy Friday, Buffet Sunday, and Happy Hour Snack Corner, but missed out on a Cowboy Hoedown where horses were advised to remove their shoes. We sipped cold drinks and watched from the boat patio as a formal wedding was celebrated on Saturday afternoon. From here we did the touristy thing and explored Hong Kong.

As to what there is to see in Hong Kong, besides the giant Buddha on a hilltop, a tram car ride for a magnificent view, temples, monasteries, parks, botanical gardens, old museums, art galleries, new museums, Hong Kong of old, statue squares, distinguished architecture old and new, galleries, financial districts, exotic islands, shopping districts, quaint fishing villages, markets large and small, floating restaurants, ferry rides, harbour cruises, walks of fame, theatres, famous hotels, infamous roads and storied homes...well, it's not a matter of what there is to see, but that it's hard to take it all in.

Of all the tours, perhaps the most rewarding is a simple ten-minute ferry ride across Victoria Harbour from the island of Hong Kong to Kowloon. It has the feel of standing on the pitcher's mound in a great stadium, with the bonus of crosswinds, salt spray, and the roll of the harbour waves. Again, it would be hard to contemplate the Zen of plus or minus zero here with the Vitruvian abandonment of the Sulu Sea; the harbor is extremely busy, but if you are going to be tempted, for my buck-ninety-nine, it beats counting zeros in a Manhattan Harbor tour, though that comes with the Brooklyn Bridge and the Statue of Liberty.

Standing midday, street level, in a grove of towers webbed with laundry several stories high, some places in Hong Kong have the appearance of approaching dusk all day long. One can see blue sky and the sun if one waits patiently for it to pass overhead, but then again, I suppose if one enters the forests of sequoias, redwoods or Douglas firs, it's the trees they've come to see and not the sky above.

After a week in Hong Kong, with all there was to do, it reminded me of Samuel Johnson's quote on London: "When a man is tired of London, he is tired of life; for there is in London all that life can afford." A modern version might read, "When a man is tired of London, he moves to Hong Kong, which are places now that few men can afford."

Rob left a day before me on a Cebu Philippines flight back to Clark International and eventually Subic, where he was hoping to take up permanent residence. There was too much to say for final goodbyes, so in the end, we said little beyond man hugs, take care, and hope to see you soon.

"I'll Skype you when you get home."

"Whoa, sounds like fun...I guess. You'll have to catch me first."

"Ha-ha, always the joker. Say hi to Lena and the kids," and with that, Captain Rob climbed the stairs from the yacht club and caught his rides to the airport.

And then there was one.

I flew out a day later than planned because my flight to Dalian, China, had been canceled. No reasons were given. It was my wife who called me and let me know.

"Remember you had me book that flight from Hong Kong to Dalian because you couldn't get the computer to work in Kota Kinta...Kona Kata...Kinta Kuna...wherever the hell you were?"

"Kota Kinabalu," I offered up to deaf ears.

"Whatever! That's why they e-mailed me and not you; crazy that I have to play travel agent here in Toronto for you there in China. Maybe someday you'll figure out how to use a computer."

"Love you too, dear. Thanks again, I'll be home in a week." Gee, maybe I should stay. Sounds a little cranky at home. It must be report card time again.

I flew off to Dalian, China, to meet my nephew Michael, who, in less than a week, introduced me to mainland China in a quick tour that took in Dalian and Beijing, where every tour of the Forbidden City and the Great Wall was offered up like Siamese twins. He was disappointed that my visit was going to be so short. There were so many places and things he wanted to show me; Shanghai, Xi'an, Guilin, Hangzhou, Chengdu, Lhasa; places outside of Shanghai I had never heard of. He assured me that they were magnificent cities with ancient histories that predated the might of Rome. The problem was they were divided by huge distances and flung to all points of the compass. I had less than a week. Beijing and the Wall became our focus.

As much as Michael was eager to begin sharing his exciting new world of China with me, he was still in the midterm of teaching math (the high kind that people require to build things and run the world) as well as holding the position of Assistant Dean of Missouri State's satellite university in Dalian. It would soon be American Thanksgiving, and most of his staff—all American—were feeling homesick for football, turkeys and pilgrims, none of which could be found in Dalian. If they were homesick for snow, however, Dalian was obliging with a dusting, a shock to my system that had not felt anything this cold since the 7-Eleven back in Singapore.

It was just as well to get myself acclimatized, I thought, since back home in Canada where I would be returning in a week, the mercury was already dipping into the brackets of *"Bloody hell, it's winter again!"* The old man responsible had frosted the pumpkins early, causing a teachers' run on Caribbean cruises for March. Whole segments of normally sedate Canadians—who wouldn't say shit if they were going through a fan—were turning the air blue with expletives... an annual festival timed to the first snowfall of the season. Others cheered and bought the Christmas turkey. And nothing takes the bloom off a southern vacation like snow. Step off the plane into a midwinter snowstorm, and the heat of that Mexican morning becomes a distant memory.

A weekend trip with a borrowed Friday to Beijing was just what was needed.

An hour's flight and we were over Beijing, where it appeared the city was engulfed in smoke from a forest fire. It was smog; a smog so thick that, once on the street, it stung the eyes and whole buildings disappeared from view.

And then, there we were, standing on the Great Wall of China. It was incredible, looking exactly as it had in my View-Master when I was ten. It had been included in the Great Wonders of the World along with the Pyramids, the Sphinx, Machu Picchu, the Parthenon, the Hanging Gardens of Babylon, some colossal harbour statue on the island of Rhodes, the Library of Alexandria, and Marilyn Monroe, though that might have been the first issue of *Playboy*...I get confused. It now ranks as a major travel highlight in my life (not Marilyn; the Wall, though Marilyn ranks up there) because standing on the Wall was something I had never imagined doing. It commanded a silent attention like no other place I had been.

But once beyond the desire for poetic dissertations, inspired by the lost-to-the-horizon size (over thirteen thousand miles in length) and history (begun centuries BC), to me, the Great Wall served as a timely reminder. Walls are an incentive for those on the perceived outside to join those on the inside...or vice versa. At some point, the unwanted catapult over, dig under, or drive through, and all that labour and death (millions, it has been said, died in the construction of the Great Wall) is for naught. The modern world should take note. Several nations and misguided individuals are in the process of building or planning to build walls to keep out the unwanted...untold millions of refugees at last count.

Standing on the Great Wall, I wondered if sailors—real sailors, not the ilk of me—would see what I saw and felt...that the sea was everything the Wall was not. It's the stillness, the cold solidity of the abandoned statue to former greatness, and the knowing fact that when the sentries had left, the conquering hordes were assimilated, and when the tourists are tucked in their beds, nothing but darkness, silence and stones remained. It is a reminder, in a dark-versus-light sort of way, that the sea was life, with all the millions of living permutations to its credit.

But maybe only sailors, familiar with movement beneath their feet, might feel that connection...or lack of such. It is a never-ending momentum that draws them back time and again, like secret lovers in a seductive tryst...waves and tides, heartbeats flowing with sustaining life. Perhaps only man can reflect upon such things, but all of earth's creatures have it coursing through their veins. In contrast, this great wall hugged the emaciated hills in all directions, like varicose veins on an ancient corpse.

And yes, the wall had seen its version of life...tides of humanity...Asian nomads, Huns, Manchus and Mongols rolled over the ramparts in tsunami force, and the zero plus or zero minus of communism, where peasants were urged to tear apart the wall towards a new beginning. In the end, the wall became a tombstone reminder that changes, like tides that circled the globe, were not hindered by the feeble attempts to hold them in or keep them out: tides trumped papers, scissors and rocks, especially rocks piled to thwart their advance.

Even though the Great Wall is a shining example of the fact that walls in the end don't work, no one should miss an opportunity to see it. That was ditto for the Forbidden City, a palace structure so large that entrance fees should include a chauffeured golf cart and a week to see it all. But nothing I can write would do them justice. Those who can should make the effort to go see for themselves. Walk the walk.

⚓ ⚓ ⚓

All too soon I was standing with Michael in another Great Wonder of the World, Terminal 3 of the Beijing Airport. It is larger than ninety-seven soccer fields combined, covering approximately two hundred acres or close to eight million square feet, spanned with a single roof. Again, nothing happens in a small way in China.

Michael was with me on his mission to return to Dalian and send me home to Toronto. He had made my few days in mainland China a perfect ending to the trip. In our final goodbyes, he had charged me with the task of going home to tell my brother—his father—to get to China for a visit, and then disappeared down a long line of inspections and melted into domestic departures. I followed in like form for international destinations, holding my pants up while shoes, belt and jacket floated through the scanner. Though it was not fact until I weighed myself back home, I had slimmed by nearly fifty pounds.

The way home was a bit of a swallow's migration route, having started in the Philippines. North to Hong Kong in the south of China to Dalian, "the southernmost city of China's northernmost warm water ports," west to Beijing, considered the hub of the Far East, and then eleven hours east over the Pacific Northwest. Home from Beijing was a total of eight and a half thousand kilometres or fifty-three hundred miles across the greatest single expanse of "no-wheels-down" ocean on the planet. At eight knots or nearly fifteen kilometres per hour, it would have taken us twenty-four days or five hundred and seventy-six hours on *Bob-the-Boat*. Adding time for strong currents, running out of fuel, drifting, several typhoon displacements, icebergs in the northwest passage, polar bears, a dog sled ride to get help and an Inuit gathering of elders— well, we would have reached home about three years after the publication of this book. Don't get me wrong, I loved every inch of the boating adventure, but thank goodness for Air Canada and its direct flight to Vancouver from Beijing.

Shortly after takeoff, nose pressed to the window, I could see the ocean, whitecaps even, and then a long scar, and another, ships with the single-minded intent of finding harbour. There were no islands or distant shores in their view; a humbling reminder of how large the ocean is and how small my journey through it was. Those scars, incisions in the flesh, healed quickly, leaving no trace of where the ships had come from and no indication of where they were going. And oh, isn't that our journey, all of us, naked sailors through life? We are launched with the splash and fizz of much ado about something, part the waters, make a noise and, if we are lucky, make port without sinking prematurely. In the end, the iceberg wins the day, and we are borne by six strong sailors who help close the open wound without a trace.

And then the gift of exhaustion...the white flag tossed at a tired mind. It drifted in fragments, particles of dust in a sunbeam, then shadows of a willow on a stream.

Cue the birds!

That's bloody cruel, let him sleep.

Cruel? Cruel? I'll tell you what's bloody cruel. He's taking us home to minus bloody cold and...

His wife.

Snow shovels...

His kids!

Snowstorms, snowdrifts, snow...

Christmas, mulled wine by the fire, Swedish meatballs...you always liked Christmas!

I could get used to colored lights on a palm tree, you know.

The family... Brown paper packages tied up with strings...

Gentle warm breezes, whispers in palms, waves breaking on shore...

Happy reunions, "Welcome Home" at the airport when they open the door...

Rolling horizons, a hot sun overhead...

Sleep undisturbed in a familiar bed...

When the cold stings!

When the shark bites!

Well, I guess...sad or not, we're heading home. Together now...

We can simply remember these wonderful things...and then we won't feel so bad.

And so, with the yin-yang choir finally agreeing, extolling the virtues of home, my mind began the dive toward a well-deserved sleep. There were detours, of course, through hearts of midnight darkness, rabbit holes, Hitchcock's *Birds*, the CIA, crazed marlins, thieves with eyes on the pearls, and the yin-yang pair playing whack-a-mole with my brain. If the steward came by offering meals, drinks or morning snacks, I missed them all. Sleep, deep REM, glorious sleep carried me until landing at Vancouver International Airport, a full thirteen hours without the urge to step out on deck to check the crosswinds once. If there were reflections in those dreams, I was none the wiser. In the darkness of that vacuum, my brain reached back in time, retrieving words of solace. Okay, people, that's a wrap.

AFT

So you might understand why I am glad I didn't hang up the phone when I got the call to sea. That "Hey, you" call was the best thing that had ever happened to me, after all the other best things that got me to that point.

Travelling can't help but alter how we view the world, change horizons and adjust the sails of life's expectations. For me, travelling by sea was extra special because it forced the writing me to stretch. The sea singularly demands your attention. It challenges you to find character in a cloud or a folding wave, to reach deep and search for your soul, one perhaps you didn't know you had.

If there had been a metamorphosis in me, I think it was the revelation that there was a kinder, more accepting side emerging that I needed to explore. It wasn't immediate or a full nelson of capitulation to the other side, and it wavered and waned on occasion. Yin, my steward of a more accepting transformation, still battled yang's view of our world that "All mankind should be invited to sea, but only a few should be given boats."

In their contrary assessments, however, I think both yin and yang might have agreed with John Donne's observation that no man was an island... Every man is a piece of the continent, a part of the main. Yin and yang were still battling as separate entities, but they joined me in silent deference to the thousands lost; lives taken by the earthquake for whom, it seemed, no bells tolled. There were also those victims of the ten-second tsunami that, in my world, had harmlessly washed over our boat; a scare of "what ifs" and little more. They were victims I had no bond with, other than perhaps I had shared the same wave of their destruction. And in some way, I felt a connection with the tenants of the hillside shantytowns and the stilted villages that hung precariously vulnerable over the water's edge. Why should their condition connect with me now, at this point in my life? I was passing through; a voyeur tourist with the promise to return to my first-world comfort, leaving third-world problems behind. And there in a moment of spiritual epiphany, from a mind not prone to such, was the answer. To invoke the big blue planet once again, viewed from space or contemplated at zero plus and zero minus, there were no first- or third-world nations: we are all, as John Donne suggested, connected on this Mother Earth.

It is impossible, I think, to focus on new horizons without first acknowledging ties to the old.

John still lives in Edmonton, happy, I believe, in the quiet peace of order. He came for my father's funeral three months after my return home. It is several years now, and we have spoken twice. Our aged vintages run the risk of passing prime. Perhaps it is time to uncork and drink.

Rob settled into the blue-green hills near Barretto and married Kim. He has since returned to Canada, where it has been a joy to watch Kim make angels in the snow.

Bob-the-Boat was sold in 2012, like a child, collateral damage of divorce.

As for Christina, there was one question I wanted to ask. It wasn't to her, but to my in-law back in Canada, the one at the Christmas party that with a twist of words had dismissed all bar girls into a whole blacklist of ugly expletives needing to be deleted.

A quote by Max Muller rose after the fact in my head… "Is it sin which makes the worm a chrysalis, the chrysalis a butterfly and the butterfly dust?"

"And what would you do to survive?" I had wanted to say, but bit my tongue knowing the conversation would be too dark for the spirit of the gathering.

Rob has informed me that someone has since come through Christina's door. She now has a home, a son and, I hope, respect and acceptance. The chrysalis has moved on to the butterfly.

Home for me has been a return to the place I started, though the bar has moved. It would be crazy to think that once you have experienced new horizons at plus or minus zero, your world would stay the same. This book is a result of that moving bar.

This is not to say that all I knew and all I had known now stood on shaky grounds; I had known for instance that the world was round before I started to travel. That is the benefit of being born in an age where man looks back from space.

And there's no peeking over horizons; there's always a shift. It is not the ever presence of near-death that drives a sailor mad; it's those horizons that never stand still. But those shifting horizons—the ones we arbitrarily set for clearing humps and hurdles—are the genesis of change; once we have accepted what might lie beyond, there is no settling for what's left behind.

For some reason, it would seem, that horizons, the arbitrary kind, are best found when one is metaphorically stripped and naked.

From inside to out, I have developed this desire to connect with a place my West calls Far East. It is a label of distance, perhaps, to justify our ignorance of their world. That might only be me, though I doubt it since barely a soul I have spoken with could pinpoint where I had been. My change might be best described by an old Hasidic parable retold by Sue Monk Kidd in her book, *First Light* (Guidepost Books, New York, New York, 2006), related to me by my wife, who found me floundering to self-assess. She assures me I have a soul, and I think she can see deeper into it than I can reach.

> *A rabbi asked his students a question. "When does night end and day begin?"*
>
> *"Is it the moment you can see the difference between an olive tree and a fig tree?" one student asked.*
>
> *"No," said the rabbi, "that's not it."*
>
> *"Is it the moment you can tell the difference between a sheep and a dog?" asked another.*
>
> *The rabbi shook his head. "No, that's not it either. Rather it is the moment you look into the face of a stranger and recognize that it is really your brother."*

That stranger, my wife suggested, might well be your surrounding world, or it just might be you, knowing she had sensed a change in vision since I returned. Perhaps it was that Vitruvian man found floating, contemplating the relevance of a grain of sand or that tsunami wash of humility, or the arrogance of fearing a *Heart of Darkness* ending while Christina, laughter and all, was navigating a bleak river of her own—or was it the sea? No one could discount the power of the sea. Perhaps in the end my whole voyage boiled down to this…

That brown man, black man, that man so white his ignorance stains his clothes, the men in turbans, women in hijabs, young boys in a kurta, kufis on the heads of the wisp of beards, those flowing gowns of white in the wind, silks of distinction and celebration, coloured veils and black-dyed hoods, the Asian, Malaysian, Indonesian, Spanish-Indo-Chinese, native Filipino, Vietnamese, Korean, north or south, those Thai men,

Thai women, tied to bars with young women and men, saints and angels good or bad, tinkers, tailors, soldiers, sailors, rich men, poor men, beggar men, thieves of hearts and thieves of souls, those refugees by boat and sea, mothers, daughters, wives and sisters, father, sons and uncles, brothers, Muslim, Christian, Buddhist, Monk, Libyan, Somalian, Syrian, the philosophic Greek, the Middle East, the Far East, and, east of where you live, the straight man singled, those gay men married and women and their wives, some lost in ignorance, some found in the know, those with holes in pockets or no pockets for holes at all, those sorry souls without new shoes, blind to the man who has no feet, the blind man blessed with vision, the deaf men to be heard, the dead man who gets the last word...

"Travel," Mark Twain has said, "is fatal to prejudice, bigotry, and narrow-mindedness."

REFERENCES

FORE

HarperCollins Publishers. (2004). Naked. *HarperCollins Canadian English Dictionary & Thesaurus* (first edition, p. 287). Glasgow.

HarperCollins Publishers. (2004). Sailor. *HarperCollins Canadian English Dictionary & Thesaurus* (first edition, p. 1063). Glasgow.

Naked Sailor. (n.d.). In *Urban Dictionary.* Retrieved 2024.05.26 from Urban Dictionary: Naked Sailor.

Conrad, J. (2007). *Heart of Darkness.* (Hampson, R. & Knowles, O. Eds.) Penguin Classic.

Barry, D. (1992). Captains Uncourageous, *Miami Herald.*

CHAPTER 8

Prostitution in the Philippines. (n.d.). From *Wikipedia.* Retrieved 2015-09-01 from https://en.wikipedia.org/wiki/Prostitution_in_the_Philippines.

CHAPTER 10

Coppola, F.F. (1979). *Apocalypse Now.* United Artists.

CHAPTER 11

Kennedy, L. (n.d.). Excerpts from an interview with Lee Kuan Yew. *New York Times.* Retrieved 2024.05.26 from https://www.nytimes.com.

CHAPTER 13

Texas City Explosion. (n.d.). From *Wikipedia.* Retrieved 13/02/2014 from http://en.wikipedia.org/wiki/Texas_City_disaster.

Halifax Explosion. (n.d.). From *Wikipedia*. Retrieved 13/02/2014 from http://en.wikipedia.org/wiki/Halifax_Explosion.

World's Tallest Tsunami. (n.d.). From *Geology.com*. Retrieved 15/02/2014 from http://geology.com/records/biggest-tsunami.shtml.

CHAPTER 15

Durian. (n.d.). From *Wikipedia*. Retrieved 28/02/2014 from http://en.wikipedia.org/wiki/Durian.

CHAPTER 16

National Oceanic and Atmospheric Administration. (n.d.). Waves. Retrieved 2024.05.26 from https://www.noaa.gov.

Names of Winds. (n.d.). From *G.G. Weather.com*. Retrieved 20/01/2014 from http://ggweather.com/winds.html.

CHAPTER 23

BrainyQuote. (n.d.). St. Augustine Quotes. Retrieved 2024.05.26 from https://www.brainyquote.com.

CHAPTER 25

Hikaru Sulu. (n.d.). From *Wikipedia*. Retrieved 2024.05.26 from http://en.wikipedia.org/wiki/Hikaru_Sulu.

CHAPTER 27

Bakla. (n.d.). From *Wikipedia*. Retrieved 25/05/2013 from http://en.wikipedia.org/wiki/Bakla_(Philippines).

CHAPTER 31

Melville, H. (2021). *Moby Dick*. Chartwell Books.

CHAPTER 34

Zollner, F., & Nathan, J. (2011). *Leonardo da Vinci, 1452-1519 Vol. II: The Graphic Work.* Taschen.

Sea level. (n.d.). From *Wikipedia.* Retrieved 10/03/2013 from http://en.wikipedia.org/wiki/Sea_level.

Diurnal cycle. (n.d.). From *Wikipedia.* Retrieved 27/01/2014 from http://en.wikipedia.org/wiki/Diurnal_cycle.

CHAPTER 35

MV Tricolor. (n.d.). From *Wikipedia.* Retrieved 15/03/2013 from http://en.wikipedia.org/wiki/MV_Tricolor.

Culion leper colony. (n.d.). From *Wikipedia.* Retrieved 25/02/2013 from http://en.wikipedia.org/wiki/Culion_leper_colony.

How many ships sink per year. (n.d.). From *WikiAnswers.* Retrieved 15/03/2013 from http://wiki.answers.com/Q/How_many_times_a_year_do_ships_sink.

CHAPTER 36

National Oceanic and Atmospheric Administration. (n.d.). Typhoons. Retrieved 2024.05.26 from https://www.noaa.gov.

Typhoons. (n.d.). From *Wikipedia.* Retrieved 2024.05.26 from http://en.wikipedia.org/wiki/Typhoon.

Eye (Cyclone). (n.d.). From *Wikipedia.* Retrieved 20/03/2013 from http://en.wikipedia.org/wiki/Eye_(cyclone).

Fujiwhara effect. (n.d.). From *Wikipedia.* Retrieved 27/05/2024 from http://en.wikipedia.org/wiki/Fujiwhara_effect.

Tropical cyclone. (n.d.). From *Wikipedia.* Retrieved 20/03/2013 from http://en.wikipedia.org/wiki/Tropical_cyclone.

Ghosh, P. (2011). Where Did The Word 'Hurricane' Come From? *International Business Times.* Retrieved 2023-06-05 from http://www.ibtimes.com/where-did-word-hurricane-come-304960.

Typhoon Yunya. (n.d.). From *Wikipedia*. Retrieved 03/09/2012 from http://en.wikipedia.org/wiki/Typhoon_Yunya_(1991).

Lahar. (n.d.). From *Wikipedia*. Retrieved 28/03/2013 from http://en.wikipedia.org/wiki/Lahar.

What are the horse latitudes? (n.d.). From *Ocean Service, National Oceanic and Atmospheric Administration*. Retrieved 2014-11-14 from http://oceanservice.noaa.gov/facts/horse-latitudes.html.

CHAPTER 37

Olongapo. (n.d.). From *Wikipedia*. Retrieved 01/06/2013 from http://en.wikipedia.org/wiki/Olongapo.

CHAPTER 38

U.S. Naval Base Subic Bay. (n.d.). From *Wikipedia*. Retrieved 25/05/2013 from http://en.wikipedia.org/wiki/U.S._Naval_Base_Subic_Bay.

CHAPTER 39

American girl in Italy: 60 years later. (n.d.). From *Yahoo*. Retrieved 03/06/2013 from http://news.yahoo.com/blogs/lookout/american-girl-italy-60-years-later-221005987.html.

CHAPTER 41

Van Biema, D. (1997). SEX IN THE MILITARY: THE RULES OF ENGAGEMENT. *Time.com*. Retrieved 6/7/2024 from https://time.com/archive/6730895/sex-in-the-military-the-rules-of-engagement/.

US Navy. Marine Corps Manual 1100.4Y. REGULATIONS 1165. Article 134, UCMJ. Fraternization. Retrieved 07/06/2024 from https://www.socom.mil/navsoc/Documents/Inspector%20General%20Library%20Documents/Fraternization.pdf.

What percentage of the US Navy is gay? From *Quora.com*. Retrieved 5/27/2024 from https://www.quora.com/What-percentage-of-the-US-navy-is-gay.

Navy Fleet Fleet Strength by Country 2024. (n.d.). From *globalfirepower.com*. Retrieved 5/27/2024 from https://www.globalfirepower.com/navy-ships.php.

ACKNOWLEDGMENTS

To my wife, Lena, who bought me a laptop and said, "Go write your book." Nearly fifty years together and we still have things to talk about. Love you lots.

To my daughter, Anna, (mother, wife, triathlete, teacher, therapist, writer, editor and multi-tasker extraordinaire), and my son, David, (the greatest personal trainer and one of the funniest guys I know). You are the best cheerleaders a dad could have.

To Elvira Purtle. You read the first half of the mud on the wall and liked it. You were the reason I continued. Sadly, it was the last thing you read before you passed. I hope the finished *Naked Sailor* would have met your expectations.

To Donna Hu, my first editor and continuous supporter. You were the perfect first willing victim.

Richard Bingham who exclaimed, "What the HELL happened?" and got me back on course, and Tuan Nguyen, a cheerleader to us both.

To Ian Ferguson who gently commented on the length, too kind to say it needed major editing.

To all those who read the *War and Peace* version before I lost two short novels to the final edit. I apologize for making you suffer.

And, of course, to the Atmosphere Press team. Thank you for the opportunity and trust, and, for making this process a joy to follow. To this end, a special thanks to Kyle McCord, Alex Kale, editor Nathanial Lee Hansen, proofreaders Erin Larson, BE Allatt, Chris Beale, Dakota Reed, Art director Ronaldo Alves, cover designer Felipe Betimi and all those specialists and special helpers in between.

ABOUT ATMOSPHERE PRESS

Founded in 2015, Atmosphere Press was built on the principles of Honesty, Transparency, Professionalism, Kindness, and Making Your Book Awesome. As an ethical and author-friendly hybrid press, we stay true to that founding mission today.

If you're a reader, enter our giveaway for a free book here:

SCAN TO ENTER
BOOK GIVEAWAY

If you're a writer, submit your manuscript for consideration here:

SCAN TO SUBMIT
MANUSCRIPT

And always feel free to visit Atmosphere Press and our authors online at atmospherepress.com. See you there soon!

ABOUT THE AUTHOR

Norm has a degree in television production and creative writing. A retired Toronto native, he has been married for over forty years and is a father of two. This is his first book.

www.ingramcontent.com/pod-product-compliance
Lightning Source LLC
Jackson TN
JSHW021925301224
76069JS00010B/9/J